WEBSTER'S
CONCISE
SPANISH–ENGLISH
ENGLISH–SPANISH
DICTIONARY

WEBSTER'S
CONCISE
SPANISH–ENGLISH
ENGLISH–SPANISH
DICTIONARY

Books Are Fun Ltd

Reader's Digest Company

This edition published 2004 for Books Are Fun by Geddes & Grosset,
David Dale House, New Lanark ML11 9DJ, Scotland

© 2004 Geddes & Grosset

This book is not published by the original publishers of
Webster's Dictionary or by their successors

ISBN 1 84205 418 X

Printed and bound in Poland, OZGraf S.A.

Spanish–English Dictionary

A

a *prep* to; in; at; according to; on; by; for; of.
abadía *f* abbey.
abajo *adv* under, underneath; below.
abalanzarse *vr* to rush forward.
abandonado/da *adj* derelict; abandoned; neglected.
abandonar *vt* to abandon; to leave: —~se *vr* ~ a to give oneself up to.
abarcar *vt* to include; to monopolize.
abarrotado/da *adj* packed.
abarrotar *vt* to tie down; (*mar*) to stow.
abastecer *vt* to purvey.
abatido/da *adj* dejected, low-spirited; abject.
abatimiento *m* low spirits *pl*, depression.
abatir *vt* to knock down; to humble.
abdicar *vt* to abdicate.
abdomen *m* abdomen.
abdominal *adj* abdominal.
abecedario *m* alphabet; spelling book, primer.
abeja *f* bee.
aberración *f* aberration.
abertura *f* aperture, chink, opening.
abeto *m* fir tree.
abierto/ta *adj* open; sincere; frank.
abismal *adj* abysmal.
abismo *m* abyss; gulf; hell.
ablandar *vt, vi* to soften.
abnegado/da *adj* selfless.
abogacía *f* legal profession.
abogado/a *m/f* lawyer; barrister.
abogar *vi* to intercede:—~ por to advocate.
abolir *vt* to abolish.
abollar *vt* to dent.
abonado/da *adj* paid-up:—*m/f* subscriber.
abonar *vt* to settle; to fertilize.
abono *m* payment; subscription; dung, manure.
aborrecer *vt* to hate, abhor.
abortar *vi* to miscarry; to have an abortion.
aborto *m* abortion; monster.
abotonar *vt* to button.
abovedado/da *adj* vaulted.
abrasar *vt* to burn; to parch:—~se *vr* to burn oneself.
abrazar *vt* to embrace; to surround; to contain.
abrazo *m* embrace.
abrebotellas *m invar* bottle opener.
abrelatas *m invar* can opener.
abreviar *vt* to abridge, cut short.
abridor *m* opener.
abrigar *vt* to shelter, to protect.
abrigo *m* shelter; protection; aid.

abril *m* April.
abrillantar *vt* to polish.
abrir *vt* to open; to unlock.
abrochar *vt* to button; to do up.
abrumar *vt* to overwhelm.
absolución *f* forgiveness, absolution.
absoluto/ta *adj* absolute.
absorber *vt* to absorb.
absorción *f* absorption; takeover.
absorto *adj* engrossed.
abstemio *adj* teetotal.
abstracción *f* abstraction.
abstracto/ta *adj* abstract.
abstraer *vt* to abstract:—~se *vr* to be absorbed.
absuelto/ta *adj* absolved.
absurdo *adj* absurd.
abuela *f* grandmother.
abuelo *m* grandfather.
abulia *f* lethargy.
abultado/da *adj* bulky, large, massive.
abultar *vt* to increase, enlarge:—*vi* to be bulky.
abundante *adj* abundant, copious.
aburrido/da *adj* boring, bored.
aburrir *vt* to bore, weary.
abusar *vt* to abuse.
acá *adv* here.
acabado/da *adj* perfect, accomplished; old.
acabar *vt* to finish, complete; to achieve: —~se *vr* to finish, expire.
academia *f* academy; literary society.
acaecer *vi* to happen.
acallar *vt* to quiet, hush; to soften, appease.
acalorado/da *adj* heated.
acampar *vt* (*mil*) to encamp.
acanalado/da *adj* grooved; fluted.
acaparar *vt* to monopolize; to hoard.
acariciar *vt* to fondle, caress.
acarrear *vt* to transport; to occasion.
acaso *m* chance:—*adv* perhaps.
acatarrarse *vr* to catch cold.
acceder *vi* to agree:—~ a to have access to.
accesible *adj* attainable; accessible.
acceso *m* access; fit.
accidentado/da *adj* uneven; hilly; eventful.
accidental *adj* accidental; casual.
accidente *m* accident.
acción *f* action, operation; share.
accionar *vt* to work.
accionista *m* shareholder.
acebo *m* holly tree.
acechar *vt* to lie in ambush for; to spy on.
aceite *m* oil.

11

aceituna *f* olive.
aceitunado/da *adj* olive-green.
aceleración *f* acceleration.
aceleradamente *adv* swiftly, hastily.
acelerar *vt* to accelerate; to hurry.
acento *m* accent.
aceptar *vt* to accept, admit.
acera *f* sidewalk.
acerca *prep* about, relating to.
acercar *vt* to move nearer:—~se *vr* ~ a to approach.
acero *m* steel.
acertar *vt* to hit; to guess right.
acertijo *m* riddle.
achacar *vt* to impute.
achaque *m* ailment; excuse; subject, matter.
achicar *vt* to diminish; to humiliate; to bale (out).
achicharrar *vt* to scorch; to overheat.
aciago/ga *adj* unlucky; ominous.
ácido *m* acid:—~/da *adj* acid, sour.
acierto *m* success; solution; dexterity.
aclamar *vt* to applaud, acclaim.
aclaración *f* clarification.
aclarar *vt* to clear; to brighten; to explain; to clarify.
acobardar *vt* to intimidate.
acodarse *vr* to lean.
acoger *vt* to receive; to welcome; to harbor:—~se *vr* to take refuge.
acogida *f* reception; asylum.
acometida *f* attack, assault.
acomodar *vt* to accommodate, arrange:—~se *vr* to comply.
acompañar *vt* to accompany; to join; (*mus*) to accompany.
acompasado/da *adj* measured; well-proportioned.
acondicionar *vt* to arrange; to condition.
acongojar *vt* to distress.
aconsejar *vt* to advise:—~se *vr* to take advice.
acontecer *vi* to happen.
acontecimiento *m* event, incident.
acoplar *vt* to couple; to fit; to connect.
acordar *vt* to agree; to remind:—~se *vr* to agree; to remember.
acorde *adj* harmonious:—*m* chord.
acordeón *m* accordion.
acorralar *vt* to round up; to intimidate.
acortar *vt* to abridge, shorten:—~se *vr* to become shorter.
acostar *vt* to put to bed; to lay down: —~se *vr* to go to bed; to lie down.
acostumbrar *vi* to be used to:—*vt* to accustom:—~se *vr* ~ a to become used to.
acotar *vt* to set bounds to; to annotate.

ácrata *m/f* anarchist.
acreditar *vt* to guarantee; to assure; to authorize.
acreedor *m* creditor.
acribillar *vt* to riddle with bullets; to molest, torment.
acta *f* act:—~s *fpl* records *pl*.
actitud *f* attitude; posture.
actividad *f* activity; liveliness.
activo/va *adj* active; diligent.
acto *m* act, action; act of a play; ceremony.
actor *m* actor; plaintiff.
actriz *f* actress.
actuación *f* action; behavior; proceedings *pl*.
actual *adj* actual, present.
actualizar *vt* to update.
actuar *vt* to work; to operate:—*vi* to work; to act.
acuarela *f* watercolor.
acudir *vi* to go to; to attend; to assist.
acuerdo *m* agreement:—**de** ~ OK.
acumular *vt* to accumulate, collect.
acurrucarse *vr* to squat; to huddle up.
adelantado/da *adj* advanced; fast.
adelantar *vt*, *vi* to advance, accelerate; to pass.
adelante *adv* forward(s):—*excl* come in!
adelanto *m* advance; progress; improvement.
adelgazar *vt* to make thin or slender; to discuss with subtlety.
además *adv* moreover, besides:—~ **de** besides.
adentro *adv* in; inside.
aderezar *vt* to dress, adorn; to prepare; to season.
adeudar *vt* to owe:—~se *vr* to run into debt.
adherir *vi*:—~ a to adhere to; to espouse.
adiestrar *vt* to guide; to teach, to instruct.
adiós *excl* goodbye; hello.
adivinar *vt* to foretell; to guess.
admirar *vt* to admire; to surprise:—~se *vr* to be surprised.
admitir *vt* to admit; to let in; to concede; to permit.
admonición *f* warning.
adobar *vt* to dress; to season.
adobe *m* adobe, sun-dried brick.
adobo *m* dressing; pickle sauce.
adolecer *vi* to suffer from.
adolescencia *f* adolescence.
adónde *adv* where.
adoptar *vt* to adopt.
adoquín *m* paving stone.
adorar *vt* to adore; to love.
adormecer *vt* to put to sleep:—~se *vr* to fall asleep.

adornar *vt* to embellish, adorn.
adosado/da *adj* semi-detached.
adquirir *vt* to acquire.
adrede *adv* on purpose.
aduana *f* customs *pl.*
adueñarse *vr*:—~ **de** to take possession of.
adular *vt* to flatter.
adulterio *m* adultery.
adulto/ta *adj, m/f* adult, grown-up.
advenedizo *m* upstart.
advenimiento *m* arrival; accession.
adversidad *f* adversity; setback.
advertencia *f* warning, foreword.
advertir *vt* to notice; to warn.
aerodeslizador *m* hovercraft.
aeronave *f* spaceship.
aeropuerto *m* airport.
afán *m* hard work; desire.
afanar *vt* to harass; (*col*) to pinch:—~**se** *vr* to strive.
afear *vt* to deform, misshape.
afección *f* affection; fondness, attachment; disease.
afectar *vt* to affect, feign.
afectuoso/sa *adj* affectionate; moving; tender.
afeitar *vt*:—~**se** *vr* to shave.
aferrar *vt* to grapple, grasp, seize.
afianzar *vt* to strengthen; to prop up.
aficionado/da *adj* keen:—*m/f* lover, devotee; amateur.
afilado *adj* sharp.
afilar *vt* to sharpen, grind.
afín *m* related; similar.
afinar *vt* to tune; to refine.
afincarse *vr* to settle.
afirmar *vt* to secure, fasten; to affirm, assure.
aflicción *f* affliction, grief.
aflictivo/va *adj* distressing.
aflojar *vt* to loosen, slacken, relax.
aflorar *vi* to emerge.
afluente *adj* flowing:—*m* tributary.
afónico/ca *adj* hoarse; voiceless.
afortunado/da *adj* fortunate, lucky.
afrenta *f* outrage; insult.
afrontar *vt* to confront; to bring face to face.
afuera *adv* out, outside.
agacharse *vr* to stoop, squat.
agarradero *m* handle.
agarrar *vt* to grasp, seize:—~**se** *vr* to hold on tightly.
agasajar *vt* to receive and treat kindly; to regale.
agenciarse *vr* to obtain.
agenda *f* diary.
agente *m* agent, policeman.
ágil *adj* agile.

agilidad *f* agility, nimbleness.
agitar *vt* to wave; to move:—~**se** *vr* to become excited; to become worried.
aglomeración *f* crowd; jam.
agobiar *vt* to weigh down; to oppress; to burden.
agolparse *vr* to assemble in crowds.
agonía *f* agony.
agorar *vt* to predict.
agostar *vt* to parch.
agosto *m* August.
agotado/da *adj* exhausted; finished; sold out.
agotar *vt* to exhaust; to drain; to misspend.
agradable *adj* pleasant; lovely.
agradar *vt* to please, gratify.
agradecer *vt* to be grateful for; to thank.
agradecido/da *adj* thankful.
agrandar *vt* to enlarge; to exaggerate.
agrario/ria *adj* agrarian; agricultural.
agravante *f* further difficulty.
agraviar *vt* to wrong; to offend:—~**se** *vr* to be aggrieved; to be piqued.
agredir *vt* to attack.
agregar *vt* to aggregate, heap together; to collate; to appoint.
agreste *adj* rustic, rural.
agrícola *adj* farming *compd.*
agricultor/ra *m/f* farmer.
agrietarse *vr* to crack.
agrimensor *m* surveyor.
agrio *adj* sour, acrid; rough, craggy; sharp, rude, unpleasant.
agrupar *vt* to group, cluster; to crowd.
agua *f* water.
aguacate *m* avocado pear.
aguacero *m* cloudburst, downpour.
aguado/da *adj* watery.
aguafuerte *m* etching.
aguamarina *f* aquamarine (gem stone).
aguanieve *f* sleet.
aguantar *vt* to bear, suffer; to hold up.
aguardar *vt* to wait for.
aguarrás *f* turpentine.
agudo/da *adj* sharp; keen-edged; smart; fine; acute; witty; brisk.
aguijón *m* sting of a bee, wasp, etc; stimulation.
águila *f* eagle; genius.
aguileño/ña *adj* aquiline; sharp-featured.
aguja *f* needle; spire; hand; magnetic needle; (*ferro*) points *pl.*
agujerear *vt* to pierce, bore.
agujero *m* hole.
ahí *adv* there.
ahijada *f* goddaughter.
ahijado *m* godson.
ahínco *m* earnestness; eagerness.

ahogar *vt* to smother; to drown; to suffocate; to oppress; to quench.

ahora *adv* now, at present; just now.

ahorrar *vt* to save; to avoid.

ahumar *vt* to smoke, cure (in smoke): —~se *vr* to fill with smoke.

ahuyentar *vt* to drive off; to dispel.

aire *m* air; wind; aspect; musical composition.

aislar *vt* to insulate; to isolate.

ajardinado/da *adj* landscaped.

ajedrez *m* chess.

ajedrezado/da *adj* chequered.

ajeno/na *adj* someone else's; foreign; ignorant; improper.

ajetreo *m* activity; bustling.

ajo *m* garlic.

ajorca *f* bracelet.

ajustar *vt* to regulate, adjust; to settle (a balance); to fit.

al = a el.

ala *f* wing; aisle; row, file; brim:—*m/f* winger.

alabar *vt* to praise; to applaud.

alacena *f* cupboard, closet.

alacrán *m* scorpion.

alambre *m* wire.

alameda *f* avenue; poplar grove.

álamo *m* poplar.

alargar *vt* to lengthen; to extend.

alarido *m* outcry, shout:—**dar ~s** to howl.

alarma *f* alarm.

alba *f* dawn.

albañil *m* mason, bricklayer.

albarán *m* invoice.

albaricoque *m* apricot.

albedrío *m* free will.

albergue *m* shelter:—~ **de juventud** youth hostel.

albóndiga *f* meatball.

albornoz *m* burnous:—~ **de baño** bath robe.

alboroto *m* noise; disturbance, riot.

alborozo *m* joy.

albricias *fpl* good news *pl*.

albufera *f* lagoon.

álbum *m* album.

alcachofa *f* artichoke.

alcalde *m* mayor.

alcaldesa *f* mayoress.

alcantarilla *m* sewer; gutter.

alcanzar *vt* to reach; to get, obtain; to hit.

alcaparra *f* caper.

alcayata *f* hook.

alcázar *m* castle, fortress.

alcornoque *m* cork tree.

aldea *f* village.

aleatorio/ria *adj* random.

aleccionar *vt* to instruct; to train.

alegar *vt* to allege; to quote.

alegrar *vt* to cheer; to poke; to liven up:—~se *vr* to get merry.

alegre *adj* happy; merry, joyful; content.

alegría *f* happiness; merriment.

alejar *vt* to remove; to estrange:—~se *vr* to go away.

alemán/ana *adj, m/f* German:—*m* German language.

alentar *vt* to encourage.

alergia *f* allergy.

alero *m* gable-end; eaves *pl*.

alertar *vt* to alert.

aleta *f* fin; wing; flipper; fender.

alfabeto *m* alphabet.

alfarería *f* pottery.

alféizar *m* window sill.

alfiler *m* pin; clip; clothes pin.

alfombra *f* carpet; rug.

alga *f* (*bot*) seaweed.

algo *pn* something; anything:—*adv* somewhat.

algodón *m* cotton; cotton plant; cotton wool.

alguien *pn* someone, somebody; anyone, anybody.

alguno/na *adj* some; any; no:—*pn* someone, somebody.

alhaja *f* jewel.

aliado/da *adj* allied.

alianza *f* alliance, league; wedding ring.

alicates *mpl* pincers *pl*, nippers *pl*.

aliciente *m* attraction; incitement.

aliento *m* breath; respiration.

aligerar *vt* to lighten; to alleviate; to hasten; to ease.

alijo *m* lightening of a ship; alleviation; cache.

alimentar *vt* to feed, nourish:—~se *vr* to feed.

aliñar *vt* to adorn; to season.

alinear *vt* to arrange in line:—~se *vr* to line up.

alisar *vt* to plane; to polish; to smooth.

aliviar *vt* to lighten; to ease; to relieve, mollify.

allá *adv* there; over there; then.

allanar *vt* to level, flatten; to subdue; to burgle.

allí *adv* there, in that place.

alma *f* soul; human being.

almacén *m* warehouse, store; magazine.

almacenar *vt* to store (up).

almeja *f* clam.

almena *f* battlement.

almendra *f* almond.

almíbar *m* syrup.

almirez *m* mortar.

almizcle *m* musk.

almohada *f* pillow; cushion.

almorranas *fpl* hemorrhoids *pl*.

almuerzo *m* lunch.

alocado/*adj* crazy; foolish; inconsiderate.

alojamiento *m* lodgings, rooming house; housing.

alpargata *f* rope-soled shoe.

alpinismo *m* mountaineering.

alquilar *vt* to let, rent; to hire.

alquitrán *m* tar, liquid pitch.

alrededor *adv* around.

alta *f* (*mil*) discharge from hospital.

altanero/**ra** *adj* haughty, arrogant, vain, proud.

altavoz *m* loudspeaker, amplifier.

alterar *vt* to alter, change; to disturb.

altercado *m* altercation, controversy; quarrel.

alterno/**na** *adj* alternate; alternating.

Alteza *f* Highness (title).

altibajos *mpl* ups and downs *pl*.

altitud *f* height; altitude.

altivo/**va** *adj* haughty, proud, high-flown.

alto/**ta** *adj* high; tall:—*m* height; story; highland; (*mil*) halt; (*mus*) alto: —**i**~**!/i**~ **ahí!** *interj* stop!

altura *f* height; depth; mountain summit; altitude.

alubia *f* kidney bean.

alucinar *vt* to blind, deceive:—*vi* to hallucinate.

alumbrado *m* lighting; illumination.

alumbrar *vt* to light:—*vi* to give birth.

alumno/**na** *m/f* student, pupil.

alza *f* rise; sight.

alzar *vt* to raise, lift up:—~**se** *vr* to get up; to rise in rebellion.

ama *f* mistress, owner; housewife; foster mother.

amable *adj* kind, nice.

amagar *vt* to threaten; to shake one's fist at:—*vi* to feint.

amamantar *vt* to suckle.

amanecer *vi* to dawn:—**al** ~ at daybreak.

amanerado/**da** *adj* affected.

amansar *vt* to tame; to soften; to subdue:— ~**se** *vr* to calm down.

amante *m/f* lover.

amapola *f* (*bot*) poppy.

amar *vt* to love.

amargo/**ga** *adj* bitter, acrid; painful:—*m* bitterness.

amarillo/**lla** *adj* yellow:—*m* yellow.

amarrar *vt* to moor; to tie, fasten.

amasar *vt* to knead; (*fig*) to arrange, settle; to prepare.

ámbar *m* amber.

ambiente *m* atmosphere; environment.

ambiguo/**gua** *adj* ambiguous; doubtful, equivocal.

ámbito *m* circuit, circumference; field; scope.

ambos/**bas** *adj, pn* both.

ambulante *adj* traveling.

ambulatorio *m* state-run clinic.

amenazar *vt* to threaten.

ameno/**na** *adj* pleasant; delicious; flowery (of language).

América *f* America:—~ **del Norte/del Sur** North/South America.

amianto *m* asbestos.

amiga *f* (female) friend.

amigo *m* friend; comrade; lover:—~/**ga** *adj* friendly.

aminorar *vt* to diminish; to reduce.

amistad *f* friendship.

amistoso/**sa** *adj* friendly, cordial.

amo *m* owner; boss.

amoldar *vt* to mold; to adapt:—~**se** *vr* to adapt oneself.

amor *m* love; fancy; lover:—~ **mio** my love:—**por** ~ **de Dios** for God's sake: —~ **propio** self-love.

amortiguador *m* shock absorber.

amortizar *vt* to redeem, pay, liquidate, discharge (a debt).

amperio *m* amp.

ampliar *vt* to amplify, enlarge; to extend; to expand.

amplificador *m* amplifier.

amplio/**lia** *adj* ample, extensive.

ampolla *f* blister; ampoule.

amueblar *vt* to furnish.

anacoreta *m* anchorite, hermit.

anacronismo *m* anachronism.

añadir *vt* to add.

analfabeto/**ta** *adj* illiterate.

analgésico *m* painkiller.

análisis *m* analysis.

anaranjado/**da** *adj* orange-colored.

anarquía *f* anarchy.

ancho/**cha** *adj* broad, wide, large:—*m* breadth, width.

anchoa *f* anchovy.

anchura *f* width, breadth.

anciano/**na** *adj* old:—*m/f* old man/woman.

ancla *f* anchor.

anclaje *m* anchorage.

andamiaje *m* scaffolding.

andar *vi* to go, walk; to fare; to act, proceed.

andén *m* sidewalk; (*ferro*) platform; quayside.

andrajo *m* rag.

anegar *vt* to inundate, submerge;.

añejo/ja *adj* old; stale, musty.

anexión *f* annexation.

anfibio/bia *adj* amphibious.

anfitrión/ona *m/f* host(ess).

ángel *m* angel.

angosto/ta *adj* narrow, close.

anguila *f* eel.

angula *f* elver.

angular *adj* angular:—**piedra ~** *f* cornerstone.

ángulo *m* angle, corner.

angustia *f* anguish; heartache.

anhelar *vi* to gasp:—*vt* to long for.

anidar *vi* to nestle, make a nest; to dwell, inhabit.

añil *m* indigo plant; indigo.

anillo *m* ring.

ánima *f* soul.

animación *f* liveliness; activity.

animado/da *adj* lively.

animal *adj, m* animal.

animar *vt* to animate, liven up; to comfort; to revive:—**~se** *vr* to cheer up.

ánimo *m* soul; courage; mind; intention:—*excl* come on!

anís *m* aniseed; anisette.

aniversario/ria *adj* annual:—*m* anniversary.

ano *m* anus.

año *m* year.

anoche *adv* last night.

anochecer *vi* to grow dark:—*m* nightfall.

anónimo/ma *adj* anonymous.

añoranza *f* longing.

anormal *adj* abnormal.

anotar *vt* to comment, note.

anquilosamiento *m* paralysis.

ánsar *m* goose.

ansiar *vt* to desire.

ansiedad *f* anxiety.

antagónico/ca *adj* antagonistic; opposed.

antaño *adv* formerly.

ante *m* suede:—*prep* before; in the presence of; faced with.

anteanoche *adv* the night before last.

anteayer *adv* the day before yesterday.

antebrazo *m* forearm.

antelación *f*:—**con ~** in advance.

antemano *adv*:—**de ~** beforehand.

antena *f* feeler, antenna; aerial.

antepasado/da *adj* passed, elapsed: **—~s** *mpl* ancestors *pl*.

anterior *adj* preceding; former.

antes *prep, adv* before:—*conj* before.

antibiótico *m* antibiotic.

anticiclón *m* anticyclone.

anticipar *vt* to anticipate; to forestall; to advance.

anticonceptivo *m* contraceptive.

anticongelante *m* antifreeze.

anticuado/da *adj* antiquated.

anticuerpo *m* antibody.

antiestético/ca *adj* unsightly.

antifaz *m* mask.

antiguamente *adv* in ancient times, of old.

antiguo/gua *adj* antique, old, ancient.

antipático/ca *adj* unpleasant.

antojo *m* whim, fancy; longing.

antorcha *f* torch; taper.

antro *m* (*poet*) cavern, den, grotto.

antropófago *m* cannibal.

antropología *f* anthropology.

anual *adj* annual.

anudar *vt* to knot; to join:—**~se** *vr* to get into knots.

anular *vt* to annul; to revoke; to cancel:—*adj* annular.

anunciar *vt* to announce; to advertise.

anuncio *m* advertisement.

anzuelo *m* hook; allurement.

apacible *adj* affable; gentle; placid, quiet.

apaciguar *vt* to appease; to pacify, calm.

apagar *vt* to put out; to turn off; to quench, extinguish.

apañar *vt* to grasp; to pick up; to patch: —**~se** *vr* to manage.

aparador *m* sideboard; store window.

aparato *m* apparatus; machine; radio or television set; ostentation, show; (*med*) bandage, dressing.

aparcamiento *m* parking lot.

aparcar *vt, vi* to park.

aparecer *vi* to appear:—**~se** *vr* to appear.

aparentar *vt* to look; to pretend; to deceive.

apariencia *f* outward appearance.

apartamento *m* flat, apartment.

apartar *vt* to separate, divide; to remove; to sort;.

aparte *adv* aside; new paragraph:—*adv* apart, separately; besides; aside.

apasionado/da *adj* passionate; devoted; fond; biased.

apeadero *m* halt, stopping place; station.

apearse *vr* to dismount; to get down/out/off.

apechugar *vt* to face up to.

apego *m* attachment, fondness.

apelar *vi* (*jur*) to appeal:—**~ a** to have recourse to.

apellido *m* surname; family name; epithet.

apenar *vt* to grieve; to embarrass:—**~se** *vr* to grieve; to be embarrassed.

apenas *adv* scarcely, hardly:—*conj* as soon as.

apéndice *m* appendix, supplement.

apercibirse *vr* to notice.
aperitivo *m* aperitif; appetizer.
apero *m* agricultural implement.
apesadumbrar *vt* to sadden.
apestar *vt* to infect:—*vi* ~ **a** to stink of.
apetito *m* appetite.
apiadarse *vr* to take pity.
apilar *vt* to pile up:—~**se** *vr* to pile up.
apiñado/da *adj* crowded; pyramidal; pine-shaped.
apio *m* (*bot*) celery.
apisonadora *f* steamroller.
aplacar *vt* to appease, pacify:—~**se** *vr* to calm down.
aplastar *vt* to flatten, crush.
aplatanarse *vr* to get weary.
aplaudir *vt* to applaud; to extol.
aplauso *m* applause; approbation, praise.
aplazar *vt* to postpone.
aplicado/da *adj* studious; industrious.
aplicar *vt* to apply; to clasp; to attribute:—~**se** *vr* ~ **a** to devote oneself to.
aplique *m* wall light.
aplomo *m* self-assurance.
apocado/da *adj* timid.
apoderado/da *adj* powerful:—*m* proxy, attorney; agent.
apodo *m* nickname, sobriquet.
apogeo *m* peak.
apósito *m* (*med*) external dressing.
aposta *adv* on purpose.
apostar *vt* to bet, wager; to post soldiers:—*vi* to bet.
apóstol *m* apostle.
apoteosis *f* apotheosis.
apoyar *vt* to rest; to favor, patronize, support:—~**se** *vr* to lean.
apreciar *vt* to appreciate; to estimate, value.
aprecio *m* appreciation; esteem.
apremiante *adj* urgent.
aprender *vt* to learn:—~ **de memoria** to learn by heart.
aprensión *f* apprehension.
apresar *vt* to seize, grasp.
apresurar *vt* to accelerate, hasten, expedite:—~**se** *vr* to hurry.
apretar *vt* to compress, tighten; to constrain:—*vi* to be too tight.
aprisa *adv* quickly, swiftly; promptly.
aprobar *vt* to approve; to pass:—*vi* to pass.
apropiado/da *adj* appropriate.
aprovechar *vt* to use; to exploit; to profit from; to take advantage of:—*vi* to be useful; to progress:—~**se** *vr* ~ **de** to use; to take advantage of.
aproximar *vt* to approach:—~**se** *vr* to approach.

aptitud *f* aptitude, fitness, ability.
apto/ta *adj* apt; fit, able; clever.
apuesta *f* bet, wager.
apuñalar *vt* to stab.
apuntar *vt* to aim; to level, point at; to mark:—*vi* to begin to appear or show itself; to prompt (theater):—~**se** *vr* to score; to enrol.
apurado/da *adj* poor, destitute of means; exhausted; hurried.
aquél/~ la *pn* that (one):—~ **los/~ las** *pl* those (ones).
aquel/~la *adj* that:—~**los/~las** *pl* those.
aquello *pn* that.
aquí *adv* here; now.
árabe *adj*, *m/f*, *m* (*ling*) Arab, Arabic.
arado *m* plough.
araña *f* spider; chandelier.
arañar *vt* to scratch; to scrape; to corrode.
arancel *m* tariff.
arandela *f* washer.
arar *vt* to plough.
árbitro *m* arbitrator; referee; umpire.
árbol *m* tree; (*mar*) mast; shaft.
arbolado/da *adj* forested; wooded: —*m* woodland.
arbusto *m* shrub.
arca *f* chest, wooden box.
arcada *f* arch; arcade:—~**s** *fpl* retching.
arce *m* maple tree.
archivar *vt* to file.
arcilla *f* clay.
arco *m* arc; arch; fiddle bow; hoop: —~**iris** rainbow.
arder *vi* to burn, blaze.
ardilla *f* squirrel.
área *f* area.
arena *f* sand; grit; arena.
arenque *m* herring:—~ **ahumado** red herring.
argolla *f* large ring.
argucia *f* subtlety.
argumentar *vt*, *vi* to argue, dispute; to conclude.
árido/da *adj* dry; barren.
arisco/ca *adj* fierce; rude; intractable.
arlequín *m* harlequin, buffoon.
arma *f* weapon, arms.
armado/da *adj* armed; reinforced.
armador *m* shipowner; privateer; jacket, jerkin.
armar *vt* to man; to arm; to fit:—~**la** to kick up a fuss.
armario *m* wardrobe; cupboard.
armazón *f* chassis; skeleton; frame.
armonía *f* harmony.
armonizar *vt* to harmonize; to reconcile.

arnés *m* harness:—**~eses** *mpl* gear, trappings *pl.*

aro *m* ring; earring.

aroma *m* aroma, fragrance.

arpa *f* harp.

arpía *f (poet)* harpy, shrew.

arpillera *f* sackcloth.

arpón *m* harpoon.

arqueado/da *adj* arched, vaulted.

arquero *m* archer.

arquitectónico/ca *adj* architectural.

arrabal *m* suburb; slum.

arraigado *adj* deep-rooted; established.

arraigar *vi* to root; to establish:—*vt* to establish;.

arrancar *vt* to pull up by the roots; to pull out:—*vi* to start; to move.

arrasar *vt* to demolish, destroy.

arrastrar *vt* to drag:—*vi* to creep, crawl; to lead a trump at cards:—**~se** *vr* to crawl; to grovel.

arrebatar *vt* to carry off, snatch; to enrapture.

arrebato *m* fury; rapture.

arrecife *m* reef.

arreglar *vt* to regulate; to tidy; to adjust:—**~se** *vr* to come to an understanding.

arrellanarse *vr* to sit at ease; to make oneself comfortable.

arrendar *vt* to rent, let out, lease.

arrendatario/ria *m/f* tenant.

arrepentirse *vr* to repent.

arrestar *vt* to arrest; to imprison.

arriate *m* flowerbed; causeway.

arriba *adv* above, over, up; high, on high, overhead; aloft.

arribista *m/f* upstart.

arriendo *m* lease; farm rent.

arriesgado *adj* risky, dangerous; daring.

arriesgar *vt* to risk, hazard; to expose to danger:—**~se** *vr* to take a chance.

arrimar *vt* to approach, draw near; *(mar)* to stow (cargo):—**~se** *vr* to sidle up; to lean.

arrinconar *vt* to put in a corner; to lay aside.

arrodillarse *vr* to kneel down.

arrogante *adj* arrogant; haughty, proud; stout.

arrojar *vt* to throw, fling; to dash; to emit; to shoot, sprout:—**~se** *vr* to hurl oneself.

arrollar *vt* to run over; to defeat heavily.

arropar *vt* to clothe, dress:—**~se** *vr* to wrap up.

arroyo *m* stream; gutter.

arroz *m* rice.

arrozal *m* ricefield.

arrugar *vt* to wrinkle; to rumple; to fold:—**~ la frente** to frown:—**~se** *vr* to shrivel.

arruinar *vt* to demolish; to ruin:—**~se** *vr* to go bankrupt.

arrullar *vt* to lull:—*vi* to coo.

artesanía *f* craftsmanship.

ártico/ca *adj* arctic, northern:—*m* **el A~** the Arctic.

articular *vt* to articulate; to joint.

artículo *m* article; clause; point; *(gr)* article; condition.

artífice *m* artisan; artist.

artificio *m* workmanship, craft; artifice, cunning trick.

artimaña *f* trap; cunning.

artista *m* artist; craftsman.

arzobispo *m* archbishop.

as *m* ace.

asa *f* handle; lever.

asado *m* roast meat; barbecue.

asaltar *vt* to assault; to storm (a position); to assail.

asamblea *f* assembly, meeting.

asar *vt* to roast.

ascender *vi* to be promoted; to rise:—*vt* to promote.

ascenso *m* promotion; ascent.

ascensor *m* elevator.

asco *m* nausea; loathing.

ascua *f* red-hot coal.

asear *vt* to clean; to tidy.

asedio *m* siege.

asegurar *vt* to secure; to insure; to affirm; to bail:—**~se** *vr* to make sure.

asentar *vt* to sit down; to affirm, assure; to note:—*vi* to suit.

asentir *vi* to acquiesce, concede.

aseo *m* cleanliness; neatness:—**~s** *mpl* rest room.

aséptico/ca *adj* germ-free.

asequible *adj* attainable; obtainable.

aserrar *vt* to saw.

aserrín *m* sawdust.

asesinar *vt* to assassinate; to murder.

asesorar *vt* to advise; to act as consultant:—**~se** *vr* to consult.

asfalto *m* asphalt.

asfixiar *vt* to suffocate:—**~se** *vr* to suffocate.

así *adv* so, thus, in this manner; like this; therefore; so that; also:—**~ que** so that; therefore:—**así/así** so-so; middling.

asiento *m* chair; bench, stool; seat; contract; entry; residence.

asignar *vt* to assign, attribute.

asignatura *f* subject; course.

asilo *m* asylum, refuge.

asimismo *adv* similarly, in the same manner.

asir *vt* to grasp, seize; to hold, grip:—*vi* to take root.

asistencia *f* audience; presence; assistance, help.

asistir *vi* to be present; to assist:—*vt* to help.

asma *f* asthma.

asno *m* ass.

asociación *f* association; partnership.

asolear *vt* to expose to the sun:—**~se** *vr* to sunbathe.

asomar *vi* to appear:—**~se** *vr* to appear, show up.

asombrar *vt* to amaze; to astonish:—**~se** *vr* to be amazed; to get a fright.

aspa *f* cross; sail.

aspecto *m* appearance; aspect.

áspero/ra *adj* rough, rugged; craggy, knotty; horrid; harsh, hard; severe, austere; gruff.

aspiración *f* breath; pause.

asqueroso/sa *adj* disgusting.

asta *f* lance; horn; handle.

astilla *f* chip (of wood), splinter.

astillero *m* dockyard.

astral *adj* astral.

astro *m* star.

astrología *m* astrology.

astronomía *f* astronomy.

astucia *f* cunning, slyness.

astuto/ta *adj* cunning, sly; astute.

asumir *vt* to assume.

asunto *m* subject, matter; affair, business.

asustar *vt* to frighten:—**~se** *vr* to be frightened.

atacar *vt* to attack.

atajo *m* short cut.

atañer *vi*:—**~ a** to concern.

atar *vt* to tie; to fasten.

atardecer *vi* to get dark:—*m* dusk; evening.

atascar *vt* to jam; to hinder:—**~se** *vr* to become bogged down.

ataúd *m* coffin.

atemorizar *vt* to frighten:—**~se** *vr* to get scared.

atención *f* attention, heedfulness; civility; observance, considcration.

atender *vi* to be attentive:—*vt* to attend to; to heed, expect, wait for; to look at.

atenerse *vr*:—**~ a** to adhere to.

atentamente *adv*:—**le saluda ~** yours faithfully.

atento/ta *adj* attentive; heedful; observing; mindful; polite, courteous, mannerly.

atenuar *vt* to diminish; to lessen.

ateo/a *adj*, *m/f* atheist.

aterciopelado/da *adj* velvety.

aterrar *vt* to terrify:—**~se** *vr* to be terrified.

aterrizar *vt* to land.

aterrorizar *vt* to frighten, terrify.

atesorar *vt* to treasure *or* hoard up (riches).

atestado/da *adj* packed:—*m* affidavit.

atestiguar *vt* to witness, attest.

atiborrar *vt* to stuff:—**~se** *vr* to stuff oneself.

ático *m* attic.

atinado/da *adj* wise; correct.

atizar *vt* to stir (the fire) with a poker; to stir up.

allántico/ca *adj* atlantic.

atleta *m* athlete.

atletismo *m* athletics.

atomizador *m* spray.

átomo *m* atom.

atónito/ta *adj* astonished, amazed.

atontado/da *adj* stunned; silly.

atornillar *vt* to screw on; to screw down.

atosigar *vt* to poison; to harass; to oppress.

atracar *vt* to moor; to rob:—**~se** *vr* **~ (de)** to stuff oneself (with).

atractivo/va *adj* attractive; magnetic:—*m* charm.

atraer *vt* to attract, allure.

atragantarse *vr* to stick in the throat, choke.

atrapar *vt* to trap; to nab; to deceive.

atrás *adv* backward(s); behind; previously: —**hacia ~** backward(s).

atrasar *vt* to be slow:—*vt* to postpone: —**el reloj** to put back a watch:—**~se** *vr* to stay behind; to be late.

atravesado/da *adj* oblique; cross; perverse; mongrel; degenerate.

atravesar *vt* to cross; to pass over; to pierce; to go through:—**~se** *vr* to get in the way; to meddle.

atreverse *vr* to dare, venture.

atribuir *vt* to attribute, ascribe; to impute.

atril *m* lectern; bookrest.

atrio *m* porch; portico.

atrocidad *f* atrocity.

atropellar *vt* to trample; to run down; to hurry; to insult:—**~se** *vr* to hurry.

atroz *adj* atrocious, heinous; cruel.

atuendo *m* attire.

atún *m* tuna (fish).

aturdir *vt* to stun, confuse; to stupefy.

audaz *adj* audacious, bold.

audiencia *f* audience.

auge *m* boom; climax.

augurio *m* omen.

aula *f* lecture room.

aullar *vi* to howl.

aumentar *vt* to augment, increase; to magnify; to put up:—*vi* to increase; to grow larger.

aún *adv* even:—**~ asi** even so.

aunque *adv* though, although.

auricular *m* receiver:—**~es** *mpl* headphones *pl*.

aurora f dawn.
ausencia f absence.
ausente adj absent.
auspicio m auspice; prediction; protection.
austero/ra adj austere, severe.
auténtico/ca adj authentic.
autoadhesivo/va adj self-adhesive.
autobús m bus.
autocar m bus, coach.
autóctono/na adj native.
autodefensa f self-defense.
autodeterminación f self-determination.
autoescuela f driving school.
automovilismo m motoring; motor racing.
autónomo/ma adj autonomous.
autopista f motorway.
autopsia f post mortem, autopsy.
autor/ra m/f author; maker; writer.
autoridad f authority.
autorizar vt to authorize.
autorretrato m self-portrait.
autoservicio m self-service store; restaurant.
autostop m hitch-hiking.
autosuficiencia f self-sufficiency.
autovía f state highway.
auxiliar vt to aid, help, assist; to attend:— adj auxiliary.
aval m guarantee; guarantor.
avanzar vt, vi to advance.
avaricia f avarice.
avaro/ra adj miserly:—m/f miser.
ave f bird; fowl.
avecinarse vr to approach.
avellana f hazelnut.
avena f oats pl.
avenida f avenue.
aventajar vt to surpass, excel.

aventura f adventure; event, incident.
avergonzar vt to shame, abash:—~se vr to be ashamed.
avería f breakdown.
averiado/da adj broken down; out of order.
averiguar vt to find out; to inquire into; to investigate.
avestruz m ostrich.
aviación f aviation; air force.
avicultura f poultry farming.
avidez f covetousness.
avinagrado/da adj sour.
avión m airplane.
avioneta f light aircraft.
avisar vt to inform; to warn; to advise.
aviso m notice; warning; hint.
avispa f wasp.
avispado/da adj lively, brisk; vivacious.
¡ay! excl alas!; ow!:—¡~ de mi! alas! poor me!
ayer adv yesterday.
ayuda f help, aid; support:—m deputy, assistant.
ayudar vt to help, assist; to further.
ayunar vi to fast, abstain from food.
ayuntamiento m town/city hall.
azabache m jet.
azafata f air hostess.
azafrán m saffron.
azahar m orange or lemon blossom.
azar m fate:—**por ~** by chance:—**al ~** at random.
azotar vt to whip, lash.
azotea f flat roof of a house.
azúcar m sugar.
azufre m sulfur, brimstone.
azul adj blue:—~ **celeste** sky blue.
azulejo m tile.

B

baba f dribble, spittle.
babero m bib.
babia f:—**estar en ~** to be absent-minded or dreaming.
baca f (auto) luggage rack.
bacalao m cod.
bache m pothole.
bachillerato m baccalaureate.
bahía f bay.
bailar vi to dance.
bailarín/ina m/f dancer.
baja f fall; casualty.
bajada f descent; inclination; slope; ebb.
bajamar f low tide.

bajar vt to lower, let down; to lessen; to humble; to go/come down.
bajo/ja adj low; abject, despicable; common; humble:—prep under, underneath, below:—adv softly; quietly:—m (mus) bass; low place.
bala f bullet.
balance m hesitation; balance sheet; balance; rolling (of a ship).
balanza f scale; balance; judgement.
balar vi to bleat.
balcón m balcony.
balde m bucket:—**de ~** adv gratis, for nothing:—**en ~** in vain.

baldío/dia *adj* waste; uncultivated.
baldosa *f* floor; tile; flagstone.
ballena *f* whale; whalebone.
balneario *m* spa.
baloncesto *m* basketball.
balonmano *m* handball.
balonvolea *m* volleyball.
balsa *f* balsa wood; pool; raft, float; ferry.
bañador *m* swimsuit.
bañar *vt* to bathe; to dip; to coat (with varnish):—**se** *vr* to bathe; to swim.
bancarrota *f* bankruptcy.
banco *m* bench; work bench; bank.
banda *f* band; sash; ribbon; troop; party; gang; touchline.
bandada *f* flock; shoal.
bandeja *f* tray, salver.
bandera *f* banner, standard; flag.
bando *m* faction, party; edict.
bandolero *m* bandit.
bañera *f* bath (tub).
baño *m* bath; dip; bathtub; varnish; crust of sugar; coating.
banqueta *f* three-legged stool; sidewalk.
banquete *m* banquet; formal dinner.
banquillo *m* dock.
bar *m* bar.
baraja *f* deck of cards.
barandilla *f* small balustrade, small railing.
barato/ta *adj* cheap:—**de ~ gratis**:—*m* cheapness; bargain sale.
barba *f* chin; beard:—**~ a ~** face to face.
barbaridad *f* barbarity, barbarism; outrage.
bárbaro/ra *adj* barbarous; cruel; rude; rough.
barbecho *m* first ploughing, fallow land.
barbero *m* barber.
barbilampiño/ña *adj* clean-shaven; (*fig*) inexperienced.
barbilla *f* chin.
barca *f* boat.
barco *m* boat; ship.
barnis *m* varnish; glaze.
barómetro *m* barometer.
barquillo *m* wafer; cornet, cone.
barra *m* bar; rod; lever; French loaf; sandbank.
barraca *f* hut.
barranco *m* gully, ravine; (*fig*) great difficulty.
barrenar *vt* to drill, bore; (*fig*) to frustrate.
barrendero *m* sweeper, garbage man.
barrer *vt* to sweep.
barrera *f* barrier; turnpike, claypit.
barriga *f* abdomen; belly.
barril *m* barrel; cask.
barrio *m* area, district.
barro *m* clay, mud.

barrote *m* ironwork of doors, windows, tables; crosspiece.
barruntar *vt* to guess; to foresee; to conjecture.
bártulos *mpl* gear, belongings *pl*.
barullo *m* uproar.
basar *vt* to base:—**se** *vr* **~ en** to be based on.
báscula *f* scales *pl*.
base *f* base, basis.
básico/ca *adj* basic.
bastante *adj* sufficient, enough:—*adv* quite.
bastar *vi* to be sufficient, be enough.
bastidor *m* embroidery frame:—**es** *mpl* scenery (on stage).
basto/ta *adj* coarse, rude, unpolished.
bastón *m* cane, stick; nightstick; (*fig*) command.
bastos *mpl* clubs *pl* (one of the four suits at cards).
basura *f* trash, garbage.
bata *f* bathrobe; overall; laboratory coat.
batalla *f* battle, combat; fight.
batata *f* sweet potato.
batería *m* battery; percussion.
batir *vt* to beat; to whisk; to dash; to demolish; to defeat.
baúl *m* trunk.
bautisar *vt* to baptize, christen.
baza *f* card-trick.
bazo *m* spleen.
beato/ta *adj* happy; blessed; devout: —*m* lay brother:—*m/f* pious person.
bebé *m/f* baby.
beber *vt* to drink.
bebida *f* drink, beverage.
beca *f* fellowship; grant, bursary, scholarship; sash; hood.
bedel *m* head porter; uniformed employee.
belén *m* nativity scene.
bélico/ca *adj* warlike, martial.
belladona *f* (*bot*) deadly nightshade.
belleza *f* beauty.
bello/lla *adj* beautiful; handsome; lovely; fine.
bellota *f* acorn.
bemol *m* (*mus*) flat.
bendecir *vt* to bless; to consecrate; to praise.
bendito/ta *adj* saintly; blessed; simple; happy.
beneficiar *vt* to benefit; to be of benefit to.
beneficio *m* benefit, advantage; profit; benefit night.
beneficioso/sa *adj* beneficial.
beneplácito *m* consent, approbation.
benévolo/la *adj* benevolent, kind-hearted.
benigno/na *adj* benign; kind; mild.

berberecho *m* cockle.
berenjena *f* eggplant.
bergantín *m* (*mar*) brig.
berrear *vi* to low, bellow.
berrinche *m* anger, rage, tantrum (applied to children).
berrinchudo/da *adj* bad-tempered.
berro *m* watercress.
berza *f* cabbage.
besar *vt* to kiss:—**~se** *vr* to kiss.
bestia *f* beast, animal; idiot.
besugo *m* sea bream.
betún *m* shoe polish.
biberón *m* feeding bottle.
bibliófilo/la *m/f* book-lover, bookworm.
bibliografía *f* bibliography.
biblioteca *f* library.
bicarbonato *m* bicarbonate.
bicho *m* small animal; bug:—**mal** ~ villain.
bici *f* (*fam*) bike.
bicicleta *f* bicycle.
bidé *m* bidet.
bien *m* good, benefit; profit:—**es** *mpl* goods *pl*, property; wealth:—*adv* well, right; very; willingly; easily:—~ **que** *conj* although:—**está** ~ very well.
bienestar *m* well-being.
bienhechor/ra *m/f* benefactor.
bienvenida *f* welcome.
bifurcación *f* fork.
bigote *m* mustache; whiskers *pl*.
bilingüe *adj* bilingual.
bilis *f* bile.
billar *m* billiards *pl*.
billete *m* note, bill; ticket; (*ferro*) ticket:—~ **sencillo** single ticket:—~ **de ida y vuelta** return ticket.
biografía *f* biography.
biología *f* biology.
biombo *m* screen.
birlar *vt* to knock down at one blow; to pinch (*fam*).
bis *excl* encore.
bisabuela *f* great-grandmother.
bisabuelo *m* great-grandfather.
bisagra *f* hinge.
bisiesto *adj*:—**año** ~ leap year.
bisnieto/ta *m/f* great-grandson/daughter.
bistec *m* steak.
bisturí *m* scalpel.
bisutería *f* costume jewelry.
bisco/ca *adj* cross-eyed.
biscocho *m* sponge cake; biscuit; ship's biscuit.
blanco/ca *adj* white; blank:—*m* whiteness, white person; blank, blank space; target (to shoot at).

blando/da *adj* soft, smooth; mild, gentle; (*fam*) cowardly.
blanquear *vt* to bleach; to whitewash; to launder (money).
blasfemar *vi* to blaspheme.
bledo *m*:—**no me importa un** ~ I don't give a damn (*sl*).
blindado/da *adj* armor-plated; bullet-proof.
bloc *m* writing pad.
bloque *m* block.
bloquear *vt* to block; to blockade.
blusa *f* blouse.
bobada *f* folly, foolishness.
bobina *f* bobbin.
bobo/ba *m/f* idiot, fool; clown, funny man:—*adj* stupid, silly.
boca *f* mouth; entrance, opening; mouth of a river:—~ **en** ~ *adv* by word of mouth:—**a pedir de** ~ to one's heart's content.
bocacalle *f* entrance to a street.
bocadillo *m* sandwich, roll.
bocado *m* mouthful.
bocazas *m invar* big-mouth.
boceto *m* sketch; design; mock-up.
bochorno *m* sultry weather, scorching heat; blush.
bocina *f* (*mus*) trumpet; (*auto*) horn.
bocinar *vi* to sound a horn, hoot.
boda *f* wedding.
bodega *f* wine cellar; warehouse; bar.
bofetada *f* slap (in the face).
boina *f* beret.
boj *m* box, box tree.
bola *f* ball; marble; globe; (*fam*) lie, fib.
bolera *f* bowling alley.
bolero *m* bolero jacket; bolero dance.
boletín *m* bulletin; journal, review.
boleto *m* ticket.
boliche *m* jack at bowls; bowls, bowling alley; dragnet.
bolígrafo *m* (ballpoint) pen.
bollo *m* bread roll; lump.
bolo *m* ninepin; (large) pill.
bolsa *f* purse; bag; pocket; sac; stock exchange.
bolsillo *m* pocket; purse.
bomba *f* pump; bomb; surprise:—**dar a la** ~ to pump:—~ **de gaso-lina** gas pump.
bombero *m* fireman.
bombilla *f* light bulb.
bombo *m* large drum.
bombón *m* chocolate.
bondad *f* goodness, kindness; courtesy.
bondadoso/sa *adj* good, kind.
boñiga *f* cow pat.
bonito *adj* pretty, nice-looking; pretty good, passable:—*m* tuna (fish).

boquerón *m* anchovy; large hole.
boquilla *f* mouthpiece of a musical instrument; nozzle.
borde *m* border; margin; (*mar*) board.
bordear *vi* (*mar*) to tack:—*vt* to go along the edge of; to flank.
bordillo *m* curb.
bordo *m* (*mar*) board of a ship.
boreal *adj* boreal, northern.
borracho/cha *adj* drunk, intoxicated; blind with passion:—*m/f* drunk, drunkard.
borrador *m* first draft; scribbling pad; eraser.
borrar *vt* to erase, rub out; to blur; to obscure.
borrasca *f* storm; violent squall of wind; hazard; danger.
borrico/ca *m/f* donkey, ass; blockhead.
borrón *m* blot, blur.
bosque *m* forest; wood.
bosquejo *m* sketch (of a painting); unfinished work.
bostezar *vi* to yawn; to gape.
bota *f* leather wine-bag; boot.
botánica *f* botany.
bote *m* bounce; thrust; tin, can; boat.
botella *f* bottle.
botijo *m* earthenware pitcher.
botín *m* high boot, half-boot; gaiter; booty.
botiquín *m* medicine chest.
botón *m* button; knob (of a radio etc); (*bot*) bud.
bóveda *f* arch; vault; crypt.
boxeo *m* boxing.
boya *f* (*mar*) buoy.
boyante *adj* buoyant, floating; (*fig*) fortunate, successful.
bozo *m* down (on the upper lip or chin); headstall (of a horse).
braga *f* sling, rope; nappy, diaper:—**s** *fpl* breeches *pl*; panties *pl*.
bragueta *f* fly, flies *pl* (of pants/trousers).
brasa *f* live coal:—**estar hecho una ~** to be very flushed.
bravío/vía *adj* ferocious, savage, wild; coarse.
bravo/va *adj* brave, valiant; bullying; savage, fierce; rough; sumptuous; excellent, fine:—*excl* well done!
braza *f* fathom.
brazo *m* arm; branch (of a tree); enterprise; courage:—**luchar a ~ par-tido** to fight hand-to-hand.
brea *f* pitch; tar.
brebaje *m* potion.
brecha *f* (*mil*) breach, gap, opening.
breva *f* early fig; early large acorn.

breve *m* papal brief:—*f* (*mus*) breve: —*adj* brief, short:—**en ~** shortly.
brezo *m* (*bot*) heather.
bribón/ona *adj* dishonest, rascally.
bricolaje *m* do-it-yourself.
brida *f* bridle; clamp, flange.
brigada *f* brigade; squad, gang.
brillante *adj* brilliant; bright, shining:—*m* diamond.
brillar *vi* to shine; to sparkle, glisten; to shine, be outstanding.
brincar *vi* to skip; to leap, jump; to gambol; to fly into a passion.
brindis *m invar* toast.
brío *m* spirit, dash.
brisca *f* card game.
broca *f* reel; drill; shoemaker's tack.
brocado *m* gold or silver brocade:—**~/ da** *adj* embroidered, like brocade.
brocha *f* large brush:—**~ de afeitar** shaving brush.
broche *m* clasp; brooch; cufflink.
broma *f* joke.
bromear *vi* to joke.
bronca *f* row.
bronceado/da *adj* tanned:—*m* bronzing, suntan.
brotar *vi* (*bot*) to bud, germinate; to gush, rush out; (*med*) to break out.
bruces *adv*:—**a ~/de ~** face down-ward(s).
bruja *f* witch.
brújula *f* compass.
bruma *f* mist; (*mar*) sea mist.
bruñir *vt* to polish; to put rouge on.
brusco/ca *adj* rude; sudden; brusque.
brutal *adj* brutal, brutish:—*m* brute.
bruto *m* brute, beast:—**~/ ta** *adj* stupid; gross; brutish.
bucal *adj* oral.
bucear *vi* to dive.
bucle *m* curl.
buen *adj* (*before m nouns*) good.
bueno/na *adj* good, perfect; fair; fit, proper; good-looking:—**¡buenos días!** good morning!:—**¡buenas tardes!** good afternoon:—**¡buenas noches!** good night!:—**¡i~!** right!
buey *m* ox, bullock.
bufanda *f* scarf.
bufete *m* desk, writing-table; lawyer's office.
bufo/fa *adj* comic:—**opera ~a** *f* comic opera.
buhardilla *f* attic.
búho *m* owl; unsocial person.
buitre *m* vulture.
bujía *f* candle; spark plug.
bullicio *m* bustle; uproar.
bulto *m* bulk; tumor, swelling; bust; baggage.

buñuelo *m* doughnut; fritter.

buque *m* vessel, ship, tonnage, capacity (of a ship); hull (of a ship).

burbuja *f* bubble.

burdel *m* brothel.

burguesía *f* bourgeoisie.

burlar *vt* to hoax; to defeat; to play tricks on, deceive; to frustrate:—**~se** *vr* to joke, laugh at.

burro *m* ass, donkey; idiot; saw-horse.

bursátil *adj* stock exchange *compd*.

buscar *vt* to seek, search for; to look for; to hunt after:—*vi* to look, search, seek.

busilis *m* difficulty, snag.

busto *m* bust.

butaca *f* armchair; seat.

butano *m* butane.

butifarra *f* Catalan sausage.

butrón *m* burglary.

buzo *m* diver.

buzón *m* mailbox; conduit, canal; cover of a jar.

C

cabalgar *vi* to ride, go riding.

cabalgata *f* procession.

caballa *f* mackerel.

caballería *f* mount, steed; cavalry; cavalry horse; chivalry; knighthood.

caballero *m* knight; gentleman; rider, horseman.

caballete *m* ridge of a roof; painter's easel; trestle; bridge (of the nose).

caballo *m* horse; (at chess) knight; queen (in cards):—**a ~** on horseback.

cabecera *f* headboard; head; far end; pillow; headline; vignette.

cabecilla *m* ringleader.

cabello *m* hair.

caber *vi* to fit.

cabeza *f* head; chief, leader; main town, chief center.

cabida *f* room, capacity.

cabildo *m* chapter (of church); meeting of a chapter; corporation of a town.

cabina *f* cabin; telephone booth.

cabizbajo/ja, cabizcaido/da *adj* crestfallen; pensive, thoughtful.

cable *m* cable, lead, wire.

cabo *m* end, extremity; cape, headland; (*mar*) cable, rope.

cabra *f* goat.

cabrón *m* cuckold:—**i~!** (*fam*) bastard! (*sl*).

cacahuete *m* peanut.

cacao *m* (*bot*) cacao tree; cocoa.

cacarear *vi* to crow; to brag, boast.

cacerola *f* pan, saucepan; casserole.

cachalote *m* sperm whale.

cacharro *m* pot.

cachivache *m* pot; piece of junk.

cachondo/da *adj* randy; funny.

cachorro/ra *m/f* puppy; cub.

caco *m* pickpocket; coward.

cada *adj invar* each; every.

cadáver *m* corpse, cadaver.

cadena *f* chain; series, link; radio or TV network.

cadera *f* hip.

caducar *vi* to become senile; to expire, lapse; to deteriorate.

caer *vi* to fall; to tumble down; to lapse; to happen; to die:—**~se** *vr* to fall down.

café *m* coffee; cafe, coffee house.

cafetera *f* coffee pot.

cagar *vi* (*fam*) to have a shit (*sl*).

caimán *m* caiman, alligator.

caja *f* box, case; casket; cashbox; cash desk; supermarket check-out:—**~ de ahorros** savings bank:—**~ de cambios** gearbox.

cajón *m* bureau; locker.

cal *f* lime:—**~ viva** quick lime.

calabacín *m* small marrow, zucchini.

calabaza *f* pumpkin, squash.

calamar *m* squid.

calar *vt* to soak, drench; to penetrate, pierce; to see through; to lower:—**~se** *vr* to stall (of a car).

calavera *f* skull; madcap.

calcar *vt* to trace, copy.

calcetín *m* sock.

calcio *m* calcium.

calcomanía *f* transfer.

calculadora *f* calculator.

calcular *vt* to calculate, reckon; to compute.

caldear *vt* to weld; to warm, heat up.

calderada *f* stew.

calderilla *f* small change.

caldo *m* stock; broth.

calefacción *f* heating.

calendario *m* calendar.

calentar *vt* to warm up, heat up:—**~se** *vr* to grow hot; to dispute.

calidad *f* grade, quality, condition; kind.

cálido/da *adj* hot; (*fig*) warm.

caliente *adj* hot; fiery:—**en ~** in the heat of the moment.

callado/da *adj* silent, quiet.
callar *vi*, ~**se** *vr* to be silent, keep quiet.
calle *f* street; road.
callejear *vi* to loiter about the streets.
callejón *m* alley.
callo *m* corn; callus:—~**s** *mpl* tripe.
calmante *m* (*med*) sedative.
calmar *vt* to calm, quiet, pacify:—*vi* to become calm.
calor *m* heat, warmth; ardor, passion.
calumnia *f* calumny, slander.
calvo/va *adj* bald; bare, barren.
calzado *m* footwear.
calzoncillos *mpl* underpants, shorts *pl*.
cama *f* bed:—**hacer la** ~ to make the bed.
cámara *f* hall; chamber; room; camera; cine camera.
camarada *m/f* comrade, companion.
camarera *f* waitress.
camarero *m* waiter.
camarón *m* shrimp, prawn.
camarote *m* berth, cabin.
cambalache *m* exchange, swap.
cambiar *vt* to exchange; to change:—*vi* to change, alter:—~**se** *vr* to move house.
cambio *m* change, exchange; rate of exchange; bureau de change.
camelar *vt* to flirt with.
camello *m* camel; drug dealer.
camilla *f* couch; cot; stretcher.
caminar *vi* to travel; to walk, go.
camino *m* road; way.
camión *m* truck.
camisa *f* shirt; chemise.
camisería *f* dry goods store.
camiseta *f* T-shirt; undershirt.
camisón *m* nightgown.
campamento *m* (*mil*) encampment.
campana *f* bell.
campanario *m* belfry.
campeón/ona *m/f* champion.
campesino/na, campestre *adj* rural.
campo *m* country; field; camp; ground; pitch.
caña *f* cane, reed; stalk; shinbone; glass of beer:—~ **dulce** sugar cane.
cañada *f* gully; glen; sheep-walk.
canal *m* channel, canal.
canalla *f* mob, rabble.
cáñamo *m* hemp.
canas *fpl* gray hair:—**peinar** ~ to grow old.
cañaveral *m* reedbed.
cancelar *vt* to cancel; to write off.
cancha *f* (tennis) court.
canción *f* song.
candado *m* padlock.
candilejas *fpl* footlights *pl*.

canela *f* cinnamon.
cangrejo *m* crab; crayfish.
canica *f* marble.
canilla *f* shinbone; arm-bone; tap of a cask; spool.
canjear *vt* to exchange.
cano/na *adj* gray-haired; white-haired.
canoso/sa *adj* gray-haired; white-haired.
cansancio *m* tiredness, fatigue.
cansar *vt* to tire, tire out; to bore:—~**se** *vr* to get tired, grow weary.
cantante *m/f* singer.
cantar *m* song:—*vt* to sing; to chant: —*vi* to sing; to chirp.
cántaro *m* pitcher; jug:—**llover a** ~**s** to rain heavily, pour.
cantera *f* quarry.
cantidad *f* quantity, amount; number.
cantina *f* buffet, refreshment room; canteen; cellar; snack bar; bar.
canto *m* stone; singing; song; edge.
canuto *m* (*fam*) joint (*sl*), marijuana cigarette.
caño *m* tube, pipe; sewer.
cañón *m* tube, pipe; barrel; gun; canyon.
caoba *f* mahogany.
caos *m* chaos; confusion.
capa *f* cloak; cape; layer, stratum; cover; pretext.
capacidad *f* capacity; extent; talent.
capataz *m* foreman, overseer.
capaz *adj* capable; capacious, spacious, roomy.
capeo *m* challenging of a bull with a cloak.
caperuza *f* hood.
capirote *m* hood.
capital *m* capital; capital sum:—*f* capital, capital city:—*adj* capital; principal.
capítulo *m* chapter of a cathedral; chapter (of a book).
capó *m* (*auto*) hood.
capote *m* greatcoat; bullfighter's cloak.
capricho *m* caprice, whim, fancy.
captar *vt* to captivate; to understand; (*rad*) to tune in to, receive.
capturar *vt* to capture.
capucha *f* cap, cowl, hood of a cloak.
capullo *m* cocoon of a silkworm; rosebud.
cara *f* face; appearance:—~ **a** ~ face to face.
cárabe *m* amber.
caracol *m* snail; seashell; spiral.
carácter *m* character; quality; condition; hand-writing.
característico/ca *adj* characteristic.
caradura *m/f*:—**es un** ~ he's got a nerve.
caramba *excl* well!

carámbano *m* icicle.
carambola *f* cannon (at billiards); trick.
caravana *f* trailer; queue; tailback (traffic).
carbón *m* coal; charcoal; carbon; carbon paper.
carboncillo *m* charcoal.
carbono *m* (*quím*) carbon.
carburador *m* carburettor.
carcajada *f* (loud) laugh.
cárcel *f* prison, penitentiary; jail.
carcoma *f* deathwatch beetle; woodworm; anxious concern.
cardenal *m* cardinal; cardinal bird; (*med*) bruise, weal.
cardo *m* thistle.
carecer *vi*:—~ **de** to want, lack.
cargar *vt* to load, burden; to charge: —*vi* to charge; to load (up); to lean.
cargo *m* burden, loading; employment; post; office; charge, care; obligation; accusation.
carguero *m* freighter.
caricia *f* caress.
caridad *f* charity.
caries *f* (*med*) tooth decay, caries.
cariño *m* fondness, tenderness; love.
carmesí *adj*, *m* crimson.
carmín *m* carmine; rouge; lipstick.
carne *f* flesh; meat; pulp (of fruit).
carné, **carnet** *m* driver's license:—~ **de identidad** identity card.
carnicería *f* butcher's (store); carnage, slaughter.
caro/ra *adj* dear; affectionate; dear, expensive:—*adv* dearly.
carpa *f* carp (fish); tent.
carpeta *f* table cover; folder, file, portfolio.
carpintero *m* carpenter.
carraca *f* carrack (ship); rattle.
carrera *f* career; course; race; run, running; route; journey:—**a** ~ **abierta**, at full speed.
carrete *m* reel, spool, bobbin.
carretera *f* highway.
carril *m* lane (of highway); furrow.
carrillo *m* cheek; pulley.
carro *m* cart; car.
carrocería *f* bodywork, coachwork.
carta *f* letter; map; document; playing card; menu:—~ **blanca** carte blanche:—~ **credencial** *o* **de creencia** credentials *pl*:—~ **certificada** registered letter:—~ **de crédito** credit card:—~ **verde** green card.
cartabón *m* square (tool).
cartel *m* placard; poster; wall chart; cartel.
cartera *f* satchel; purse, handbag; briefcase.
carterista *m/f* pickpocket.

cartero *m* mailman.
cartón *m* cardboard, pasteboard; cartoon.
casa *f* house; home; firm, company:—~ **de campo** country house:—~ **de moneda** mint:—~ **de huéspedes** boarding house, rooming house.
casar *vt* to marry; to couple; to abrogate; to annul:—~**se** *vr* to marry, get married.
cascabel *m* small bell; rattlesnake.
cascada *f* cascade, waterfall.
cascanueces *m invar* nutcracker.
cascar *vt* to crack, break into pieces; (*fam*) to beat:—~**se** *vr* to be broken open.
cáscara *f* rind, peel; husk, shell; bark.
casco *m* skull; helmet; fragment; shard; hulk (of a ship); crown (of a hat); hoof; empty bottle, returnable bottle.
cascote *m* rubble, fragment of material used in building.
caserío *m* country house; hamlet.
casero *m* landlord; janitor:—~/**ra**, *adj* domestic; household *compd*; home-made.
caset(t)e *m* cassette:—*f* cassette-player.
casi *adv* almost, nearly:—~ **nada** next to nothing:—~ **nunca** hardly ever, almost never.
caso *m* case; occurrence, event; hap, casuality; occasion; (*gr*) case:—**en ese** ~ in that case:—**en todo** ~ in any case:—~ **que** in case.
caspa *f* dandruff; scurf.
castaño *m* chestnut tree:—~/ **na** *adj* chestnut(-colored), brown.
castañuela *f* castanet.
castellano *m* Castilian, Spanish.
castigar *vt* to castigate, punish; to afflict.
castillo *m* castle.
castizo/za *adj* pure, thoroughbred.
casto/ta *adj* pure, chaste.
castor *m* beaver.
castrar *vt* to geld, castrate; to prune; to cut the honeycombs out of (beehives).
casualidad *f* chance, accident.
cataplasma *f* poultice.
catar *vt* to taste; to inspect, examine; to look at; to esteem.
catarata *f* cataract; waterfall.
catarro *m* catarrh; cold.
cátedra *f* professor's chair.
categoría *f* category; rank.
católico/ca *adj*, *m/f* catholic.
catorce *adj*, *m* fourteen.
catre *m* cot.
cauce *m* riverbed; (*fig*) channel.
caucho *m* rubber; tire.
caudal *m* volume, flow; property, wealth; plenty.

causa f cause; motive, reason; lawsuit:—**a ~ de** considering, because of.

causar vt to cause; to produce; to occasion.

cautela f caution, cautiousness.

cautivar vt to take prisoner in war; to captivate, charm.

caulo/ta adj cautious, wary.

cavar vt to dig up, excavate:—vi to dig, delve; to think profoundly.

caverna f cavern, cave.

cavidad f cavity, hollow.

cavilar vt to ponder, consider carefully.

cazador/ra m/f hunter; m huntsman: — **~ furtivo** poacher.

cazar vt to chase, hunt; to catch.

cazo m saucepan; ladle.

cazuela f casserole; pan.

cebada f barley.

cebar vt to feed (animals), fatten.

cebo m feed, food; bait, lure; priming.

cebolla f onion; bulb.

cebra f zebra.

cedazo m sieve, strainer.

ceder vt to hand over; to transfer, make over; to yield, give up:—vi to submit, comply, give in; to diminish, grow less.

cedro m cedar.

cédula f certificate; document; slip of paper; bill:—**~ de cambio** bill of exchange.

cegar vi to grow blind:—vt to blind; to block up.

ceja f eyebrow.

cejar vi to go backward(s); to slacken, give in.

celebrar vt to celebrate; to praise:—**~ misa** to say mass.

célebre adj famous, renowned; witty, funny.

celeste adj heavenly; sky-blue.

celestial adj heavenly; delightful.

celo m zeal; rut (in animals):—**~s** mpl jealousy.

celoso/sa adj zealous; jealous.

célula f cell.

cementerio m graveyard.

cena f supper.

cenar vt to have for dinner:—vi to have supper, have dinner.

cenegal m quagmire.

cenicero m ashtray.

ceniza f ashes pl:—**miércoles de ~** Ash Wednesday.

censo m census; tax; ground rent:—**~ electoral** electoral roll.

censurar vt to review, criticize; to censure, blame.

centella f lightning; spark.

centenar m hundred.

centeno m rye.

centésimo/ma adj hundredth:—m hundredth.

centígrado m centigrade.

centímetro m centimeter.

céntimo m cent.

centinela f sentry, guard.

central adj central.—f head office, headquarters; (telephone) exchange.

centro m center:—**~ comercial** shopping center.

centuplicar vt to increase a hundredfold.

ceñido/da adj tight-fitting; sparing, frugal.

ceñudo/da adj frowning, grim.

cepa f stock (of a vine); origin (of a family).

cepillo m brush; plane (tool).

cepo m branch, bough; trap; snare; poorbox.

cera f wax:—**~s** fpl honeycomb.

cerámica f pottery.

cerca f enclosure; fence:—**~s** mpl objects pl in the foreground of a painting:—adv near, at hand, close by:—**~ de** close, near.

cercano/na adj near, close by; neighboring, adjoining.

cerciorar vt to assure, ascertain, affirm:—**~se** vr to find out.

cerdo m pig, hog.

cerebro m brain.

cereza f cherry.

cerilla f wax taper; ear wax:—**~s** fpl matches, safety matches pl.

cero m nothing, zero.

cerrado/da adj closed, shut; locked; overcast, cloudy; broad (of accent).

cerrajero m locksmith.

cerrar vt to close, shut; to block up; to lock:—**~ la cuenta** to close an account:—**~se** vr to close; to heal; to cloud over:—vi to close, shut; to lock.

cerro m hill; neck (of an animal); backbone; combed flax or hemp:—**en ~** bareback.

cerrojo m bolt (of a door).

certamen m competition, contest.

certero adj accurate; well-aimed.

certeza, certidumbre f certainty.

certificado m certificate:—**~/ da** adj registered (of a letter).

cerveza f beer.

cesar vt to cease, stop; to fire (sl); to remove from office:—vi to cease, stop; to retire.

cese m suspension; dismissal.

cesión f cession; transfer.

césped m grass; lawn.

cesta f basket, pannier.

chabola *f* shack.
chal *m* shawl.
chalado/da *adj* crazy.
chale(t) *m* detached house.
chaleco *m* vest.
champán *m* champagne.
champiñón *m* mushroom.
champú *m* shampoo.
chamuscar *vt* to singe, scorch.
chantaje *m* blackmail.
chapa *f* metal plate; panel; (*auto*) license plate.
chaparrón *m* heavy shower (of rain).
chapuza *f* badly done job.
chaqueta *f* jacket.
charco *m* pool, puddle.
charcutería *f* store selling pork meat products.
charlar *vi* to chat.
charlatán/ana *m/f* chatterbox.
charol *m* varnish; patent leather.
chasco *m* disappointment; joke, jest.
chasis *m invar* (*auto*) chassis.
chasquido *m* crack; click.
chatarra *f* scrap.
chato/ta *adj* flat, flattish; snub-nosed.
chaval/la *m/f* lad/lass.
chicle *m* chewing gum.
chico/ca *adj* little, small:—*m/f* boy/girl.
chiflado/da *adj* crazy.
chile *m* chilli pepper.
chillar *vi* to scream, shriek; to howl; to creak.
chimenea *f* chimney; fireplace.
china *f* pebble; porcelain, chinaware; China silk.
chincheta *f* thumbtack.
chino/na *adj*, *m/f* Chinese:—*m* Chinese language.
chirriar *vi* to hiss; to creak; to chirp.
chisme *m* tale; thingummyjig.
chispa *f* spark, sparkle; wit; drop (of rain); drunkenness.
chiste *m* funny story, joke.
chivo/va *m/f* billy/nanny goat.
chocar *vi* to strike, knock; to crash:—*vt* to shock.
chochear *vi* to dodder, be senile; to dote.
chocolate *m* chocolate.
chófer *m* driver.
chopo *m* (*bot*) black poplar.
chorizo *m* pork sausage.
chorro *m* gush; jet; stream:—**a ~s** abundantly.
chuchería *f* trinket.
chulear *vi* to brag.
chuleta *f* chop.

chulo *m* rascal; pimp.
chupar *vt* to suck; to absorb.
churro *m* fritter.
ciática *f* sciatica.
cicatriz *f* scar.
cicatrizar *vt* to heal.
ciclista *m/f* cyclist.
ciclo *m* cycle.
cicuta *f* (*bot*) hemlock.
ciego/ga *adj* blind.
cielo *m* sky; heaven; atmosphere; climate.
ciempiés *m invar* centipede.
cien *adj*, *m* a hundred.
ciénaga *f* swamp.
ciencia *f* science.
cieno *m* mud; mire.
cierto/ta *adj* certain, sure; right, correct:—**por ~** certainly.
ciervo *m* deer, hart, stag:—**~ volante** stag beetle.
cierzo *m* cold northerly wind.
cifra *f* number, numeral; quantity; cipher; abbreviation.
cigarra *f* cicada.
cigarro *m* cigar; cigarette.
cigüeña *f* stork; crank (of a bell).
cilindro *m* cylinder.
cima *f* summit; peak; top.
cimiento *m* foundation, groundwork; basis, origin.
cinc *m* zinc.
cincelar *vt* to chisel, engrave.
cinco *adj*, *m* five.
cincuenta *adj*, *m* fifty.
cine *m* cinema.
cínico/ca *adj* cynical.
cinta *f* band, ribbon; reel.
cintura *f* waist.
cinturón *m* belt, girdle; (*fig*) zone:—**~ de seguridad** seatbelt.
ciprés *m* cypress tree.
circo *m* circus.
circuito *m* circuit; circumference.
circular *adj* circular; circulatory:—*vt* to circulate:—*vi* (*auto*) to drive.
círculo *m* circle; (*fig*) scope, compass.
circunspecto/ta *adj* circumspect, cautious.
circunstancia *f* circumstance.
circunvalacion *f*:—**carretera de ~** bypass.
cirio *m* wax candle.
ciruela *f* plum:—**~ pasa** prune.
cirugía *f* surgery.
cisne *m* swan.
citar *vt* to make an appointment with; to quote; (*jur*) to summon.
ciudad *f* city; town.
ciudadano/na *m/f* citizen:—*adj* civic.

clamor *m* clamor, outcry; peal of bells.
clandestino/na *adj* clandestine, secret, concealed.
clara *f* egg-white.
claraboya *f* skylight.
clarear *vi* to dawn:—~**se** *vr* to be transparent.
clarín *m* bugle; bugler.
clarinete *m* clarinet:—*m/f* clarinetist.
claro/ra *adj* clear, bright; evident, manifest:—*m* opening; clearing (in a wood).
clase *f* class; rank; order.
clasificar *vt* to classify.
claudicar *vi* to limp; to act deceitfully; to back down.
claustro *m* cloister; faculty (of a university).
cláusula *f* clause.
clavar *vt* to nail.
clave *f* key; (*mus*) clef:—*m* harpsichord.
clavel *m* (*bot*) carnation.
clavicordio *m* clavichord.
clavícula *f* clavicle, collar bone.
clavija *f* pin, peg.
clavo *m* nail; corn (on the feet); clove.
clemente *adj* clement, merciful.
clérigo *m* priest; clergyman.
cliente *m/f* client.
clima *m* climate.
climatizado/da *adj* air-conditioned.
clínica *f* clinic; private hospital.
clip *m* paper clip.
cloaca *f* sewer.
coacción *f* coercion, compulsion.
coagular *vt*, ~**se** *vr* to coagulate; to curdle.
coartada *f* (*jur*) alibi.
coartar *vt* to limit, restrict, restrain.
cobalto *m* cobalt.
cobarde *adj* cowardly, timid.
cobaya *f* guinea pig.
cobertizo *m* small shed; shelter.
cobijar *vt* to cover; to shelter.
cobrar *vt* to recover:—~**se** *vr* (*med*) to come to.
cobre *m* copper; kitchen utensils *pl*; (*mus*) brass.
cocear *vt* to kick; (*fig*) to resist.
cocer *vt* to boil; to bake (bricks):—*vi* to boil; to ferment:—~**se** *vr* to suffer intense pain.
cochambroso/sa *adj* nasty; filthy, stinking.
coche *m* car; coach, carriage; pram, baby carriage:—(*ferro*) ~ **cama** sleeping car:—~ **restaurante** restaurant car.
cochino/na *adj* dirty, filthy; nasty:—*m* pig, hog.
cocina *f* kitchen; stove; cookery.
cocinero/ra *m/f* cook.

coco *m* coconut; bogeyman.
cocodrilo *m* crocodile.
codazo *m* blow given with the elbow.
codear *vt*, *vi* to elbow:—~**se** *vr* ~**se con** to rub shoulders with.
codiciar *vt* to covet, desire.
código *m* code; law; set of rules.
codillo *m* knee of a four-legged animal; angle; (*tec*) elbow (joint).
codo *m* elbow.
codorniz *f* quail.
coetáneo/nea *adj* contemporary.
coexistir *vi* to coexist.
cofia *f* (nurse's) cap.
cofradía *f* brotherhood, fraternity.
cofre *m* trunk.
coger *vt* to catch, take hold of; to occupy, take up:—~**se** *vr* to catch.
cogollo *m* heart of a lettuce or cabbage; shoot of a plant.
cogote *m* back of the neck.
cohecho *m* bribery.
coherencia *f* coherence.
cohete *m* rocket.
cohibido/da *adj* shy.
coincidir *vi* to coincide.
coito *m* intercourse, coitus.
cojear *vi* to limp, hobble; (*fig*) to go astray.
cojín *m* cushion.
cojo/ja *adj* lame, crippled.
col *f* cabbage.
cola *f* tail; queue; last place; glue.
colaborar *vi* to collaborate.
colada *f* wash, washing; (*quím*) bleach; sheep run.
colador *m* sieve.
colar *vt* to strain, filter:—*vi* to ooze: —~**se en** to get into without paying.
colcha *f* bedspread, counterpane.
colchón *m* mattress.
coleccionar *vt* to collect.
colecta *f* collection (for charity).
colectivo/va *adj* collective.
colega *m/f* colleague.
colegial *m* schoolboy.
colegiala *f* schoolgirl.
colegio *m* college; school.
colegir *vt* to collect; to deduce, infer.
cólera *f* bile; anger; fury, rage; cholera.
coleta *f* pigtail.
colgar *vt* to hang; to suspend; to decorate with tapestry:—*vi* to be suspended.
colibrí *m* hummingbird.
coliflor *m* cauliflower.
colina *f* hill.
colisión *f* collision; friction.
colmar *vt* to heap up:—*vi* to fulfill, realize.

colmena f hive, beehive.
colmillo m eyetooth; tusk.
colmo m height; summit; extreme:—**a ~** plentifully.
colocar vt to arrange; to place; to provide with a job:—**se** vr to get a job.
collar m necklace; (dog) collar.
colono m colonist; farmer.
coloquio m conversation; conference.
color m color, hue; dye; rouge; suit (of cards).
colorado/da adj ruddy; red.
colorete m rouge.
columna f column.
columpio m swing, seesaw.
colza f (bot) rape; rape seed.
coma f (gr) comma:—m (med) coma.
comadreja f weasel.
comandante m commander.
comarca f territory, district.
combatir vt to combat, fight; to attack:—vi to fight.
combinar vi to combine.
combustible adj combustible:—m fuel.
comedia f comedy; play, drama.
comedido/da adj moderate, restrained.
comedor/ra m/f glutton:—m dining room.
comentar vt to comment on, expound.
comentario m comment, remark; commentary.
comenzar vi to commence, begin.
comer vt to eat; to take (a piece at chess):—vi to have lunch.
comercial adj commercial.
comercio m trade, commerce; business.
comestible adj eatable:—mpl **~s** food, foodstuffs pl.
cometa m comet:—f kite.
cometer vt to commit, charge; to entrust.
cómico/ca adj comic, comical.
comida f food; eating; meal; lunch.
comillas fpl quotation marks pl.
comino m cumin (plant or seed).
comisaría f police station; commissariat.
como adv as; like; such as.
cómo adv how?; why?:—excl what?
cómoda f bureau.
cómodo/da adj convenient; comfortable.
compacto/ta adj compact; close, dense.
compadecer vt to pity:—**se** vr to agree with each other.
compaginar vt to arrange, put in order:—**se** vr to tally.
compañero/ra m/f companion, friend; comrade; partner.
compañía f company.
comparar vt to compare.

compartimento m compartment.
compartir vt to share.
compás m compass; pair of compasses; (mus) measure, beat.
compatible adj:—**~ con** compatible with, consistent with.
compensar vt to compensate; to recompense.
competencia f competition, rivalry; competence.
competente adj competent; adequate.
compilar vt to compile.
compinche m pal, mate (sl).
complacencia f pleasure; indulgence.
complacer vt to please:—**se** vr to be pleased with.
complejo m complex:—**~/ja** adj complex.
complementario/ria adj complementary.
complemento m complement.
completar vt to complete.
completo/ta adj complete; perfect.
complicar vt to complicate.
cómplice m/f accomplice.
complot m plot.
componer vt to compose; to constitute; to mend, repair; to strengthen, restore; to compose, calm:—**se** vr **~se de** to consist of.
comportamiento m behavior.
compostura f composition, composure; mending, repairing; discretion; modesty, demureness.
compota f stewed fruit.
comprar vt to buy, purchase.
comprender vt to include, contain; to comprehend, understand.
compresa f sanitary napkin.
comprimido m pill.
comprimir vt to compress; to repress, restrain.
comprobar vt to verify, confirm; to prove.
comprometer vt to compromise; to embarrass; to implicate; to put in danger:—**se** vr to compromise oneself.
compuerta f hatch; sluice.
compuesto m compound:—**~/ta** adj composed; made up of.
compulsar vt to collate, compare; to make an authentic copy.
compungirse vr to feel remorseful.
comulgar vt to administer communion to:—vi to receive communion.
común adj common, usual, general: —m community; public:—**en ~** in common.
comunicar vt to communicate:—**se** vr to communicate (with each other).
comunidad f community.

con prep with; by:—~ **que** so then, providing that.

coñac m brandy, cognac.

cóncavo/va adj concave.

concebir vt to conceive:—vi to become pregnant.

conceder vt to give; to grant; to concede, allow.

concejal/la m/f member of a council.

concentrar vt:—~se vr to concentrate.

concepto m conceit, thought; judgement, opinion.

concernir v imp to regard, concern.

concertar vt to coordinate; to settle; to adjust; to agree; to arrange, fix up:—vi (mus) to harmonize, be in tune.

concesión f concession.

concha f shell; tortoise-shell.

conciencia f conscience.

concienciar vt to make aware:—~se vr to become aware.

concierto m concert; agreement; concerto: —**de** ~ in agreement, in concert.

conciliar vt to reconcile:—adj conciliar, council.

conciso/sa adj concise, brief.

concluir vt to conclude, end, complete; to infer, deduce:—~se vr to conclude.

concordar vt to reconcile, make agree:—vi to agree, correspond.

concordia f conformity, agreement.

concretar vt to make concrete; to specify.

concubina f concubine.

concurrido/da adj busy.

concursante m/f competitor.

concurso m crowd; competition; help, cooperation.

conde m earl, count.

condenable adj culpable.

condenar vt to condemn; to find guilty:— ~se vr to blame oneself; to confess (one's guilt).

condensar vt to condense.

condescender vi to acquiesce, comply.

condición f condition, state; quality; status; rank; stipulation.

condimentar vt to flavor, season.

condolerse vr to sympathize.

condón m condom.

conducir vt to convey, conduct; to drive; to manage:—vi to drive:—~ (a) to lead (to):—~se vr to conduct oneself.

conducta f conduct, behavior; management.

conducto m conduit, pipe; drain; (fig) channel.

conductor/ra m/f conductor, guide; (ferro) guard; driver.

conectar vt to connect.

conejo m rabbit.

conexión f connection; plug; relationship.

confección f preparation; clothing industry.

conferencia f conference; telephone call.

confesar vt to confess; to admit.

confianza f trust; confidence; conceit; familiarity:—**en** ~ confidential.

confiar vt to confide, entrust:—vi to trust.

configurar vt to shape, form.

confinar vt to confine:—vi ~ **con** to border upon.

confirmar vt to confirm; to corroborate.

confiscar vt to confiscate.

confitería f sweet store.

confitura f preserve; jam.

conflicto m conflict.

conformar vt to shape; to adjust, adapt:—vi to agree:—~se vr to conform; to resign oneself.

conforme adj alike, similar; agreed: —prep according to.

confortar vt to comfort; to strengthen; to console.

confundir vt to confound, jumble; to confuse:—~se vr to make a mistake.

confusión f confusion.

congelado/da adj frozen:—mpl ~s frozen food.

congelar vt to freeze:—~se vr to congeal.

congeniar vi to get on well.

congoja f anguish, distress, grief.

congraciarse vr to ingratiate oneself.

congregar(se) vt (vr) to assemble, meet, collect.

conjetura f conjecture, guess.

conjugar vt (gr) to conjugate; to combine.

conjunto/ta adj united, joint:—m whole; (mus) ensemble, band; team.

conjurar vt to exorcize:—vi to conspire, plot.

conmemorar vt to commemorate.

conmigo pn with me.

conmover vt to move; to disturb.

conmutador m switch.

conmutar vt (jur) to commute; to exchange.

connotar vt to imply.

cono m cone.

conocer vt to know, understand:—~se vr to know one another.

conocimiento m knowledge, understanding; (med) consciousness; acquaintance; (mar) bill of lading.

conquistar vt to conquer.

consabido/da adj well-known; above-mentioned.

consagrar vt to consecrate.

consanguíneo/nea *adj* related by blood.
consecuencia *f* consequence; conclusion; consistency:—por ~ therefore.
consecuente *adj* consistent.
conseguir *vt* to attain; to get, obtain.
consejo *m* advice; council.
consentir *vt* to consent to; to allow; to admit; to spoil (a child).
conserje *m* doorman; janitor.
conservar *vt* to conserve; to keep; to preserve (fruit).
conservas *fpl* canned food.
conservatorio *m* (*mus*) conservatoire.
consideración *f* consideration; respect.
considerar *vt* to consider.
consigna *f* (*mil*) watchword; order, instruction; (*ferro*) left-luggage office.
consignar *vt* to consign, dispatch; to assign; to record, register.
consigo *pn* (*m*) with him; (*f*) with her; (*vd*) with you; (*refl*) with oneself.
consiguiente *adj* consequent.
consistente *adj* consistent; firm, solid.
consistir *vi*:—~ en to consist of; to be due to.
consola *f* control panel.
consolar *vt* to console, comfort, cheer.
consolidar *vt* to consolidate.
consonante *m* rhyme:—*f* (*gr*) consonant:— *adj* consonant, harmonious.
consorcio *m* partnership.
consorte *m/f* consort, companion, partner; accomplice.
conspirar *vi* to conspire, plot.
constante *adj* constant; firm.
constar *vi* to be evident, be certain; to be composed of, consist of.
constatar *vt* to note; to check.
consternar *vt* to dismay; to shock.
constipado/da *adj*:—estar ~ to have a cold.
constituir *vt* to constitute; to establish; to appoint.
construir *vt* to form; to build, construct; to construe.
consuegro/gra *m/f* father-in-law/mother-in-law of one's son or daughter.
consuelo *m* consolation, comfort.
cónsul *m* consul.
consultar *vt* to consult, ask for advice.
consultor/ra *m/f* adviser, consultant.
consultorio *m* (*med*) consulting room, doctor's rooms.
consumar *vt* to consummate, finish; to carry out.
consumir *vt* to consume; to burn, use; to waste, exhaust:—~se *vr* to waste away, be consumed.
contabilidad *f* accounting; bookkeeping.

contacto *m* contact; (*auto*) ignition.
contado/da *adj*:—~s scarce, few:—*m* pagar al ~ to pay (in) cash.
contador *m* meter; counter in a cafe: — ~/ ~a *m/f* accountant.
contagiar *vt* to infect:—~se *vr* to get infected.
contaminar *vt* to contaminate; to pollute; to corrupt.
contar *vt* to count, reckon; to tell:—*vi* to count:—~ con to rely upon.
contemplar *vt* to look at; to contemplate, consider; to meditate.
contemporáneo/nea *adj* contemporary.
contenedor *m* container.
contener *vt* to contain, hold; to hold back; to repress:—~se *vr* to control oneself.
contentar *vt* to content, satisfy; to please:— ~se *vr* to be pleased or satisfied.
contento/ta *adj* glad; pleased; content:—*m* contentment; (*jur*) release.
contestador *m*:—~ automatico answering machine.
contestar *vt* to answer, reply; to prove, corroborate.
contienda *f* contest, dispute.
contigo *pn* with you.
contiguo/gua *adj* contiguous, close.
continente *m* continent, mainland:—*adj* continent.
contingencia *f* risk; contingency.
continuar *vt*, *vi* to continue.
continuo/nua *adj* continuous.
contorno *m* environs *pl*; contour, outline: —en ~ round about.
contra *prep* against; contrary to; opposite.
contrabajo *m* (*mus*) double bass; bass guitar; low bass.
contrabando *m* contraband; smuggling.
contrachapado *m* plywood.
contradecir *vt* to contradict.
contraer *vt* to contract, shrink; to make (a bargain):—~se *vr* to shrink, contract.
contrahecho/cha *adj* deformed; hunchbacked; counterfeit, fake, false.
contralto *m* (*mus*) contralto.
contrapartida *f* (*com*) balancing entry.
contrapelo *adv*:—a ~ against the grain.
contrapeso *m* counterpoise; counterweight.
contraproducente *adj* counterproductive.
contrariar *vt* to contradict, oppose; to vex.
contrariedad *f* opposition; setback; annoyance.
contrario/ria *m/f* opponent:—*adj* contrary, opposite:—por el ~ on the contrary.
contrarrestar *vt* to return a ball; (*fig*) to counteract.

contraseña f countersign; (*mil*) watch word.
contrasentido m contradiction.
contrastar vt to resist; to contradict; to assay (metals); to verify (measures and weights): —vi to contrast.
contratar vt to contract; to hire, engage.
contratiempo m setback; accident.
contrato m contract, agreement.
contravenir vi to contravene, transgress; to violate.
contraventana f shutter.
contribución f contribution; tax.
contribuir vt, vi to contribute.
contrincante m competitor.
controlar vt to control; to check.
contumaz adj obstinate, stubborn; (*jur*) guilty of contempt of court.
contundente adj overwhelming; blunt.
contusión f bruise.
convalecer vi to recover from sickness, convalesce.
convencer vt to convince.
conveniencia f suitability; usefulness; agreement:—s fpl property.
convenir vi to agree, suit.
convento m convent, nunnery; monastery.
conversar vi to talk, converse.
convicto/ta adj convicted (found guilty).
convidar vt to invite.
convocar vt to convoke, assemble.
convocatoria f summons; notice of a meeting.
conyugal adj conjugal, married.
cónyuge m/f spouse.
cooperar vi to cooperate.
coordinar vt to arrange, coordinate.
copa f cup; glass; top of a tree; crown of a hat:—s fpl hearts pl (at cards).
copiar vt to copy; to imitate.
copla f verse; (*mus*) popular song, folk song.
copo m small bundle; flake of snow.
coquetear vi to flirt.
coraje m courage; anger, passion.
coral m coral; choir:—adj choral.
corazón m heart; core:—de ~ willingly.
corazonada f inspiration; quick decision; presentiment.
corbata f tie.
corchete m clasp; hook and eye.
corcho m cork; float (for fishing); cork bark.
cordel m cord, rope; (*mar*) line.
cordero m lamb; lambskin; meek, gentle person.
cordial adj cordial, affectionate:—m cordial.
cordillera f range of mountains.
cordón m cord, string; lace; cordon.
cornada f thrust with a bull's horn.

coro m choir; chorus.
corona f crown; coronet; top of the head; crown (of a tooth); tonsure; halo.
coronilla f crown of the head.
corpiño m bodice.
corporal adj corporal.
corpulento/ta adj corpulent, bulky.
corral m yard; farmyard; corral; playpen.
correa f leather strap, thong; flexibility.
correcto/ta adj exact, correct.
corregir vt to correct, amend; to reprehend: —se vr to reform.
correo m post, mail; courier; mailman:—a vuelta de ~ by return of post:—s mpl post office.
correr vt to run; to flow; to travel over; to pull (a drape):—vi to run, rush; to flow; to blow (applied to the wind):—se vr to be ashamed; to slide, move; to run (of colors).
correspondencia f correspondence; communication; agreement.
corresponder vi to correspond; to answer; to be suitable; to belong; to concern:— ~se vr to love one another.
corresponsal m/f correspondent.
corriente f current; course, progression; (electric) current:—adj current; common, ordinary, general; fluent; flowing, running.
corro m circle of people.
corroer vt to corrode, erode.
corromper vt to corrupt; to rot; to turn bad; to seduce; to bribe:—se vr to rot; to become corrupted:—vi to stink.
cortacesped m lawn mower.
cortado m coffee with a little milk:—~/ da adj cut; sour; embarrassed.
cortar vt to cut; to cut off, curtail; to intersect; to carve; to chop; to cut (at cards); to interrupt:—se vr to be ashamed or embarrassed; to curdle.
corte m cutting; cut; section, length (of cloth); style:—f (royal) court; capital (city): —C~s fpl Spanish Parliament.
cortejo m entourage; courtship; procession; lover.
cortés/esa adj courteous, polite.
cortesía f courtesy, good manners pl.
corteza f bark; peel; crust; (*fig*) outward appearance.
cortina f curtain.
corto/ta adj short; scanty, small; stupid; bashful:—a la ~a o a la larga sooner or later.
corzo/za m/f roe deer, fallow deer.
cosa f thing; matter; affair:—no hay tal ~ nothing of the sort!

cosecha *f* harvest; harvest time:—**de su ~** of one's own invention.

coser *vt* to sew; to join.

cosquillas *fpl* tickling; (*fig*) agitation.

costa *f* cost, price; charge, expense; coast, shore:—**a toda ~** at all events.

costado *m* side; (*mil*) flank; side of a ship.

costal *m* sack, large bag.

costar *vt* to cost; to need.

coste *m* cost, expense.

costero/ra *adj* coastal; (*mar*) coasting.

costilla *f* rib; cutlet:—**~s** *fpl* back, shoulders *pl*.

costra *f* crust; (*med*) scab.

costumbre *f* custom, habit.

cotejar *vt* to compare.

cotidiano/na *adj* daily.

cotilla *m/f* gossip.

cotizar *vt* to quote:—**~se** *vr* **~ a** to sell at; to be quoted at.

coto *m* enclosure; reserve; boundary stone.

cotorra *f* small parrot; (*col*) chatterbox.

covacha *f* small cave, grotto.

coyuntura *f* joint, articulation; juncture.

coz *f* kick; recoil (of a gun); ebbing (of a flood); (*fig*) insult.

cráneo *m* skull.

crear *vt* to create, make; to establish.

crecer *vi* to grow, increase; to rise.

crecida *f* swell (of rivers).

creciente *f* crescent (moon); (*mar*) flood tide:—*adj* growing; crescent.

crecimiento *m* increase; growth.

crédito *m* credit; belief, faith; reputation.

creer *vt, vi* to believe, to think; to consider.

crema *f* cream; custard.

cremallera *f* zipper.

crepúsculo *m* twilight.

cresta *f* crest (of birds).

creyente *m/f* believer.

cría *f* breeding; young.

criadero *m* (*bot*) nursery; breeding place.

criadilla *f* testicle; small loaf; truffle.

crianza *f* breeding, rearing.

criar *vt* to create, produce; to breed; to breast-feed; to bring up.

criatura *f* creature; child.

crimen *m* crime.

criminal *adj, m/f* criminal.

crin *f* mane; horsehair.

crío/a *m/f* (*fam*) kid.

cripta *f* crypt.

crisis *f invar* crisis.

crisol *m* crucible; melting pot.

crispar *vt* to set on edge; to tense up.

cristal *m* crystal; glass; pane; lens.

cristalino/na *adj* crystalline.

cristalizar *vt* to crystallize.

cristiano/na *adj, m/f* Christian.

criterio *m* criterion.

crítica *m/f* criticism.

criticar *vt* to criticize.

croar *vi* to croak.

cromo *m* chrome.

crónica *f* chronicle; news report; feature.

crónico/ca *adj* chronic.

cronista *m/f* chronicler; reporter, columnist.

cronómetro *m* stopwatch.

cruce *m* crossing; crossroads.

crucero *m* cruiser; cruise; transept; crossing.

crucifijo *m* crucifix.

crucigrama *m* crossword.

crudo/da *adj* raw; green, unripe; crude; cruel; hard to digest.

cruel *adj* cruel.

crueldad *f* cruelty.

crujiente *adj* crunchy.

crujir *vi* to crackle; to rustle.

crustáceo *m* crustacean.

cruz *f* cross; tails (of a coin).

cruzar *vt* to cross; (*mar*) to cruise:—**~se** *vr* to cross; to pass each other.

cuaderno *m* notebook; exercise book; logbook.

cuadra *f* block; stable.

cuadrado/da *adj, m* square.

cuadrante *m* quadrant; dial.

cuadrar *vt, vi* to square; to fit, suit, correspond.

cuadrilátero/ra *adj, m* quadrilateral.

cuadrilla *f* party, group; gang, crew.

cuadro *m* square; picture, painting; window frame; scene; chart.

cuadrúpedo/da *adj* quadruped.

cuajar *vt* to coagulate; to thicken; to adorn; to set:—**~se** *vr* to coagulate, curdle; to set; to fill up.

cual *pn* which; who; whom:—*adv* as; like:—*adj* such as.

cuál *pn* which (one).

cualidad *f* quality.

cualquier *adj* any.

cualquiera *adj* anyone, anybody; someone, somebody; whoever; whichever.

cuando *adv* when; if; even:—*conj* since:—**de ~ en ~** from time to time:—**~ más/~ mucho** at most, at best:—**~ menos** at least.

cuándo *adv* when:—**¿de cuándo acá?** since when?

cuánto *adj* what a lot of; how much?:—**¿~s?** how many?:—*pn, adv* how; how much; how many.

cuanto/ta *adj* as many as; as much as; all; whatever:—*adv* **en ~** as soon as:—**en ~ a** as regards:—**~ más** moreover, the more as.
cuarenta *adj, m* forty.
cuaresma *f* Lent.
cuarto *m* fourth part; quarter; room, apartment; span:—**~s** *mpl* cash, money: **~/ta** *adj* fourth.
cuarzo *m* quartz.
cuatro *adj, m* four.
cuatrocientos/tas *adj* four hundred.
cuba *f* cask; tub; (*fig*) drunkard.
cubierta *f* cover; deck of a ship; (*auto*) hood; tire; pretext.
cubierto *m* cover; shelter; place at table; meal at a fixed charge:—**~s** *mpl* cutlery, silverware.
cubo *m* cube; bucket; can:—**~ de la basura** garbage can.
cubrir *vt* to cover; to disguise; to protect; to roof a building:—**~se** *vr* to become overcast.
cucaracha *f* cockroach.
cuchara *f* spoon.
cucharada *f* spoonful; ladleful.
cucharadita *f* teaspoonful.
cuchichear *vi* to whisper.
cuchillo *m* knife.
cuclillas *adv*:—**en ~** squatting.
cuclillo *m* cuckoo; (*fig*) cuckold.
cuello *m* neck; collar.
cuenca *m* bowl, deep valley; hollow; socket of the eye.
cuenta *f* calculation; account; check, bill (in a restaurant); count, counting; bead; importance.
cuento *m* tale, story, narrative.
cuerda *f* rope; string; spring.
cuerdo/da *adj* sane; prudent, judicious.
cuerno *m* horn.

cuero *m* hide, skin, leather.
cuerpo *m* body; cadaver, corpse.
cuesta *f* slope, hill; incline:—**ir ~ abajo** to go downhill:—**~ arriba** uphill.
cuestión *f* question, matter; dispute; quarrel; problem.
cueva *f* cave; cellar.
cuidado *m* care, worry, concern; charge.
cuidar *vt* to care for; to mind, look after.
culebra *f* snake.
culo *m* backside; bum (*sl*); bottom.
culpa *f* fault, blame; guilt.
culpable *adj* culpable; guilty:—*m/f* culprit.
cultivar *vt* to cultivate.
culto/ta *adj* cultivated, cultured; refined, civilized:—*m* culture; worship.
cumbre *f* top, summit.
cumplir *vt* to carry out, fulfil; to serve (a prison sentence); to carry out (death penalty); to attain, reach (a certain age):—**~se** *vr* to be fulfilled; to expire, be up.
cuna *f* cradle.
cuña *f* wedge.
cuñado/da *m/f* brother/sister-in-law.
cura *m* priest:—*f* cure; treatment.
curar *vt* to cure; to treat, dress (a wound); to salt; to dress; to tan.
curioso/sa *adj* curious:—*m/f* bystander.
currar *vi* (*fam*) to work.
curso *m* course, direction; year (at university); subject.
curtir *vt* to tan leather:—**~se** *vr* to become sunburned; to become inured.
curva *f* curve, bend.
custodia *f* custody, safekeeping, care; monstrance.
cutis *m* skin.
cutre *adj* (*fam*) mean, grotty.
cuyo/ya *pn* whose, of which, of whom.

D

dado *m* die (*pl* dice).
daga *f* dagger.
dama *f* lady, gentlewoman; mistress; queen; actress of principal parts.
damnificar *vt* to hurt, injure, damage.
dañar *vt* to hurt, injure; to damage.
dañino/na *adj* harmful; noxious; mischievous.
danza *f* dance.
dar *vt* to give; to supply, administer, afford; to deliver.
dátil *m* (*bot*) date.

dato *m* fact.
de *prep* of; from; for; by; on; to; with.
debajo *adv* under, underneath, below.
debatir *vt* to debate, argue, discuss.
debe *m* (*com*) debit:—**~ y haber** debit and credit.
deber *m* obligation, duty; debt:—*vt* to owe; to be obliged to:—*vi* **debe (de)** it must, it should.
debidamente *adv* justly, duly; exactly, perfectly.
débil *adj* feeble, weak; sickly; frail.

debilitar *vt* to debilitate, weaken.
decadencia *f* decay, decline.
decena *f* ten.
decencia *f* decency.
decepción *f* disappointment.
decidir *vt* to decide, determine.
décimo/ma *adj, m* tenth.
decir *vt* to say; to tell; to speak; to name.
decisión *f* decision; determination, resolution; sentence.
declamar *vi* to declaim; to harangue.
declarar *vt* to declare; to manifest; to expound; to explain; (*jur*) to decide:—~se *vr* to declare one's opinion:—*vi* to testify.
declinar *vi* to decline; to decay, degenerate:—*vt* (*gr*) to decline.
declive *m* slope; decline.
decorar *vt* to decorate, adorn; to illustrate.
decrecer *vi* to decrease.
decrépito/ta *adj* decrepit, worn out with age.
decretar *vt* to decree, determine.
dedal *m* thimble; very small drinking glass.
dedicar *vt* to dedicate, devote; to consecrate:—~se *vr* to apply oneself to.
dedo *m* finger; toe; small bit:—~ **meñique** little finger:—~ **pulgar** thumb:—~ **del corazón** middle finger:—~ **anular** ring finger.
deducir *vt* to deduce, infer; to allege in pleading; to subtract.
defecto *m* defect; defectiveness.
defectuoso/sa *adj* defective, imperfect, faulty.
defender *vt* to defend, protect; to justify, assert; to resist, oppose.
defensor/ra *m/f* defender, protector; lawyer, defense counsel.
deferir *vi* to defer; to yield (to another's opinion):—*vt* to communicate.
deficiente *adj* defective.
definir *vt* to define, describe, explain; to decide.
definitivo/va *adj* definitive; positive.
deformar *vt* to deform:—~se *vr* to become deformed.
deforme *adj* deformed; ugly.
defraudar *vt* to defraud, cheat; to usurp; to disturb.
defunción *f* death; funeral.
degenerar *vi* to degenerate.
degollar *vt* to behead; to destroy, ruin.
degradar *vt* to degrade:—~se *vr* to degrade or demean oneself.
degustar *vt* to taste.
dehesa *f* pasture.
dejadez *f* slovenliness, neglect.

dejar *vt* to leave, quit; to omit; to let; to permit, allow; to forsake; to bequeath; to pardon:—~ **de** to stop; to fail to:—~se *vr* to abandon oneself.
del *adj* of the (contraction of *de* and *el*).
delantal *m* apron.
delante *adv* in front; opposite; ahead: —~ **de** in front of; before.
delantero/ra *adj* front:—*m* forward.
delegar *vt* to delegate; to substitute.
deleitar *vt* to delight.
deletrear *vt* to spell; to examine; to conjecture.
delfín *m* dolphin; dauphin.
delgado/da *adj* thin; delicate, fine; light; slender, lean.
deliberadamente *adv* deliberately.
deliberar *vi* to consider, deliberate: —*vt* to debate; to consult.
delicado/da *adj* delicate, tender; faint; exquisite; delicious, dainty; slender, subtle.
delicioso/sa *adj* delicious; delightful.
delincuencia *f* delinquency.
delineante *m/f* draftsman/woman.
delirar *vi* to rave; to talk nonsense.
delito *m* offence; crime.
demacrado/da *adj* pale and drawn.
demandar *vt* to demand; to ask; to claim; to sue.
demarcar *vt* to mark out (limits).
demás *adj* other; remaining:—*pn* **los/las** ~ the others, the rest:—**estar** ~ to be over and above; to be useless or superfluous:—**por** ~ in vain.
demasiado/da *adj* too; excessive:—*adv* too, too much.
demencia *f* madness.
demoler *vt* to demolish; to destroy.
demonio *m* demon.
demorar *vt* to delay:—~se *vr* to be delayed:—*vi* to linger.
demostrar *vt* to prove, demonstrate; to manifest.
denegar *vt* to deny; to refuse.
denigrar *vt* to blacken; to insult.
denominar *vt* to name; to designate.
denotar *vt* to denote; to express.
denso/sa *adj* dense, thick; compact.
dentado/da *adj* toothed; indented.
dentadura *f* set of teeth.
dentífrico *m* toothpaste.
dentista *m/f* dentist.
dentro *adv* within:—*pn* ~ **de** in, inside.
denunciar *vt* to advise; to denounce; to report.
depender *vi*:—~ **de** to depend on, be dependent on.

dependiente *m* sales clerk:—*adj* dependent.

depilatorio *m* hair remover.

deponer *vt* to depose; to declare; to displace; to deposit.

deportar *vt* to deport.

deporte *m* sport.

deportista *m/f* sportsman/woman.

depositar *vt* to deposit; to confide; to put away for safekeeping.

depravación *f* depravity.

deprimir *vt* to depress:—~**se** *vr* to become depressed.

deprisa *adv* quickly.

depurar *vt* to cleanse, purify; to filter.

derecho/cha *adj* right; straight; just; perfect; certain:—*m* right, justice; law; just claim; tax, duty; fee:—*adv* straight.

derivar *vt, vi* to derive; (*mar*) to drift.

derogar *vt* to derogate, abolish; to reform.

derramar *vt* to drain off (water); to spread; to spill, scatter; to waste, shed: —~**se** *vr* to pour out.

derretir *vt* to melt; to consume; to thaw:— ~**se** *vr* to melt.

derribar *vt* to demolish; to flatten.

derrochar *vt* to dissipate; to squander.

derrotar *vt* to destroy; to defeat.

derruir *vt* to demolish.

derrumbar *vt* to throw down:—~**se** *vr* to collapse.

desabrido/da *adj* tasteless, insipid; rude; unpleasant.

desacato *m* disrespect, incivility.

desacertado/da *adj* mistaken; unwise; inconsiderate.

desaconsejar *vt* to advise against.

desacostumbrado/da *adj* unusual.

desacuerdo *m* blunder; disagreement; forgetfulness.

desafiar *vt* to challenge; to defy.

desafinar *vi* to be out of tune.

desafuero *m* outrage; excess.

desagradable *adj* disagreeable, unpleasant.

desagradecido/da *adj* ungrateful.

desagüe *m* channel, drain; drainpipe; drainage.

desahogar *vt* to ease; to vent:—~**se** *vr* to recover; to relax.

desahuciar *vt* to cause to despair; to give up; to evict.

desajustar *vt* to make uneven; to unbalance:—~**se** *vr* to get out of order.

desalentar *vt* to put out of breath; to discourage.

desaliño *m* slovenliness; carelessness.

desalmado/da *adj* cruel, inhuman.

desalojar *vt* to eject; to move out:—*vi* to move out.

desamparar *vt* to forsake, abandon; to relinquish.

desangrar *vt* to bleed; to drain (a pond); (*fig*) to exhaust (one's means):—~**se** *vr* to lose a lot of blood.

desanimar *vt* to discourage:—~**se** *vr* to lose heart.

desaparecer *vi* to disappear.

desapercibido/da *adj* unnoticed.

desaprobar *vt* to disapprove; to condemn; to reject.

desaprovechado/da *adj* useless; unprofitable; backward; slack.

desaprovechar *vt* to waste, turn to a bad use.

desarmar *vt* to disarm; to disband (troops); to dismantle; (*fig*) to pacify.

desarraigar *vt* to uproot; to root out; to extirpate.

desarrollar *vt* to develop; to unroll; to unfold:—~**se** *vr* to develop; to be unfolded; to open.

desasosiego *m* restlessness; anxiety.

desastre *m* disaster; misfortune.

desatar *vt* to untie, loose; to separate; to solve:—~**se** *vr* to come undone; to break.

desatascar *vt* to unblock; to clear.

desatender *vt* to pay no attention to; to disregard.

desatinar *vi* to talk nonsense; to reel, stagger.

desatornillar *vt* to unscrew.

desayunar *vt* to have for breakfast:—~**se** *vr* to breakfast:—*vi* to have breakfast.

desazón *f* disgust; uneasiness; annoyance.

desbarrar *vi* to talk nonsense.

desbordar *vt* to exceed:—~**se** *vr* to overflow.

descalabrado/da *adj* wounded on the head; imprudent.

descalificar *vt* to disqualify; to discredit.

descalzo/za *adj* barefooted; (*fig*) destitute.

descaminado/da *adj* (*fig*) misguided.

descansar *vt* to rest:—*vi* to rest; to lie down.

descansillo *m* landing.

descapotable *m* convertible.

descarado/da *adj* cheeky, barefaced.

descargar *vt* to unload, discharge:—~**se** *vr* to unburden oneself.

descarriar *vt* to lead astray; to misdirect:— ~**se** *vr* to lose one's way; to stray; to err.

descarrilar *vi* (*ferro*) to leave or run off the rails.

descartar *vt* to discard; to dismiss; to rule out.

descendencia *f* descent, offspring.

descender *vt* to take down:—*vi* to descend, walk down; to flow; to fall:—~ **de** to be derived from.

descenso *m* descent; drop.

descifrar *vt* to decipher; to unravel.

descollar *vi* to excel.

descolorido/da *adj* pale, colorless.

descomunal *adj* uncommon; huge.

desconcertar *vt* to disturb; to confound; to disconcert:—~**se** *vr* to be bewildered; to be upset.

desconectar *vt* to disconnect.

desconfiar *vi*:—~ **de** to mistrust, suspect.

descongelar *vt* to defrost.

desconocer *vt* to disown, disavow; to be totally ignorant of (a thing); not to know (a person); not to acknowledge (a favor received).

desconsuelo *m* distress; trouble; despair.

descontar *vt* to discount; to deduct.

descontento *m* dissatisfaction; disgust.

descortés/esa *adj* impolite, rude.

descoser *vt* to unseam; to separate:—~**se** *vr* to come apart at the seams.

descreído/da *adj* incredulous.

descremado/da *adj* skimmed.

describir *vt* to describe; to draw, delineate.

descuartizar *vt* to quarter; to carve.

descubrir *vt* to discover, disclose; to uncover; to reveal; to show:—~**se** *vr* to reveal oneself; to take off one's hat; to confess.

descuento *m* discount; decrease.

descuidado/da *adj* careless, negligent.

descuidar *vt* to neglect:—*vi* ~**se** *vr* to be careless.

desde *prep* since; after; from:—~ **lue-go** of course:—~ **entonces** since then.

desdén *m* disdain, scorn.

desdeñar *vt* to disdain, scorn:—~**se** *vr* to be disdainful.

desdentado/da *adj* toothless.

desdicha *f* misfortune, calamity; great poverty.

desdoblar *vt* to unfold, spread open.

desear *vt* to desire, wish; to require, demand.

desecar *vt* to dry up.

desechar *vt* to depreciate; to reject; to refuse; to throw away.

desecho *m* residue:—~**s** *mpl* trash.

desembarcar *vt* to unload, disembark:—*vi* to disembark, land.

desembolsar *vt* to pay out.

desempatar *vi* to hold a play-off.

desempeñar *vt* to redeem; to extricate from debt; to fulfil (any duty or promise); to acquit:—~**se** *vr* to get out of debt.

desempleo *m* unemployment.

desencadenar *vt* to unchain:—~**se** *vr* to break loose; to burst.

desencajar *vt* to disjoint; to dislocate; to disconnect.

desencanto *m* disenchantment.

desenchufar *vt* to unplug.

desenfado *m* ease; facility; calmness, relaxation.

desenfocado/da *adj* out of focus.

desenfreno *m* wildness; lack of self-control.

desengañar *vt* to disillusion:—~**se** *vr* to become disillusioned.

desenganchar *vt* to unhook; to uncouple.

desengrasar *vt* to take the grease off.

desenlace *m* climax; outcome.

desenredar *vt* to disentangle.

desenroscar *vt* to untwist; to unroll.

desentenderse *vr* to feign not to understand; to pass by without noticing.

desenterrar *vt* to exhume; to dig up.

desentonar *vi* to be out of tune; to clash.

desenvolver *vt* to unfold; to unroll; to decipher, unravel; to develop:—~**se** *vr* to develop; to cope.

deseo *m* desire, wish.

desequilibrado/da *adj* unbalanced.

desertar *vt* to desert; (*jur*) to abandon (a cause).

desesperar *vi*, ~**se** *vr* to despair:—*vt* to make desperate.

desestabilizar *vt* to destabilize.

desfachatez *f* impudence.

desfalco *m* embezzlement.

desfallecer *vi* to get weak; to faint.

desfasado/da *adj* old-fashioned.

desfavorable *adj* unfavorable.

desfiladero *m* gorge.

desfilar *vi* (*mil*) to parade.

desfogarse *vr* to give vent to one's passion or anger.

desgana *f* disgust; loss of appetite; aversion, reluctance.

desgañitarse *vr* to scream, bawl.

desgarrar *vt* to tear; to shatter.

desgaste *m* wear (and tear).

desgracia *f* misfortune; disgrace; accident; setback.

desgreñado/da *adj* disheveled.

deshabitado/da *adj* deserted, uninhabited; desolate.

deshacer *vt* to undo, destroy; to cancel; to efface; to rout (an army); to solve; to melt; to break up, divide; to dissolve in a liquid;

to violate (a treaty); to diminish; to disband (troops):—~se *vr* to melt; to come apart.
deshelar *vt* to thaw:—~se *vr* to thaw, melt.
desheredar *vt* to disinherit.
deshidratar *vt* to dehydrate.
deshinchar *vt* to deflate:—~se *vr* to go flat, go down.
deshonesto/ta *adj* indecent.
deshonrar *vt* to affront, insult, defame; to dishonor.
deshuesar *vt* to rid of bones; to stone.
desidia *f* idleness, indolence.
desierto/ta *adj* deserted; solitary:—*m* desert; wilderness.
designar *vt* to design; to intend; to appoint; to express, name.
desigual *adj* unequal, unlike; uneven, craggy, cliffy.
desilusionar *vt* to disappoint:—~se *vr* to become disillusioned.
desinfectar *vt* to disinfect.
desinflar *vt* to deflate.
desinteresado/da *adj* disinterested; unselfish.
desistir *vi* to desist, cease.
desleal *adj* disloyal; unfair.
desleír *vt* to dilute; to dissolve.
deslenguado/da *adj* foul-mouthed.
desligar *vt* to untie; to separate.
deslizar *vt* to slip, slide; to let slip (a comment):—~se *vr* to slip; to skid; to flow softly; to creep in.
deslumbrar *vt* to dazzle; to puzzle.
desmayar *vi* to be dispirited or faint-hearted:—~se *vr* to faint.
desmedido/da *adj* disproportionate.
desmemoriado/da *adj* forgetful.
desmentir *vt* to give the lie to:—~se *vr* to contradict oneself.
desmenuzar *vt* to crumble; to chip at; to fritter away; to examine minutely.
desmesurado/da *adj* excessive; huge; immeasurable.
desmoralizar *vt* to demoralize.
desnatado/da *adj* skimmed.
desnivel *m* unevenness of the ground.
desnudar *vt* to undress; to strip; to discover, reveal:—~se *vr* to undress.
desnutrido/da *adj* undernourished.
desobedecer *vt, vi* to disobey.
desocupar *vt* to vacate; to empty:—~se *vr* to retire from a business; to withdraw from an arrangement.
desodorante *m* deodorant.
desolado/da *adj* desolate, disconsolate.
desordenar *vt* to disorder; to untidy: —~se *vr* to get out of order.
desorganizar *vt* to disorganize.

desorientar *vt* to mislead; to confuse: —~se *vr* to lose one's way.
desovar *vi* to spawn.
despabilado/da *adj* watchful, vigilant; wide-awake.
despacho *m* dispatch, expedition; cabinet; office; commission; warrant, patent; expedient; smart answer.
despachurrar *vt* to squash, crush; to mangle.
despacio *adv* slowly, leisurely; little by little:—¡~! softly!, gently!
desparramar *vt* to disseminate, spread; to spill; to squander, lavish: —~se *vr* to be dissipated.
despavorido *adj* frightened.
despecho *m* indignation; displeasure; spite; dismay, despair; deceit; derision, scorn: —a ~ de in spite of.
despectivo/va *adj* pejorative, derogatory.
despedir *vt* to discharge; to dismiss (from office); to see off:—~se *vr* ~ de to say goodbye to.
despegar *vt* to unglue; to take off:—~se *vr* to come loose.
despegue *m* take-off.
despeinar *vt* to ruffle.
despejado/da *adj* sprightly, quick; clear.
despellejar *vt* to skin.
despensa *f* pantry, larder; provisions *pl*.
desperdiciar *vt* to squander.
desperdigar *vt* to separate; to scatter.
desperfecto *m* slight damage; flaw.
despertador *m* alarm clock.
despertar *vt* to wake up, rouse from sleep; to excite:—*vi* to wake up; to grow lively or sprightly:—~se *vr* to wake up.
despiadado/da *adj* heartless; merciless.
despido *m* dismissal.
despierto/ta *adj* awake; vigilant; fierce; brisk, sprightly.
despistar *vt* to mislead; to throw off the track:—~se *vr* to take the wrong way; to become confused.
desplazar *vt* to move; to scroll:—~se *vr* to travel.
desplegar *vt* to unfold, display; to explain, elucidate; (*mar*) to unfurl:—~se *vr* to open out; to travel.
desplomarse *vr* to fall to the ground; to collapse.
despoblar *vt* to depopulate; to desolate: —~se *vr* to become depopulated.
despojar *vt*:—~ (de) to strip (of); to deprive (of):—~se *vr* to undress.
desposar *vt* to marry, betroth:—~se *vr* to be betrothed or married.
desposeer *vt* to dispossess.

déspota *m* despot.

despreciar *vt* to offend; to despise.

desprender *vt* to unfasten, loosen; to separate:—**~se** *vr* to give way; to fall down; to extricate oneself.

despreocupado/da *adj* careless; unworried.

desprevenido/da *adj* unawares, unprepared.

desproporcionado/da *adj* disproportionate.

desprovisto/ta *adj* unprovided.

después *adv* after, afterwards; next.

despuntar *vt* to blunt:—*vi* to sprout; to dawn:—**al ~ del día** at break of day.

desquiciar *vt* to upset; to discompose; to disorder.

desquite *m* recovery of a loss; revenge, retaliation.

destacamento *m* (*mil*) detachment.

destacar *vt* to emphasize; to (*mil*) detach (a body of troops):—**~se** *vr* to stand out.

destajo *m* piecework.

destapar *vt* to uncover; to open:—**~se** *vr* to be uncovered.

destartalado/da *adj* untidy.

destello *m* signal light; sparkle.

desteñir *vt* to discolor:—**~se** *vr* to fade.

desternillarse *vr*:—**~ de risa** to roar with laughter.

desterrar *vt* to banish; to expel, drive away.

destetar *vt* to wean.

destilar *vt*, *vi* to distil.

destinar *vt* to destine for, intend for.

destinatario/a *m/f* addressee.

destino *m* destiny; fate, doom; destination; office.

destornillador *m* screwdriver.

destreza *f* dexterity, cleverness, cunning, expertness, skill.

destrozar *vt* to destroy, break into pieces; (*mil*) to defeat.

destruir *vt* to destroy.

desvalido/da *adj* helpless; destitute.

desvalijar *vt* to rob; to burgle.

desván *m* garret.

desvanecer *vt* to dispel:—**~se** *vr* to grow vapid, become insipid; to vanish; to be affected with giddiness.

desvarío *m* delirium; giddiness; inconstancy, caprice; extravagance.

desvelar *vt* to keep awake:—**~se** *vr* to stay awake.

desventaja *f* disadvantage; damage.

desventura *f* misfortune; calamity.

desvergüenza *f* impudence; shamelessness.

desvestir *vt*:—**~se** *vr* to undress.

desviar *vt* to divert; to dissuade; to parry (at fencing):—**~se** *vr* to go off course.

detallar *vt* to detail, relate minutely.

detener *vt* to stop, detain; to arrest; to keep back; to reserve; to withhold:—**~se** *vr* to stop; to stay.

detenidamente *adv* carefully.

detergente *m* detergent.

deteriorar *vt* to damage.

determinar *vt* to determine:—**~se** *vr* to decide.

detestar *vt* to detest, abhor.

detonar *vi* to detonate.

detrás *adv* behind; at the back, in the back.

deuda *f* debt; fault; offence.

devanar *vt* to reel; to wrap up.

devastar *vt* to devastate.

devengar *vt* to accrue.

devoción *f* devotion, piety; strong affection; ardent love.

devolver *vt* to return; to send back; to refund:—*vi* to be sick.

devorar *vt* to devour, swallow up.

día *m* day.

diablo *m* devil.

diablura *f* prank.

diana *f* (*mil*) reveille; bull's-eye.

diapositiva *f* transparency, slide.

diario *m* journal, diary; daily newspaper; daily expenses *pl*:—**/ ria** *adj* daily.

diarrea *f* diarrhea.

dibujar *vt* to draw, design.

diccionario *m* dictionary.

dicha *f* happiness, good fortune:—**por ~** by chance.

diciembre *m* December.

dictamen *m* opinion, notion; suggestion; judgement.

dictar *vt* to dictate.

diecinueve *adj*, *m* nineteen.

dieciocho *adj*, *m* eighteen.

dieciséis *adj*, *m* sixteen.

diecisiete *adj*, *m* seventeen.

diente *m* tooth; fang; tusk.

diestro/tra *adj* right; dexterous, skillful, clever; sagacious, prudent; sly, cunning: —*m* skillful fencer; halter; bridle.

dieta *f* diet, regimen; diet, assembly; daily salary of judges.

diez *adj*, *m* ten.

diezmar *vt* to decimate.

difamar *vt* to defame, libel.

diferencia *f* difference.

diferenciar *vt* to differentiate, distinguish: —**~se** *vr* to differ, distinguish oneself.

diferente *adj* different, unlike.

diferido/da *adj* recorded.

difícil *adj* difficult.

dificultad *f* difficulty.

difundir *vt* to diffuse, spread; to divulge:— **~se** *vr* to spread (out).

difunto/ta *adj* dead, deceased; late.

digerir *vt* to digest; to bear with patience; to adjust, arrange.

dignarse *vr* to condescend, deign.

digno/na *adj* worthy; suitable.

dilatado/da *adj* large; numerous; prolix; spacious, extensive.

dilatar *vt* to dilate, expand; to spread out; to defer, protract.

dilema *m* dilemma.

diligencia *f* diligence; affair, business; call of nature; stage coach.

dilucidar *vt* to elucidate, explain.

diluir *vt* to dilute.

diluviar *vi* to rain in torrents.

diminuto/ta *adj* minute, small.

dimitir *vt* to give up:—*vi* to resign.

dinamita *f* dynamite.

dinamo *f* dynamo.

dineral *m* large sum of money.

dinero *m* money.

dios *m* god.

diosa *f* goddess.

diplomado/da *adj* qualified.

dique *m* dam.

dirección *f* direction, guidance; administration; steering.

directo/ta *adj* direct, straight; apparent, evident; live.

director/ra *m/f* director; conductor; president; manager.

dirigir *vt* to direct; to conduct; to regulate, govern:—~se *vr* to go towards; to address oneself to.

discernir *vt* to discern, distinguish.

discípulo *m* disciple; scholar.

disco *m* disc; record; discus; light; face (of the sun or moon); lens (of a telescope).

díscolo/la *adj* ungovernable; peevish.

discordante *adj* dissonant, discordant.

discreción *f* discretion; acuteness of mind.

discrepar *vi* to differ.

discreto/ta *adj* discreet; ingenious; witty, eloquent.

disculpar *vt* to exculpate, excuse; to acquit, absolve:—~se *vr* to apologize; to excuse oneself.

discurrir *vi* to ramble about; to run to and fro; to discourse (on a subject):—*vt* to invent, contrive; to meditate.

discurso *m* speech; conversation; dissertation; space of time.

discutir *vt*, *vi* to discuss.

disecar *vt* to dissect; to stuff.

diseminar *vt* to scatter; to disseminate, propagate.

diseñar *vt* to draw; to design.

disentir *vi* to dissent, disagree.

disfrazar *vt* to disguise, conceal; to cloak, dissemble:—~se *vr* to disguise oneself as.

disfrutar *vt* to enjoy:—~se *vr* to enjoy oneself.

disgustar *vt* to disgust; to offend:—~se *vr* to be displeased; to fall out.

disidente *adj* dissident:—*m/f* dissident, dissenter.

disimular *vt* to hide; to tolerate.

disipar *vt* to dissipate, disperse, scatter; to lavish.

dislocarse *vr* to be dislocated or out of joint.

disminuir *vt* to diminish; to decrease.

disolver *vt* to loosen, untie; to dissolve; to disunite; to melt, liquefy; to interrupt.

disparar *vt* to shoot, discharge, fire; to let off; to throw with violence:—*vi* to shoot, fire.

disparate *m* nonsense, absurdity, extravagance.

displicencia *f* displeasure; dislike.

disponer *vt* to arrange, prepare; to dispose.

disponible *adj* available; disposable.

dispositivo *m* device.

disputar *vt* to dispute, controvert, question:—*vi* to debate, argue.

disquete *m* floppy disk.

distancia *f* distance; interval; difference.

distante *adj* distant, far off.

distinguido/da *adj* distinguished, conspicuous.

distinguir *vt* to distinguish; to discern:—~se *vr* to distinguish oneself.

distinto/ta *adj* distinct, different; clear.

distraer *vt* to distract:—~se *vr* to be absent-minded, be inattentive.

distraído/da *adj* absent-minded, inattentive.

distribuir *vt* to distribute.

distrito *m* district; territory.

disturbio *m* riot; disturbance, interruption.

disuadir *vt* to dissuade.

diurno/na *adj* daily.

diva *f* prima donna.

divagar *vt* to digress.

divergencia *f* divergence.

diversidad *f* diversity; variety of things.

diversificar *vt* to diversify; to vary.

diversión *f* diversion; sport; amusement; (*mil*) diversion.

divertir *vt* to divert (the attention); to amuse, entertain; (*mil*) to draw off:—~se *vr* to amuse oneself.

dividir *vt* to divide; to disunite; to separate; to share out.

divieso *m* (*med*) boil.
divino/na *adj* divine, heavenly; excellent.
divorcio *m* divorce; separation, disunion.
divulgar *vt* to publish, divulge.
dobladillo *m* hem; turn-up.
doblar *vt* to double; to fold; to bend: —*vi* to turn; to toll:—**se** *vr* to bend, bow, submit.
doble *adj* double; dual; deceitful:—**al ~** doubly:—*m* double.
doblegar *vt* to bend:—**se** *vr* to yield.
doblez *m* crease; fold; turn-up:—*f* duplicity.
doce *adj*, *m* twelve.
docena *f* dozen.
dócil *adj* docile, tractable.
doctor/ra *m/f* doctor.
documento *m* document; record.
dogma *m* dogma.
dólar *m* dollar.
doler *vt*, *vi* to feel pain; to ache:—**se** *vr* to feel for the sufferings of others; to complain.
dolor *m* pain; aching, ache; affliction.
domar *vt* to tame; to subdue, master.
domesticar *vt* to domesticate.
domicilio *m* domicile; home, abode.
dominar *vt* to dominate; to be fluent in:— **se** *vr* to moderate one's passions.
domingo *m* Sunday; (Christian) Sabbath.
donar *vt* to donate; to bestow.
donativo *m* contribution.
doncella *f* virgin, maiden; lady's maid.
donde *relative adv* where

¿dónde? *interrogative adv* where?:—**¿de dónde?** from where?
dondequiera *adv* wherever.
dorado/da *adj* gilt *compd*; golden:—*m* gilding.
dormir *vi* to sleep:—**se** *vr* to fall asleep.
dos *adj*, *m* two.
doscientos/tas *adj pl* two hundred.
dosis *f invar* dose.
dotado/da *adj* gifted.
drama *m* drama.
dramatizar *vt* to dramatize.
droga *f* drug; stratagem; artifice, deceit.
droguería *f* hardware store.
ducha *f* shower; (*med*) douche.
ducho/cha *adj* skilled, experienced.
dudar *vt* to doubt.
duelo *m* grief, affliction; mourning.
duende *m* elf, hobgoblin.
dueño/ña *m/f* owner; landlord/lady; employer.
dulce *adj* sweet; mild, gentle, meek; soft:— *m* sweet, candy.
dúo *m* (*mus*) duo, duet.
duodécimo/ma *adj* twelfth.
duplicar *vt* to duplicate; to repeat.
duradero/ra *adj* lasting, durable.
durante *adv* during.
durar *vi* to last, continue.
durazno *m* peach; peach tree.
dureza *f* hardness; harshness:—**~ de oido** hardness of hearing.
duro/ra *adj* hard; cruel; harsh, rough: —*m* five peseta coin:—*adv* hard.

E

e *conj* and (before words starting with *i* and *hi*).
ébano *m* ebony.
ebrio/ia *adj* drunk.
ebullición *f* boiling.
echar *vt* to throw; to add; to pour out; to mail:—**se** *vr* to lie down.
eco *m* echo.
económico/ca *adj* economic; cheap; thrifty; financial; avaricious.
ecuánime *adj* level-headed.
ecuménico/ca *adj* ecumenical; universal.
edad *f* age.
edición *f* edition; publication.
edificar *vt* to build, construct; to edify.
edificio *m* building; structure.
editar *vt* to edit; to publish.
educación *f* education; upbringing; (good) manners *pl*.

educar *vt* to educate, instruct; to bring up.
efectivamente *adv* exactly; really; in fact.
efecto *m* effect; consequence; purpose: — **~s** *mpl* effects *pl*, goods *pl*:—**en ~** in fact, really.
efectuar *vt* to effect, carry out.
eficaz *adj* efficient; effective.
eficiente *adj* efficient.
egoísta *m/f* self-seeker:—*adj* selfish.
eje *m* axle; axis.
ejecutar *vt* to execute, perform; to put to death; (*jur*) to distrain, seize.
ejecutivo/va *adj* executive:—*m/f* executive.
ejemplar *m* specimen; copy; example:— *adj* exemplary.
ejemplo *m* example:—**por ~** for example, for instance.
ejercer *vt* to exercise; *vi* to apply oneself to the functions of an office.

ejercicio *m* exercise.
ejercitar *vt* to exercise.
ejército *m* army.
el *art, m* the.
él *pn* he, it.
elaborar *vt* to elaborate.
elástico/ca *adj* elastic.
elección *f* election; choice.
eléctrico/ca *adj* electric, electrical.
electrocutar *vt* to electrocute.
electrodomesticos *mpl* (electrical) household appliances *pl*.
electrotecnia *f* electrical engineering.
elefante *m* elephant.
elegante *adj* elegant, fine.
elegir *vt* to choose, elect.
elemento *m* element:—**s** *mpl* elements, rudiments, first principles *pl*.
elevar *vt* to raise; to elevate:—**se** *vr* to rise; to be enraptured; to be conceited.
eliminar *vt* to eliminate, remove.
eliminatoria *f* preliminary (round).
ella *pn* she; it.
ello *pn* it.
elogiar *vt* to praise, eulogize.
eludir *vt* to elude, escape.
emanar *vi* to emanate.
embadurnar *vt* to smear, bedaub.
embalaje *m* packing, package.
embaldosar *vt* to pave with tiles.
embalse *m* reservoir.
embarazada *f* pregnant woman:—*adj* pregnant.
embarazoso/sa *adj* difficult; intricate; entangled.
embarcación *f* embarkation; any vessel or ship.
embarcar *vt* to embark:—**se** *vr* to go on board; (*fig*) to get involved (in a matter).
embargo *m* embargo:—**sin** — still, however.
embarque *m* embarkation.
embaucar *vt* to deceive; to trick.
embeber *vt* to soak; to saturate:—*vi* to shrink:—**se** *vr* to be enraptured; to be absorbed.
embeleso *m* amazement, enchantment.
embellecer *vt* to embellish, beautify.
embestir *vt* to assault, attack.
emblanquecer *vt* to whiten:—**se** *vr* to grow white; to bleach.
embobado/da *adj* amazed; fascinated.
émbolo *m* plunger; piston.
embolsar *vt* to put money into (a purse); to pocket.
emborrachar *vt* to intoxicate, inebriate:—**se** *vr* to get drunk.
emboscada *f* (*mil*) ambush.

embotar *vt* to blunt:—**se** *vr* to go numb.
embotellamiento *m* traffic jam.
embotellar *vt* to bottle (wine).
embozar *vt* to muffle (the face); (*fig*) to cloak, conceal.
embrague *m* clutch.
embriagar *vt* to intoxicate, inebriate; to transport, enrapture.
embrión *m* embryo.
embrollo *m* muddle.
embromar *vt* to tease; to cajole, wheedle.
embrujar *vt* to bewitch.
embrutecer *vt* to brutalize:—**se** *vr* to become depraved.
embudo *m* funnel.
embustero/ra *m/f* impostor, cheat; liar:—*adj* deceitful.
embutido *m* sausage; inlay.
emerger *vi* to emerge, appear.
emigrar *vi* to emigrate.
eminente *adj* eminent, high; excellent, conspicuous.
emisora *f* broadcasting station.
emitir *vt* to emit; to issue; to broadcast.
emoción *f* emotion; feeling; excitement.
emocionar *vt* to excite; to move, touch.
emotivo/va *adj* emotional.
empacho *m* (*med*) indigestion.
empalagoso/sa *adj* cloying; tiresome.
empalmar *vt* to join.
empanada *f* (meat) pie.
empanar *vt* to cover with bread-crumbs.
empantanarse *vr* to get swamped; to get bogged down.
empapar *vt* to soak; to soak up:—**se** *vr* to soak.
empapelar *vt* to paper.
empaquetar *vt* to pack, parcel up.
emparedado *m* sandwich.
emparrado *m* vine arbor.
empastar *vt* to paste; to fill (a tooth).
empatar *vi* to draw.
empedernido/da *adj* inveterate; heartless.
empedrado *m* paving.
empeine *m* instep.
empellón *m* push; heavy blow.
empeñar *vt* to pawn, pledge:—**se** *vr* to pledge oneself to pay debts; to get into debt:—**se en algo** to insist on something.
empeorar *vt* to make worse:—*vi* ~**se** *vr* to grow worse.
empequeñecer *vt* to dwarf; (*fig*) to belittle.
empezar *vt* to begin, start.
emplazamiento *m* summons; location.
empleado/da *m/f* official; employee.
emplear *vt* to employ; to occupy; to commission.

empobrecer *vt* to reduce to poverty: —*vi* to become poor.

empollar *vt* to incubate; to hatch; (*fam*) to swot (up).

empolvar *vt* to powder; to sprinkle powder upon.

empotrado/da *adj* built-in.

emprender *vt* to embark on; to tackle; to undertake.

empresa *f* (*com*) company; enterprise, undertaking.

empujar *vt* to push; to press forward.

empujón *m* push; impulse:—**a ~ones** in fits and starts.

emular *vt* to emulate, rival.

en *prep* in; for; on, upon.

enaguas *fpl* petticoat.

enamorado/da *adj* in love, lovesick.

enamorar *vt* to inspire love in:—**~se** *vr* to fall in love.

enano/na *adj* dwarfish:—*m* dwarf.

enardecer *vt* to fire with passion, inflame.

enarenar *vt* to fill with sand.

encabezar *vt* to head; to put a heading to; to lead.

encadenar *vt* to chain, link together; to connect, unite.

encajar *vt* to insert; to drive in; to encase; to intrude:—*vi* to fit (well).

encaje *m* lace.

encalar *vt* to whitewash.

encallar *vi* (*mar*) to run aground.

encaminar *vt* to guide, show the way: — **~se** *vr* **a** to take the road to.

encandilar *vt* to dazzle.

encanecer *vi* to grow gray; to grow old.

encantado/da *adj* bewitched; delighted; pleased.

encantador/ra *adj* charming:—*m/f* magician.

encantar *vt* to enchant, charm; (*fig*) to delight.

encarcelar *vt* to imprison.

encarecimiento *m* price increase:—**con ~** insistently.

encargado/da *adj* in charge:—*m/f* representative; person in charge.

encargar *vt* to charge; to commission.

encariñarse *vr*:—**~ con** to grow fond of.

encarnar *vt* to embody, personify.

encasillar *vt* to pigeonhole; to typecast.

encastillarse *vr* to refuse to yield.

encausar *vt* to prosecute.

encauzar *vt* to channel.

encebollado *m* casseroled beef or lamb and onions, seasoned with spice.

encenagado/da *adj* muddy, mud-stained.

encendedor *m* lighter.

encender *vt* to kindle, light, set on fire; to inflame, incite; to switch on, to turn on:—**~se** *vr* to catch fire; to flare up.

encerado *m* blackboard.

encerar *vt* to wax; to polish.

encerrar *vt* to shut up, confine; to contain: **~se** *vr* to withdraw from the world.

enchufar *vt* to plug in; to connect.

enchufe *m* plug; outlet, socket; connection; (*fam*) contact, connection.

encía *f* gum (of the teeth).

encierro *m* confinement; enclosure; prison, penitentiary; bull-pen; penning (of bulls).

encima *adv* above; over; at the top; besides:—**~ de** *prep* above; over; at the top of; besides.

encina *f* evergreen oak.

encinta *adj* pregnant.

enclenque *adj* weak, sickly:—*m* weakling.

encoger *vt* to contract, shorten; to shrink; to discourage:—**~se** *vr* to shrink; (*fig*) to cringe.

encolar *vt* to glue.

encolerizar *vt* to provoke, irritate:—**~se** *vr* to get angry.

encomendar *vt* to recommend; to entrust: **~se** *vr* **~ a** to entrust oneself to; to put one's trust in.

encontrar *vt* to meet, encounter:—*vr* **~ con** to run into:—*vi* to assemble, come together.

encrucijada *f* four way stop, intersection; junction.

encuadernar *vt* to bind (books).

encubierto/ta *adj* hidden, concealed.

encubrir *vt* to hide, conceal.

encuesta *f* inquiry; opinion poll.

encurtir *vt* to pickle.

endeble *adj* feeble, weak.

endemoniado/da *adj* possessed with the devil; devilish.

enderezar *vt* to straighten out; to set right: **~se** *vr* to stand upright.

endeudarse *vr* to get into debt.

endosar *vt* to endorse.

endrino *m* blackthorn, sloe.

endulzar *vt* to sweeten; to soften.

endurecer *vt* to harden, toughen:—**~se** *vr* to become cruel; to grow hard.

enebro *m* (*bot*) juniper.

enemistar *vt* to make an enemy:—**~se** *vr* to become enemies; to fall out.

energía *f* energy, power, drive; strength of will.

energúmeno/na *m/f* (*fam*) madman/woman.

enero *m* January.

enfadar *vt* to anger, irritate; to trouble:— **~se** *vr* to become angry.

énfasis *m* emphasis.

enfermar *vi* to fall ill:—*vt* to make sick; to weaken.

enfermedad *f* illness.

enfermero/ra *m/f* nurse.

enfermo/ma *adj* sick, ill:—*m/f* invalid, sick person; patient.

enfocar *vt* to focus; to consider (a problem).

enfoque *m* focus.

enfrentar *vt* to confront; to put face to face:—~**se** *vr* to face each other; to meet (two teams).

enfrente *adv* over against, opposite; in front.

enfriar *vt* to cool; to refrigerate:—~**se** *vr* to cool down; (*med*) to catch a cold.

enfurecer *vt* to madden, enrage:—~**se** *vr* to get rough (of the wind and sea); to become furious or enraged.

enfurruñarse *vr* to get sulky; to frown.

engañar *vt* to deceive, cheat:—~**se** *vr* to be deceived; to make a mistake.

enganchar *vt* to hook, hang up; to hitch up; to couple, connect; to recruit into military service:—~**se** *vr* (*mil*) to enlist.

engañoso/sa *adj* deceitful, artful, false.

engastar *vt* to set, mount.

engatusar *vt* to coax.

engendrar *vt* to beget, engender; to produce.

englobar *vt* to include.

engordar *vt* to fatten:—*vi* to grow fat; to put on weight.

engorroso/sa *adj* troublesome, cumbersome.

engranaje *m* gear; gearing.

engrasar *vt* to grease, lubricate.

engreído/da *adj* conceited, vain.

engullir *vt* to swallow; to gobble, devour.

enharinar *vt* to cover or sprinkle with flour.

enhebrar *vt* to thread.

enhorabuena *f* congratulations *pl*:—*adv* all right; well and good.

enhoramala *interj* good riddance!

enjalbegar *vt* to whitewash.

enjambre *m* swarm of bees; crowd, multitude.

enjuagar *vt* to rinse out; to wash out.

enjuiciar *vt* to prosecute, try; to pass judgement on, judge.

enlace *m* connection, link; relationship.

enladrillar *vt* to pave with bricks.

enlazar *vt* to join, unite; to tie.

enlodar *vt* to cover in mud; (*fig*) to stain.

enloquecer *vt* to madden, drive crazy:—*vi* to go mad.

enmarañar *vt* to entangle; to complicate; to confuse:—~**se** *vr* to become entangled; to get confused.

enmendar *vt* to correct; to reform; to repair, compensate for; to amend:—~**se** *vr* to mend one's ways.

enmohecer *vt* to make moldy; to rust:—~**se** *vr* to grow moldy or musty; to rust.

enmudecer(se) *vt* to silence:—~**se** *vr* to grow dumb; to be silent.

ennegrecer *vt* to blacken; to darken; to obscure.

enojar *vt* to irritate, make angry; to annoy; to upset; to offend:—~**se** *vr* to get angry.

enorgullecerse *vr*:—~ **(de)** to be proud (of).

enorme *adj* enormous, vast, huge; horrible.

enredadera *f* climbing plant; bindweed.

enredar *vt* to entangle, ensnare, confound, perplex; to puzzle; to sow discord among:—~**se** *vr* to get entangled; to get complicated; to get embroiled.

enrejado *m* trelliswork.

enrevesado/da *adj* complicated.

enriquecer *vt* to enrich; to adorn:—~**se** *vr* to grow rich.

enrojecer *vt* to redden:—*vi* to blush.

enrolar *vt* to recruit:—~**se** *vr* (*mil*) to join up.

enrollar *vt* to roll (up).

enroscar *vt* to twist:—~**se** *vr* to curl or roll up.

ensalada *f* salad.

ensalmo *m* enchantment, spell.

ensalzar *vt* to exalt, aggrandize; to exaggerate.

ensamblar *vt* to assemble.

ensañar *vt* to irritate, enrage:—~**se con** *vr* to treat brutally.

ensanchar *vt* to widen; to extend; to enlarge:—~**se** *vr* to expand; to assume an air of importance.

ensangrentar *vt* to stain with blood.

ensartar *vt* to string (beads, etc).

ensayar *vt* to test; to rehearse.

ensayo *m* test, trial; rehearsal of a play; essay.

enseñar *vt* to teach, instruct; to show

ensimismarse *vr* to be or become lost in thought.

ensordecer *vt* to deafen:—*vi* to grow deaf.

ensuciar *vt* to stain, soil; to defile:—~**se** *vr* to wet oneself; to dirty oneself.

ensueño *m* fantasy; daydream; illusion.

entablar *vt* to board (up); to strike up (conversation).

entablillar *vt* (*med*) to put in a splint.

entallar *vt* to tailor (a suit):—*vi* to fit.

ente *m* organization; entity, being; (*fam*) odd character.

entender *vt, vi* to understand, comprehend; to remark, take notice (of); to reason, think:—**a mi** ~ in my opinion: —~**se** *vr* to understand each other.

enterar vt to inform; to instruct:—~**se** vr to find out.

enternecer vt to soften; to move (to pity):—~**se** vr to be moved.

entero/ra adj entire, complete; perfect; honest; resolute:—**por** ~ entirely, completely.

enterrar vt to inter, bury.

entidad f entity; company; body; society.

entierro m burial; funeral.

entonar vt to tune, intonate; to intone; to tone:—vi to be in tune:—~**se** vr to give oneself airs.

entonces adv then, at that time.

entornar vt to half close.

entorpecer vt to dull; to make lethargic; to hinder; to delay.

entrada f entrance, entry; (com) receipts pl; entree; ticket (for cinema, theater, etc).

entrampar vt to trap, snare; to mess up; to burden with debts:—~**se** vr get into debt.

entrañable adj intimate; affectionate.

entrañas fpl entrails pl, intestines pl.

entrar vi to enter, go in; to commence.

entre prep between; among(st); in:—~**manos** in hand.

entrecejo m space between the eyebrows; frown.

entredicho m (jur) injunction:—**estar en** ~ to be banned:—**poner en** ~ to cast doubt on.

entregar vt to deliver; to hand over: —~**se** vr to surrender; to devote oneself.

entremeses mpl hors d'oeuvres.

entrenarse vr to train.

entrepierna f crotch.

entresuelo m entresol; mezzanine.

entretanto adv meanwhile.

entretejer vt to interweave.

entretela f interfacing, stiffening, interlining.

entretener vt to amuse; to entertain, divert; to hold up; to maintain:—~**se** vr to amuse oneself; to linger.

entrever vt to have a glimpse of.

entrevistar vt to interview:—~**se** vr to have an interview.

entristecer vt to sadden.

entrometer vt to put (one thing) between (others):—~**se** vr to interfere.

entumecido/da adj numb, stiff.

enturbiar vt to make cloudy; to obscure, confound:—~**se** vr to become cloudy; (fig) to get confused.

entusiasmar vt to excite, fill with enthusiasm; to delight.

enumerar vt to enumerate.

envalentonar vt to give courage to:—~**se** vr to boast.

envanecer vt to make vain; to swell with pride:—~**se** vr to become proud.

envaramiento m stiffness; numbness.

envasar vt to pack; to bottle; to can.

envase m packing; bottling; canning; container; package; bottle; can.

envejecer vt to make old:—vi ~**se** vr to grow old.

envenenar vt to poison; to embitter.

envés m wrong side (of material).

enviar vt to send, transmit, convey, dispatch.

enviciar vt to vitiate, corrupt:—~**se** vr to get corrupted.

envidia f envy; jealousy.

envidiar vt to envy; to grudge; to be jealous of.

envilecer vt to vilify, debase:—~**se** vr to degrade oneself.

envío m (com) dispatch, remittance of goods; consignment.

enviudar vi to become a widower or widow.

envolver vt to involve; to wrap up.

enyesar vt to plaster; (med) to put in a plaster cast.

enzarzarse vr to get involved in a dispute; to get oneself into trouble.

épico/ca adj epic.

epígrafe f epigraph, inscription; motto; headline.

episodio m episode, installment.

época f epoch; period, time.

epopeya f epic.

equidad f equity, honesty; impartiality, justice.

equilibrar vt to balance; to poise.

equilibrio m balance, equilibrium.

equipaje m luggage; equipment.

equipar vt to fit out, equip, furnish.

equipararse vr:—~ **con** to be on a level with.

equipo m equipment; team; shift.

equitación f horsemanship; riding.

equitativo/va adj equitable; just.

equivaler vi to be of equal value.

equivocación f mistake, error; misunderstanding.

equivocar vt to mistake:—~**se** vr to make a mistake, be wrong.

equívoco/ca adj equivocal, ambiguous:—m equivocation; quibble.

era f era, age; threshing floor.

erario m treasury, public funds pl.

erguir vt to erect, raise up straight:—~**se** vr to straighten up.

erial m fallow land.

erigir vt to erect, raise, build; to establish.

erizarse vr to bristle; to stand on end.

erizo m hedgehog:—~ **de mar** sea urchin.

ermita f hermitage.

erotismo m eroticism.

errar vi to be mistaken; to wander.

errata f misprint.

erre: —~ **que** ~ adv obstinately.

error m error, mistake, fault.

eructar vi to belch, burp.

esbelto/ta adj slim, slender.

esbirro m bailiff; henchman; killer.

esbozo m outline.

escabeche m pickle; pickled fish.

escabroso/sa adj rough, uneven; craggy; rude, risqué, blue.

escabullirse vr to escape, evade; to slip through one's fingers.

escafandra f diving suit; space suit.

escala f ladder; (mus) scale; stopover.

escalar vt to climb.

escalera f staircase; ladder.

escalfar vt to poach (eggs).

escalofriante adj chilling.

escalón m step of a stair; rung.

escama f (fish) scale.

escamar vt to scale, take off scales:—~**se** vr to flake off; to become suspicious.

escamotear vt to swipe; to make disappear.

escampar vi to stop raining.

escándalo m scandal; uproar.

escaño m bench with a back; seat (parliament).

escapar vi to escape:—~**se** vr to get away; to leak (water, etc).

escaparate m store window; wardrobe.

escape m escape, flight; leak; exhaust (of motor).

escarabajo m beetle.

escaramuza f skirmish; dispute, quarrel.

escarbar vt to scratch (the earth as hens do); to inquire into.

escarcha f white frost.

escarlata f scarlet.

escarlatina f scarlet fever.

escarmentar vi to learn one's lesson: —vt to punish severely.

escarola f (bot) endive.

escarpado/da adj sloped; craggy.

escaso/sa adj small, short, little; sparing; scarce; scanty.

escenario m stage; set.

escéptico/ca adj sceptic, sceptical.

esclarecer vt to lighten; to illuminate; to illustrate; to shed light on (problem, etc)

esclavo/va m/f slave; captive.

esclusa f sluice, floodgate.

escoba f broom, brush.

escocer vt to sting; to burn:—~**se** vr to chafe.

escoger vt to choose, select.

escolar m/f schoolboy/girl:—adj scholastic.

escollo m reef, rock.

escoltar vt to escort.

escombros mpl trash; debris.

esconder vt to hide, conceal:—~**se** vr to be hidden.

escondite m hiding place:—**juego de** ~ hide-and-seek.

escoplo m chisel.

escorbuto m scurvy.

escote m low neck (of a dress).

escribir vt to write; to spell.

escrito m document; manuscript, text.

escritor/ra m/f writer, author.

escritorio m writing desk; office, study.

escrúpulo m doubt, scruple, scrupulousness.

escuchar vt to listen to, heed.

escudilla f bowl.

escudo m shield.

escudriñar vt to search, examine; to pry into.

escuela f school.

esculpir vt to sculpt.

escupir vt to spit.

escurreplatos m invar plate rack.

escurrir vt to drain; to drip:—~**se** vr to slip away; to slip, slide:—vi to wring out.

ese/esa adj that:—**esos/as** pl those.

ése/ésa pn that (one):—**ésos/as** pl those (ones).

esencial adj essential; principal.

esfera f sphere; globe.

esforzarse vr to exert oneself, make an effort.

esfuerzo m effort.

esfumarse vr to fade away.

esgrima f fencing.

esguince m (med) sprain.

eslabón m link of a chain; steel; shackle.

esmalte m enamel.

esmerado/da adj careful, neat.

esmeralda m emerald.

esmero m careful attention, great care.

eso pn that.

esos/as; ésos/as pl of **ese/a; ése/a**.

espabilar vt to wake up:—~**se** vr to wake up; (fig) to get a move on.

espaciar vt to spread out; to space (out).

espacio m space; (radio or TV) program.

espada f sword; ace of spades.

espalda f back, back-part:—~**s** fpl shoulders pl.

español/la adj Spanish:—m/f Spaniard:—m Spanish language.

espantajo *m* scarecrow; bogeyman.

espantar *vt* to frighten; to chase or drive away.

esparadrapo *m* adhesive tape.

esparcir *vt* to scatter; to divulge:—~se *vr* to amuse oneself.

espárrago *m* asparagus.

espátula *f* spatula.

especia *f* spice.

especial *adj* special; particular:—en ~ especially.

especie *f* species; kind, sort; matter.

especificar *vt* to specify.

espectáculo *m* spectacle; show.

espectador/ra *m/f* spectator.

especular *vt* to speculate.

espejismo *m* mirage.

espejo *m* mirror.

espeluznante *adj* horrifying.

esperanza *f* hope.

esperar *vt* to hope; to expect, wait for.

esperma *f* sperm.

espeso/sa *adj* thick, dense.

espesor *m* thickness.

espía *m/f* spy.

espiga *f* ear (of corn).

espigón *m* ear of corn; sting; (*mar*) breakwater.

espina *f* thorn; fishbone.

espinaca *f* (*bot*) spinach.

espinilla *f* shinbone.

espino *m* hawthorn.

espiral *adj*, *f* spiral.

espirar *vt* to exhale.

espíritu *m* spirit, soul; mind; intelligence:—el E~ Santo the Holy Ghost:—~s *pl* demons, hobgoblins *pl*.

espléndido/da *adj* splendid.

espliego *m* (*bot*) lavender.

espolón *m* spur (of a cock); spur (of a mountain range); sea wall; jetty; (*mar*) buttress.

espolvorear *vt* to sprinkle.

esponja *f* sponge.

espontáneo/nea *adj* spontaneous.

esposa *f* wife.

esposas *fpl* handcuffs *pl*.

esposo *m* husband.

espuma *f* froth, foam.

espumar *vt* to skim, take the scum off.

espumoso/sa *adj* frothy, foamy; sparkling (wine).

esputo *m* spit, saliva.

esqueje *m* cutting (of plant).

esquela *f* note, slip of paper.

esqueleto *m* skeleton.

esquema *m* scheme; diagram; plan.

esquí *m* ski; skiing.

esquina *f* corner, angle.

esquirol *m* blackleg.

esquivar *vt* to shun, avoid, evade.

esta *adj f* this:—~s *pl* these.

ésta *pn f* this:—~s *pl* these.

estable *adj* stable.

establecer *vt* to establish.

establo *m* stable.

estaca *f* stake; stick; post.

estación *f* season (of the year); station; railroad station, terminus:—~ de autobuses bus station:—~ de servicio service station.

estacionar *vt* to park; (*mil*) to station.

estadio *m* phase; stadium.

estado *m* state, condition.

Estados Unidos *mpl* United States (of America).

estafar *vt* to deceive, defraud.

estallar *vi* to crack; to burst; to break out.

estambre *m* stamen.

estamento *m* estate; body; layer; class.

estampa *f* print; engraving; appearance.

estampar *vt* to print.

estancar *vt* to check (a current); to monopolize; to prohibit, suspend:—~se *vr* to stagnate.

estancia *f* stay; bedroom; ranch; (*poet*) stanza.

estanco *m* tobacconist's (store):—~/ca *adj* watertight.

estándar *adj*, *m* standard.

estaño *m* tin.

estanque *m* pond, pool; reservoir.

estantería *f* shelves *pl*, shelving.

estar *vi* to be; to be (in a place).

estatua *f* statue.

este[1] *m* east;

este[2]/ta *adj* this:—estos/tas *pl* these.

estéreo *adj invar*, *m* stereo.

estereotipo *m* stereotype.

estéril *adj* sterile, infertile.

esterlina *adj*:—libra ~ pound sterling.

estético/ca *adj* esthetic:—*f* esthetics.

estiércol *m* dung; manure.

estilo *m* style; fashion; stroke (swimming).

estima *f* esteem.

estimar *vt* to estimate, value; to esteem; to judge; to think.

estimular *vt* to stimulate, excite; to goad.

estío *m* summer.

estipular *vt* to stipulate.

estirar *vt* to stretch out.

esto *pn* this.

estofado *m* stew.

estómago *m* stomach.

estopa *f* tow.

estorbar *vt* to hinder; (*fig*) to bother: —*vi* to be in the way.

estornudar *vi* to sneeze.

estos/as, éstos/tas *pl* of **este/ta, éste/ta.**

estrado *m* drawing room; stage, platform.

estrafalario/ria *adj* slovenly; eccentric.

estrago *m* ruin, destruction; havoc.

estrangular *vt* to strangle; (*med*) to strangulate.

estraperlo *m* black market.

estratagema *f* stratagem, trick.

estrato *m* stratum, layer.

estraza *f* rag:—**papel de ~** brown paper.

estrechar *vt* to tighten; to contract, constrain; to compress:—**~se** *vr* to grow narrow; to embrace:—**~ la mano** to shake hands.

estrecho *m* straits *pl*:—**~/cha** *adj* narrow, close; tight; intimate; rigid, austere; short (of money).

estrella *f* star.

estrellar *vt* to dash to pieces:—**~se** *vr* to smash; to crash; to fail.

estremecer *vt* to shake, make tremble:—**~se** *vr* to shake, tremble.

estrenar *vt* to wear for the first time; to move into (a house); to show (a movie) for the first time:—**~se** *vr* to make one's debut.

estreñido/da *adj* constipated.

estrépito *m* noise; racket; fuss.

estribillo *m* chorus.

estribo *m* buttress; stirrup; running board: —**perder los ~s** to fly off the handle (*fam*).

estribor *m* (*mar*) starboard.

estricto/ta *adj* strict; severe.

estrofa *f* (*poet*) verse, strophe.

estropajo *m* scourer.

estropear *vt* to spoil; to damage:—**~se** *vr* to get damaged.

estructura *f* structure.

estruendo *m* clamor, noise; confusion; uproar; pomp, ostentation.

estuche *m* case (for scissors, etc); sheath.

estudiar *vt* to study.

estufa *f* heater, fire.

estupefaciente *m* narcotic.

estupefacto *adj* speechless; thunderstruck.

estupendo/da *adj* terrific, marvelous.

estúpido *adj* stupid.

etapa *f* stage; stopping place; (*fig*) phase.

etcétera *adv* etcetera, and so on.

eterno/na *adj* eternal.

ético/ca *adj* ethical, moral.

etiqueta *f* etiquette; label.

evacuar *vt* to evacuate, empty.

evadir *vt* to evade, escape.

evaluar *vt* to evaluate.

evaporar *vt* to evaporate:—**~se** *vr* to vanish.

eventual *adj* possible; temporary, casual (worker).

evidente *adj* evident, clear.

evitar *vt* to avoid.

evolucionar *vi* to evolve.

ex *adj* ex.

ex profeso *adv* on purpose.

exacerbar *vt* to exacerbate; to irritate.

exacto/ta *adj* exact; punctual; accurate.

exagerar *vt* to exaggerate.

exaltar *vt* to exalt, elevate; to praise, extol: —**~se** *vr* to get excited.

examen *m* exam, examination, test, inquiry.

examinar *vt* to examine.

exasperar *vt* to exasperate, irritate.

excavar *vt* to excavate, dig out.

exceder *vt* to exceed, surpass, excel, outdo.

excelente *adj* excellent.

excéntrico/ca *adj* eccentric.

excepto *adv* excepting, except (for).

exceso *m* excess.

excitar *vt* to excite:—**~se** *vr* to get excited.

exclamar *vt* to exclaim, cry out.

excluir *vt* to exclude.

excremento *m* excrement.

excursión *f* excursion, trip.

excusa *f* excuse, apology.

excusado *m* bathroom.

excusar *vt* to excuse; to avoid:—**~ de** to exempt from:—**~se** *vr* to apologize.

exento/ta *adj* exempt, free.

exhalar *vt* to exhale; to give off; to heave (a sigh).

exhausto/ta *adj* exhausted.

exhibir *vt* to exhibit.

exhortar *vt* to exhort.

exhumar *vt* to disinter, exhume.

exigir *vt* to demand, require.

exiliado/da *adj* exiled:—*m/f* exile.

existir *vi* to exist, be.

éxito *m* outcome; success; (*mus,etc*) hit:— **tener ~** to be successful.

exorbitante *adj* exhorbitant, excessive.

exótico/ca *adj* exotic.

expandir *vt* to expand.

expatriarse *vr* to emigrate; to go into exile.

expectativa *f* expectation; prospect.

expedición *f* expedition.

expediente *m* expedient; means; (*jur*) proceedings *pl*; dossier, file.

expedir *vt* to send, forward, dispatch.

expensas *fpl*:—**a ~ de** at the expense of.

experimentar *vt* to experience:—*vi* **~ con** to experiment with.

experto/ta *adj* expert; experienced.
expiar *vt* to atone for; to purify.
expirar *vi* to expire.
explayarse *vr* to speak at length.
explicar *vt* to explain, expound:—~**se** *vr* to explain oneself.
explorar *vt* to explore.
explotar *vt* to exploit; to run:—*vi* to explode.
exponer *vt* to expose; to explain.
exportar *vt* to export.
exposición *f* exposure; exhibition; explanation; account.
expresar *vt* to express.
expreso/sa *adj* express, clear, specific; fast (train).
exprimir *vt* to squeeze out.
expropriar *vt* to expropriate.
expulsar *vt* to expel, drive out.
éxtasis *m* ecstasy, enthusiasm.
extender *vt* to extend, stretch out:—~**se** *vr* to extend; to spread.
extenso/sa *adj* extensive.
extenuar *vt* to exhaust, debilitate.

exterior *adj* exterior, external:—*m* exterior, outward appearance.
exterminar *vt* to exterminate.
externo/na *adj* external, outer:—*m/f* day pupil.
extinguir *vt* to wipe out; to extinguish.
extintor *m* (fire) extinguisher.
extra *adj invar* extra; good quality:—*m/f* extra:—*m* bonus.
extraer *vt* to extract.
extrañar *vt* to find strange; to miss: —~**se** *vr* to be surprised; to grow apart.
extranjero/ra *m/f* stranger; foreigner:—*adj* foreign, alien.
extraño/ña *adj* foreign; rare; singular; strange, odd.
extraviar *vt* to mislead:—~**se** *vr* to lose one's way.
extremidad *f* extremity; brim; tip:—~**es** *fpl* extremities *pl.*
extremo/ma *adj* extreme, last:—*m* extreme, highest degree:—**en** ~/**por** ~ extremely.
extrovertido/da *adj*, *m/f* extrovert.
exuberancia *f* exuberance; luxuriance.

F

fábrica *f* factory.
fabricar *vt* to build, construct; to manufacture; (*fig*) to fabricate.
fábula *f* fable; fiction; rumor, common talk.
fabuloso/sa *adj* fabulous, fictitious.
facción *f* (political) faction; feature.
fachada *f* facade, face, front.
fácil *adj* facile, easy.
facilitar *vt* to facilitate.
fácilmente *adv* easily.
factor *m* (*mat*) factor; (*com*) factor, agent.
factura *f* invoice.
facultativo/va *adj* optional:—*m/f* doctor, practitioner.
faena *f* task, job; hard work.
faisán *m* pheasant.
fajo *m* bundle; wad.
falaz *adj* deceitful, fraudulent; fallacious.
falda *f* skirt; lap; flap; train; slope, hillside.
fallar *vt* (*jur*) to pronounce sentence on, judge:—*vi* to fail.
fallecer *vi* to die.
falso/sa *adj* false, untrue; deceitful; fake.
falta *f* fault, defect; want; flaw, mistake; (*dep*) foul.
faltar *vi* to be wanting; to fail; not to fulfil one's promise; to need; to be missing.
fama *f* fame; reputation, name.

familia *f* family.
familiar *adj* familiar; homely, domestic:— *m/f* relative, relation.
famoso/sa *adj* famous.
fanfarrón *m* bully, braggart.
fango *m* mire, mud.
fantasía *f* fancy; fantasy; caprice; presumption.
fantasma *f* phantom, ghost.
fardo *m* bale, parcel.
farmacia *f* drugstore.
faro *m* (*mar*) lighthouse; (*auto*) headlamp; floodlight.
farola *f* street light.
fascículo *m* part, installment.
fascinar *vt* to fascinate; to enchant.
fase *f* phase.
fastidiar *vt* to annoy; to offend; to spoil.
fatal *adj* fatal; mortal; awful.
fatiga *f* weariness, fatigue.
fatuo/tua *adj* fatuous, stupid, foolish; conceited.
fauces *fpl* jaws *pl*, gullet.
favor *m* favor; protection; good turn.
favorecer *vt* to favor, protect.
fe *f* faith, belief.
febrero *m* February.
fecha *f* date (of a letter etc).

fecundar *vt* to fertilize.
felicitar *vt* to congratulate.
feliz *adj* happy, fortunate.
felpa *f* plush; toweling.
felpudo *m* doormat.
femenino/na *adj* feminine; female.
feo/ea *adj* ugly; bad, nasty.
feria *f* fair, rest day; village market.
fermentar *vi* to ferment.
feroz *adj* ferocious, savage; cruel.
ferretería *f* hardware store.
ferrocarril *m* railway.
fértil *adj* fertile, fruitful.
festejo *m* courtship; feast.
festivo/va *adj* festive, merry; witty: **—dia ~** holiday.
feto *m* fetus.
fiable *adj* trustworthy; reliable.
fiambre *m* cold meat.
fianza *f* (*jur*) surety.
fiar *vt* to entrust, confide; to bail; to sell on credit:**—se** *vr* to trust.
fibra *f* fibre.
ficha *f* token, counter (at games); (index) card.
fidelidad *f* fidelity; loyalty.
fideos *mpl* noodles *pl*.
fiebre *f* fever.
fiel *adj* faithful, loyal:**—mpl los ~es** the faithful *pl*.
fieltro *m* felt.
fiera *f* wild beast.
fiesta *f* party; festivity:**—s** *fpl* vacations *pl*.
figura *f* figure, shape.
figurar *vt* to figure:**—se** *vr* to fancy, imagine.
fijar *vt* to fix, fasten:**—se** *vr* to become fixed:**—se en** to notice.
fijo/ja *adj* fixed, firm; settled, permanent.
fila *f* row, line; (*mtl*) rank:**—en ~** in a line, in a row.
filete *m* fillet; fillet steak.
filmar *vt* to film.
filo *m* edge, blade.
filosofía *f* philosophy.
filtro *m* filter.
fin *m* end; termination, conclusion; aim, purpose:**—al ~** at last:**—en ~** (*fig*) well then:**—por ~** finally, lastly.
finalmente *adv* finally, at last.
financiar *vt* to finance.
finca *f* land, property, real estate; country house; farm.
fingir *vt* to feign, fake:**—se** *vr* to pretend to be:**—vi** to pretend.
fino/na *adj* fine, pure; slender; polite; acute; dry (of sherry).

firma *f* signature; (*com*) company.
firmamento *m* firmament, sky, heaven.
firme *adj* firm, stable, strong, secure; constant; resolute:**—m** road surface.
fiscal *adj* fiscal:**—m/f** district attorney.
fisco *m* treasury, exchequer.
fisgar *vt* to pry into.
física *f* physics.
flaco/ca *adj* lean, skinny; feeble.
flan *m* crème caramel.
flauta *f* (*mus*) flute.
flecha *f* arrow.
flequillo *m* fringe (of hair).
flete *m* (*mar*) freight; charter.
flexible *adj* flexible; compliant; docile.
flojo/ja *adj* loose; flexible; slack; lazy.
flor *f* flower.
florecer *vi* to blossom.
florero *m* vase.
flotador *m* float; rubber ring.
flotar *vi* to float.
fluctuar *vi* to fluctuate; to waver.
fluir *vi* to flow.
foco *m* focus; center; source; floodlight; (light)bulb.
fogón *m* stove; hearth.
fogoso/sa *adj* fiery; ardent, fervent; impetuous, boisterous.
folleto *m* pamphlet; folder, brochure.
follón *m* (*fam*) mess; fuss.
fomentar *vt* to encourage; to promote.
fondo *m* bottom; back; background; space:**—s** *mpl* stock, funds *pl*, capital:**—a ~** perfectly, completely.
fontanero/ra *m/f* plumber.
forjar *vt* to forge; to frame; to invent.
forma *f* form, shape; pattern; (*med*) fitness; (*dep*) form; means, method: **—de ~ que** in such a manner that.
formación *f* formation; form, figure; education; training.
formar *vt* to form, shape.
fornido/da *adj* well-built.
forro *m* lining; book jacket.
fortuna *f* fortune; wealth.
forzar *vt* to force.
forzoso/sa *adj* indispensable, necessary.
fosa *f* grave; pit.
fósforo *m* phosphorus:**—s** *mpl* matches *pl*.
fotocopia *f* photocopy.
fotografía *f* photography; photograph.
fracasar *vi* to fail.
frágil *adj* fragile, frail.
fraguar *vt* to forge; to contrive:**—vi** to solidify, harden.
fraile *m* friar, monk.

frambuesa f raspberry.
francés/sa adj French:—m French language:—m/f Frenchman/woman.
frasco m flask.
frase f phrase.
fraternal adj fraternal, brotherly.
fraude m fraud, deceit; cheat.
frazada f blanket.
frecuencia f frequency.
fregar vt to scrub; to wash up.
freír vt to fry.
frenar vt to brake; (fig) to check.
frenesí m frenzy.
freno m bit; brake; (fig) check.
frente f front; face:—— a ~ face to face:—en ~ opposite; (mil) front:—m forehead.
fresa f strawberry.
fresco/ca adj fresh; cool; new; ruddy: —m fresh air:—m/f (fam) shameless or impudent person.
fresno m ash tree.
frigorífico m fridge.
frijol m kidney bean.
frío/fría adj cold; indifferent:—m cold; indifference.
friso m frieze; wainscot.
frito/ta adj fried.
frívolo/la adj frivolous.
frondoso/sa adj leafy.
frontera f frontier.
frontón m (dep) pelota court; pelota.
frotar vt to rub.
fructificar vi to bear fruit; to come to fruition.
frugal adj frugal, sparing.
fruncir vt to pleat; to knit; to contract:—~ las cejas to knit the eyebrows.

frustrar vt to frustrate.
fruta f fruit:—~ del tiempo seasonal fruit.
frutal m fruit tree.
frutilla f strawberry.
fuego m fire.
fuente f fountain; spring; source; large dish.
fuera adv out(side); away:—~ de prep outside:—i~! out of the way!
fuerte m (mil) fortification, fort; forte: — adj vigorous, tough; strong; loud; heavy: —adv strongly; hard.
fuerza f force, strength; (elec) power; violence:—a ~ de by dint of:—~s mpl troops pl.
fugarse vr to escape, flee.
fugaz adj fleeting.
fullero m cardsharper, cheat.
fumar vt, vi to smoke.
función f function; duties pl; show, performance.
funcionar vi to function; to work (of a machine).
funcionario/ria m/f official; civil servant.
funda f case, sheath:—~ de almohada pillowcase.
fundar vt to found; to establish; to ground.
fundir vt to fuse; to melt; to smelt; (com) to merge; to bankrupt; (elec) to fuse, blow.
fúnebre adj mournful, sad; funereal.
furgoneta f pick-up (truck).
furioso/sa adj furious.
furtivo/va adj furtive.
fusible m fuse.
fusión f fusion; (com) merger.
fútbol m soccer.
futuro/ra adj, m future.

G

gabardina f gabardine; raincoat.
gabinete m (pol) cabinet, study; office (of solicitors, etc).
gafas fpl glasses pl, spectacles pl.
gafe m jinx.
gai (fam) adj invar, m gay (sl), homosexual.
gajo m segment (of orange).
galápago m tortoise.
galardón m reward, prize.
galbana f laziness, idleness.
galera f (mar) galley; wagon; galley (of type).
galería f gallery.
galgo m grayhound.
gallardo/da adj graceful, elegant; brave, daring.

galleta f biscuit.
gallina f hen:—m/f (fig) coward:—~ ciega blindman's buff.
gallo m cock.
gama f (mus) scale; (fig) range, gamut; doe.
gamba f shrimp.
gamberro/rra m/f hooligan.
gamuza f chamois.
gana f desire, wish; appetite; will, longing:—de buena ~ with pleasure, voluntarily:—de mala ~ unwillingly, with reluctance.
ganado m livestock, cattle pl:—~ mayor horses and mules pl:—~ menor sheep, goats and hogs pl.
ganar vt to gain; to win; to earn:—vi to win.

gancho *m* hook; crook.
gandul *adj*, *m/f* layabout.
ganga *f* bargain.
ganso/sa *m/f* gander; goose; (*fam*) idiot.
garabatear *vi*, *vt* to scrawl, scribble.
garaje *m* garage.
garantía *f* warranty, guarantee.
garbanzo *m* chickpea, garbanzo.
garbo *m* gracefulness, elegance; stylishness; generosity.
garganta *f* throat, gullet; instep; neck (of a bottle); narrow pass between mountains or rivers.
gárgara *f* gargling, gargle.
garra *f* claw; talon; paw.
garrafa *f* carafe; (gas) cylinder.
garrafal *adj* great, vast, huge.
garrotillo *m* (*med*) croup.
garrucha *f* pulley.
garza *f* heron.
gasa *f* gauze.
gaseoso/sa *adj* fizzy:—*f* lemonade.
gasoil *m* diesel (oil).
gasolina *f* gas.
gasolinera *f* gas station.
gastar *vt* to spend; to expend; to waste; to wear away; to use up:—~se *vr* to wear out; to waste.
gata *f* she-cat:—**a ~s** on all fours.
gato *m* cat; jack.
gavilán *m* sparrow hawk.
gavilla *f* sheaf of corn.
gaviota *f* seagull.
gazpacho *m* Spanish cold tomato soup.
gelatina *f* jelly; gelatine.
gemelo/la *m/f* twin.
gemir *vi* to groan, moan.
generación *f* generation; progeny, race.
general *m* general:—*adj* general:—**en ~** generally, in general.
género *m* genus; kind, type; gender; cloth, material:—~**s** *mpl* goods, commodities *pl*.
generoso/sa *adj* noble, generous.
genio *m* nature, character; genius.
genital *adj* genital:—*mpl* ~**es** genitals *pl*.
gente *f* people; nation; family.
gentileza *f* grace; charm; politeness.
genuino/na *adj* genuine; pure.
geografía *f* geography.
geología *f* geology.
geometría *f* geometry.
geranio *m* (*bot*) geranium.
gerente *m/f* manager; director.
germinar *vi* to germinate, bud.
gestión *f* management; negotiation.
gesto *m* face; grimace; gesture.
gigante *m* giant:—*adj* gigantic.

gilipollas *adj invar* (*fam*) stupid:—*m/f invar* wimp (*sl*).
gimnasia *f* gymnastics.
ginebra *f* gin.
ginecólogo/ga *m/f* gynecologist.
gira *f* trip, tour.
girar *vt* to turn around; to swivel:—*vi* to go round, revolve.
girasol *m* sunflower.
gitano/na *m/f* Gipsy.
glacial *adj* icy.
glándula *f* gland.
globo *m* globe; sphere; orb; balloon: —~ **aerostatico** air balloon.
glorieta *f* bower, arbor; traffic circle.
glosar *vt* to gloss; to comment on.
glotón/ona *m/f* glutton.
gobierno *m* government.
goce *m* enjoyment.
gol *m* goal.
golondrina *f* swallow.
golosina *f* dainty, titbit; sweet.
golpe *m* blow, stroke, hit; knock; clash; coup:—**de ~** suddenly.
goma *f* gum; rubber; elastic.
gordo/da *adj* fat, plump, big-bellied; first, main; (*fam*) enormous.
gorjear *vi* to twitter, chirp.
gorrión *m* sparrow.
gorro *m* cap; bonnet.
gorrón/ona *m/f* scrounger.
gota *f* drop; (*med*) gout.
gotera *f* leak.
gozar *vt* to enjoy, have, possess:—~se *vr* to enjoy oneself, rejoice.
gozne *m* hinge.
gozo *m* joy, pleasure.
grabado *m* engraving.
grabar *vt* to engrave; to record.
gracia *f* grace, gracefulness; wit:—**i(muchas) ~s!** thanks (very much): —**tener ~** to be funny.
gracioso/sa *adj* graceful; beautiful; funny; pleasing:—*m* comic character.
grada *f* step of a staircase; tier, row:—~**s** *fpl* seats *pl* of stadium or theater.
grado *m* step; degree:—**de buen ~** willingly.
gráfico/ca *adj* graphic:—*m* diagram: —*f* graph.
grajo *m* rook.
gramo *m* gram(me).
gran *adj* = **grande**.
granada *f* pomegranate.
granate *m* garnet (precious stone).
grande *adj* great; big; tall; grand:—*m/f* adult.
grandioso/sa *adj* grand, magnificent.
granel *adv*:—**a ~** in bulk.

granizado *m* iced drink.
granizo *m* hail.
granja *f* farm.
grano *m* grain.
granuja *m/f* rogue; urchin.
grapa *f* staple; clamp.
grasa *f* suet; fat; grease.
gratis *adj* free.
grato/ta *adj* pleasant, agreeable.
gravamen *m* charge, obligation; nuisance; tax.
grave *adj* weighty, heavy; grave, important; serious.
gravilla *f* gravel.
gravoso/sa *adj* onerous, burdensome; costly.
graznar *vi* to croak; to cackle; to quack.
gremio *m* union, guild; society; company, corporation.
greña *f* tangle; shock of hair.
gresca *f* clatter; outcry; confusion; wrangle, quarrel.
grieta *f* crevice, crack, chink.
grifo *m* faucet, tap; gas station.
grillo *m* cricket; bud, shoot.
gripe *f* flu, influenza.
gris *adj* gray.
gritar *vi* to cry out, shout, yell.
grosella *f* redcurrant:—~ **negra** blackcurrant.
grosero/ra *adj* coarse; rude, bad-mannered.
grúa *f* crane (machine); derrick.
grueso/sa *adj* thick, bulky; large; coarse:—*m* bulk.
grulla *f* crane (bird).
gruñir *vi* to grunt, to grumble; to creak (of hinges, etc).

grupo *m* group.
gruta *f* grotto.
guadaña *f* scythe.
guante *m* glove.
guapo/pa *adj* good-looking; handsome; smart.
guardabosque *m* gamekeeper; ranger.
guardacostas *m invar* coastguard vessel.
guardaespaldas *m/f invar* bodyguard.
guardar *vt* to keep, preserve; to save (money); to guard:—~**se** *vr* to be on one's guard:—~**se de** to avoid, abstain from.
guardarropa *f* wardrobe; cloakroom.
guardia *f* guard; (*mar*) watch; care, custody: —*m/f* guard; police officer: —*m* (*mil*) guardsman.
guarecer *vt* to protect; to shelter:—~**se** *vr* to take refuge.
guarnecer *vt* to provide, equip; to reinforce; to garnish, set (in gold, etc); to adorn.
guasa *f* joke.
gubernativo/va *adj* governmental.
guía *m/f* guide:—*f* guidebook.
guiar *vt* to guide; (*auto*) to steer.
guijarro *m* pebble.
guiñar *vt* to wink.
guinda *f* cherry.
guindilla *f* chilli pepper.
guión *m* hyphen; script (of movie).
guisante *m* (*bot*) pea.
guisar *vt* to cook.
guitarra *f* guitar.
gula *f* gluttony.
gusano *m* maggot, worm.
gustar *vt* to taste; to sample:—*vi* to please, be pleasing:—**me gusta. . .** I like. . .

H

haba *f* bean.
haber *vt* to get, lay hands on; to occur:—*v imp* **hay** there is, there are: —*v aux* to have:—~**se** *vr* **habérselas con uno** to have it out with somebody:—*m* income, salary; assets *pl*; (*com*) credit.
hábil *adj* able, clever, skillful, dexterous, apt.
habitación *f* habitation, abode, rooming house, dwelling, residence; room.
habitar *vt* to inhabit, live in.
hábito *m* dress; habit, custom.
habitual *adj* habitual, customary.
hablar *vt*, *vi* to speak; to talk.
hacendoso/sa *adj* industrious.
hacer *vt* to make; to do; to put into practice; to perform; to effect; to prepare; to

imagine; to force; (*mat*) to amount to, make:—*vi* to act, behave:—~**se** *vr* to become.
hacha *f* torch; ax, hatchet.
hacia *adv* toward(s); about:—~ **arriba/abajo** up(wards)/down(wards).
hada *f* fairy.
halagar *vt* to cajole, flatter.
halcón *m* falcon.
hallar *vt* to find; to meet with; to discover:—~**se** *vr* to find oneself; to be.
hambre *f* hunger; famine; longing.
harina *f* flour.
harto/ta *adj* full; fed up:—*adv* enough.
hasta *prep* up to; down to; until, as far as:— *adv* even.

haya f beech tree.
hazaña f exploit, achievement.
hebilla f buckle.
hebra f thread; vein of minerals or metals; grain of wood.
hebreo/ea m/f, adj Hebrew; Israeli:—m Hebrew language.
hechizar vt to bewitch, enchant; to charm.
hecho/cha adj made; done; mature; ready-to-wear; cooked:—m action; act; fact; matter; event.
hectárea f hectare.
helado/da adj frozen; glacial, icy; astonished; astounded:—m ice cream.
helar vt to freeze; to congeal; to astonish, amaze:—se vr to be frozen; to turn into ice; to congeal:—vi to freeze; to congeal.
helecho m fern.
hélice f helix; propeller.
hembra f female.
heno m hay.
heredar vt to inherit.
hereje m/f heretic.
herir vt to wound, hurt; to beat, strike; to affect, touch, move; to offend.
hermana f sister.
hermano m brother:—/na adj matched; resembling.
hermético/ca adj hermetic, airtight.
hermoso/sa adj beautiful, handsome, lovely; large, robust.
héroe m hero.
herradura f horseshoe.
herrero m smith.
hervir vt to boil; to cook:—vi to boil; to bubble; to seethe.
hiedra f ivy.
hiel f gall, bile.
hielo m frost; ice.
hierba f grass; herb.
hierro m iron.
hígado m liver; (fig) courage, pluck.
higiene f hygiene.
higo m fig.
hijo/ja m/f son/daughter; child; offspring.
hilera f row, line, file.
hilo m thread; wire.
hincar vt to thrust in, drive in.
hinchar vt to swell; to inflate; (fig) to exaggerate:—se vr to swell; to become vain.
hinojo m (bot) fennel.
hipo m hiccups pl.
hipócrita adj hypocritical:—m/f hypocrite.
hipódromo m racetrack.
hipoteca f mortgage.

historia f history; tale, story.
historieta f short story; short novel; comic strip.
hocico m snout:—**meter el ~ en todo** to meddle in everything.
hogar m hearth, fireplace; (fig) house, home; family life.
hogaza f large loaf of bread.
hoguera f bonfire; blaze.
hoja f leaf; petal; sheet of paper; blade.
hojalata f tin (plate).
hojaldre f puff pastry.
hojear vt to turn the pages of.
hola excl hello!
holgado/da adj loose, wide, baggy; at leisure; idle, unoccupied; well-off.
hollín m soot.
hombre m man; human being.
hombro m shoulder.
homenaje m homage.
homicidio m murder.
hondo/da adj deep, profound.
honesto/ta adj honest; modest.
hongo m mushroom; fungus.
honor m honor.
honorario/ria adj honorary:—s mpl fees pl.
honra f honor, reverence; self-esteem; reputation; integrity:—s funebres pl funeral honors pl.
hora f hour; time.
horario/ria adj hourly, hour compd: —m schedule.
horchata f tiger-nut milk.
horma f mold, form.
hormiga f ant.
hormigón m concrete.
horno m oven; furnace.
horquilla f pitchfork; hairpin.
hórreo m granary.
horrible adj horrid, horrible.
horror m horror, fright; atrocity.
hortaliza f vegetable.
hospedar vt to put up, lodge; to entertain.
hospicio m orphanage; hospice.
hospital m hospital.
hostal m small hotel.
hostelería f hotel business or trade.
hostia f host; wafer; (fam) whack (sl), punch.
hostil adj hostile; adverse.
hotel m hotel.
hoy adv today; now, nowadays:—**de ~ en adelante** from now on, henceforward.
hoyo m hole, pit; excavation.
hoz f sickle; gorge.
hucha f money-box.

hueco/ca adj hollow, concave; empty; vain, ostentatious:—m interval; gap, hole; vacancy.
huelga f strike.
huella f track, footstep.
huérfano/na adj, m/f orphan.
huerta f market garden; irrigated region.
hueso m bone; stone, core.
huésped/da m/f guest, lodger, roomer; innkeeper.
huevo m egg.
huir vi to flee, escape.
humano/na adj human; humane, kind.

húmedo/da adj humid; wet; damp.
humilde adj humble.
humillar vt to humble; to subdue:—~se vr to humble oneself.
humo m smoke; fumes pl.
humor m mood, temper; humor.
hundir vt to submerge; to sink; to ruin:—~se vr to sink, go to the bottom; to collapse; to be ruined.
huraño/ña adj shy; unsociable.
hurtadillas adv:—a ~ by stealth.
hurtar vt to steal, rob.
husmear vt to scent; to pry into.

I

ictericia f jaundice.
ida f departure, going:—(viaje de) ~ outward journey:—~ y vuelta round trip:—~s y venidas comings and goings pl.
idea f idea; scheme.
ídem pn ditto.
idéntico/ca adj identical.
idioma m language.
idiota m/f idiot.
idóneo/nea adj suitable, fit.
iglesia f church.
ignorar vt to be ignorant of, not to know.
igual adj equal; similar; the same:—al ~ equally.
ilegal adj illegal, unlawful.
ileso/sa adj unhurt.
ilimitado/da adj unlimited.
iluminar vt to illumine, illuminate, enlighten.
ilusión f illusion; hope:—hacerse ~ones to build up one's hopes.
ilustre adj illustrious, famous.
imagen f image.
imaginar vt to imagine; to think up:—vi ~se vr to imagine.
imán m magnet.
imitar vt to imitate, copy; to counterfeit.
impaciente adj impatient.
impar adj odd.
imparcial adj impartial.
impedir vt to impede, hinder; to prevent.
impeler vt to drive, propel; to impel; to incite, stimulate.
impenetrable adj impenetrable, impervious; incomprehensible.
impenitente adj impenitent.
imperdible m safety pin.
imperdonable adj unforgivable.
imperfecto/ta adj imperfect.
impermeable adj waterproof:—m raincoat.

imperturbable adj imperturbable; unruffled.
implacable adj implacable, inexorable.
implicar vt to implicate, involve.
imponer vt to impose; to command: —~se vr to assert oneself; to prevail.
impopular adj unpopular.
importante adj important, considerable.
importar vi to be important, matter: —vt to import; to be worth.
importe m amount, cost.
importunar vt to bother, pester.
imposible adj impossible; extremely difficult; slovenly.
impostor/ra m/f impostor, fraud.
impotencia f impotence.
impracticable adj impracticable, unworkable.
impreciso/sa adj imprecise, vague.
imprenta f printing; press; printing office.
imprescindible adj essential.
impresión f impression; stamp; print; edition.
impresionar vt to move; to impress:—~se vr to be impressed; to be moved.
imprevisto/ta adj unforeseen, unexpected.
imprimir vt to print; to imprint; to stamp.
improbable adj improbable, unlikely.
improvisar vt to extemporize; to improvise.
improviso/sa adj:—de ~ unexpectedly.
imprudente adj imprudent; indiscreet; unwise.
impúdico/ca adj shameless; lecherous.
impuesto/ta adj imposed:—m tax, duty.
impulso m impulse; thrust; (fig) impulse.
impune adj unpunished.
impuro/ra adj impure; foul.
inaccesible adj inaccessible.
inadvertido/da adj unnoticed.
inagotable adj inexhaustible.

inaguantable *adj* unbearable, intolerable.
inalterable *adj* unalterable.
inapreciable *adj* imperceptible; invaluable.
inaudito/ta *adj* unheard-of.
inaugurar *vt* to inaugurate.
incalculable *adj* incalculable.
incansable *adj* untiring, tireless.
incapaz *adj* incapable, unable.
incauto/ta *adj* incautious, unwary.
incendio *m* fire.
incentivo *m* incentive.
incertidumbre *f* doubt, uncertainty.
incierto/ta *adj* uncertain, doubtful.
incineración *f* incineration; cremation.
incitar *vt* to incite, excite.
inclemencia *f* inclemency, severity; inclem-
    ency (of the weather).
inclinar *vt* to incline; to nod, bow (the
    head):—**~se** *vr* to bow; to stoop.
incluir *vt* to include, comprise; to incorp-
    orate; to enclose.
incluso/sa *adj* included:—*adv* inclusively;
    even.
incógnito/ta *adj* unknown:—**de ~** incognito.
incombustible *adj* incombustible, fireproof.
incómodo/da *adj* uncomfortable; annoy-
    ing; inconvenient.
incomparable *adj* incomparable, matchless.
incompasivo *adj* unsympathetic.
incompleto/ta *adj* incomplete.
incomunicado/da *adj* isolated, cut off; in
    solitary confinement.
inconcebible *adj* inconceivable.
incondicional *adj* unconditional; whole-
    hearted; staunch.
inconfundible *adj* unmistakable.
inconsciente *adj* unconscious; thoughtless.
inconstante *adj* inconstant, variable, fickle.
incorporar *vt* to incorporate:—**~se** *vr* to
    sit up; to join (an organization), become
    incorporated.
incorrecto/ta *adj* incorrect.
incrédulo/la *adj* incredulous.
increíble *adj* incredible.
incremento *m* increment, increase; growth;
    rise.
inculcar *vt* to inculcate.
inculto/ta *adj* uncultivated; uneducated;
    uncouth.
incumbencia *f* obligation; duty.
incurable *adj* incurable; irremediable.
indagar *vt* to inquire into.
indebido/da *adj* undue; illegal, unlawful.
indeciso/sa *adj* hesitant; undecided.
indefenso/sa *adj* defenseless.
indemnizar *vt* to indemnify, compensate.
independiente *adj* independent.

indeterminado/da *adj* indeterminate; indef-
    inite.
indicador *m* indicator; gage.
indicar *vt* to indicate.
índice *m* ratio, rate; hand (of a watch or
    clock); index, table of contents; catalog;
    forefinger, index finger.
indicio *m* indication, mark; sign, token; clue.
indiferencia *f* indifference, apathy.
indígena *adj* indigenous, native:—*m/f* native.
indignar *vt* to irritate; to provoke, tease:—
    ~se *vr* **~ por** to get indignant about.
indigno/na *adj* unworthy, contemptible, low.
indirecta *f* innuendo, hint.
indiscreción *f* indiscretion, tactlessness; gaffe.
individual *adj* individual; single (of a
    room):—*m* (*dep*) singles.
individuo *m* individual.
índole *f* disposition, nature, character; soft,
    kind.
indolente *adj* indolent, lazy.
indómito/ta *adj* untamed, ungoverned.
inducir *vt* to induce, persuade.
indudable *adj* undoubted; unquestionable.
indultar *vt* to pardon; to exempt.
industria *f* industry; skill.
inédito/ta *adj* unpublished; (*fig*) new.
ineficaz *adj* ineffective; inefficient.
inepto/ta *adj* inept, unfit, useless.
inercia *f* inertia, inactivity.
inerte *adj* inert, dull; sluggish, motionless.
inesperado/da *adj* unexpected, unforeseen.
inevitable *adj* unavoidable.
inexacto/ta *adj* inaccurate, untrue.
inexperto/ta *adj* inexperienced.
infame *adj* infamous.
infancia *f* infancy, childhood.
infantil *adj* infantile; childlike; children's.
infarto *m* heart attack.
infatigable *adj* tireless, untiring.
infectar *vt* to infect.
infeliz *adj* unhappy, unfortunate.
inferior *adj* inferior.
infernal *adj* infernal, hellish.
infiel *adj* unfaithful; disloyal; inaccurate.
infierno *m* hell.
infiltrarse *vr* to infiltrate.
ínfimo/ma *adj* lowest; of very poor quality.
infinidad *f* infinity; immensity.
infinito/ta *adj* infinite; immense.
inflamable *adj* inflammable.
inflar *vt* to inflate, blow up; (*fig*) to exag-
    gerate.
inflexible *adj* inflexible.
influir *vt* to influence.
información *f* information; news; (*mil*)
    intelligence; investigation, judicial inquiry.

informal *adj* irregular, incorrect; untrustworthy; informal.

informar *vt* to inform; to reveal, make known:—**~se** *vr* to find out: —*vi* to report; (*jur*) to plead; to inform.

informática *f* computer science, information technology.

informe *m* report, statement; piece of information, account:—*adj* shapeless, formless.

infortunio *m* misfortune, ill luck.

infracción *f* infraction; breach, infringement.

infructuoso/sa *adj* fruitless, unproductive, unprofitable.

infundado/da *adj* groundless.

ingeniero/ra *m/f* engineer.

ingenio *m* talent; wit; ingenuity; engine:— ~ **de azúcar** sugar mill.

ingenuo/nua *adj* naive.

ingerir *vt* to ingest; to swallow; to consume.

ingle *f* groin.

inglés/esa *adj* English:—*m* English language: —*m/f* Englishman/woman.

ingratar *vt* to deposit:—*vi* to come in.

ingrato/ta *adj* ungrateful, thankless; disagreeable.

inhabilitar *vt* to disqualify, disable.

inhabitable *adj* uninhabitable.

inhibir *vt* to inhibit; to restrain.

iniciar *vt* to initiate; to begin.

ininteligible *adj* unintelligible.

injertar *vt* to graft.

injuriar *vt* to insult, wrong.

injusto/ta *adj* unjust.

inmediaciones *fpl* neighborhood.

inmediatamente *adv* immediately, at once.

inmobiliario/ria *adj* real-estate *compd*:—*f* estate agency.

inmortal *adj* immortal.

inmóvil *adj* immovable, still.

inmueble *m* property:—*adj* **bienes ~s** real estate.

inmundo/da *adj* filthy, dirty; nasty.

inmune *adj* (*med*) immune; free, exempt.

innato/ta *adj* inborn, innate.

innecesario/ria *adj* unnecessary.

innegable *adj* undeniable.

innumerable *adj* innumerable, countless.

inocente *adj* innocent.

inodoro *m* washroom:—**~/ra** *adj* odorless, without smell.

inofensivo/va *adj* harmless.

inolvidable *adj* unforgettable.

inoxidable *adj*:—**acero ~** stainless steel.

inquietar *vt* to worry, disturb:—**~se** *vr* to worry, get worried.

inquilino/na *m/f* tenant; roomer, lodger.

inquirir *vt* to inquire into, investigate.

inscribir *vt* to inscribe; to list, register.

insecto *m* insect.

insensato/ta *adj* senseless, stupid; mad.

insensible *adj* insensitive; imperceptible; numb.

inseparable *adj* inseparable.

insertar *vt* to insert.

inservible *adj* useless.

insignia *f* badge:—**~s** *fpl* insignia *pl*.

insinuar *vt* to insinuate:—**~se** *vr* ~ **en** to worm one's way into.

insípido/da *adj* insipid.

insistir *vi* to insist.

insolación *f* (*med*) sunstroke.

insolencia *f* insolence, rudeness, effrontery.

insólito/ta *adj* unusual.

insolvente *adj* insolvent.

insomnio *m* insomnia.

insondable *adj* unfathomable; inscrutable.

insoportable *adj* unbearable.

inspeccionar *vt* to inspect; to supervize.

inspector/ra *m/f* inspector; superintendent.

inspirar *vt* to inspire; (*med*) to inhale.

instalar *vt* to install.

instantáneo/nea *adj* instantaneous: —*f* snap(shot):—**café ~** instant coffee.

instante *m* instant:—**al ~** immediately, instantly.

instigar *vt* to instigate.

instinto *m* instinct.

instructivo/va *adj* instructive; educational.

instrumento *m* instrument; tool, implement.

insuficiente *adj* insufficient, inadequate.

insulso/sa *adj* insipid; dull.

insultar *vt* to insult.

insuperable *adj* insuperable, insurmountable.

intacto/ta *adj* untouched; entire; intact.

integral *adj* integral, whole:—**pan ~** wholewheat bread.

intemperie *f*:—**a la ~** out in the open.

intencionado/da *adj* meaningful; deliberate.

intenso/sa *adj* intense, strong; deep.

intentar *vt* to try, attempt.

intercalar *vt* to insert.

intercambio *m* exchange, swap.

interés *m* interest; share, part; concern, advantage; profit.

interesar *vt* to be of interest to, interest:— **~se** *vr* ~ **en** *o* **por** to take an interest in:—*vi* to be of interest.

interferir *vt* to interfere with; to jam (a telephone):—*vi* to interfere.

interfono *m* intercom.

interino/na *adj* provisional, temporary:—*m/f* temporary holder of a post; stand-in.
interior *adj* interior, internal:—*m* interior, inside.
intermedio/dia *adj* intermediate:—*m* interval.
interminable *adj* interminable, endless.
intermitente *adj* intermittent; *m* (*auto*) indicator.
internado *m* boarding school.
interno/na *adj* interior, internal:—*m/f* boarder.
interpretar *vt* to interpret, explain; (*teat*) to perform; to translate.
interrogación *f* interrogation; question mark.
interrogatorio *m* questioning; (*jur*) examination; questionnaire.
interrumpir *vt* to interrupt.
interruptor *m* switch.
intervenir *vt* to control, supervise; (*com*) to audit; (*med*) to operate on: —*vi* to participate; to intervene.
intestino/na *adj* internal, interior:—*m* intestine.
íntimo/ma *adj* internal, innermost; intimate, private.
intranquilo/la *adj* worried.
intransitable *adj* impassable.
intrépido/da *adj* intrepid, daring.
intrigar *vt, vi* to intrigue.
introducir *vt* to introduce; to insert.
introvertido/da *adj, m/f* introvert.
intruso/sa *adj* intrusive:—*m/f* intruder.
inundar *vt* to inundate, overflow; to flood.
inusitado/da *adj* unusual.
inútil *adj* useless.

inválido/da *adj* invalid, null and void:—*m/f* invalid.
invencible *adj* invincible.
invernadero *m* greenhouse.
inverosímil *adj* unlikely, improbable.
inverso/sa *adj* inverse; inverted; contrary.
invertir *vt* (*com*) to invest; to invert.
investigar *vt* to investigate; to do research into.
invierno *m* winter.
invitar *vt* to invite; to entice; to pay for.
invocar *vt* to invoke.
ir *vi* to go; to walk; to travel:—~**se** *vr* to go away, depart.
ira *f* anger, wrath.
iris *m* iris (eye):—**arco ~** rainbow.
ironía *f* irony.
irracional *adj* irrational.
irreal *adj* unreal.
irreflexión *f* rashness, thoughtlessness.
irregular *adj* irregular; abnormal.
irremediable *adj* irremediable; incurable.
irresistible *adj* irresistible.
irreverente *adj* irreverent; disrespectful.
irrisorio/ria *adj* derisory, ridiculous.
irritar *vt* to irritate, exasperate; to stir up; to inflame.
isla *f* island, isle.
istmo *m* isthmus.
italiano/na *adj* Italian:—*m* Italian language:—*m/f* Italian.
itinerario *m* itinerary.
izquierdo/da *adj* left; left-handed:—*f* left; left(-wing).

J

jabalí *m* wild boar.
jabón *m* soap.
jaca *f* pony.
jacinto *m* hyacinth.
jadear *vi* to pant.
jaleo *m* racket, uproar.
jamás *adv* never:—**para siempre ~** for ever.
jamón *m* ham:—~ **de York** cooked ham:—~ **serrano** cured ham.
jaque *m* check (at game of chess):—~ **mate** checkmate.
jaqueca *f* migraine.
jarabe *m* syrup.
jardín *m* garden.
jarra *f* jug, jar, pitcher:—**en ~s, de ~s** with hands to the sides.

jaula *f* cage; cell for mad people.
jazmín *m* jasmin.
jefe *m* chief, head, leader:—(*ferro*) ~ **de tren** guard, conductor.
jerarquía *f* hierarchy.
jerigonza *f* jargon, gibberish.
jeringa *f* syringe.
jeroglífico/ca *adj* hieroglyphic:—*m* hieroglyph, hieroglyphic.
jersey *m* sweater, pullover.
jilguero *m* goldfinch.
jinete/ta *m/f* horseman/woman, rider.
jipijapa *m* straw hat.
jirón *m* rag, shred.
jornada *f* journey; day's journey; working day.
jornal *m* day's wage.

jornalero *m* (day) laborer.
joroba *f* hump:—*m/f* hunchback.
jota *f* jot, iota; Spanish dance.
joven *adj* young:—*m/f* youth; young woman.
jovial *adj* jovial, cheerful.
joya *f* jewel:—**~s** *fpl* jewelry.
juanete *m* (*med*) bunion.
jubilar *vt* to pension off; to superannuate; to discard:—**~se** *vr* to retire.
júbilo *m* joy, rejoicing.
judía *f* bean:—**~ verde** French bean.
judicial *adj* judicial.
judío/día *adj* Jewish:—*m/f* Jewish man/woman.
juego *m* play; amusement; sport; game; gambling.
jueves *m invar* Thursday.
juez *m/f* judge.
jugar *vt*, *vi* to play, sport, gamble.
jugo *m* sap, juice.
juguete *m* toy, plaything.

juicio *m* judgement, reason; sanity; opinion.
julio *m* July.
junco *m* (*bot*) rush; junk (Chinese ship).
junio *m* June.
junta *f* meeting; assembly; congress; council.
juntar *vt* to join; to unite:—**~se** *vr* to meet, assemble; to draw closer.
junto/ta *adj* joined; united; near; adjacent:—**~s** together:—*adv* **todo ~** all at once.
jurar *vt*, *vi* to swear.
jurídico/ca *adj* lawful, legal; juridical.
justicia *f* justice; equity.
justificante *m* voucher; receipt.
justo/ta *adj* just; fair, right; exact, correct; tight:—*adv* exactly, precisely; just in time.
juventud *f* youthfulness, youth; young people *pl*.
juzgado *m* tribunal; court.

K

kilogramo *m* kilogram(me).
kilómetro *m* kilometer.

kiosco *m* kiosk.

L

la *art f* the:—*pn* her; you; it.
labio *m* lip; edge.
labor *f* labor, task; needlework; farmwork; ploughing.
laborioso/sa *adj* laborious; hard-working.
labrar *vt* to work; to carve; to farm; (*fig*) to bring about.
laca *f* lacquer; hairspray.
lacio/cia *adj* faded, withered, languid; lank (hair).
lacrar *vt* to seal (with sealing wax).
lactancia *f* lactation; breast-feeding.
lácteo/tea *adj*:—**productos ~s** dairy products.
ladera *f* slope.
ladino/na *adj* cunning, crafty.
lado *m* side; faction, party; favor, protection; (*mil*) flank:—**al ~ de** beside:—**poner a un ~** to put aside:—**por todos ~s** on all sides.
ladrar *vt* to bark.
ladrillo *m* brick.
ladrón/ona *m/f* thief, robber.

lagar *m* wine press.
lagartija *f* (small) lizard.
lagarto *m* lizard.
lago *m* lake.
lágrima *f* tear.
laguna *f* lake; lagoon; gap.
laico/ca *adj* lay.
lamentar *vt* to be sorry about; to lament, regret:—*vi* **~se** *vr* to lament, complain; to mourn.
lamer *vt* to lick, lap.
lámina *f* plate, sheet of metal; engraving.
lámpara *f* lamp.
lana *f* wool.
lancha *f* barge, lighter; launch.
langosta *f* locust; lobster.
lanzar *vt* to throw; (*dep*) to bowl, pitch; to launch, fling; (*jur*) to evict.
lápida *f* flat stone, tablet.
lápiz *m* pencil; mechanical pencil.
largamente *adv* for a long time.
largo/ga *adj* long; lengthy, generous; copious:—**a la ~a** in the end, eventually.

las *art fpl* the:—*pn* them; you.
lascivo/va *adj* lascivious; lewd.
láser *m* laser.
lástima *f* compassion, pity; shame.
lastimar *vt* to hurt; to wound; to feel pity for:—**~se** *vr* to hurt oneself.
lastre *m* ballast.
lata *f* tin; tin can; (*fam*) nuisance.
latido *m* (heart)beat.
latifundio *m* large estate.
latir *vi* to beat, palpitate.
latitud *f* latitude.
latón *m* brass.
latoso/sa *adj* annoying; boring.
laúd *f* lute (musical instrument).
laudable *adj* laudable, praise-worthy.
laurel *m* (*bot*) laurel; reward.
lavabo *m* washbasin; washroom.
lavadora *f* washing machine.
lavanda *f* lavender.
lavar *vt* to wash; to wipe away:—**~se** *vr* to wash oneself.
laxante *m* (*med*) laxative.
lazarillo *m*:—**perro ~** guide dog.
lazo *m* knot; bow; snare, trap; tie; bond.
le *pn* him; you; (*dativo*) to him; to her; to it; to you.
leal *adj* loyal; faithful.
lebrel *m* greyhound.
lección *f* reading, lesson; lecture; class.
leche *f* milk.
lecho *m* bed; layer.
lechón *m* sucking pig.
lechuga *f* lettuce.
lechuza *f* owl.
leer *vt, vi* to read.
legado *m* bequest, legacy; legate.
legal *adj* legal; trustworthy.
legaña *f* sleep (in eyes).
legislar *vt* to legislate.
legítimo/ma *adj* legitimate, lawful; authentic.
legumbres *fpl* pulses *pl*.
lejano/na *adj* distant, remote; far.
lejía *f* bleach.
lejos *adv* at a great distance, far off.
lelo/la *adj* stupid, ignorant:—*m/f* idiot.
lema *m* motto; slogan.
leña *f* firewood, kindling.
lencería *f* linen, drapery.
lengua *f* tongue; language.
lenguado *m* sole.
lenguaje *m* language.
lente *m/f* lens.
lenteja *f* lentil.
lentilla *f* contact lens.
lento/ta *adj* slow.
león *m* lion.

leopardo *m* leopard.
leotardos *mpl* tights, pantihose.
lesión *f* wound; injury; damage.
letal *adj* mortal, deadly.
letanía *f* litany.
letargo *m* lethargy.
letra *f* letter; handwriting; printing type; draft of a song; bill, draft:—**~s** *fpl* letters *pl*, learning.
letrero *m* sign; label.
leucemia *f* leukemia.
levadura *f* yeast; brewer's yeast.
levantar *vt* to raise, lift up; to build; to elevate; to hearten, cheer up:—**~se** *vr* to get up; to stand up.
levante *m* Levant; east; east wind.
levantisco *adj* turbulent, restless.
leve *adj* light; trivial.
léxico *m* vocabulary.
ley *f* law; standard (for metal).
leyenda *f* legend.
liar *vt* to tie, bind; to confuse.
libélula *f* dragonfly.
liberal *adj* liberal, generous:—*m/f* liberal.
libertad *f* liberty, freedom.
libra *f* pound:—**~ esterlina** pound sterling.
libre *adj* free; exempt; vacant.
librería *f* book store.
libreta *f* notebook:—**~ de ahorros** savings book.
libro *m* book.
licencia *f* license; licentiousness.
licenciado/da *adj* licensed:—*m/f* graduate.
lícito/ta *adj* lawful, fair; permissible.
líder *m/f* leader.
liebre *f* hare.
lienzo *f* linen; canvas; face or front of a building.
liga *f* suspender; birdlime; league; coalition; alloy.
ligar *vt* to tie, bind, fasten:—**~se** *vr* to commit oneself:—*vi* to mix, blend; (*fam*) to pick up.
ligero/ra *adj* light, swift; agile; superficial.
liguero *m* suspender belt.
lijar *vt* to smooth, sandpaper.
lima *f* file.
límite *m* limit, boundary.
limón *m* lemon.
limosna *f* alms *pl*, charity.
limpiar *vt* to clean; to cleanse; to purify; to polish; (*fig*) to clean up.
linaza *f* linseed.
lince *m* lynx.
lindar *vi* to be adjacent.
lindo/da *adj* pretty; lovely.
línea *f* line; cable; outline.

lino *m* flax.
linterna *f* lantern, lamp; torch.
lío *m* bundle, parcel; (*fam*) muddle, mess.
liquidar *vt* to liquidate; to settle (accounts).
líquido/da *adj* liquid.
lirio *m* (*bot*) iris.
lirón *m* dormouse; (*fig*) sleepy- head.
liso/sa *adj* plain, even, flat, smooth.
lisonja *f* adulation, flattery.
lista *f* list; register; catalog; menu.
listo/ta *adj* ready; smart, clever.
litera *f* berth; bunk, bunk bed.
litigio *m* lawsuit.
litoral *adj* coastal:—*m* coast.
litro *m* liter (measure).
liviano/na *adj* light; fickle; trivial.
llama *f* flame; llama (animal).
llamar *vt* to call; to name; to summon; to ring up, telephone:—*vi* to knock at the door; to ring up, telephone:—**~se** *vr* to be named.
llano/na *adj* plain; even, level, smooth; clear, evident:—*m* plain.
llanta *f* (wheel) rim; tire; inner (tube).
llanura *f* evenness, flatness; plain, prairie.
llave *f* key:—**~ maestra** master key.
llegar *vi* to arrive:—**~ a** to reach:—**~se** *vr* to come near, approach.
llenar *vt* to fill; to cover; to fill out (a form); to satisfy, fulfil:—**~se** *vr* to gorge oneself.
llevar *vt* to take; to wear; to carry; to convey, transport; to drive; to lead; to bear:—**~se** *vr* to carry off, take away.
llorar *vt, vi* to weep, cry.
llover *vi* to rain.
lluvia *f* rain.
lo *pn* it; him; you:—*art* the.
lobo *m* wolf.
lóbulo *m* lobe.
local *adj* local:—*m* place, site.

loco/ca *adj* mad:—*m/f* mad person.
locutor/ra *m/f* (*rad*) announcer; (*TV*) news-reader.
lodo *m* mud, mire.
lograr *vt* to achieve; to gain, obtain.
lombarda *f* red cabbage.
lombriz *f* worm.
lomo *m* loin; back (of an animal); spine (of a book):—**llevar** o **traer a ~** to carry on the back.
lona *f* canvas.
loncha *f* slice; rasher.
longaniza *f* pork sausage.
longitud *f* length; longitude.
loro *m* parrot.
los *art mpl* the:—*pn* them; you.
losa *f* flagstone.
lote *m* lot; portion.
loza *f* crockery.
lucero *m* morning star, bright star.
luchar *vi* to struggle; to wrestle.
luciérnaga *f* glowworm.
lucir *vt* to light (up); to show off:—*vi* to shine:—**~se** *vr* to make a fool of oneself.
luego *adv* next; afterward(s):—**desde ~** of course.
lugar *m* place, spot; village; reason: —**en ~ de** instead of, in lieu of.
lúgubre *adj* lugubrious; sad, gloomy.
lujo *m* luxury; abundance.
lujuria *f* lust.
lumbre *f* fire; light.
luna *f* moon; glass plate for mirrors; lens.
lunar *m* mole, spot:—*adj* lunar.
lunes *m invar* Monday.
lupa *f* magnifying glass.
lupanar *m* brothel.
luto *m* mourning (dress); grief.
luz *f* light.

M

maceta *f* flowerpot.
machacar *vt* to pound, crush:—*vi* to insist, go on.
macho *adj* male; (*fig*) virile:—*m* male; (*fig*) he-man.
macizo/za *adj* massive; solid:—*m* mass, chunk.
madera *f* wood; lumber.
madrastra *f* stepmother.
madre *f* mother; womb.
madreselva *f* honeysuckle.
madriguera *f* burrow; den.
madrugar *vi* to get up early; to get ahead.

maduro/ra *adj* ripe, mature.
maestro *m* master; teacher:—**~/tra** *adj* masterly, skilled; principal.
magia *f* magic.
magisterio *m* teaching; teaching profession; teachers *pl*.
magnetófon, magnetófono *m* tape recorder.
magnífico/ca *adj* magnificent, splendid.
mago/ga *m/f* magician.
magullar *vt* to bruise; to damage; to bash (*sl*).
mahometano/na *m/f, adj* Muslim.
maíz *m* maize, Indian corn.
majadero/ra *adj* dull; silly, stupid:—*m* idiot.

majo/ja *adj* nice; attractive; smart.

majuelo *m* vine newly planted; hawthorn.

mal *m* evil; hurt; harm, damage; misfortune; illness:—*adj* (before masculine nouns) bad.

malcriado/da *adj* rude, ill-behaved; naughty; spoiled.

maldad *f* wickedness.

maldecir *vt* to curse.

maldito/ta *adj* wicked; damned, cursed.

malecón *m* pier.

maleducado/da *adj* bad-mannered, rude.

malestar *m* discomfort; (*fig*) uneasiness; unrest.

maleta *f* suitcase; (*auto*) trunk.

maleza *f* weeds *pl*; thicket.

malgastar *vt* to waste, ruin.

malhablado/da *adj* foul-mouthed.

malhechor/ra *m/f* malefactor; criminal.

malhumorado/da *adj* cross, bad-tempered.

malla *f* mesh, network:—~**s** *fpl* leotard.

malo/la *adj* bad; ill; wicked:—*m/f* villain.

maltratar *vt* to ill-treat, abuse, mistreat.

malva *f* (*bot*) mallow.

malvado/da *adj* wicked, villainous.

mama *f* teat; breast.

mamá *f* (*fam*) mum, mummy.

mamar *vt, vi* to suck.

mamífero *m* mammal.

manada *f* flock, herd; pack; crowd.

manantial *m* source, spring; origin.

manchar *vt* to stain, soil.

manco/ca *adj* one-armed; one-handed; maimed; faulty.

mancomunidad *f* union, fellowship; community; (*jur*) joint responsibility.

mandar *vt* to command, order; to bequeath; to send.

mandarina *f* tangerine.

mandíbula *f* jaw.

mandil *m* apron.

manera *f* manner, way; fashion; kind.

manga *f* sleeve; hose.

mango *m* handle; mango.

manguera *f* hose; pipe.

maní *m* peanut.

manifestación *f* manifestation; show; demonstration; mass meeting.

manifestar *vt* to manifest, declare.

maniobrar *vt* to maneuvre; to handle.

manipular *vt* to manipulate.

maniquí *m* dummy:—*m/f* model.

manivela *f* crank.

mano *f* hand; hand (of clock, etc); foot, paw (of animal); coat (of paint); lot, series; hand (at game):—**a ~** by hand:—**a ~s llenas** liberally, generously.

manojo *m* handful, bunch.

manopla *f* wash cloth; mitten; gauntlet.

manosear *vt* to handle; to mess up.

manso/sa *adj* tame; gentle, soft.

manta *f* blanket.

manteca *f* fat:—~ **de cerdo** lard.

mantel *m* tablecloth.

mantener *vt* to maintain, support; to nourish; to keep:—~**se** *vr* to hold one's ground; to support oneself.

mantequilla *f* butter.

manzana *f* apple.

manzanilla *f* camomile; camomile tea; manzanilla sherry.

maña *f* handiness, dexterity, cleverness, cunning; habit, custom; trick.

mañana *f* morning:—*adv* tomorrow.

mapa *m* map.

maquillar *vt* to make up:—~**se** *vr* to put on make-up.

máquina *f* machine; (*ferro*) engine; camera; (*fig*) machinery; plan, project.

maquinilla *f*:—~ **de afeitar** razor.

maquinista *m* (*ferro*) train driver; operator; (*mar*) engineer.

mar *m/f* sea.

maravilla *f* wonder.

marca *f* mark; stamp; make, brand.

marcar *vt* to mark; to dial; to score; to record; to set (hair):—*vi* to score; to dial.

marchar *vi* to go; to work:—~**se** *vr* to go away.

marco *m* frame; framework; (*dep*) goalposts *pl*.

marea *f* tide.

marear *vt* (*mar*) to sail, navigate; to annoy, upset:—~**se** *vr* to feel sick; to feel faint; to feel dizzy.

marfil *m* ivory.

margarita *f* daisy.

margen *m* margin; border:—*f* bank (of river).

marido *m* husband.

marinero/ra *adj* sea *compd*; seaworthy:—*m* sailor.

marioneta *f* puppet.

mariposa *f* butterfly.

mariquita *f* ladybird.

marisco *m* shellfish *pl*.

mármol *m* marble.

marrano *m* hog, boar.

marrón *adj* brown.

martes *m invar* Tuesday.

martillo *m* hammer.

marzo *m* March.

mas *adv* but, yet.

más *adv* more; most; besides, moreover:— **a ~ tardar** at latest:—**sin ~ ni ~** without more ado.

masa *f* dough, paste; mortar; mass.
mascar *vt* to chew.
máscara *m/f* masked person:—*f* mask.
mascullar *vt* to mumble, mutter.
mástil *m* (*mar*) mast.
mastín *m* mastiff.
mata *f* shrub; sprig, blade; grove, group of trees; mop of hair.
matadero *m* slaughterhouse.
matar *vt* to kill; to execute; to murder:—~se *vr* to kill oneself, commit suicide.
matasellos *m invar* postmark.
mate *m* checkmate:—*adj* matt.
material *adj* material, physical:—*m* equipment, materials *pl*.
maternidad *f* motherhood.
matinal *adj* morning *compd*.
matiz *m* shade of color; shading.
matrícula *f* register, list; (*auto*) registration number; license plate.
matrimonio *m* marriage, matrimony.
matriz *f* matrix; womb; mold, form.
maullar *vi* to mew.
mayo *m* May.
mayor *adj* main, chief; (*mus*) major; biggest; eldest; greater, larger; elderly:—*m* chief, boss; adult:—**al por** ~ wholesale:—~**es** *mpl* forefathers.
mayoría *f* majority, greater part:—~ **de edad** coming of age.
mayúsculo/la *adj* (*fig*) tremendous: —*f* capital letter.
mazo *m* bunch; club, mallet; bat.
mazorca *f* ear of corn.
me *pn* me; to mc.
mear *vi* (*fam*) to pee, piss (*sl*).
mecanógrafo/fa *m/f* typist.
mecer *vt* to rock; to dandle (a child).
mechar *vt* to lard; to stuff.
mechón *m* lock of hair; large bundle of threads or fibres.
media *f* stocking; sock; average.
medianoche *f* midnight.
mediante *prep* by means of.
mediar *vi* to intervene; to mediate.
medicamento *m* medicine.
médico/ca *adj* medical:—*m/f* doctor.
medida *f* measure.
medio/dia *adj* half:—**a medias** partly:—*m* middle; average; way, means; medium.
mediodía *m* noon, midday.
medir *vt* to measure:—~**se** *vr* to be moderate.
medrar *vi* to grow, thrive, prosper; to improve.
médula *f* marrow; essence, substance; pith.
medusa *f* jellyfish.
mejilla *f* cheek.
mejillón *m* mussel.

mejor *adj, adv* better; best.
mejorar *vt* to improve, ameliorate; to enhance:—*vi* to improve; (*med*) to recover, get better:—~**se** *vr* to improve, get better.
melenudo/da *adj* long-haired.
melindroso/sa *adj* prudish, finicky.
mella *f* notch in edged tools; gap.
mellizo/za *adj, m/f* twin.
melocotón *m* peach.
meloso/sa *adj* honeyed; mellow.
membrete *m* letter head.
membrillo *m* quince; quince tree.
memoria *f* memory; report; record:—~**s** *fpl* memoirs *pl*.
mendigar *vt* to beg.
menear *vt* to move from place to place; (*fig*) to handle:—~**se** *vr* to move; to shake; to sway.
menguante *f* waning.
meñique *m* little finger.
menor *m/f* young person, juvenile:—*adj* less; smaller; minor:—**al por** ~ retail.
menos *adv* less; least:—**a lo** ~ *o* **por lo** ~ at least:—*prep* except; minus.
menospreciar *vt* to undervalue; to despise, scorn.
mensaje *m* message.
mensual *adj* monthly.
menta *f* mint.
mente *f* mind; understanding.
mentecato/ta *adj* silly, stupid:—*m/f* idiot.
mentir *vt* to feign; to pretend:—*vi* to lie.
mentira *f* lie, falsehood.
menudo/da *adj* small; minute; petty, insignificant:—**a** ~ frequently, often.
mercader *m* dealer, trader.
mercado *m* market; marketplace.
mercancía *f* commodity:—~**s** *fpl* goods *pl*, merchandise.
mercurio *m* mercury.
merecer *vt* to deserve, merit.
meridional *adj* southern.
merienda *f* (light) tea; afternoon snack; picnic.
merluza *f* hake.
mermelada *f* jam.
mero *m* pollack (fish):—~/**ra** *adj* mere, pure.
mes *m* month.
mesa *f* table; desk; plateau:—~ **redonda** round table.
mestizo/za *adj* of mixed race; crossbred:—*m/f* half-caste.
meta *f* goal; finish.
metal *m* metal; (*mus*) brass; timbre (of voice).
meter *vt* to place, put; to insert, put in; to involve; to make, cause:—~**se** *vr* to meddle, interfere.

método *m* method.

metro *m* meter; subway.

mezclar *vt* to mix:—**~se** *vr* to mix; to mingle.

mezquino/na *adj* mean; small-minded, petty; wretched.

mezquita *f* mosque.

mi *adj* my.

mí *pn* me; myself.

miedo *m* fear, dread.

miel *f* honey.

miembro *m* member.

mientras *adv* meanwhile:—*conj* while; as long as.

miércoles *m invar* Wednesday.

mierda *f* (*fam*) shit (*sl*).

miga *f* crumb:—**~s** *fpl* fried bread-crumbs *pl*.

mijo *m* (*bot*) millet.

mil *m* one thousand.

milagro *m* miracle, wonder.

milésimo/ma *adj, m* thousandth.

milímetro *m* millimeter.

milla *f* mile.

millón *m* million.

mimar *vt* to spoil, pamper.

mimbre *m* wicker.

mimo *m* caress, spoiling; mime.

mina *f* mine; underground passage.

minero/ra *m/f* miner.

minifalda *f* miniskirt.

mínimo/ma *adj* minimum.

minoría *f* minority.

minucioso/sa *adj* meticulous; very detailed.

minúsculo/la *adj* minute:—*f* small letter.

minusválido/da *adj* (physically) handicapped: —*m/f* (physically) handicapped person.

minuto *m* minute.

mío/mía *adj* mine.

miope *adj* short-sighted.

mirar *vt* to look at; to observe; to consider: —*vi* to look:—**~se** *vr* to look at oneself; to look at one another.

mirlo *m* blackbird.

misa *f* mass:—**~ del gallo** midnight mass.

miserable *adj* miserable; mean; squalid (place); (*fam*) despicable:—*m/f* rotter.

misericordia *f* mercy.

mismo/ma *adj* same; very.

mitad *f* half; middle.

mitin *m* (political) rally.

mixto/ta *adj* mixed.

mobiliario *m* furniture.

mochila *f* backpack.

mochuelo *m* red owl.

moco *m* snot (*sl*), mucus.

moda *f* fashion, style.

modales *mpl* manners *pl*.

modelo *m* model, pattern.

módico/ca *adj* moderate.

modificar *vt* to modify.

modisto/ta *m/f* dressmaker.

modo *m* mode, method, manner.

modorra *f* drowsiness.

mofarse *vr*:—**~ de** to mock, scoff at.

moflete *m* fat cheek.

moho *m* rust; mold, mildew.

mojar *vt* to wet, moisten:—**~se** *vr* to get wet.

mojón *m* landmark.

molde *m* mold; pattern; model.

moler *vt* to grind, pound; to tire out; to annoy, bore.

molestar *vt* to annoy, bother; to trouble:— *vi* to be a nuisance.

molino *m* mill.

momentáneo/nea *adj* momentary.

momento *m* moment.

momia *f* mummy.

mondadientes *m invar* toothpick.

mondar *vt* to clean; to cleanse; to peel:— **~se** *vr* **~ de risa** (*fam*) to split one's sides laughing.

mondo/da *adj* clean; pure:—**~ y lirondo** bare, plain; pure and simple.

moneda *f* money; currency; coin.

monja *f* nun.

mono/na *adj* lovely; pretty; nice:—*m/f* monkey; ape:—*mpl* dungarees *pl*; overalls *pl*.

monstruo *m* monster.

montaje *m* assembly; decor (of theater); montage.

montaña *f* mountain.

montar *vt* to mount, get on (a bicycle, horse, etc); to assemble, put together; to overlap; to set up (a business); to beat, whip (in cooking):—*vi* to mount; to ride: **~ a** to amount to.

monte *m* mountain; woodland:—**~ alto** forest:—**~ bajo** scrub.

montón *m* heap, pile; mass:—**a ~ones**, abundantly, by the score.

montura *f* mount; saddle.

monzón *m* monsoon.

mora *f* blackberry.

morado/da *adj* violet, purple.

morcilla *f* blood sausage.

mordaz *adj* biting, scathing; pungent.

mordaza *f* gag; clamp.

morder *vt* to bite; to nibble; to corrode, eat away.

moreno/na *adj* brown; swarthy; dark-skinned.

morir *vi* to die; to expire; to die down: — **~se** *vr* to die; (*fig*) to be dying.

morisco/ca *adj* Moorish.

moroso/sa *adj* slow, sluggish; (*com*) slow to pay up.

morral *m* haversack.

morro *m* snout; nose (of plane, etc).

morsa *f* walrus.

mortal *adj* mortal; fatal, deadly.

mosca *f* fly.

mosquearse *vr* (*fam*) to get cross; (*fam*) to take offence.

mosquitero *m* mosquito net.

mosquito *m* gnat, mosquito.

mostaza *f* mustard.

mosto *m* must, grape juice.

mostrador *m* counter.

mostrar *vt* to show, exhibit; to explain: —~se *vr* to appear, show oneself.

mote *m* nickname.

motivo *m* motive, cause, reason.

moto (*fam*), **motocicleta** *f* motorcycle.

motor *m* engine, motor.

mover *vt* to move; to shake; to drive; (*fig*) to cause:—~se *vr* to move; (*fig*) to get a move on.

móvil *adj* mobile, movable; moving: —*m* motive.

mozo/za *adj* young:—*m/f* youth, young man/girl; waiter/waitress.

muchacho/a *m/f* boy/girl:—*f* maid, maidservant.

mucho/cha *adj* a lot of, much:—*adv* much, a lot; long.

mudar *vt* to change; to shed:—~se *vr* to change one's clothes; to change house:—*vi* to change;

mudo/da *adj* dumb; silent, mute.

mueble *m* piece of furniture:—~s *mpl* furniture.

mueca *f* grimace, funny face.

muela *f* tooth, molar.

muelle *m* spring; regulator; quay.

muérdago *m* (*bot*) mistletoe.

muerte *f* death.

mujer *f* woman.

mulato *adj* mulatto.

muleta *f* crutch.

mullido/da *adj* soft; springy.

mulo/la *m/f* mule.

multa *f* fine, penalty.

mundial *adj* worldwide; world *compd*.

mundo *m* world.

muñeca *f* wrist; child's doll.

municipio *m* town council; municipality.

murciélago *m* bat.

murmullo *m* murmur, mutter.

murmurar *vi* to murmur; to gossip.

muro *m* wall.

músculo *m* muscle.

museo *m* museum.

musgo *m* moss.

música *f* music.

muslo *m* thigh.

mustio/tia *adj* parched, withered; sad, sorrowful.

mutuo/tua *adj* mutual, reciprocal.

muy *adv* very; too; greatly:—~ **ilustre** most illustrious.

N

nabo *m* turnip.

nácar *m* mother-of-pearl, nacre.

nacer *vi* to be born; to bud, shoot (of plants); to rise; to grow.

nacimiento *m* birth; nativity.

nada *f* nothing:—*adv* no way, not at all, by no means.

nadar *vi* to swim.

nadie *pn* nobody, no one.

nafta *f* gas.

nalgas *fpl* buttocks *pl*.

naranja *f* orange.

nariz *f* nose.

narrar *vt* to narrate, tell.

nata *f* cream.

natillas *fpl* custard.

naturaleza *f* nature.

naufragar *vi* to be shipwrecked; to suffer ruin in one's affairs.

náutica *f* navigation.

navaja *f* penknife; razor.

nave *f* ship; nave; warehouse.

navegar *vt, vi* to navigate; to sail; to fly.

Navidad *f* Christmas.

nebuloso/sa *adj* misty; cloudy; nebulous; foggy; hazy; drizzling:—*f* nebula.

neceser *m* toilet bag; holdall.

necesitar *vt* to need:—*vi* to want, to need.

necio/cia *adj* ignorant; stupid, foolish; imprudent.

nefasto/ta *adj* unlucky.

negado/da *adj* incapable, unfit.

negar *vt* to deny; to refuse:—~se *vr* ~ **a hacer** to refuse to do.

negocio *m* business, affair; transaction; firm; place of business.

negro/gra *adj* black:—*m* black:—*m/f* Black.

nene, na *m/f* baby.

neto/ta *adj* neat, pure; net.

neumático/ca *adj* pneumatic:—*m* tire.

neutro/tra *adj* neutral; neuter.
nevar *vi* to snow.
nevera *f* icebox.
ni *conj* neither, nor.
nido *m* nest; hiding place.
niebla *f* fog; mist.
nieta *f* granddaughter.
nieto *m* grandson.
nieve *f* snow.
niña *f* little girl; pupil, (of eye).
ningún, ninguno/na *adj* no:—*pn* nobody; none; not one; neither.
niño/ña *adj* childish:—*m/f* child; infant:— **desde ~** from infancy, from a child:—*m* boy.
nitidez *f* clarity; brightness; sharpness.
nivel *m* level; standard; height:—**a ~** perfectly level.
no *adv* no; not:—*excl* no!
no obstante *adv* nevertheless, notwithstanding.
noche *f* night; evening; darkness:—**~ buena** Christmas Eve:—**~ vieja** New Year's Eve: —**¡buenas ~s!** good night!
noción *f* notion, idea.
nocivo/va *adj* harmful.
nogal *m* walnut tree.
nombrar *vt* to name; to nominate; to appoint.
nombre *m* name; title; reputation.
nómina *f* list; (com) payroll.
non *adj* odd, uneven:—*m* odd number.
nor(d)este *adj* northeast, northeastern:—*m* northeast.
nórdico/ca *adj* northern; Nordic.
noria *f* water wheel; big wheel.
noroeste *adj* northwest, northwestern:—*m* northwest.

norte *adj* north, northern:—*m* north; (*fig*) rule, guide.
nos *pn* us; to us; for us; from us; to ourselves.
nosotros/tras *pn* we; us.
nostalgia *f* homesickness.
notar *vt* to note; to mark; to remark:—**~se** *vr* to be obvious.
noticia *f* information; note:—**~s** *fpl* news.
noticiario *m* newsreel; news bulletin.
notificar *vt* to notify, inform.
novato/ta *adj* inexperienced:—*m/f* beginner.
novecientos/tas *adj* nine hundred.
novedad *f* novelty; modernness; newness; piece of news; change.
noveno/na *adj* ninth.
noventa *adj, m* ninety.
novia *f* bride; girlfriend; fiancée.
noviembre *m* November.
novio *m* bridegroom; boyfriend; fiancé.
nube *f* cloud.
nublado/da *adj* cloudy:—*m* storm cloud.
nuca *f* nape (of the neck); scruff of the neck.
nudillo *m* knuckle.
nudo *m* knot.
nuera *f* daughter-in-law.
nuestro/tra *adj* our:—*pn* ours.
nueve *m, adj* nine.
nuevo/va *adj* new; modern; fresh:—*f* piece of news:—**¿que hay de ~?** is there any news?, what's new?
nuez *f* nut; walnut; Adam's apple:—**~ moscada** nutmeg.
número *m* number; cipher.
nunca *adv* never.
nutria *f* otter.
nutrir *vt* to nourish; to feed.

Ñ

ñato/ta *adj* snub-nosed.
ñoño/ña *adj* insipid; spineless; silly.

ñoñeria *f* insipidness.

O

o *conj* or; either.
obedecer *vt* to obey.
obeso/sa *adj* obese, fat.
objetar *vi* to object.
objeto *m* object; aim.

obligar *vt* to force:—**~se** *vr* to bind oneself.
obra *f* work; building, construction; play:— **por ~ de** thanks to.
obrero/ra *adj* working; labor *compd*:—*m/f* worker; laborer.

obsequiar vt to lavish attention on:— ~**con** to present with.
observar vt to observe; to notice.
obstáculo m obstacle, impediment.
obstinarse vr to be obstinate:—~ **en** to persist in.
obstruir vt to obstruct:—~**se** vr to be blocked up, be obstructed.
obtener vt to obtain; to gain.
ocasión f occasion, opportunity.
ocasionar vt to cause, occasion.
occidente m occident, west.
océano m ocean.
ochenta m, adj eighty.
ocho m, adj eight.
ochocientos m, adj eight hundred.
ocio m leisure; pastime.
octavilla f pamphlet.
octavo/va adj eighth.
octubre m October.
ocultar vt to hide, conceal.
ocupar vt to occupy; to hold (office): —~**se** vr ~ **de**, ~ **en** to concern oneself with; to look after.
ocurrencia f event; bright idea.
ocurrir vi to occur, happen.
odiar vt to hate:—~**se** vr to hate one another.
oeste adj west, western:—m west.
ofender vt to offend; to injure:—~**se** vr to be vexed; to take offence.
oficina f office.
oficio m employment, occupation; ministry; function; trade, business.
ofrecer vt to offer; to present; to exhibit:— ~**se** vr to offer oneself; to occur, present itself.
oído m hearing; ear.
oír vt, vi to hear; to listen (to).
ojal m buttonhole.
ojalá conj if only!, would that!
ojear vt to eye, view; to glance.
ojera f bag under the eyes.
ojo m eye; sight; eye of a needle; arch of a bridge.
ola f wave.
oler vt to smell, scent:—vi to smell:—~ **a** to smack of.
olfato m sense of smell.
olivo m olive tree.
olla f pan; stew:—~ **exprés**, ~ **a presion** pressure cooker.
olmo m elm tree.
olor m smell, odor; scent.
olvidar vt to forget.
ombligo m navel.
once m, adj eleven.

onda f wave.
opaco/ca adj opaque; dark.
opinar vt to think:—vi to give one's opinion.
oponer vt to oppose:—~**se** vr to be opposed:—~ **a** to oppose.
oposición f opposition:—~**ones** fpl public examinations pl.
oprimir vt to oppress; to crush; to press; to squeeze.
optar vt to choose, elect.
optativo/va adj optional.
óptimo/ma adj best.
opuesto/ta adj opposite; contrary; adverse.
orar vi to pray.
ordenado/da adj methodical; tidy.
ordenador m computer.
ordenanza f order; statute, ordinance; ordination.
ordenar vt to arrange; to order; to ordain: —~**se** vr to take holy orders.
ordeñar vt to milk.
oreja f ear.
orgullo m pride, haughtiness.
oriental adj oriental, eastern.
orientar vt to orient; to point; to direct; to guide:—~**se** vr to get one's bearings; to decide on a course of action.
orificio m orifice; mouth; aperture.
orilla f limit, border, margin; edge (of cloth); shore.
orín m rust.
orina f urine.
orinal m chamber pot.
oro m gold; ~**s** mpl diamonds pl (cards).
ortiga f (bot) nettle.
oruga f (bot) caterpillar.
orzuelo m (med) stye.
os pn you; to you.
osa f she-bear:—**O**~ **Mayor/Menor** Great/ Little Bear.
osar vi to dare, venture.
oscuro/ra adj obscure; dark.
oso m bear:—~ **blanco** polar bear.
ostentar vt to show:—vi to boast, brag.
ostra f oyster.
otoño m fall, autumn.
otorgar vt to concede; to grant.
otorrino/na, otorrinolaringólogo/ga m/f ear, nose and throat specialist.
otro/tra adj another; other.
oveja f sheep.
ovillo m ball of wool.
óvulo m ovum.
oxidar vt to rust:—~**se** vr to go rusty.
oyente m/f listener, hearer.

P

pacificar *vt* to pacify, appease.
pacotilla *f*:—**de ~** third-rate; cheap.
pactar *vt* to covenant; to contract; to stipulate.
padecer *vt* to suffer; to sustain (an injury); to put up with.
padrastro *m* stepfather.
padre *m* father:—**~s** *mpl* parents *pl*.
pagar *vt* to pay; to pay for; (*fig*) to repay:—*vi* to pay.
página *f* page.
pago *m* payment; reward.
país *m* country; region.
paisaje *m* landscape.
paisano/na *adj* of the same country: —*m/f* fellow countryman/woman.
paja *f* straw; (*fig*) trash.
pájaro *m* bird; sly, acute fellow.
pajita *f* (drinking) straw.
pala *f* spade, shovel.
palabra *f* word:—**de ~** by word of mouth.
paladar *m* palate; taste, relish.
palanca *f* lever.
palangana *f* basin.
palco *m* box (in a theater).
paleto/ta *m/f* rustic.
pálido/da *adj* pallid, pale.
palillo *m* small stick; toothpick:—**~s** *mpl* chopsticks *pl*.
paliza *f* beating, thrashing.
palma *f* palm tree; palm of the hand; palm leaf.
palmada *f* slap, clap:—**~s** *fpl* clapping of hands, applause.
palmera *f* palm tree.
palo *m* stick; cudgel; blow given with a stick; post; mast; bat; suit (at cards):—**~s** *mpl* masting.
paloma *f* pigeon, dove:—**~ torcaz** ring dove:—**~ zorita** wood pigeon.
palomilla *f* moth; wing nut; angle iron.
palpar *vt* to feel, touch.
palta *f* avocado (pear).
pámpano *m* vine branch.
pan *m* bread; loaf; food in general.
pana *f* corduroy.
pañal *m* diaper, nappy.
pandereta *f* tambourine.
pandilla *f* group; gang; clique.
paño *m* cloth; piece of cloth; duster, rag.
pantalla *f* screen; lampshade.
pantalón *m*, **pantalones** *mpl* trousers, pants *pl*.
pantano *m* marsh; reservoir; obstacle, difficulty.

pantorrilla *f* calf (of the leg).
pañuelo *m* handkerchief.
panza *f* belly, paunch.
papá *m* (*fam*) dad, pop.
papada *f* double chin.
papel *m* paper; writing; part, role (in a play):—**~ de estraza** brown paper: —**~ sellado** stamped paper.
papeleo *m* red tape.
paperas *fpl* mumps.
paquete *m* packet; parcel; package tour.
par *adj* equal; alike; even:—*m* pair; couple; peer:—**sin ~** matchless.
para *prep* for; to, in order to; towards.
parabrisas *m invar* windshield.
paracaídas *m invar* parachute.
parada *f* halt; suspension; pause; stop; shutdown; stopping place:—**~ de autobús** bus stop.
parado/da *adj* motionless; at a standstill; stopped; standing (up); unemployed.
paraguas *m invar* umbrella.
parar *vi* to stop, halt:—*vt* to stop, detain:—**sin ~** instantly, without delay: —**~se** *vr* to stop, halt; to stand up.
parecer *m* opinion, advice, counsel; countenance, air, mien:—*vi* to appear; to seem:—**~se** *vr* **a** to resemble.
parecido/da *adj* resembling, like.
pared *f* wall:—**~ medianera** party wall.
pareja *f* pair, couple, brace.
pariente/ta *m/f* relative, relation.
parir *vt* to give birth to:—*vi* to give birth.
paro *m* strike; unemployment.
párpado *m* eyelid.
parra *f* vine raised on stakes or nailed to a wall.
párrafo *m* paragraph.
parrilla *f* grill; grille.
parte *m* message; report:—*f* part; side; party:—**de ocho días a esta ~** within these last eight days:—**de ~ a ~** from side to side, through and through.
partera *f* midwife.
particular *adj* particular, special:—*m* private individual; particular matter or subject treated upon.
partida *f* departure; party; item in an account; parcel; game.
partido *m* party; match; team.
partir *vt* to part; to divide, separate; to cut; to break:—*vi* to depart:—**~se** *vr* to break (in two, etc).
parvulario *m* nursery school.

pasa f raisin.
pasadizo m narrow passage; narrow, covered way.
pasado/da adj past; bad; overdone; out of date:—~ **mañana** the day after tomorrow:—**la semana pasada** last week:—m past.
pasaje m passage; fare; passengers pl.
pasajero/ra adj transient, transitory; fugitive:—m/f traveler; passenger.
pasamanos m invar (hand)rail; bannister.
pasar vt to pass; to surpass; to suffer; to strain; to dissemble:—vi to pass; to happen:—~se vr to go over (to another party); to go bad or off.
pasarela f footbridge; gangway.
pasatiempo m pastime, amusement.
Pascua f Passover; Easter.
pasear vt to walk:—vi ~se vr to walk; to walk about.
pasmar vt to amaze; to numb; to chill:—~se vr to be astonished.
paso m pace, step; passage; manner of walking; flight of steps; accident:—(ferro) ~ **a nivel** grade crossing:—**al** ~ on the way, in passing.
pasta f paste; dough; pastry; (fam) dough:—~s fpl pastries pl; pasta:—~ **de dientes** toothpaste.
pastel m cake; pie; crayon (for drawing).
pastilla f bar (of soap); tablet, pill.
pastor m shepherd; pastor.
pata f leg (of animal or furniture); foot:—**meter la** ~ to put one's foot in it.
patata f potato.
patear vt to kick; to stamp on.
patillas fpl sideburns pl.
patín m skate; runner.
patinar vi to skate; to skid; (fam) to blunder.
patio m courtyard; playground.
pato m duck.
patoso/sa adj (fam) clumsy.
patraña f lie.
patrocinar vt to sponsor; to back, support.
patrón/ona m/f boss, master/mistress; landlord/lady; patron saint:—m pattern.
patronal adj:—**la clase** ~ management.
patrulla f patrol.
paulatino/na adj gradual, slow.
pausar vi to pause.
pauta f guideline.
pavo m turkey:—~ **real** peacock.
pavor m dread, terror.
payaso/sa m/f clown.
payo/ya m/f non-Gipsy (for a Gipsy).
paz f peace; tranquillity; ease.
peaje m toll.

peana f pedestal; footstool.
peatón m pedestrian.
peca f freckle; spot.
pecado m sin.
pecho m chest; breast(s) (pl); teat; (fig) courage, valor:—**dar el** ~ **a** to suckle:—**tomar a** ~ to take to heart.
pechuga f breast of a fowl; (fam) bosom.
pedazo m piece, bit.
pedernal m flint.
pediatra m/f pediatrician.
pedicuro/ra m/f chiropodist.
pedir vt to ask for; to petition; to beg; to order; to need; to solicit:—vi to ask.
pedo m (fam) fart (sl):—**tirarse un** ~ to fart (sl).
pegamento m glue.
pegar vt to cement; to join, unite; to beat:—~ **fuego a** to set fire to:—vi to stick; to match:—~se vr to intrude; to steal in.
pegatina f sticker.
peinar vt to comb; to style.
peine m comb.
pelar vt to cut (hair); to strip off (feathers); to peel:—~se vr to peel off; to have one's hair cut.
peldaño m step (of a flight of stairs).
pelear vt to fight, combat:—~se vr to scuffle.
pelele m dummy; man of straw.
película f film, thin covering; movie.
peligro m danger, peril; risk.
pelirrojo/ja m/f redhead:—adj red-haired.
pellejo m skin; hide, pelt; peel; wine skin; oilskin; drunkard.
pellizcar vt to pinch.
pelo m hair; pile; flaw (in precious stones).
pelota f ball.
peluca f wig.
peluquería f hairdresser's/barber's premises.
pelusa f bloom (on fruit); fluff.
pena f punishment, pain:—**a duras** ~s with great difficulty or trouble.
pendiente f slope, declivity:—m earring:—adj pending; unsettled.
pene m penis.
penetrante adj deep; sharp; piercing; searching; biting.
penique m penny.
penoso/sa adj painful.
pensar vi to think.
pensativo/va adj pensive, thoughtful.
pensión f guest-house; pension.
penúltimo/ma adj penultimate, last but one.
penumbra f half-light.
penuria f penury, poverty, neediness, extreme want.

peña f rock, large stone.
peón m (day) laborer; foot soldier; pawn (at chess).
peor adj, adv worse:—~ que ~ worse and worse.
pepino m cucumber.
pepita f kernel; pip.
pequeño/ña adj little, small; young.
pera f pear.
percatarse vr:—~ de to notice.
percha f coat hook; coat hanger; perch.
percibir vt to receive; to perceive, comprehend.
perder vt to lose; to waste; to miss:—~se vr to go astray; to be lost; to be spoiled.
perdiz f partridge.
perdón m pardon; mercy:—¡~! sorry!
perdonar vt to pardon, forgive; to excuse.
perdurar vi to last; to still exist.
perecedero/ra adj perishable.
peregrino/na adj (fig) strange:—m pilgrim.
perejil m parsley.
pereza f laziness, idleness.
perfil m profile.
perforar vt to perforate; to drill; to punch a hole in:—vi to drill.
perfume m perfume.
pergamino m parchment.
periódico/ca adj periodical:—m newspaper.
periodista m/f journalist.
peripecia f vicissitude; sudden change.
periquito m budgie.
perito/ta adj skillful, experienced:—m/f expert; skilled worker; technician.
perjudicar vt to prejudice, damage; to injure, hurt.
perjurar vi to perjure, swear falsely; to swear.
perla f pearl:—de ~s fine.
permanecer vi to stay; to continue to be.
permiso m permission, leave, license.
permitir vt to permit, allow.
permutar vt to exchange, permute.
pernera f trouser leg.
perno m bolt.
pernoctar vi to spend the night.
pero m kind of apple:—conj but, yet.
perogrullada f truism, platitude.
perol m large metal pan.
perro m dog.
perseguir vt to pursue; to persecute; to chase after.
perseverar vi to persevere, persist.
persiana f (Venetian) blind.
persistir vi to persist.
persona f person:—de ~ a ~ from person to person.

personaje m celebrity; character.
persuadir vt to persuade:—~se vr to be persuaded.
pertenecer vi:—~ a to belong to; to appertain, concern.
pértiga f long pole or rod.
pertinaz adj pertinacious; obstinate.
pertinente adj relevant; appropriate.
perturbar vt to perturb, disturb.
pervertir vt to pervert; to corrupt.
pesa f weight.
pesadez f heaviness, weight; gravity; slowness; peevishness, fretfulness; trouble; fatigue.
pesadilla f nightmare.
pesado/da adj peevish; troublesome; cumbersome; tedious; heavy, weighty.
pesar m sorrow, grief; repentance:—a ~ de in spite of, not withstanding:—vi to weigh; to repent:—vt to weigh.
pescado m fish (in general).
pescar vt to fish for, catch (fish):—vi to fish.
pescuezo m neck.
pésimo/ma adj very bad.
peso m weight, heaviness; balance scales pl.
pesquisa f inquiry, examination.
pestaña f eyelash.
pestañear vi to blink.
pestillo m bolt.
petróleo m crude oil, petroleum.
pez m fish:—f pitch.
pezón m nipple.
pezuña f hoof.
piadoso/sa adj pious; mild; merciful; moderate.
piar vi to squeak; to chirp.
pibe/ba m/f boy/girl.
picado/da adj pricked; minced, chopped; bad (tooth); cross.
picante adj hot, spicy; racy.
picaporte m doorhandle; latch.
picar vt to prick; to sting; to mince; to nibble:—vi to prick; to sting; to itch:—~se vr to be piqued; to take offence; to be moth-eaten; to begin to rot.
pícaro/ra adj roguish; mischievous; malicious; sly:—m/f rogue, knave.
pico m beak; bill, nib; peak; pick-ax.
pie m foot; leg; basis; trunk (of trees); foundation; occasion:—a ~ on foot.
piedad f piety; mercy, pity.
piedra f stone.
piel f skin; hide; peel.
pienso m fodder.
pierna f leg (human).
pieza f piece; room.

pila f battery; trough; font; sink; pile, heap:—**nombre de ~** first name.
píldora f pill.
pileta f basin; swimming pool.
pimentón m paprika.
pimienta f pepper.
pimiento m pepper, pimiento.
piña f pineapple; fir cone; group.
pincel m paintbrush.
pinchar vt to prick; to puncture.
pincho m thorn; snack.
ping-pong m table tennis.
pino m (bot) pine.
piñón m pine nut; pinion.
pintar vt to paint; to picture; to describe; to exaggerate:—vi to paint; (fam) to count, to be important:—**~se** vr to put on make-up.
pintura f painting.
pinza f claw; clothes pin; pincers pl: —**~s** fpl tweezers pl.
piojo m louse; troublesome hanger-on.
pipa f pipe; sunflower seed.
pipí m (fam):—**hacer ~** to have to go (wee-wee).
piquete m prick, jab; hole; (mil) squad.
piragua f canoe.
piropo m compliment; flattery.
pisar vt to tread, trample; to stamp on (the ground); to hammer down:—vi to tread, walk.
piscina f swimming pool.
piso m apartment; tread, trampling; floor, sidewalk; floor, story.
pisotear vt to trample, tread under foot.
pista f trace, footprint; clue.
pita f (bot) agave.
pitar vt to blow; to whistle at:—vi to whistle; to toot one's horn; to smoke.
pito m whistle; horn.
pizarra f slate.
pizca f mite; pinch.
placa f plate; badge.
placer m pleasure; delight:—vt to please.
plan m plan; design; plot; scheme.
plancha f plate; iron; gangway.
planear vt to plan:—vi to glide.
planicie f plain.
planificación f planning:—**~ familiar** family planning.
plano/na adj plain, level, flat:—m plan; ground plot, map:—**~ inclinado** (ferro) dead level.
plantación f plantation.
plantar vt to plant; to fix upright; to strike or hit (a blow); to found; to establish:— **~se** vr to stand upright.

plantilla f personnel; insole of a shoe.
plata f silver; plate (wrought silver); cash:— **en ~** briefly.
plátano m banana; plane tree.
plateado/da adj silvered; plated.
platicar vi to converse.
platillo m saucer:—**~s** mpl cymbals pl: —**~ volador/~ volante** flying saucer.
platino m platinum:—**~s** mpl contact points pl.
plato m dish; plate.
playa f beach.
playera f T-shirt:—**~s** fpl sneakers pl.
plaza f square; place; office, employment; room; seat.
plazo m term; installment; expiry date.
plegar vt to fold; to crease.
pleito m contract, bargain; dispute, controversy, debate; lawsuit.
plenilunio m full moon.
pleno/na adj full; complete:—m plenum.
pliego m sheet of paper.
pliegue m fold; pleat.
plisado/da adj pleated:—m pleating.
plomero m plumber.
plomo m lead:—**a ~** perpendicularly.
pluma f feather, plume.
población f population; town.
pobre adj poor.
poco/ca adj little, scanty; (pl) few:—adv little:—**a ~** gently; little by little:—m small part; little.
podar vt to prune.
poder m power, authority; command; force:—vi to be able to; to possess the power of doing or performing.
podrido/da adj rotten, bad; (fig) rotten.
poesía f poetry.
polea f pulley, (mar) tackle-block.
polideportivo m sports center.
polilla f moth.
pollera f skirt.
pollo m chicken.
polo m pole; ice lolly; polo; polo neck.
polvo m powder, dust.
pólvora f gunpowder.
pomada f cream, ointment.
pomelo m grapefruit.
pómez f:—**piedra ~** pumice stone.
pompa f pomp; bubble.
pómulo m cheekbone.
poner vt to put, place; to put on; to impose; to lay (eggs):—**~se** vr to oppose; to set (of stars); to become.
poniente m west; west wind.
ponzoña f poison.
popa f (mar) poop, stern.

por *prep* for; by; about; by means of; through; on account of.

porción *f* part, portion; lot.

porfiar *vt* to dispute obstinately; to persist in a pursuit.

pormenor *f* detail.

poro *m* pore.

porque *conj* because; since; so that.

porquería *f* nastiness, foulness; brutishness, rudeness; trifle; dirty action.

porrón *m* spouted wine jar.

portada *f* portal, porch; frontispiece.

portaequipajes *m invar* trunk (in car); baggage rack.

portarse *vr* to behave.

portátil *adj* portable.

portavoz *m/f* spokesman/woman.

porte *m* transportation (charges *pl*); deportment, demeanor, conduct.

portero *m* porter, gatekeeper.

porvenir *m* future.

posar *vi* to sit, pose:—*vt* to lay down (a burden):—**se** *vr* to settle; to perch; to land.

posdata *f* postscript.

poseer *vt* to hold, possess.

posesivo/va *adj* possessive.

posibilitar *vt* to make possible; to make feasible.

poso *m* sediment, dregs *pl*.

posponer *vt* to postpone.

postal *adj* postal:—*f* postcard.

poste *m* post, pillar.

postergar *vt* to leave behind; to postpone.

posterioridad *f*:—**con ~** subsequently, later.

postigo *m* wicket; postern; shutter.

postizo/za *adj* artificial (not natural): —*m* wig.

postrar *vt* to humble, humiliate:—**se** *vr* to prostrate oneself.

postre *m* dessert.

postura *f* posture, position; attitude; bet, wager; agreement, convention.

potable *adj* drinkable.

potaje *m* pottage; drink made up of several ingredients; medley of various useless things.

potro/ra *m/f* colt; foal.

pozo *m* well.

practicar *vt* to practice.

práctico/ca *adj* practical; skillful, experienced.

prado *m* lawn; meadow.

precaver *vt* to prevent; to guard against.

preceder *vt* to precede, go before.

preciado/da *adj* esteemed, valued.

precinto *m* seal.

precio *m* price; value.

precioso/sa *adj* precious; (*fam*) beautiful.

precisamente *adv* precisely; exactly.

precisar *vt* to compel, oblige; to need.

preciso/sa *adj* necessary, requisite; precise, accurate; abstracted.

precoz *adj* precocious.

precursor/ra *m/f* harbinger, forerunner.

predecir *vt* to foretell.

predicar *vt* to preach.

predilecto/ta *adj* darling, favorite.

predisponer *vt* to predispose; to prejudice.

predominar *vi* to predominate, prevail.

preferir *vt* to prefer.

pregón *m* proclamation; hue and cry.

preguntar *vt* to ask; to question; to demand; to inquire.

prejuicio *m* prejudgement; preconception; prejudice.

premiar *vt* to reward, remunerate.

premura *f* pressure, haste, hurry.

preñada *adj* pregnant.

prenda *f* pledge; garment; sweetheart; person or thing dearly loved: —**s** *fpl* accomplishments, talents *pl*.

prender *vt* to seize, catch, lay hold of; to imprison:—**se** *vr* to catch fire:—*vi* to take root.

prensar *vt* to press.

preocupar(se) *vt* (*vr*) to worry.

preparar *vt* to prepare:—**se** *vr* to be prepared.

prepucio *m* foreskin.

presa *f* capture, seizure; dike, dam.

presagio *m* omen.

prescindir *vi*:—**~ de** to do without; to dispense with.

presenciar *vt* to attend; to be present at; to witness.

presentar *vt* to present; to introduce; to offer; to show:—**se** *vr* to present oneself; to appear, to run (as candidate); to apply.

presentir *vt* to have a premonition of.

preservativo *m* condom, sheath.

presidiario *m* convict.

presilla *f* clip; loop (in clothes).

presión *f* pressure, pressing.

presionar *vt* to press; (*fig*) to put pressure on.

preso/sa *m/f* prisoner.

prestar *vt* to lend.

presto/ta *adj* quick; prompt; ready: —*adv* soon; quickly.

presumir *vt* to presume, conjecture: —*vi* to be conceited.

presunto/ta *adj* supposed; so-called.

presupuesto *m* presumed cost; budget.
pretender *vt* to claim; to try, attempt.
pretendiente *m* pretender; suitor.
pretexto *m* pretext; pretence, excuse.
prevalecer *vi* to prevail; to triumph; to take root.
prevenir *vt* to prepare; to foresee, know in advance; to prevent; to warn:—~**se** *vr* to be prepared; to be predisposed.
prever *vt* to foresee, forecast.
previo/via *adj* previous.
previsión *f* foresight, prevision; forecast.
prima *f* bonus; (female) cousin.
primario/ria *adj* primary.
primavera *f* spring (the season).
primer(o)/ra *adj* first; prior; former:—*adv* first; rather, sooner.
primicias *f* first fruits *pl*.
primo/ma *m* cousin.
primogénito/ta *adj*, *m/f* first-born.
príncipe *m* prince.
principiante *m* beginner, learner.
principio *m* beginning, commencement; principle.
pringoso/sa *adj* greasy; sticky.
prisa *f* speed; hurry; urgency; promptness.
prismáticos *mpl* binoculars *pl*.
privación *f* deprivation, want.
privado/da *adj* private; particular.
proa *f* (*mar*) prow.
probador *m* fitting room.
probar *vt* to try; to prove; to taste:—*vi* to try.
probeta *f* test tube.
procedente *adj* reasonable; proper:—~ **de** coming from.
procesador *m*:—~ **de textos** word processor.
procesar *vt* to put on trial.
procurar *vt* to try; to obtain; to produce.
prodigar *vt* to waste, lavish.
producir *vt* to produce; (*jur*) to produce as evidence:—~**se** *vr* to come about; to arise; to be made; to break out.
proeza *f* prowess, valor, bravery.
profanar *vt* to profane, desecrate.
profesor/ra *m/f* teacher.
prófugo *m* fugitive.
profundo/da *adj* profound.
programa *m* program(me).
prohibir *vt* to prohibit, forbid; to hinder.
prójimo *m* fellow creature; neighbor.
prole *f* offspring, progeny; race.
prolijidad *f* prolixity; minute attention to detail.
prólogo *m* prolog.
promedio *m* average; middle.
prometer *vt* to promise; to assure:—~**se** *vr* to become engaged.

promiscuo/cua *adj* promiscuous; confusedly mingled.
promover *vt* to promote, advance; to stir up.
promulgar *vt* to promulgate, publish.
pronosticar *vt* to predict, foretell; to conjecture.
pronto/ta *adj* prompt; ready:—*adv* promptly.
pronunciamiento *m* (*jur*) publication; insurrection, sedition.
pronunciar *vt* to pronounce; to deliver: —~**se** *vr* to rebel.
propaganda *f* propaganda; advertising.
propagar *vt* to propagate.
propasar *vt* to go beyond, exceed.
propenso/sa *adj* prone, inclined.
propiamente *adv* properly; really.
propiciar *vt* to favor; to cause.
propiedad *f* property, possessions *pl*; right of property; propriety.
propina *f* tip.
propio/pia *adj* proper; own; typical; very.
proponer *vt* to propose.
proporcionar *vt* to provide.
propósito *m* aim, purpose:—**a ~** on purpose.
propuesta *f* proposal, offer; representation.
propulsar *vt* to propel; (*fig*) to promote.
prórroga *f* prolongation; extension; extra time.
prorrumpir *vi* to break forth, burst forth.
prosa *f* prose.
proscrito/ta *adj* banned.
proseguir *vt* to continue:—*vi* to continue, go on.
prospección *f* exploration; prospecting.
prosperar *vi* to prosper, thrive.
proteger *vt* to protect.
protestar *vt* to protest; to make public declaration (of faith):—*vi* to protest.
provecho *m* profit; advantage.
proveedor/ra *m/f* purveyor, supplier.
provenir *vi* to arise, originate; to issue.
provocar *vt* to provoke; to lead to; to excite.
próximamente *adv* soon.
próximo/ma *adj* next; neighboring; close, nearby.
proyectar *vt* to throw; to cast; to screen; to plan.
prueba *f* proof; reason; argument; token; experiment; essay; attempt; relish, taste.
púa *f* sharp point, prickle; shoot; pick.
pubertad *f* puberty.
publicar *vt* to publish; to make public.
publicidad *f* publicity; advertising.
público/ca *adj* public:—*m* public; audience; crowd.
puchero *m* pot; stew.
púdico/ca *adj* chaste, pure.

pudiente *adj* rich, opulent.
pudor *m* bashfulness.
pudrir *vt* to rot, putrefy:—**se** *vr* to decay, rot.
pueblo *m* people *pl*; town, village; population; populace.
puente *m* bridge.
puerco/ca *adj* nasty; filthy, dirty; rude, coarse:—*m* pig, hog:—**espín** porcupine.
pueril *adj* childish; puerile.
puerro *m* leek.
puerta *f* door; doorway; gateway:—**trasera** back door.
puerto *m* port, harbor; haven; pass.
pues *adv* then; therefore; well:—**i~!** well, then.
puesto *m* place; particular spot; post, employment; barracks *pl*; stand.
púgil *m* boxer.
pujante *adj* powerful, strong, robust; stout, strapping.
pulga *f* flea:—**tener malas ~s** to be easily piqued; to be ill-tempered.
pulgada *f* inch.
pulgar *m* thumb.
pulir *vt* to polish; to put the last touches to.
pulmón *m* lung.
pulpa *f* pulp; soft part (of fruit).
pulpería *f* small grocery store.

pulpo *m* octopus.
pulsar *vt* to touch; to play; to press.
pulsera *f* bracelet.
pulso *m* pulse; wrist; firmness or steadiness of the hand.
pulular *vi* to swarm.
pulverizador *m* spray gun.
puna *f* (*med*) mountain sickness.
puñado *m* handful.
puñal *m* dagger.
puño *m* fist; handful; wrist-band; cuff; handle.
punta *f* point; end; trace.
puntada *f* stitch.
puntal *m* prop, stay; buttress.
puntapié *m* kick.
puntería *f* aiming.
puntiagudo/da *adj* sharp-pointed.
puntilla *f* narrow lace edging:—**de ~s** on tiptoe.
punto *m* point; end; spot; stitch; full stop.
puntual *adj* punctual; exact; reliable.
punzada *f* prick; sting; pain; compunction.
punzante *adj* sharp.
pupila *f* pupil (of eye).
puro/ra *adj* pure; mere; clear; genuine.
púrpura *f* purple.
purulento/ta *adj* purulent.
puta *f* whore.

Q

que *pn* that; who; which; what:—*conj* that; than.
¿qué? *adj* what?; which?:—*pn* what?; which?.
quebrantar *vt* to break; to crack; to burst; to pound, grind; to violate; to fatigue; to weaken.
quedar *vi* to stay:—**se** *vr* to remain.
quedo/da *adj* quiet, still:—*adv* softly, gently.
quejarse *vr* to complain of.
quemar *vt* to burn; to kindle:—**se** *vr* to be parched with heat; to burn oneself:—*vi* to be too hot.
querella *f* charge; dispute; complaint.
querer *vt* to want; to desire; to will; to love:—*m* will, desire.
querido/da *adj* dear, beloved:—*m/f* darling; lover:—**mio, ~da mia** my dear, my love, my darling.
queso *m* cheese.
quicio *m* hook, hinge (of a door).
quien *pn* who; whom.

¿quién? *pn* who?; whom?.
quienquiera *adj* whoever.
quieto/ta *adj* still, peaceable.
quilla *f* keel.
química *f* chemistry.
quina *f* Peruvian bark, quinine.
quince *adj, m* fifteen; fifteenth.
quincena *f* fortnight.
quinientos/tas *adj* five hundred.
quinta *f* country house; levy, drafting of soldiers.
quinto *adj* fifth:—*m* fifth; drafted soldier.
quiosco *m* bandstand; news stand.
quirúrgico/ca *adj* surgical.
quiste *m* cyst.
quitamanchas *m invar* stain remover.
quitanieves *m invar* snowplough.
quitar *vt* to take away, remove; to take off; to relieve; to annul:—**se** *vr* to take off (clothes, etc); to withdraw.
quitasol *m* parasol.
quizá/quizás *adv* perhaps.

R

rábano *m* radish.
rabia *f* rage, fury.
rabo *m* tail.
racha *f* gust of wind:—**buena/mala ~** spell of good/bad luck.
racimo *m* bunch of grapes.
radiografía *f* x-ray.
ráfaga *f* gust; flash; burst.
raído/da *adj* scraped; worn-out; impudent.
raíz *f* root; base, basis; origin:—**bienes raíces** *mpl* landed property.
raja *f* splinter, chip (of wood); chink, fissure.
rajatabla *f*:—**a ~** *adv* strictly.
rallar *vt* to grate.
rama *f* branch (of tree, of family).
ramo *m* branch (of tree).
rampa *f* ramp.
rana *f* frog.
rancho *m* grub; ranch; small farm.
rancio/cia *adj* rank; rancid.
ranura *f* groove; slot.
rapar *vt* to shave; to plunder.
rapaz/za *adj* rapacious:—*m/f* young boy/girl.
rápido/da *adj* quick, rapid, swift.
rapiña *f* robbery.
raptar *vt* to kidnap.
raquítico/ca *adj* stunted; (*fig*) inadequate.
raro/ra *adj* rare, scarce; extraordinary.
ras *m*:—**a ~ de** level with:—**a ~ de tierra** at ground level.
rascacielos *m invar* skyscraper.
rascar *vt* to scratch, scrape.
rasgar *vt* to tear, rip.
rasgo *m* dash, stroke; grand or magnanimous action:—**~s** *mpl* features *pl*.
rasguño *m* scratch.
raso *m* satin; glade:—**~/sa** *adj* plain; flat:—**al ~** in the open air.
raspa *f* beard (of an ear of corn); backbone (of fish); stalk (of grapes); rasp.
raspar *vt* to scrape, rasp.
rastrear *vt* to trace; to inquire into:—*vi* to skim along close to the ground (of birds).
rastrillo *m* rake.
rastro *m* track; rake; trace.
rata *f* rat.
ratificar *vt* to ratify, confirm.
rato *m* moment:—**a ~s perdidos** in leisure time.
ratón *m* mouse.
raya *f* stroke; line; part; frontier; ray (fish); roach (fish).
rayar *vt* to draw lines on; to cross out; to underline; to cross; to rifle.

rayo *m* ray, beam (of light).
raza *f* race, lineage; quality; crack, fissure.
razonar *vi* to reason; to discourse, talk.
reaccionar *vi* to react.
real *adj* real, actual; royal:—*m* (*mil*) camp.
realidad *f* reality; sincerity.
realizador/ra *m/f* producer (in TV, etc).
realzar *vt* to raise, elevate; to emboss; to heighten.
reanimar *vt* to cheer, encourage; to reanimate.
reanudar *vt* to resume.
rebaja *f* abatement; deduction:—**~s** *fpl* sale.
rebanada *f* slice.
rebaño *m* flock (of sheep), herd (of cattle).
rebasar *vt* to exceed.
rebatir *vt* to resist; to parry, ward off; to refute; to repress.
rebeca *f* cardigan.
rebelarse *vr* to revolt; to rebel; to resist.
rebosar *vi* to run over, overflow; to abound.
rebotar *vt* to bounce; to clinch; to repel:—*vi* to rebound.
rebozar *vt* to wrap up; to fry in batter or breadcrumbs.
rebuznar *vi* to bray.
recado *m* message; errand.
recaer *vi* to relapse.
recaída *f* relapse.
recalcar *vt* to stress, emphasize.
recalentar *vt* to heat again; to overheat.
recambio *m* spare; refill.
recapacitar *vt* to reflect.
recargar *vt* to overload; to recharge; to charge again.
recatado/da *adj* prudent; circumspect; modest.
recaudar *vt* to gather; to obtain; to recover.
recelo *m* dread; suspicion, mistrust.
receta *f* recipe; prescription.
rechazar *vt* to refuse; to repulse; to contradict.
recibir *vt* to receive, accept; to let in; to go to meet:—**~se** *vr* **~ de** to qualify as.
recibo *m* receipt.
recién *adv* recently, lately.
reciente *adj* recent; new, fresh; modern.
recio/cia *adj* stout; strong, robust; coarse, thick; rude; arduous, rigid:—*adv* strongly, stoutly:—**hablar ~** to talk loud.
recipiente *m* container.
reclamación *f* claim; reclamation; protest.
recluir *vt* to shut up.
reclutar *vt* to recruit.

recobrar *vt* to recover:—**~se** *vr* to recover (from sickness).

recodo *m* corner or angle jutting out.

recoger *vt* to collect; to take back; to get; to gather; to shelter; to compile: —**~se** *vr* to take shelter or refuge; to retire; to withdraw from the world.

recompensa *f* compensation; recompense, reward.

reconfortar *vt* to comfort.

reconocer *vt* to recognize; to examine closely; to acknowledge; to consider; (*mil*) to reconnoiter.

reconstituyente *m* tonic.

reconversión *f*:—**~ industrial** industrial rationalization.

recopilar *vt* to compile.

recordar *vt* to remember; to remind: —*vi* to remember.

recorrer *vt* to run over, peruse; to cover.

recortar *vt* to cut out.

recostar *vt* to lean, recline:—**~se** *vr* to lie down.

recoveco *m* cubby hole; bend.

recreo *m* recreation; playtime (school).

recta *f* straight line.

rectángulo/la *adj* rectangular:—*m* rectangle.

rectitud *f* straightness; rectitude; justness, honesty; exactitude.

recto/ta *adj* straight; right; just, honest:—*m* rectum.

rector/ra *m/f* superior of a community or establishment; rector (of a university); curate, rector:—*adj* governing.

recuadro *m* box; inset.

recuento *m* inventory.

recuerdo *m* souvenir; memory.

recuperar *vt* to recover:—**~se** *vr* to recover (from sickness).

recurrir *vi*:—**~ a** to resort to.

red *f* net; network; snare.

redactar *vt* to draft; to edit.

redada *f*:—**~ policial** police raid.

redimir *vt* to redeem; to ransom.

redoblar *vt* to redouble; to rivet.

redondo/da *adj* round; complete.

reducir *vt* to reduce; to limit:—**~se** *vr* to diminish.

redundancia *f* superfluity, redundancy, excess.

reembolso *m* reimbursement; refund: —**contra ~** C.O.D.

referir *vt* to refer, relate, report:—**~se** *vr* to refer or relate to.

refinado/da *adj* refined; subtle, artful.

reflejar *vt* to reflect.

reflejo *m* reflex; reflection.

reflujo *m* reflux, ebb:—**flujo y ~** the tides *pl*.

reformar *vt* to reform; to correct; to restore:—**~se** *vr* to mend; to have one's manners reformed or corrected.

reforzar *vt* to strengthen, fortify; to encourage.

refrán *m* proverb.

refrescar *vt* to refresh:—**~se** *vr* to get cooler; to go out for a breath of fresh air:—*vi* to cool down.

refriega *f* affray, skirmish, fray.

refrigerador *m*, **refrigeradora** *f* refrigerator, fridge.

refuerzo *m* reinforcement.

refugiar *vt* to shelter:—**~se** *vr* to take refuge.

refunfuñar *vi* to snarl; to growl; to grumble.

regadera *f* watering can.

regalar *vt* to give (as present); to give away; to pamper; to caress.

regaliz *m* licorice.

regalo *m* present, gift; pleasure; comfort.

regañadientes: —**a ~** *adv* reluctantly.

regañar *vt* to scold:—*vi* to growl; to grumble; to quarrel.

regar *vt* to water, irrigate.

regata *f* irrigation ditch; regatta.

regatear *vt* (*com*) to bargain over; to be mean with:—*vi* to haggle; to dribble (in sport).

regazo *m* lap.

regentar *vt* to rule; to govern.

régimen *m* regime, management; diet; (*gr*) rules *pl* of verbs.

registrar *vt* to survey; to inspect, examine; to record, enter in a register: —**~se** *vr* to register; to happen.

regla *f* rule, ruler; period.

reglamentar *vt* to regulate.

regocijar *vt* to gladden:—**~se** *vr* to rejoice.

regordete *adj* chubby, plump.

regresar *vi* to return, go back.

reguero *m* small rivulet; trickle of spilt liquid; drain, gutter.

regular *vt* to regulate, adjust:—*adj* regular; ordinary.

rehén *m* hostage.

rehuir *vt* to avoid.

rehusar *vt* to refuse, decline.

reimpresión *f* reprint.

reina *f* queen.

reincidir *vi*:—**~ en** to relapse into, fall back into.

reino *m* kingdom, reign.

reintegrar *vt* to reintegrate, restore:—**~se** *vr* to be reinstated or restored.

reír(se) *vi* (*vr*) to laugh.

reiterar vt to reiterate, repeat.
reivindicar vt to claim.
reja f ploughshare; lattice, grating.
rejoneador m mounted bullfighter.
relación f relation; relationship; report; account.
relajar vt to relax, slacken:—~se vr to relax.
relamerse vr to lick one's lips; to relish.
relámpago m flash of lightning.
relatar vt to relate, tell.
relato m story; recital.
relegar vt to relegate; to banish, exile.
relente m evening dew.
relieve m relief; (fig) prominence.
relinchar vi to neigh.
reliquia f residue, remains pl; (saintly) relic.
rellano m landing (of stairs).
rellenar vt to fill up; to stuff.
reloj m clock; watch.
relucir vi to shine, glitter; to excel, be brilliant.
relumbrar vi to sparkle, shine.
remachar vt to rivet; (fig) to drive home.
remache m rivet; clinch; obstinacy.
remanente m remainder; (com) balance; surplus.
remanso m stagnant water; quiet place.
remar vi to row.
rematar vt to terminate, finish; to sell off cheaply:—vi to end.
remedar vt to copy, imitate; to mimic.
remediar vt to remedy; to assist, help; to free from danger; to avoid.
remesa f shipment; remittance.
remilgado/da adj prim; affected.
remitente m sender.
remojar vt to steep; to dunk.
remolacha f beet.
remolcar vt to tow.
remordimiento m remorse.
remoto/ta adj remote, distant; far.
remover vt to stir; to move around.
remozar vt to rejuvenate; to renovate.
renacer vi to be born again; to revive.
renacuajo m tadpole.
rendija f crevice, crack, cleft.
rendir vt to subject, subdue:—~se vr to yield; to surrender; to be tired out.
renegar vt to deny; to disown; to detest, abhor:—vi to apostatize; to blaspheme, curse.
renglón m line; item.
reñir vt, vi to wrangle, quarrel; to scold, chide.
renombre m renown.
renovar vt to renew; to renovate; to reform.

renta f income; rent; profit.
reo m offender, criminal.
reparar vt to repair; to consider, observe; to parry:—vi ~ en to notice; to pass (at cards).
repartir vt to distribute; to deliver.
repasar vt to revise; to check; to mend.
repente:—de ~ adv suddenly.
repercutir vi to reverberate; to rebound.
repetir vt, vi to repeat.
repiquetear vt to ring merrily.
repisa f pedestal, stand; shelf; windowsill.
repleto/ta adj replete, very full.
replicar vi to reply.
repoblar vt to repopulate; to reafforest.
repollo m cabbage.
reponer vt to replace; to restore:—~se vr to recover lost health or property.
reportaje m report, article.
reposar vi to rest, repose.
repostería f confectioner's (store).
reprender vt to reprimand.
represa f dam; lake.
representar vt to represent; to play on the stage; to look (age).
reprimir vt to repress; to check; to contain.
reprobable adj reprehensible.
reprochar vt to reproach.
repuesto m supply; spare part.
repugnancia f reluctance; repugnance; disgust.
requerir vt to intimate, notify; to request; to require, need; to summon.
requesón m cottage cheese.
requiebro m endearing expression.
res f head of cattle.
resabio m (unpleasant) aftertaste; vicious habit, bad custom.
resaca f surge, surf; (fig) backlash; (fam) hangover.
resaltar vi to rebound; to jut out; to be evident; to stand out.
resbaladizo/za adj slippery.
resbalar(se) vi (vr) to slip, slide.
rescindir vt to rescind, annul.
rescoldo m embers pl, cinders pl.
resecarse vr to dry up.
reseña f review; account.
resentirse vr:—~ de to suffer:—~ con to resent.
reservar vt to keep; to reserve:—~se vr to preserve oneself; to keep to oneself.
resfriado m cold.
resguardar vt to preserve, defend:—~se vr to be on one's guard.
residir vi to reside, dwell.
residuo m residue, remainder.

resistir vt to resist, oppose; to put up with:—vi to resist; to hold out.

resol m glare (of the sun).

resollar vi to wheeze; to take breath.

resolver vt to resolve, decide; to analyse:—~se vr to resolve, determine.

resoplar vi to snore; to snort.

resorte m spring.

respaldo m backing; endorsement; back of a seat.

respetar vt to respect; to revere.

respingo m start; jump.

respiradero m vent, breathing hole; rest, repose.

respirar vi to breathe.

resplandecer vi to shine; to glisten.

resplandor m splendor, brilliance.

responder vt to answer:—vi to answer; to correspond:—~ de to be responsible for.

responso m prayer for the dead.

respuesta f answer, reply.

resquemor m resentment.

restablecer vt to re-establish:—~se vr to recover.

restallar vi to crack; to click.

restar vt to subtract, take away:—vi to be left.

restaurar vt to restore.

restituir vt to restore; to return.

resto m remainder, rest.

restregar vt to scrub, rub.

restringir vt to restrict, limit; to restrain.

resuelto/ta adj resolute, determined; prompt.

resultar vi to be; to turn out; to amount to.

resumir vt to abridge; to summarize.

retahíla f range, series.

retal m remnant.

retar vt to challenge.

retener vt to retain, keep back.

retentiva f memory.

retirar vt to withdraw, retire; to remove:—~se vr to retire, retreat; to go to bed.

reto m challenge; threat, menace.

retocar vt to retouch; to mend; to finish off (work).

retoñar vi to sprout.

retorcer vt to twist; to wring.

retozar vi to frisk, skip.

retraído/da adj shy.

retransmitir vt to broadcast; to relay; to retransmit.

retraso m delay; slowness; backwardness; lateness:—(ferro) **el tren ha tenido ~** the train is overdue or late.

retrato m portrait, effigy.

retrete m lavatory.

retribuir vt to repay.

retroceder vi to go backwards, fly back; to back down.

retrovisor m rear-view mirror.

retumbar vi to resound, jingle.

reúma f rheumatism.

reunir vt to reunite; to unite:—~se vr to gather, meet.

revancha f revenge.

revelar vt to reveal; to develop (photographs).

reventar vi to burst, crack; to explode; to toil, drudge.

reverdecer vi to grow green again; to revive.

revés m back; wrong side; disappointment, setback.

revisar vt to revise, review.

revisor m inspector; ticket collector.

revista f review, revision; magazine.

revolcarse vr to wallow.

revolotear vi to flutter.

revoltijo m confusion, disorder.

revoltoso/sa adj rebellious, unruly.

revolver vt to move about; to turn around; to mess up; to revolve; ~se vr to turn round; to change (of the weather).

revuelta f turn; disturbance, revolt.

rey m king; king (in cards or chess).

rezagar vt to leave behind; to defer:—~se vr to remain behind.

rezar vi to pray, say one's prayers.

rezumar vt to ooze, leak.

ría f estuary.

riada f flood.

ribera f shore, bank.

rico/ca adj rich; delicious; lovely; cute.

riego m irrigation.

rienda f rein of a bridle:—**dar ~ suelta** to give free rein to.

riesgo m risk, danger.

rifa f raffle, lottery.

rígido/da adj rigid, inflexible; severe.

riguroso/sa adj rigorous.

rimar vi to rhyme.

rímel, rimmel m mascara.

riña f quarrel, dispute.

rincón m (inside) corner.

rinoceronte m rhinoceros.

riñón m kidney.

río m river, stream.

riqueza f riches pl, wealth.

risa f laugh, laughter.

risco m steep rock.

ritmo m rhythm.

rizo m curl; ripple (on water).

robar vt to rob; to steal; to break into.

roble m oak tree.

robusto/ta *adj* robust, strong.
roca *f* rock.
rociar *vt* to sprinkle; to spray.
rocío *m* dew.
rodaja *f* slice.
rodaje *m* filming:—**en ~** (*auto*) running in.
rodear *vt* to make a detour:—*vt* to surround, enclose.
rodilla *f* knee:—**de ~s** on one's knees.
rodillo *m* roller; rolling pin.
roer *vt* to gnaw; to corrode.
rogar *vt*, *vi* to ask for; to beg, entreat; to pray.
rojizo/za *adj* reddish.
rojo/ja *adj* red; ruddy.
rol *m* list, roll, catalog; role.
rollo *m* roll; coil.
romería *f* pilgrimage.
romero *m* (*bot*) rosemary.
rompecabezas *m invar* riddle; jigsaw.
romper *vt* to break; to tear up; to wear out; to break up (land):—*vi* to break (of waves); to break through.
ron *m* rum.
roña *f* scab, mange; grime; rust.
roncar *vi* to snore; to roar.
ronco/ca *adj* hoarse; husky; raucous.
ronda *f* night patrol; round (of drinks, cards, etc).
ronronear *vi* to purr.
ropa *f* clothes *pl*; clothing; dress.
rosa *f* rose; birthmark.
rosado/da *adj* pink; rosy.
rosca *f* thread (of a screw); coil, spiral.
rosquilla *f* doughnut.

rostro *m* face.
roto/ta *adj* broken, destroyed; debauched.
rótula *f* kneecap; ball-and-socket joint.
rotulador *m* felt-tip pen.
rótulo *m* inscription; label, ticket; placard, poster.
rotundo/da *adj* round; emphatic.
rozar *vt* to rub; to chafe; to nibble (the grass); to scrape; to touch lightly.
rubio/bia *adj* fair-haired, blond(e): —*m/f* blond/blonde.
rudimento *m* principle; beginning:—**~s** *mpl* rudiments *pl*.
rudo/da *adj* rough, coarse; plain, simple; stupid.
rueda *f* wheel; circle; slice, round.
ruedo *m* rotation; border, selvage; arena, bullring.
ruego *m* request, entreaty.
rufián *m* pimp, pander; lout.
rugir *vi* to roar, bellow.
rugoso/sa *adj* wrinkled.
ruido *m* noise, sound; din, row; fuss.
ruin *adj* mean, despicable; stingy.
ruina *f* ruin, collapse; downfall, destruction: —**~s** *fpl* ruins *pl*.
ruiseñor *m* nightingale.
rulo *m* curler.
rumbo *m* (*mar*) course, bearing; road, route, way; course of events, pomp, ostentation.
rumboso/sa *adj* generous, lavish.
rústico/ca *adj* rustic:—*m/f* peasant.
ruta *f* route, itinerary.
rutina *f* routine; habit.

S

sábado *m* Saturday; (*jewish*) Sabbath.
sábana *f* sheet; altar cloth.
sabañón *m* chilblain.
sabelotodo *m/f invar* know-all.
saber *vt* to know; to be able to; to find out, learn; to experience:—*vi* **~ a** to taste of: —*m* learning, knowledge.
sabiduría *f* learning, knowledge; wisdom.
sabio/bia *adj* sage, wise:—*m/f* sage, wise person.
sablazo *m* sword wound; (*fam*) sponging, scrounging.
sabor *m* taste, savor, flavor.
sabroso/sa *adj* tasty, delicious; pleasant; salted.

sabueso *m* bloodhound.
sacacorchos *m invar* corkscrew.
sacapuntas *m invar* pencil sharpener.
sacar *vt* to take out, extract; to get out; to bring out (a book etc); to take off (clothes); to receive, get; (*dep*) to serve.
sacerdote *m* priest.
saco *m* bag, sack; jacket.
sacudir *vt* to shake, jerk; to beat, hit.
sagaz *adj* shrewd, clever, sagacious.
sagrado/da *adj* sacred, holy.
sal *f* salt.
sala *f* large room; (*teat*) house, auditorium; public hall; (*jur*) court; (*med*) ward.
salado/da *adj* salted; witty, amusing.

salario *m* salary.

salchicha *f* sausage.

salchichón *m* (salami-type) sausage.

saldo *m* settlement; balance; remainder:— **~s** *mpl* sale.

salida *f* exit, way out; leaving, departure; production, output; (*com*) sale; sales outlet.

saliente *adj* projecting; rising; (*fig*) outstanding.

salir *vi* to go out, leave; to depart, set out; to appear; to turn out, prove:—**~se** *vr* to escape, leak.

salmo *m* psalm.

salmonete *m* red mullet.

salmuera *f* brine.

salón *m* living room, lounge; public hall.

salpicadero *m* dashboard.

salpicar *vt* to sprinkle, splash, spatter.

salsa *f* sauce.

saltamontes *m invar* grasshopper.

saltar *vt* to jump, leap; to skip, miss out:— *vi* to leap, jump; to bounce; (*fig*) to explode, blow up.

saltimbanqui *m/f* acrobat.

salubre *adj* healthy.

salud *f* health.

saludar *vt* to greet; (*mil*) to salute.

salvado *m* bran.

salvaguardar *vt* to safeguard.

salvaje *adj* savage.

salvar *vt* to save; to rescue; to overcome; to cross, jump across; to cover, travel; to exclude:—**~se** *vr* to escape from danger.

salvavidas *adj invar:*—**bote/chaleco/cinturón ~** lifeboat/life preserver/life belt.

salvia *f* (*bot*) sage.

salvo/va *adj* safe:—*adv* save, except (for).

San *adj* Saint (as title).

saña *f* anger, passion.

sanar *vt, vi* to heal.

sandalia *f* sandal.

sandez *f* folly, stupidity.

sandía *f* watermelon.

sangre *f* blood:—**a ~ fria** in cold blood:—**a ~ y fuego** without mercy.

sangriento/ta *adj* bloody, blood-stained, gory; cruel.

sano/na *adj* healthy, fit; intact, sound.

sapo *m* toad.

saquear *vt* to ransack, plunder.

sarampión *m* measles.

sarna *f* itch; mange; (*med*) scabies.

sarpullido *m* (*med*) rash.

sarro *m* (*med*) tartar.

sarta *f* string of beads, etc; string, row.

sartén *f* frying pan.

sastre *m* tailor.

satisfacer *vt* to satisfy; to pay (a debt):— **~se** *vr* to satisfy oneself; to take revenge.

sauce *m* (*bot*) willow.

saúco *m* (*bot*) elder.

savia *f* sap.

sazonar *vt* to ripen; to season.

se *pn reflexivo* himself; herself; itself; yourself; themselves; yourselves; each other; one another; oneself.

se(p)tiembre *m* September.

sebo *m* fat, grease.

secano *m* dry, arable land which is not irrigated.

secar *vt* to dry:—**~se** *vr* to dry up; to dry oneself.

seco/ca *adj* dry; dried up; skinny; cold (of character); brusque, sharp; bare.

secuestrar *vt* to kidnap; to confiscate.

sed *f* thirst:—**tener ~** to be thirsty.

seda *f* silk.

sedal *m* fishing line.

sede *f* see; seat; headquarters.

sediento/ta *adj* thirsty; eager.

seducir *vt* to seduce; to bribe; to charm, attract.

segar *vt* to reap, harvest; to mow.

seguido/da *adj* continuous; successive; long-lasting:—*adv* straight (on); after; often.

seguir *vt* to follow, pursue; to continue:— *vi* to follow; to carry on:—**~se** *vr* to follow, ensue.

según *prep* according to.

segundo/da *adj* second:—*m* second (of time).

seguro/ra *adj* safe, secure; sure, certain; firm, constant:—*adv* for sure:—*m* safety device; insurance; safety, certainty.

seis *adj, m* six; sixth.

seiscientos/tas *adj* six hundred.

seísmo *m* earthquake.

sello *m* seal; stamp.

seleccionar *vt* to select, chose, pick.

selectivo *adj* selective.

selva *f* forest.

semáforo *m* traffic lights *pl*; signal.

semana *f* week.

sembrar *vt* to sow; to sprinkle, scatter.

semejante *adj* similar, like:—*m* fellow man.

semestral *adj* half-yearly.

semilla *f* seed.

sémola *f* semolina.

sempiterno/na *adj* everlasting.

seña *f* sign, mark, token; signal; (*mil*) password:—**~s** *fpl* address.

señal f sign, token; symptom; signal; landmark; (*com*) deposit.

señalar vt to stamp, mark; to signpost; to point out; to fix, settle:—**~se** vr to distinguish oneself, excel.

sencillo/lla adj simple; natural; unaffected; single.

senda f, **sendero** m path, trail.

seno m bosom; lap; womb; hole, cavity; sinus:—**~s** mpl breasts pl.

señor m man; gentleman; master; Mr; sir.

señora f lady; Mrs; madam; wife.

señorita f Miss; young lady.

señorito m young gentleman; rich kid.

sensación f sensation, feeling; sense.

sensato/ta adj sensible.

sensible adj sensitive; perceptible, appreciable; regrettable.

sentado/da adj sitting, seated; sedate; settled.

sentar vt to seat; (*fig*) to establish:—vi to suit:—**~se** vr to sit down.

sentido m sense; feeling; meaning:—**~/da** adj regrettable; sensitive.

sentir vt to feel; to hear; to perceive; to sense; to suffer from; to regret, be sorry for:—**~se** vr to feel; to feel pain; to crack (of walls, etc):—m opinion, judgement.

separar vt to separate:—**~se** vr to separate; to come away, come apart; to withdraw.

septentrional adj north, northern.

séptimo/ma adj seventh.

sepultar vt to bury, inter.

sequía f dryness; thirst; drought.

séquito m retinue, suite; group of supporters; aftermath.

ser vi to be; to exist:—**~ de** to come from; to be made of; to belong to:—m being.

serenata f (*mus*) serenade.

sereno m night watchman:—**~/na** adj serene, calm, quiet.

serie f series; sequence.

serio/ria adj serious; grave; reliable.

serpentear vi to wriggle; to wind, snake.

serpiente f snake.

serranía f range of mountains; mountainous country.

serrar vt to saw.

serrín m sawdust.

servicial adj helpful, obliging.

servilleta f napkin, serviette.

servir vt to serve; to wait on:—vi to serve; to be of use; to be in service:—**~se** vr to serve oneself, help oneself; to deign, please; to make use of.

sesenta m, adj sixty; sixtieth.

seso m brain.

sestear vi to take a nap.

seta f mushroom.

setecientos/tas adj seven hundred.

setenta adj, m seventy.

setiembre m September.

seto m fence; enclosure; hedge.

severo/ra adj severe, strict; grave, serious.

sexto/ta adj, m sixth.

si conj whether; if.

sí adv yes; certainly; indeed:—pn oneself; himself; herself; itself; yourself; themselves; yourselves; each other; one another.

siderúrgico/ca adj iron and steel compd:—f **la siderúrgica** the iron and steel industry.

sidra f cider.

siempre adv always; all the time; ever; still:—**~ jamás** for ever and ever.

sien f temple (of the head).

sierra f saw; range of mountains.

siete adj, m seven.

sigilo m secrecy.

sigla f acronym; abbreviation.

siglo m century.

significado m significance, meaning.

significativo/va adj significant.

signo m sign, mark.

siguiente adj following, successive, next.

silbar vt, vi to hiss; to whistle.

silencio m silence:—**~!** silence! quiet!

silla f chair; saddle; seat:—**~ de ruedas** wheelchair.

silo m silo; underground wheat store.

silueta f silhouette; outline; figure.

silvestre adj wild, uncultivated; rustic.

símbolo m symbol.

simio m ape.

simpático/ca adj pleasant; kind.

simpatizar vi:—**~ con** to get on well with.

simular vt to simulate.

sin prep without.

sindicato m trade(s) union; syndicate.

sinfín m:—**un ~ de** a great many.

singular adj singular; exceptional; peculiar, odd.

siniestro/tra adj left; (*fig*) sinister:—m accident.

sino conj but; except; save; only:—m fate.

sinsabor m unpleasantness; disgust.

sinuoso/sa adj sinuous; wavy; winding.

sinvergüenza m/f rogue.

siquiera conj even if, even though:—adv at least.

sitio m place; spot; site, location; room, space; job, post; (*mil*) siege, blockade.

situar vt to place, situate; to invest:—**~se** vr to be established in place or business.

smoking m tuxedo.

sobaco m armpit, armhole.

sobar vt to handle, soften; to knead; to massage, rub hard; to rumple (clothes); to fondle.

soberbia f pride, haughtiness; magnificence.

sobornar vt to suborn, bribe.

sobrante adj remaining.—m surplus, remainder.

sobrar vt to exceed, surpass;—vi to be more than enough; to remain, be left.

sobre prep on; on top of; above, over; more than; besides:—m envelope.

sobrecargar vt to overload; (com) to surcharge.

sobredosis f overdose.

sobreentender vt to deduce:—~se vr se sobreentiende que . . . it is implied that.

sobrellevar vt to carry; to tolerate.

sobremesa f:—de ~ immediately after dinner.

sobrenombre m nickname.

sobrepasar vt to surpass.

sobresalto m start, scare; sudden shock.

sobrevenir vi to happen, come unexpectedly; to supervene.

sobrevivir vi to survive.

sobrevolar vt to fly over.

sobrino/na m/f nephew/niece.

sobrio/ria adj sober, frugal.

socarrón/ona adj sarcastic; ironic(al).

socavar vt to undermine.

socio/cia m/f associate, member.

socorrista m first aider; lifeguard.

socorro m help, aid, assistance, relief.

soez adj dirty, obscene.

sofá m sofa.

soga f rope.

soja f soya.

sol m sun; sunshine, sunlight.

solamente adv only, solely.

solapa f lapel.

solar m building site; piece of land; ancestral home of a family:—adj solar.

soldado m/f soldier:—~ raso private.

soldar vt to solder; to weld; to unite.

soledad f solitude; loneliness.

soler vi to be accustomed to, be in the habit of.

solicitar vt to ask for, seek; to apply for (a job); to canvass for; to chase after, pursue.

solidario/ria adj joint; mutually binding.

soliloquio m soliloquy, monologue.

solista m/f soloist.

solitario/ria adj solitary:—m solitaire:—m/f hermit.

sollozar vi to sob.

solo m (mus) solo:—~la adj alone, single:—a solas alone, unaided.

sólo adv only.

solomillo m sirloin.

soltar vt to untie, loosen; to set free, let out:—~se vr to get loose; to come undone.

soltero/ra m/f bachelor/single woman: —adj single, unmarried.

soltura f looseness, slackness; agility, activity; fluency.

solucionar vt to solve; to resolve.

sombra f shade; shadow.

sombrero m hat.

sombrilla f parasol.

sombrío/bría adj shady, gloomy; sad.

somero/ra adj superficial.

someter vt to conquer (a country); to subject to one's will; to submit; to subdue:—~se vr to give in, submit.

somnífero m sleeping pill.

sonar vt to ring:—vi to sound; to make a noise; to be pronounced; to be talked of; to sound familiar:—~se vr to blow one's nose.

soñar vt, vi to dream.

sondeo m sounding; boring; (fig) poll.

soneto m sonnet.

sonido m sound.

sonreír(se) vi (vr) to smile.

sonrisa f smile.

sonrojarse vr to blush.

sonsacar vt to wheedle; to cajole; to obtain by cunning.

sopa f soup; sop.

sopetón m:—de ~ suddenly.

soplar vt to blow away, blow off; to blow up, inflate:—vi to blow, puff.

soplón/ona m/f telltale.

soportal m portico.

soportar vt to suffer, tolerate; to support.

sorber vt to sip; to inhale; to swallow; to absorb.

sorbete m sherbet; iced fruit drink.

sordo/da adj deaf; silent, quiet:—m/f deaf person.

sorprender vt to surprise.

sorteo m draw; raffle.

sortija f ring; ringlet, curl.

sortilegio m sorcery.

sosegar vt to appease, calm:—vi to rest.

soso/sa adj insipid, tasteless; dull.

sospechar vt to suspect.

sostén m support; bra; sustenance.

sostener vt to sustain, maintain:—~se vr to support or maintain oneself; to contrive, remain.

sota f knave (at cards).

sótano m basement, cellar.

su pn his, her, its, one's; their; your.

suave *adj* smooth, soft; delicate; gentle; mild, meek.

subalterno/na *adj* secondary; auxiliary.

subasta *f* auction.

subcampeón/ona *m/f* runner-up.

subestimar *vt* to underestimate.

subir *vt, vi* to raise, lift up; to go up; to climb, ascend, mount; to increase, swell; to get in, get on, board; to rise (in price).

súbito/ta *adj* sudden, hasty; unforeseen.

sublevar *vt* to excite (a rebellion); to incite (a revolt):—~**se** *vr* to revolt.

submarino/na *adj* underwater:—*m* submarine.

subrayar *vt* to underline.

subsanar *vt* to excuse; to mend, repair; to overcome.

subsidio *m* subsidy, aid; benefit, allowance.

su(b)stancia *f* substance.

su(b)straer *vt* to remove; (*mat*) to subtract:—~**se** *vr* to avoid; to withdraw.

subterráneo/nea *adj* subterranean; underground:—*m* underground passage; (*ferro*) underground (railway).

suburbio *m* slum quarter; suburbs *pl*.

subvencionar *vt* to subsidize.

sucedáneo/nea *adj* substitute:—*m* substitute (food).

suceder *vt* to succeed, inherit:—*vi* to happen.

suceso *m* event; incident.

sucesor/ra *m/f* successor; heir.

sucio/cia *adj* dirty, filthy; obscene; dishonest.

sucursal *f* branch (office).

sudar *vt, vi* to sweat.

sudeste *adj* southeast, southeastern: —*m* southeast.

sudoeste *adj* southwest, southwestern:—*m* southwest.

suegra *f* mother-in-law.

suegro *m* father-in-law.

suela *f* sole of the shoe.

sueldo *m* wages *pl*, salary.

suelo *m* ground; floor; soil, surface.

suelto/ta *adj* loose; free; detached; swift:—*m* loose change.

sueño *m* sleep; dream.

suero *m* (*med*) serum; whey.

suerte *f* fate, destiny, chance, lot, fortune, good luck; kind, sort.

sufrir *vt* to suffer; to bear, put up with; to support.

sugerir *vt* to suggest.

sugetador *m* fastener; bra.

sujetar *vt* to fasten, hold down; to subdue; to subject:—~**se** *vr* to subject oneself.

sujeto/ta *adj* fastened, secure; subject, liable:—*m* subject; individual.

sumamente *adv* extremely.

sumar *vt* to add, add up; to collect, gather: —*vi* to add up.

sumergir *vt* to submerge, sink; to immerse.

sumidero *m* sewer, drain.

suministrar *vt* to supply, furnish.

sumiso/sa *adj* submissive, docile.

sumo/ma *adj* great, extreme; highest, greatest:—**a lo ~** at most.

súper *f* four-star (gas).

superar *vt* to surpass; to overcome; to exceed, go beyond.

superficial *adj* superficial; shallow.

superficie *f* surface; area.

superintendente *m/f* superintendent, supervisor; floorwalker.

superior *adj* superior; upper; higher; better: —*m/f* superior.

supermercado *m* supermarket.

superviviente *m/f* survivor:—*adj* surviving.

suplente *m/f* substitute.

suplicar *vt* to beg (for), plead (for); to beg; to plead with.

suplicio *m* torture.

suplir *vt* to supply; to make good, make up for; to replace.

suponer *vt* to suppose:—*vi* to have authority.

suprimir *vt* to suppress; to abolish; to remove; to delete.

supuesto *m* assumption:—~**/ta** *adj* supposed:—~ **que** *conj* since, granted that.

sur *adj* south, southern:—*m* south; south wind.

surco *m* furrow; groove.

surgir *vi* to emerge; to crop up.

surtido *m* assortment, supply.

surtir *vt* to supply, furnish, provide: —*vi* to spout, spurt.

suscitar *vt* to excite, stir up.

susodicho/cha *adj* above-mentioned.

suspender *vt* to suspend, hang up; to stop; to fail (an exam etc).

suspicaz *adj* suspicious, mistrustful.

suspirar *vi* to sigh.

sustentar *vt* to sustain; to support, nourish.

susto *m* fright, scare.

sustraer *vt* to take away; to subtract.

susurrar *vi* to whisper; to murmur; to rustle: —~**se** *vr* to be whispered about.

sutil *adj* subtle; thin; delicate; very soft; keen, observant.

suyo/ya *adj* his; hers; theirs; one's; his; her; its own; one's own; their own:—**de ~** per se:—**los ~s** *mpl* his own, near friends, relations, family, supporters.

T

tabaco *m* tobacco; (*fam*) cigarettes *pl*.

tabique *m* thin wall; partition wall.

tabla *f* board; shelf; plank; slab; index of a book; bed of earth in a garden.

tablero *m* plank, board; chessboard; dashboard; bulletin board; gambling den.

taburete *m* stool.

tacaño/ña *adj* mean, stingy; crafty.

tachar *vt* to find fault with; to erase.

tachuela *f* tack, nail.

tácito/ta *adj* tacit, silent; implied.

taco *m* stopper, plug; heel (of a shoe); wad; book of coupons; billiard cue.

tacón *m* heel.

tacto *m* touch, feeling; tact.

tahona *f* bakery.

taimado/da *adj* sly, cunning, crafty.

tajo *m* cut, incision; cleft, sheer drop; working area; chopping block.

tal *adj* such:—**con ~ que** provided that:—**no hay ~** no such thing.

taladro *m* drill; borer, gimlet.

talante *m* mood; appearance; aspect; will.

talar *vt* to fell (trees); to desolate.

talega *f*, **talego** *m* bag; bagful.

talla *f* raised work; sculpture; stature, size; measure (of anything); hand, draw, turn (at cards).

tallar *vt* to cut, chop; to carve in wood; to engrave; to measure.

taller *m* workshop, laboratory.

tallo *m* shoot, sprout.

talón *m* heel; receipt; cheque.

tamaño *m* size, shape, bulk.

tambalearse *vr* to stagger, waver.

también *adv* also, as well; likewise; besides.

tambor *m* drum; drummer; eardrum.

tamiz *m* fine sieve.

tampoco *adv* neither, nor.

tan *adv* so.

tanto *m* certain sum or quantity; point; goal:—**~/ta** *adj* so much, as much; very great:—*adv* so much, as much; so long, as long.

tapar *vt* to stop up, cover; to conceal, hide.

tapia *f* wall.

tapicería *f* tapestry; upholstery; upholsterer's (store).

tapiz *m* tapestry; carpet.

tapón *m* cork, plug, bung.

taquigrafía *f* shorthand.

taquilla *f* booking office; takings *pl*.

tardar *vi* to delay; to take a long time; to be late.

tarde *f* afternoon; evening:—*adv* late.

tarea *f* task.

tarima *f* platform; step.

tarjeta *f* card; visiting card:—**~ postal** postcard.

tarro *m* pot.

tarta *f* cake.

tartamudear *vi* to stutter, stammer.

tarugo *m* wooden peg or pin.

tasar *vt* to appraise, value.

tatarabuelo/la *m/f* great-great-grandfather/mother.

tataranieto/ta *m/f* great-great-grandson/daughter.

tatuaje *m* tattoo; tattooing.

taurino/na *adj* bullfighting *compd*.

taza *f* cup; basin of a fountain.

te *pn* you.

té *m* (*bot*) tea.

teatro *m* theater, playhouse.

tebeo *m* comic.

techo *m* roof; ceiling.

tecla *f* key (of an organ, piano, etc).

técnico/ca *adj* technical.

tedio *m* boredom; dislike, abhorrence.

tejado *m* roof covered with tiles.

tejer *vt* to weave.

tejo *m* quoit; yew tree.

tejón *m* badger.

tela *f* cloth; material.

telaraña *f* cobweb.

telefax *m invar* fax; fax (machine).

televisor *m* television set.

telón *m* curtain, drape.

tema *m* theme.

temblar *vi* to tremble.

temer *vt* to fear, doubt:—*vi* to be afraid.

temerario/ria *adj* rash.

temible *adj* dreadful, terrible.

témpano *m* ice-floe.

templado/da *adj* temperate, tempered.

templar *vt* to temper, moderate, cool; to tune:—**~se** *vr* to be moderate.

temple *m* temperature; tempera; temperament; tuning:—**al ~** painted in distemper.

temporada *f* time, season; epoch, period.

temprano/na *adj* early, anticipated: —*adv* early; very early, prematurely.

tenaz *adj* tenacious; stubborn.

tenaza(s) *f* (*pl*) tongs *pl*, pincers *pl*.

tender *vt* to stretch out; to expand; to extend; to hang out; to lay:—**~se** *vr* to stretch oneself out.

tendero/ra *m/f* shop-keeper.

tendón *m* tendon, sinew.

tenebroso/sa *adj* dark, obscure.

tenedor *m* holder, keeper, tenant; fork.

tener *vt* to have; to take; to hold; to possess:
—**~se** *vr* to stand upright; to stop, halt;
to resist; to adhere.

tenia *f* tapeworm.

teñir *vt* to tinge, dye.

tensar *vt* to tauten.

tentar *vt* to touch; to try; to tempt; to
attempt.

tentempié *m* (*fam*) snack.

tenue *adj* thin; tenuous, slender.

terapia *f* therapy.

tercer(o)/ra *adj* third:—*m* (*jur*) third party.

tercio/cia *adj* third:—*m* third part.

terciopelo *m* velvet.

terco/ca *adj* obstinate.

tergiversar *vt* to distort.

terminante *adj* decisive; categorical.

terminar *vt* to finish; to end; to terminate:
—*vi* to end; to stop.

termo *m* flask.

ternero/ra *m/f* calf; veal; heifer.

ternilla *f* gristle.

ternura *f* tenderness.

terrado *m* terrace.

terrateniente *m/f* landowner.

terraza *f* balcony; (flat) roof; terrace (in
fields).

terremoto *m* earthquake.

terreno/na *adj* earthly, terrestrial:—*m* land,
ground, field.

terrón *m* clod of earth; lump:—**~ones** *mpl*
landed property.

terror *m* terror, dread.

terso/sa *adj* smooth, glossy.

tertulia *f* club, assembly, circle.

tesorero *m* treasurer.

tesoro *m* treasure; exchequer.

testamento *m* will, testament.

testar *vt*, *vi* to make one's will.

testarudo/da *adj* obstinate.

testificar *vt* to attest, witness.

testigo *m* witness, deponent.

teta *f* breast.

tetera *f* teapot.

tetilla *f* nipple; teat (of a bottle).

tétrico/ca *adj* gloomy, sullen, surly.

tez *f* complexion, hue.

ti *pn* you; yourself.

tía *f* aunt; (*fam*) bird.

tibio/bia *adj* lukewarm.

tiburón *m* shark.

tiempo *m* time; term; weather; (*gr*) tense;
occasion, opportunity; season.

tienda *f* tent; awning; tilt; shop.

tierno/na *adj* tender.

tierra *f* earth; land, ground; native country.

tieso/sa *adj* stiff, hard, firm; robust; valiant;
stubborn.

tiesto *m* earthen pot.

tigre *m* tiger.

tijeras *fpl* scissors *pl*.

tilde *f* tilde (ñ).

tilo *m* lime tree.

timar *vt* to con; to swindle.

timbre *m* stamp; bell; timbre; stamp duty.

tímido/da *adj* timid; cowardly.

timón *m* helm, rudder.

tímpano *m* ear-drum; small drum.

tina *f* tub; bath (tub).

tinieblas *fpl* darkness; shadows *pl*.

tino *m* skill; judgement, prudence.

tinta *f* ink; tint, dye; color.

tinte *m* tint, dye; dry cleaner's.

tinto/ta *adj* dyed:—*m* red wine.

tío *m* uncle; (*fam*) guy.

tiovivo *m* merry-go-round.

típico/ca *adj* typical; characteristic; picturesque; traditional; regional.

tipo *m* type; norm; pattern; guy.

tiquismiquis *m invar* fussy person.

tira *f* abundance; strip.

tirachinas *m invar* slingshot.

tirado/da *adj* dirt-cheap; (*fam*) very easy:
—*f* cast; distance; series; edition.

tirano/na *m/f* tyrant.

tirante *m* joist; stay; strap; brace:—*adj* taut,
extended, drawn.

tirar *vt* to throw; to pull; to draw; to drop;
to tend, aim at:—*vi* to shoot; to pull; to
go; to tend to.

tirita *f* (sticking) plaster.

tiritar *vi* to shiver.

títere *m* puppet; ridiculous little fellow.

titubear *vi* to stammer; to stagger; to
hesitate.

titular *adj* titular:—*m/f* occupant:—*m* headline:—*vt* to title:—**~se** *vr* to obtain a title.

tiza *f* chalk.

tiznar *vt* to stain; to tarnish.

tizón *m* half-burnt wood.

toalla *f* towel.

tobillo *m* ankle.

tobogán *m* toboggan; roller-coaster; slide.

tocadiscos *m invar* record player.

tocado *m* headdress, headgear.

tocar *vt* to touch; to strike; (*mus*) to play;
to ring (a bell):—*vi* to belong; to concern; to knock; to call; to be a duty or
obligation.

tocino *m* bacon.

todavía *adv* even; yet, still.

todo/da *adj* all, entire; every:—*pn* everything, all:—*m* whole.

todopoderoso/sa *adj* almighty.

toldo *m* awning; parasol.

tomar *vt* to take; to seize, grasp; to understand; to interpret, perceive; to drink; to acquire:—*vi* to drink; to take.

tomavistas *m invar* cine-camera.

tomillo *m* thyme.

tomo *m* bulk; tome; volume.

tonada *f* tune, melody.

tonel *m* cask, barrel.

tonelada *f* ton; (*mar*) tonnage duty.

tónico/ca *adj* tonic, strengthening:—*m* tonic:—*f* tonic (water); (*mus*) tonic; (*fig*) keynote.

tontería *f* foolery, nonsense.

tonto/ta *adj* stupid, foolish.

topar *vt* to run into; to find.

topo *m* mole; stumbler.

toquilla *f* head-scarf; shawl.

tórax *m* thorax.

torbellino *m* whirlwind.

torcer *vt* to twist, curve; to turn; to sprain:—**~se** *vr* to bend; to go wrong:—*vi* to turn off.

torcido/da *adj* oblique; crooked.

tordo *m* thrush:—**~/da** *adj* speckled black and white.

torear *vt* to avoid; to tease:—*vi* to fight bulls.

tormenta *f* storm, tempest.

tornar *vt* to return; to restore:—**~se** *vr* to become:—*vi* to return:—**~ a hacer** to do again.

tornasolado *adj* iridescent; shimmering.

torneo *m* tournament.

tornillo *m* screw.

torno *m* winch; revolution.

toro *m* bull.

toronja *f* grapefruit.

torpe *adj* dull, heavy; stupid.

torre *f* tower; turret; steeple.

torrefacto/ta *adj* roasted.

torta *f* cake; (*fam*) slap.

tortilla *f* omelet; pancake.

tortuga *f* tortoise; turtle.

tos *f* cough.

tosco/ca *adj* coarse, ill-bred, clumsy.

toser *vi* to cough.

tostado/da *adj* parched; sunburnt; light-yellow; light-brown.

tostar *vt* to toast, roast.

total *m* whole, totality:—*adj* total, entire:—*adv* in short.

tóxico/ca *adj* toxic:—*m* poison.

trabajar *vt* to work, labor; to persuade; to push:—*vi* to strive.

trabalenguas *m invar* tongue twister.

trabar *vt* to join, unite; to take hold of; to fetter, shackle.

tracción *f* traction:—**~ delantera/trasera** front-wheel/rear-wheel drive.

traducir *vt* to translate.

traer *vt* to bring, carry; to attract; to persuade; to wear; to cause.

traficar *vi* to trade, do business, deal.

tragaluz *m* skylight.

tragaperras *m o f invar* slot machine.

tragar *vt* to swallow; to swallow up.

trago *m* drink; gulp; adversity, misfortune.

traicionar *vt* to betray.

traje *m* suit; dress; costume.

trajinar *vt* to carry:—*vi* to bustle about; to travel around.

trama *f* plot; weft, woof.

tramitar *vt* to transact; to negotiate; to handle.

tramo *m* section; piece of ground; flight of stairs.

tramoya *f* scene, theatrical decoration; trick.

trampa *f* trap, snare; trapdoor; fraud.

trampolín *m* trampoline; diving board.

tramposo/sa *adj* deceitful, swindling.

tranca *f* bar, crossbeam.

trance *m* danger; last stage of life; trance.

tranquilizar *vt* to calm; to reassure.

tranquilo/la *adj* tranquil, calm, quiet.

transbordador *m* ferry.

transbordo *m* transfer:—**hacer ~** to change (trains).

transcurrir *vi* to pass; to turn out.

transeúnte *adj* transitory:—*m* passer-by.

transigir *vi* to compromise.

tránsito *m* passage; transition; road, way; change; removal; death of holy or virtuous persons.

transmitir *vt* to transmit; to broadcast.

transparente *adj* transparent; see-through.

transpirar *vi* to perspire; to transpire.

tranvía *m* tram.

trapo *m* rag, tatter.

tráquea *f* windpipe.

tras *prep* after, behind.

trascender *vi* to smell; to come out: —**~ de** to go beyond.

trasegar *vt* to move about; to decant.

trasero/ra *adj* back:—*m* bottom.

trasfondo *m* background.

trasgredir *vt* to contravene.

trashumante *adj* migrating.

trasladar *vt* to transport; to transfer; to postpone; to transcribe, copy:—**~se** *vr* to move.

trasnochar *vi* to watch, sit up the whole night.

traspasar *vt* to remove, transport; to transfix; pierce; to return; to exceed (the proper bounds); to transfer.

traste *m* fret (of a guitar):—**dar al ~ con algo** to ruin something.

trastero *m* lumber room.

trastienda *f* back room behind a shop.

trasto *m* piece of junk; useless person.

trastornar *vt* to overthrow, overturn; to confuse:—**~se** *vr* to go crazy.

trastrocar *vt* to invert (the order of).

tratar *vt* to traffic, trade; to use; to treat; to handle; to address; **~se** *vr* to treat each other.

trato *m* treatment; manner, address; trade, traffic; conversation; (*com*) agreement.

través *m* (*fig*) reverse:—**de o al ~** across, crossways:—**a ~ de** *prep* across; over; through.

travesía *f* crossing; cross-street; trajectory; (*mar*) side wind.

travieso/sa *adj* restless, uneasy, fidgety; lively; naughty.

trayecto *m* road; journey; stretch; course.

trazar *vt* to plan out; to project; to trace.

trébedes *fpl* trivet, tripod.

trébol *m* trefoil, clover.

trece *adj, m* thirteen; thirteenth.

trecho *m* space, distance of time or place:—**a ~s** at intervals.

tregua *f* truce, cessation of hostilities.

treinta *adj, m* thirty.

tremendo/da *adj* terrible, formidable; awful, grand.

tren *m* train, retinue; show, ostentation; (*ferro*) train:—**~ de gran velocidad** fast or express train:—**~ de mercancías** freight train.

trenza *f* braid (in hair), plaited silk.

trepar *vi* to climb; to crawl.

tres *adj, m* three.

tresillo *m* three-piece suite; (*mus*) triplet.

tricotar *vi* to knit.

trigésimo/ma *adj, m* thirtieth.

trigo *m* wheat.

trillado/da *adj* beaten; trite, hackneyed:—**camino ~** common routine.

trinar *vi* to trill, quaver; to be angry.

trinchar *vt* to carve, divide (meat).

trineo *m* sled.

trino *m* trill.

tripa *f* gut, intestine:—**~s** *fpl* guts; tripe.

tripulación *f* crew.

tripular *vt* to man; to drive.

tris *m invar*:—**estar en un ~ de** to be on the point of.

triste *adj* sad, mournful, melancholy.

triturar *vt* to reduce to powder; to grind, pound.

triza *f*:—**hacer ~s** to smash to bits; to tear to shreds.

trocar *vt* to exchange.

trompa *f* trumpet; proboscis; large top.

trompazo *m* heavy blow; accident.

trompeta *f* trumpet:—*m* trumpeter.

tronar *vi* to thunder; to rage.

tronco *m* trunk; log of wood; stock.

tropel *m* confused noise; hurry; bustle, confusion; heap; crowd:—**en ~** in a tumultuous and confused way.

tropezar *vi* to stumble:—*vt* to meet accidentally.

trotamundos *m invar* globetrotter.

trotar *vi* to trot.

trozo *m* piece.

trucha *f* trout.

truco *m* knack; trick.

trueno *m* thunderclap.

trueque *m* exchange.

truncar *vt* to truncate, maim.

tu *adj* your.

tú *pn* you.

tubería *f* pipe; pipeline.

tubo *m* tube.

tuerca *f* nut.

tumba *f* tomb.

tumbar *vt* to knock down:—*vi* to fall down:—**~se** *vr* to lie down to sleep.

tumbona *f* easy chair; beach chair.

tunda *f* beating.

tupido/da *adj* dense.

turbar *vt* to disturb, trouble:—**~se** *vr* to be disturbed.

turbio/bia *adj* muddy; troubled.

turno *m* turn; shift; opportunity.

turrón *m* nougat (almond cake).

tutear *vt* to address as 'tu'.

tutor *m* guardian, tutor.

tuyo/ya *adj* yours:—**~s** *pl* friends and relations of the party addressed.

U

u *conj* or (instead of *o* before an *o* or *ho*).

ubicar *vt* to place:—**~se** to be located.

ufanarse *vr* to boast.

últimamente *adv* lately.

ultimar *vt* to finalize; to finish.
último/ma *adj* last; latest; bottom; top.
ultrajar *vt* to outrage; to despise; to abuse.
ultramar *adj, m* overseas.
ultramarinos *mpl* groceries.
umbral *m* threshold.
un/una *art* a, an.—*adj, m* one (for **uno**).
uña *f* nail; hoof; claw, talon.
ungir *vt* to anoint.
ungüento *m* ointment.
únicamente *adv* only, simply.
único/ca *adj* only; singular, unique.
unidad *f* unity; unit; conformity; union.
unificar *vt* to unite.
unir *vt* to join, unite; to mingle; to bind,
tie:—**~se** *vr* to associate.
uno *m* one:—**~/una** *adj* one; sole, only:—
~ a otro one another:—**~ a ~** one by
one:—**a una** jointly together.

untar *vt* to anoint; to grease; (*fam*) to bribe.
urbanidad *f* urbanity, politeness.
urbanismo *m* town planning.
urbanización *f* housing estate.
urdir *vt* to warp; to contrive.
urgencia *f* urgency; emergency; need,
necessity.
urinario/ria *adj* urinary:—*m* urinal.
urna *f* urn; ballot box.
urraca *f* magpie.
usado/da *adj* used; experienced; worn.
usar *vt* to use, make use of; to wear: —**~se**
vr to be used.
usted *pn* you.
usuario *m* user.
útero *m* uterus, womb.
útil *adj* useful, profitable:—*m* utility.
utilizar *vt* to use; to make useful.
uva *f* grape.

V

vaca *f* cow; beef.
vacaciones *fpl* vacation; holidays *pl*.
vacante *adj* vacant:—*f* vacancy.
vaciar *vt* to empty, clear; to mold:—*vi* to
fall, decrease (of waters):—**~se** *vr* to empty.
vacilar *vi* to hesitate; to falter; to fail.
vacío/cía *adj* void, empty; unoccupied; concave; vain; presumptuous: —*m* vacuum;
emptiness.
vacuna *f* vaccine.
vacuno/na *adj* bovine, cow *compd*.
vagar *vi* to rove or loiter about; to wander.
vago/ga *adj* vagrant; restless; vague.
vagón *m* (*ferro*) wagon; carriage:—**~ de
mercancias** goods wagon.
vaho *m* steam, vapor.
vaina *f* pod, husk.
vaivén *m* fluctuation, instability; giddiness.
vajilla *f* crockery.
vale *m* OK; promissory note, IOU.
valer *vi* to be valuable; to be deserving; to
cost; to be valid; to be worth; to produce;
to be current:—*vt* to protect, favor; to be
worth; to be equivalent to:—**~se** *vr* to
employ, make use of; to have recourse to.
valiente *adj* robust, vigorous; valiant,
brave; boasting.
valija *f* suitcase.
valioso/sa *adj* valuable.
valla *f* fence; hurdle; barricade.
valle *m* valley.
valor *m* value; price; validity; force; power;
courage, valor.

valorar *vt* to value; to evaluate.
vals *m invar* waltz.
valsar *vi* to waltz
válvula *f* valve.
vanidoso/sa *adj* vain, showy; haughty;
conceited.
vano/na *adj* vain; useless, frivolous;
arrogant, futile:—**en ~** in vain.
vapor *m* vapor, steam; breath.
vaquero *m* cow-herd:—**~/ra** *adj* belonging
to a cowman:—**~s** *mpl* jeans *pl*.
vara *f* rod; pole, staff; stick.
variar *vt* to vary; to modify; to change: —*vi*
to vary.
varices *fpl* varicose veins *pl*.
varilla *f* small rod; curtain rod; spindle,
pivot.
vario/ria *adj* varied, different; vague; varie-
gated:—**~s** *pl* some; several.
varón *m* man, male.
vasco/ca *adj, m/f* Basque.
vasija *f* vessel.
vaso *m* glass; vessel; vase.
vástago *m* bud; shoot; offspring.
vasto/ta *adj* vast, huge.
vaticinar *vt* to divine, foretell.
vatio *m* watt.
vecindad *f* inhabitants of a place; neighborhood.
vecino/na *adj* neighboring; near:—*m*
neighbor, inhabitant.
veinte *adj, m* twenty.
veintena *f* twentieth part; score.

vejar *vt* to vex; to humiliate.
vejez *f* old age.
vejiga *f* bladder.
vela *f* watch; watchfulness; night-guard; candle; sail:—**hacerse a la ~** to set sail.
velar *vi* to stay awake; to be attentive: —*vt* to guard, watch.
velero/ra *adj* swift-sailing.
veleta *f* weather cock.
vello *m* down; gossamer; short downy hair.
velo *m* veil; pretext.
velocidad *f* speed; velocity.
vena *f* vein.
venado *m* deer; venison.
vencer *vt* to defeat; to conquer, vanquish:—*vi* to win; to expire.
vendaje *m* bandage, dressing for wounds.
vendaval *m* gale.
vender *vt* to sell.
vendimia *f* grape harvest; vintage.
vendimiar *vt* to harvest, gather; to profit from (something).
veneno *m* poison, venom.
venerar *vt* to venerate, worship.
vengar *vt* to revenge, avenge:—**~se** *vr* to take revenge.
venida *f* arrival; return; overflow of a river.
venidero/ra *adj* future:—**~s** *mpl* posterity.
venir *vi* to come, arrive; to follow, succeed; to happen; to spring from: —**~se** *vr* to ferment.
venta *f* sale.
ventaja *f* advantage.
ventana *f* window; window shutter; nostril.
ventilar *vt* to ventilate; to fan; to discuss.
ventisca *f*, **ventisco** *m* snowstorm.
ventosidad *f* flatulence.
ventura *f* happiness; luck, chance, fortune: —**por ~** by chance.
ver *vt* to see, look at; to observe; to visit:—*vi* to understand; to see:—**~se** *vr* to be seen; to be conspicuous; to find oneself: —**~se con uno** to have a bone to pick with someone: —*m* sense of sight; appearance.
veraneo *m* summer vacation.
verano *m* summer.
veras *fpl* truth, sincerity:—**de ~** in truth, really.
veraz *adj* truthful.
verbena *f* fair; dance.
verdad *f* truth, veracity; reality; reliability.
verdadero/ra *adj* true; real; sincere.
verde *m*, *adj* green.
verdura *f* verdure; vegetables *pl*, greens *pl*.
vereda *f* path, trail; sidewalk.
vergüenza *f* shame; bashfulness; confusion.

verificar *vt* to check, verify:—**~se** *vr* to happen.
verruga *f* wart.
vertedero *m* sewer, drain; tip.
verter *vt* to pour; to spill; to empty:—*vi* to flow.
vértice *m* vertex, zenith; crown (head).
vertiente *f* slope; waterfall, cascade.
vertiginoso/sa *adj* giddy.
vespertino/na *adj* evening *compd*.
vestíbulo *m* vestibule, lobby.
vestido *m* dress; clothes *pl*.
vestir *vt* to put on; to wear; to dress; to adorn; to cloak, disguise:—*vi* to dress: —**~se** *vr* to get dressed.
vestuario *m* clothes *pl*; uniform; vestry; changing room.
veta *f* vein (in mines, wood, etc); streak; grain.
veteado/da *adj* veined; striped:—*m* veining, streaks.
veterano/na *adj* experienced, practiced: —*m* veteran, old soldier.
veterinaria *f* veterinary medicine.
veterinario/ria *m/f* veterinary surgeon.
vez *f* time; turn; return:—**cada ~** each time: —**una ~** once:—**a veces** sometimes, by turns.
veza *f* (*bot*) vetch.
vía *f* way; road, route; mode, manner, method; (*ferro*) railway line.
viajante *m* sales representative.
viajar *vi* to travel.
víbora *f* viper.
vibrar *vt*, *vi* to vibrate.
vicio *m* vice.
vid *f* (*bot*) vine.
vida *f* life.
vídeo *m* video.
vidriera *f* stained-glass window; shop window.
vidrio *m* glass.
vieira *f* scallop.
viejo/ja *adj* old; ancient, antiquated.
viento *m* wind; air.
vientre *m* belly.
viernes *m invar* Friday:—**V ~ Santo** Good Friday.
viga *f* beam; girder.
vigente *adj* in force.
vigésimo/ma *adj*, *m* twentieth.
vigía *f* (*mar*) lookout:—*m* watchman.
vigilar *vt* to watch over:—*vi* to keep watch.
vil *adj* mean, sordid, low; worthless; infamous; ungrateful.
vilipendiar *vt* to despise, revile.
villancico *m* Christmas carol.

vilo: —**en ~** *adv* in the air; in suspense.
vinagre *m* vinegar.
vincular *vt* to link.
viñedo *m* vineyard.
vino *m* wine:—**~ tinto** red wine.
violar *vt* to rape; to violate; to profane.
violentar *vt* to force.
violento/ta *adj* violent; forced; absurd; embarrassing.
violeta *f* violet.
violón *m* double bass.
virar *vi* to swerve.
viril *adj* virile, manly.
virtud *f* virtue.
viruela *f* smallpox.
visa *f*, **visado** *m* visa.
viscoso/sa *adj* viscous, glutinous.
visillos *mpl* net curtains *pl*.
visión *f* sight, vision; fantasy.
visitar *vt* to visit.
vislumbrar *vt* to catch a glimpse of; to perceive indistinctly.
visón *m* mink.
víspera *f* eve; evening before:—**~s** *pl* vespers.
vista *f* sight, view; vision; eyesight; appearance; looks *pl*; prospect; intention; (*jur*) trial:—*m* customs officer.
vistazo *m* glance.
vistoso/sa *adj* colorful, attractive, lively.
vitalicio/cia *adj* for life.
vitorear *vt* to shout, applaud.
vitrina *f* showcase.
viudo/a *f* widower, widow.
vivaz *adj* lively.
víveres *mpl* provisions.
vivero *m* nursery (for plants); fish farm.
vivienda *f* housing; flat, apartment.
viviente *adj* living.

vivir *vt* to live through; to go through: —*vi* to live; to last.
vivo/va *adj* alive; lively:—**al ~** to the life; very realistically.
vocablo *m* word, term.
vocal *f* vowel:—*m/f* member (of a committee):—*adj* vocal, oral.
vociferar *vt* to shout; to proclaim in a loud voice:—*vi* to yell.
volante *adj* flying:—*m* (*auto*) steering wheel; note; pamphlet; shuttlecock.
volar *vi* to fly; to pass swiftly (of time); to rush, hurry:—*vt* to blow up, explode.
volcán *m* volcano.
volcar *vt* to upset, overturn; to make giddy; to empty out; to exasperate:—**se** *vr* to tip over.
volquete *m* tipcart; dump truck.
voltear *vt* to turn over; to overturn:—*vi* to roll over, tumble.
voltereta *f* tumble; somersault.
voluble *adj* unpredictable; fickle.
volumen *m* volume; size.
voluntad *f* will, willpower; wish, desire.
volver *vt* to turn (over); to turn upside down; to turn inside out:—*vi* to return, go back:—**se** *vr* to turn around.
vórtice *m* whirlpool.
vos *pn* you.
vosotros/tras *pn pl* you.
votar *vt* to vow; to vote.
voz *f* voice; shout; rumor; word, term.
vuelo *m* flight; wing; projection of a building; ruffle, frill:—**cazar al ~** to catch in flight:—**~ chárter** charter flight.
vuelta *f* turn; circuit; return; row of stitches; cuff; change; bend, curve; reverse, other side; return journey.
vuestro/tra *adj* your:—*pn* yours.

WXYZ

xenofobia *f* xenophobia.
xilófono *m* xylophone.
y *conj* and.
ya *adv* already; now; immediately; at once; soon:—*conj* **~ que** since, seeing that:—**i~!** of course!, sure!
yacimiento *m* deposit.
yate *m* yacht, sailing boat.
yedra *f* ivy.
yegua *f* mare.
yema *f* bud; leaf; yolk:—**~ del dedo** tip of the finger.

yerno *m* son-in-law.
yeso *m* gypsum; plaster:—**~ mate** plaster of Paris.
yo *pn* I:—**~ mismo** I myself.
yodo *m* iodine.
yogur *m* yogurt.
yunque *m* anvil.
yute *m* jute.
zafiro *m* sapphire.
zaguán *m* porch, hall.
zalamero/ra *adj* flattering:—*m/f* wheedler.
zamarra *f* sheepskin (*f*acket).

zambullirse *vr* to plunge into water, dive.

zampar *vt* to gobble down; to put away hurriedly:—**~se** *vr* to thrust oneself suddenly into any place; to crash, hurtle.

zanahoria *f* carrot.

zancada *f* stride.

zancudo/da *adj* long legged:—*m* mosquito.

zángano *m* drone; idler, slacker.

zanja *f* ditch, trench.

zapata *f* boot:—**~ de freno** (*auto*) brake shoe.

zapatilla *f* slipper; pump (shoe); (*dep*) trainer, training shoe.

zapato *m* shoe.

zarandear *vt* to shake vigorously.

zarcillo *m* earring; tendril.

zarpar *vi* to weigh anchor.

zarza *f* bramble.

zarzuela *f* Spanish light opera.

zócalo *m* plinth, base; baseboard.

zona *f* zone; area, belt.

zopenco/ca *adj* dull, very stupid.

zoquete *m* block; crust of bread; (*fam*) blockhead.

zorro/a *m* fox; cunning person.

zozobrar *vi* (*mar*) to founder; to capsize; (*fig*) to fail; to be anxious.

zueco *m* wooden shoe; clog.

zumbar *vt* to hit:—**~se** *vr* to hit each other:—*vi* to buzz.

zumo *m* juice.

zurcir *vt* to darn; (*fig*) to join, unite; to hatch (lies).

zurdo/da *adj* left; left-handed.

zurrar *vt* (*fam*) to flog, lay into; (*fig*) to criticize harshly.

English–Spanish

A

a *art* un, uno, una:—*prep* a, al, en.
abandon *vt* abandonar, dejar.
abash *vt* avergonzar, causar confusión,
abbey *n* abadía *f*.
abbot *n* abad *m*.
abbreviate *vt* abreviar, acortar.
abbreviation *n* abreviatura *f*.
abdicate *vt* abdicar; renunciar.
abdication *n* abdicación *f*; renuncia *f*.
abdomen *n* abdomen, bajo vientre *m*.
abduct *vt* secuestrar.
aberration *n* error *m*; aberración *f*.
abet *vt*:—**to aid and ~** ser cómplice de.
abide *vt* soportar, sufrir.
ability *n* habilidad, capacidad.
ablaze *adj* en llamas.
able *adj* capaz, hábil.
able-bodied *adj* robusto/ta, vigoroso/sa.
ably *adv* con habilidad.
abnormal *adj* anormal.
abnormality *n* anormalidad *f*.
aboard *adv* a bordo.
abode *n* domicilio *m*.
abolish *vt* abolir, anular.
abolition *n* abolición, anulación *f*.
abominable *adj* abominable.
abomination *n* abominación *f*.
aboriginal *adj* aborigen.
abort *vi* abortar.
abortion *n* aborto *m*.
abound *vi* abundar.
about *prep* acerca de, acerca.
above *prep* encima.
aboveboard *adj* legítimo/ma.
abrasion *n* abrasión *f*.
abrasive *adj* abrasivo/va.
abroad *adv* en el extranjero.
abrupt *adj* brusco/ca.
abscess *n* absceso *m*.
abscond *vi* esconderse; huirse.
absence *n* ausencia *f*.
absent *adj* ausente.
absentee *n* ausente *m*.
absent-minded *adj* distraído/da.
absolute *adj* absoluto/ta.
absorb *vt* absorber.
abstain *vi* abstenerse.
abstinence *n* abstinencia *f*.
abstinent *adj* abstinente.
abstract *adj* abstracto/ta:—*n* extracto *m*.
abstraction *n* abstracción *f*.
absurd *adj* absurdo/da.
abundance *n* abundancia *f*.
abundant *adj* abundante.

abuse *vt* abusar; maltratar.
abusive *adj* abusivo/va, ofensivo/va.
abysmal *adj* abismal.
abyss *n* abismo *m*.
acacia *n* acacia *f*.
academic *adj* académico/ca.
academy *n* academia *f*.
accede *vi* acceder.
accelerate *vt* acelerar.
accelerator *n* acelerador *m*.
accent *n* acento *m*; tono *m*.
accentuate *vt* acentuar.
accept *vt* aceptar; admitir.
acceptable *adj* aceptable.
acceptance *n* aceptación *f*.
access *n* acceso *m*; entrada *f*.
accessible *adj* accesible.
accession *n* aumento.
accessory *n* accesorio *m*.
accident *n* accidente *m*; casualidad *f*.
acclaim *vt* aclamar, aplaudir.
accommodate *vt* alojar; complacer.
accommodation *n* alojamiento *m*.
accompany *vt* acompañar.
accomplice *n* cómplice *m*.
accomplish *vt* efectuar, completar.
accord *n* acuerdo, convenio *m*.
accordance *n*:—**in ~ with** de acuerdo con.
according *prep* segun, conforme.
accordion *n* (*mus*) acordeón *m*.
account *n* cuenta *f*.
accountability *n* responsabilidad *f*.
accountancy *n* contabilidad *f*.
accountant *n* contable, contador *m*.
accrue *vi* resultar, provenir.
accumulate *vt* acumular; amontonar.
accuracy *n* exactitud *f*.
accurate *adj* exacto/ta.
accursed *adj* maldito/ta.
accuse *vt* acusar; culpar.
accustom *vt* acostumbrar.
ache *n* dolor *m*:—*vi* doler.
achieve *vt* realizar; obtener.
achievement *n* realización *f*.
acid *adj* ácido/da; agrio/ria:—*n* ácido *m*.
acknowledge *vt* reconocer, confesar.
acne *n* acne *m*.
acorn *n* bellota *f*.
acoustics *n* acústica *f*.
acquaint *vt* informar, avisar.
acquaintance *n* conocimiento *m*; conocido *m*.
acquire *vt* adquirir.
acquisition *n* adquisición
acquit *vt* absolver.

acquittal *n* absolución *f.*
acre *n* acre *m.*
acrid *adj* acre.
acrimony *n* acrimonio *m.*
across *adv* de través.
action *n* acción *f.*
activate *vt* activar.
active *adj* activo/va.
activity *n* actividad *f.*
actor *n* actor *m.*
actress *n* actriz *f.*
actual *adj* real; efectivo/va.
actuary *n* actuario de seguros *m.*
acumen *n* agudeza *f.*
acute *adj* agudo/da; ingenioso/sa.
ad *n* aviso *m.*
adage *n* proverbio *m.*
adamant *adj* inflexible.
adapt *vt* adaptar.
adaptor *n* adaptador *m.*
add *vt* añadir, agregar:—to ~ up sumar.
adder *n* culebra *f*; víbora *f.*
addict *n* drogadicto *m.*
addiction *n* dependencia *f.*
addition *n* adición *f.*
additional *adj* adicional.
additive *n* aditivo *m.*
address *vt* dirigir:—*n* dirección *f.*
adenoids *npl* vegetaciones adenoideas *fpl.*
adept *adj* hábil.
adequacy *n* suficiencia *f.*
adequate *adj* adecuado/da; suficiente.
adhere *vi* adherir.
adhesion *n* adhesión *f.*
adhesive *adj* pegajoso/sa.
adhesiveness *n* adhesividad *f.*
adieu *adv* adiós:—*n* despedida *f.*
adjacent *adj* adyacente, contiguo/gua.
adjective *n* adjetivo *m.*
adjoining *adj* contiguo/gua.
adjournment *n* prorroga *f.*
adjudicate *vt* adjudicar.
adjust *vt* ajustar, acomodar.
adjustable *adj* ajustable.
adjustment *n* ajustamiento *m.*
ad lib *vt* improvisar.
administer *vt* administrar.
administration *n* administración *f.*
administrative *adj* administrativo/va.
admirable *adj* admirable.
admiral *n* almirante *m.*
admire *vt* admirar.
admirer *n* admira/a *m/f.*
admission *n* entrada *f.*
admit *vt* admitir.
admittance *n* entrada *f.*
admittedly *adj* de acuerdo que.

admonish *vt* amonestar.
ad nauseam *adv* hasta el cansancio.
adolescence *n* adolescencia *f.*
adopt *vt* adoptar.
adorable *adj* adorable.
adore *vt* adorar.
adorn *vt* adornar.
adrift *adv* a la deriva.
adult *adj* adulto/ta.
adulterate *vt* adulterar, corromper.
adulterer *n* adultero *m.*
adultery *n* adulterio *m.*
advance *vt* avanzar; promover.
advantage *n* ventaja *f.*
advantageous *adj* ventajoso/sa.
adventure *n* aventura *f.*
adventurous *adj* intrépido/da.
adverb *n* adverbio *m.*
adversary *n* adversario enemigo *m.*
adversity *n* calamidad *f*; infortunio *m.*
advertise *vt* anunciar.
advertisement *n* aviso *m.*
advice *n* consejo *m*; aviso *m.*
advisability *n* prudencia *f.*
advise *vt* aconsejar; avisar.
advocacy *n* defensa *f.*
advocate *n* abogado *m*; protector *m.*
aerial *n* antena *f.*
aerobics *npl* aerobic *m.*
aerometer *n* areómetro *m.*
aerosol *n* aerosol *m.*
afar *adv* lejos, distante.
affair *n* asunto *m*; negocio *m.*
affect *vt* conmover; afectar.
affection *n* cariño *m.*
affidavit *n* declaración jurada *f.*
affiliate *vt* afiliar.
affiliation *n* afiliación *f.*
affinity *n* afinidad *f.*
affirm *vt* afirmar, declarar.
affirmation *n* afirmación *f.*
affirmative *adj* afirmativo/va.
affix *vt* pegar:—*n* (*gr*) afijo *m.*
afflict *vt* afligir.
affliction *n* aflicción *f*; dolor *m.*
affluence *n* opulencia *f.*
affluent *adj* opulento/ta.
affray *n* asalto *m*; tumulto *m.*
aflame *adv* en llamas.
afloat *adv* flotante, a flote.
afore *prep* antes:—*adv* primero.
afraid *adj* espantado/da.
afresh *adv* de nuevo, otra vez.
after *prep* después.
afterbirth *n* secundinas *fpl.*
after-effects *npl* consecuencias *fpl.*
afterlife *n* vida venidera *f.*

aftermath *n* consecuencias *fpl*.
afternoon *n* tarde *f*.
aftershave *n* aftershave *m*.
aftertaste *n* resabio *m*.
afterwards *adv* después.
again *adv* otra vez.
against *prep* contra.
agate *n* ágata *f*.
age *n* edad *f*; vejez *f*.
agency *n* agencia *f*.
agenda *n* orden del día *m*.
agent *n* agente *m*.
aggrandizement *n* engrandecimiento *m*.
aggravate *vt* agravar, exagerar.
aggregate *n* agregado *m*.
aggregation *n* agregación *f*.
aggression *n* agresión *f*.
aggressor *n* agresor *m*.
aggrieved *adj* ofendido/da.
aghast *adj* horrorizado/da.
agile *adj* ágil; diestro/tra.
agitate *vt* agitar.
ago *adv* pasado.
agonizing *adj* atngustioso.
agony *n* agonía *f*.
agree *vt* convenir:—*vi* estar de acuerdo/da.
agreeable *adj* agradable; amable.
agreement *n* acuerdo *m*.
agriculture *n* agricultura *f*.
ah! *excl* ¡ah! ¡ay!
ahead *adv* más allá, delante de otro.
aid *vt* ayudar, socorrer.
AIDS *n* SIDA *m*.
ail *vt* afligir, molestar.
ailment *n* dolencia, indisposición *f*.
aim *vt* apuntar aspirar a; intentar.
air *n* aire *m*:—*vt* airear; ventilar.
air balloon *n* globo aerostático *m*.
airborne *adj* aerotransportado/da.
air-conditioning *n* climatización *f*.
aircraft *n* avión *m*.
air force *n* fuerzas aéreas *fpl*.
airline *n* línea aérea *f*.
airmail *n*:—**by ~** por avión,
airplane *n* avión *m*.
airport *n* aeropuerto *m*.
airstrip *n* pista de aterrizaje *f*.
airy *adj* bien ventilado/da.
aisle *n* nave de una iglesia *f*.
akin *adj* parecido/da.
alabaster *n* alabastro *m*.
alarm *n* alarma *f*:—*vt* alarmar; inquietar.
alas *adv* desgraciadamente.
albeit *conj* aunque.
album *n* álbum *m*.
alchemy *n* alquimia *f*.
alcohol *n* alcohol *m*.

alcoholic *adj* alcohólico/ca:—*n* alcoholizado *m*.
alcove *n* nicho *m*.
alder *n* aliso *m*.
ale *n* cerveza *f*.
alert *adj* vigilante; alerto/ta.
algae *npl* alga *f*.
algebra *n* álgebra *f*.
alias *adj* alias.
alibi *n* (*law*) coartada *f*.
alien *adj* ajeno/na.
alienate *vt* enajenar.
alight *vi* apearse.
align *vt* alinear.
alike *adj* semejante, igual.
alive *adj* vivo/va, viviente; activo/va.
alkali *n* álcali *m*.
alkaline *adj* alcalino/na.
all *adj* todo/da.
allay *vt* aliviar.
allegation *n* alegación *f*.
allege *vt* alegar; declarar.
allegiance *n* lealtad, fidelidad *f*.
allegorical *adj* alegórico/ca.
allegory *n* alegoría *f*.
allergy *n* alergia *f*.
alley *n* callejuela *f*.
alliance *n* alianza *f*.
allied *adj* aliado/da.
alligator *n* caimán *m*.
allocate *vt* repartir.
allot *vt* asignar.
allow *vt* conceder; permitir; dar.
allowance *n* concesión *f*.
alloy *n* liga, mezcla *f*.
allspice *n* pimienta de Jamaica *f*.
allude *vt* aludir.
allure *n* fascinación *f*.
allusion *n* alusión *f*.
allusive *adj* alusivo/va.
alluvial *adj* aluvial.
ally *n* aliado *m*:—*vt* aliar.
almanac *n* almanaque *m*.
almighty *adj* omnipotente, todopoderoso/sa.
almond *n* almendra *f*.
almost *adv* casi; cerca de.
aloft *prep* arriba.
alone *adj* solo.
along *adv* a lo largo.
aloof *adv* lejos.
alphabet *n* alfabeto *m*.
alphabetical *adj* alfabético/ca.
alpine *adj* alpino/na.
already *adv* ya.
also *adv* también, además.
altar *n* altar *m*.
altarpiece *n* retablo *m*.

alter vt modificar.
alteration n alteración f.
alternate adj alterno/na:—vt alternar, variar.
alternator n alternador m.
alternative n alternativa f.
although conj aunque, no obstante.
altitude n altitud, altura f.
altogether adv del todo.
aluminum n aluminio m.
always adv siempre, constantemente.
a.m. adv de la mañana.
amalgam n amalgama f.
amalgamate vt vi amalgamar(se).
amaryllis n (bot) amarillas f.
amass vt acumular, amontonar.
amateur n aficionado m.
amateurish adj torpe.
amaze vt asombrar.
amazon n amazona f.
ambassador n embajador m.
amber n ámbar m.
ambidextrous adj ambidextro/tra.
ambiguity n ambigüedad, duda f.
ambiguous adj ambiguo:—~ly adv ambiguamente.
ambition n ambición f.
amble vi andar sin prisa.
ambulance n ambulancia f.
ambush n emboscada f.
amenable adj sensible.
amend vt enmendar.
amendment n enmienda f.
amends npl compensación f.
amenities npl comodidades fpl.
America n América f.
amethyst n amatista f.
amiable adj amable.
amiableness n amabilidad f.
amiably adv amablemente.
amicable adj amigable.
amid(st) prep entre, en medio de.
amiss adv:—something's ~ pasa algo malo.
ammonia n amoníaco m.
ammunition n municiones fpl.
amnesia n amnesia f.
amnesty n amnistía f.
amoral adv amoral.
amorous adj amoroso/sa.
amount n importe m; cantidad f.
amp(ere) n amperio m.
amphibian n anfibio m.
amphibious adj anfibio/bia.
amphitheater n anfiteatro m.
ample adj amplio/lia.
ampleness n amplitud, abundancia f.
amplifier n amplificador m
amplify vt ampliar, extender.

amplitude n amplitud, extensión f.
amputate vt amputar.
amuse vt entretener, divertir.
amusement n diversión f.
amusing adj divertido/da.
an art un, uno, una.
anachronism n anacronismo m.
anemia n anemia f.
anesthetic n anestesia f.
analogy n analogía f.
analyse vt analizar.
anarchy n anarquía f.
anatomical adj anatómico/ca.
anatomy n anatomía f
ancestor n:—~s pl antepasados mpl.
ancestral adj hereditario/ria.
ancestry n raza, alcurnia f.
anchor n ancla f:—vi anclar.
anchovy n anchoa f.
ancient adj antiguo.
and conj y, e.
anecdote n anécdota f
anemone n (bot) anémona f
angel n ángel m
anger n cólera f:—vt enojar, irritar.
angle n ángulo m:—vt pescar con cana.
anglicism n anglicismo m.
angry adj enojado/da.
anguish n ansia, angustia f
angular adj angular.
animal n adj animal m.
animation n animación f
aniseed n anís m
ankle n tobillo m.
annals n anales mpl.
annex vt anejar:—n anejo m.
annihilate vt aniquilar.
annihilation n aniquilación f.
anniversary n aniversario m.
annotate vi anotar.
announce vt anunciar, publicar.
announcement n anuncio m.
annoy vt molestar.
annual adj anual.
annunciation n anunciación f
anoint vt untar, ungir.
anomaly n anomalía, irregularidad f.
anon adv más tarde.
anonymity n anonimato m.
anonymous adj anónimo/ma.
anorexia n anorexia f.
another adj otro/tra.
answer vt responder.
answering machine n contestador automático m.
ant n hormiga f.
antagonize vt provocar.

antarctic *adj* antártico/ca.
antelope *n* antílope *m*.
antenna *npl* antena *f*.
anterior *adj* anterior, precedente.
anthem *n* himno *m*.
anthology *n* antología *f*.
anthropology *n* antropología *f*
antibiotic *n* antibiótico *m*.
antibody *n* anticuerpo *m*.
Antichrist *n* Anticristo *m*.
anticipate *vt* anticipar, prevenir.
anticipation *n* anticipación *f*.
antidote *n* antídoto *m*.
antipodes *npl* antípodas *fpl*
antiquarian *n* anticuario *m*.
antiquated *adj* antiguo/gua.
antiquity *n* antigüedad *f*.
antiseptic *adj* antiséptico/ca.
antler *n* cuerna *f*.
anvil *n* yunque *m*.
anxiety *n* ansiedad, ansia *f*.
anxious *adj* ansioso/sa.
any *adj pn* cualquier, cualquiera; alguno,
   alguna
apart *adv* aparte, separadamente.
apartment *n* departamento *m*.
apathy *n* apatía *f*.
ape *n* mono *m*.
apologize *vt* disculpar.
apology *n* apología, defensa *f*.
apostrophe *n* apóstrofe *m*.
appall *vt* espantar, aterrar.
apparatus *n* aparato *m*.
apparent *adj* evidente, aparente.
apparition *n* aparición, visión *f*.
appeal *vi* apelar.
appear *vi* aparecer.
appease *vt* aplacar.
append *vt* anejar.
appendicitis *n* apendicitis *f*.
appendix *n* apéndice *m*.
appetite *n* apetito *m*.
applaud *vi* aplaudir.
apple *n* manzana *f*.
appliance *n* aparato *m*.
applicable *adj* aplicable.
applicant *n* aspirante, candidato *m*.
application *n* aplicación *f*; solicitud *f*.
applied *adj* aplicado/da.
apply *vt* aplicar.
appoint *vt* nombrar.
appointment *n* cita *f*; nombramiento *m*.
apportion *vt* repartir.
appraisal *n* estimación *f*.
appraise *vt* tasar; estimar.
appreciate *vt* apreciar; agradecer.
apprehend *vt* arrestar.

apprehension *n* aprensión *f*.
apprehensive *adj* aprensivo/va.
apprentice *n* aprendiz *m*.
approach *vt vi* aproximar(se).
appropriate *vt* apropiarse de:—*adj* apro-
   piado/da.
approve (of) *vt* aprobar.
April *n* abril *m*.
apron *n* delantal *m*.
apse *n* ábside *m*.
apt *adj* apto/ta, idóneo/nea.
aptitude *n* aptitud *f*.
aquarium *n* acuario *m*.
Aquarius *n* Acuario *m*.
aqueduct *n* acueducto *m*.
arable *adj* labrantío/tía.
arbitrate *vt* arbitrar.
arcade *n* galería *f*.
arch *n* arco *m*.
archeology *n* arqueología *f*.
archaic *adj* arcaico/ca.
archbishop *n* arzobispo *m*.
archer *n* arquero *m*.
architect *n* arquitecto/ta *m/f*.
architecture *n* arquitectura *f*.
archives *npl* archivos *mpl*.
arctic *adj* ártico/ca.
area *n* área *f*; espacio *m*.
arena *n* arena *f*.
arguably *adv* posiblemente.
argue *vi* discutir.
argument *n* argumento *m*, controversia *f*.
arid *adj* árido/da, estéril.
aridity *n* sequedad *f*.
Aries *n* Aries *m*.
arise *vi* levantarse.
aristocracy *n* aristocracia *f*.
arithmetic *n* aritmética *f*.
ark *n* arca *f*.
arm *n* brazo *m*; arma *f*.
armament *n* armamento *m*.
armchair *n* sillón *m*.
armor *n* armadura *f*.
armpit *n* sobaco *m*.
army *n* ejercito *m*.
aroma *n* aroma *m*.
around *prep* alrededor de.
arouse *vt* despertar; excitar.
arraign *vt* acusar.
arraignment *n* acusación *f*; proceso criminal *m*.
arrange *vt* organizar.
arrangement *n* colocación *f*; arreglo.
arrant *adj* consumado/da.
array *n* serie *f*.
arrears *npl* resto de una deuda *m*; atraso *m*.
arrest *n* arresto *m*:—*vt* detener, arrestar.

arrival n llegada f.
arrive vi llegar.
arrogance n arrogancia, presunción f.
arrogant adj arrogante, presuntuoso/sa:—
~ly adv arrogantemente.
arrogate vt arrogarse.
arrogation n arrogación f.
arrow n flecha f.
arsenal n (mil) arsenal m; (mar) atarazana,
armería f.
arsenic n arsénico m.
art n arte m.
arterial adj arterial.
artery n arteria f.
artful adj ingenioso/sa.
art gallery n pinacoteca f.
arthritis n artritis f.
artichoke n alcachofa f.
article n artículo m.
articulate vt articular.
artifice n artificio m.
artillery n artillería f.
artisan n artesano/na m/f.
artist n artista m.
artistry n habilidad f.
artless adj sencillo, simple.
artlessness n sencillez f.
as conj como; mientras.
asbestos n asbesto m.
ascend vi ascender, subir.
ascribe vt atribuir.
ash n (bot) fresno m; ceniza f
ashamed adj avergonzado/da.
ashtray n cenicero m.
Ash Wednesday n miércoles de ceniza m.
ask vt pedir, rogar, preguntar por.
askew adv de lado.
asleep adj dormido/da.
asparagus n espárrago m.
aspect n aspecto m.
aspen n álamo temblón m.
asphalt n asfalto m.
asphyxia n (med) asfixia f.
asphyxiate vt asfixiar.
asphyxiation n asfixia f.
aspiration n aspiración f.
aspire vi aspirar, desear.
aspirin n aspirina f.
ass n asno m:—she ~ burra f.
assassin n asesino m.
assassinate vt asesinar.
assault n asalto m.
assemble vt reunir, convocar.
assembly n asamblea f.
assert vt sostener, mantener.
assess vt valorar.
assessment n valoración f.

assets npl bienes mpl.
assign vt asignar.
assimilate vt asimilar.
assist vt asistir, ayudar.
assistance n asistencia f.
assistant n asistente, ayudante m.
associate vt asociar.
association n asociación, sociedad f.
assortment n surtido m.
assume vt asumir; suponer.
assurance n seguro m.
assure vt asegurar.
asterisk n asterisco m.
asthma n asma f.
asthmatic adj asmático/ca.
astonish vt pasmar, sorprender.
astringent adj astringente.
astrologer n astrólogo/ga m/f.
astrology n astrología f.
astronaut n astronauta m/f.
astronomer n astrónomo m.
astronomy n astronomía f.
astute adj astuto/ta.
asylum n asilo, refugio m.
at prep a; en.
atheism n ateísmo m.
atheist n ateo m, atea f.
athlete n atleta m/f.
atlas n atlas m.
atmosphere n atmósfera f.
atom n átomo m.
atomic adj atómico/ca.
atrocious adj atroz.
atrocity n atrocidad, enormidad f.
attach vt adjuntar.
attaché n agregado m.
attack vt atacar; acometer.
attempt vt intentar; probar, experimentar.
attend vt servir; asistir.
attendant n sirviente m.
attention n atención f; cuidado m.
attentive adj atento/ta; cuidadoso/sa.
attest vt atestiguar.
attic n desván m; guardilla f.
attorney n abogado m.
attract vt atraer.
attraction n atracción f; atractivo m.
auburn adj moreno/na, castaño/ña.
auction n subasta f.
auctioneer n subastador/a.
audacious adj audaz.
audible adj perceptible al oído.
audience n audiencia f.
audit n auditoría f.
augment vt aumentar, acrecentar.
August n agosto m.
august adj augusto/a.

aunt *n* tía *f*.
au pair *n* au pair *f*.
aura *n* aura *f*.
auspicious *adj* propicio/cia.
austere *adj* austero/ra, severo/ra;
authentic *adj* auténtico/ca.
authenticate *vt* autenticar.
authenticity *n* autenticidad *f*.
author *n* autor *m*; escritor *m*.
authorization *n* autorización *f*.
authorize *vt* autorizar.
authority *n* autoridad *f*.
auto *n* carro, coche *m*.
autograph *n* autógrafo *m*.
automatic *adj* automático/ca.
autonomy *n* autonomía *f*.
autopsy *n* autopsia *f*.
auxiliary *adj* auxiliar, asistente.
available *adj* disponible.
avalanche *n* alud *m*.

avarice *n* avaricia *f*.
avenue *n* avenida *f*.
avert *vt* desviar, apartar.
aviary *n* pajarera *f*.
avoid *vt* evitar, escapar.
await *vt* aguardar.
awake *vt* despertar.
award *vt* otorgar:—*n* premio *m*.
aware *adj* consciente; vigilante.
away *adv* ausente, fuera.
awe *n* miedo, temor *m*.
awful *adj* tremendo/da; horroroso/sa.
awhile *adv* un rato, algún tiempo.
awkward *adj* torpe, rudo/da.
awning *n* (*mar*) toldo *m*.
awry *adv* oblicuamente, torcidamente.
axe *n* hacha *f*.
axiom *n* axioma *m*.
axis *n* eje *m*.
axle *n* eje *m*.

B

baboon *n* cinocéfalo *m*.
baby *n* niño pequeño *m*.
bachelor *n* soltero *m*; bachiller *m*.
back *n* dorso *m*.
backbone *n* hueso dorsal, espinazo *m*.
backer *n* partidario/ria *m*.
backgammon *n* juego de chaquete o tablas *m*.
background *n* fondo *m*.
backlash *n* reacción *f*.
backpack *n* mochila *f*.
backside *n* trasero *m*.
backward *adj* tardo/da, lento/ta.
bacon *n* tocino *m*.
bad *adj* mal, malo.
badge *n* señal *f*; símbolo *m*.
badger *n* tejón *m*.
badminton *n* bádminton *m*.
baffle *vt* confundir.
bag *n* saco *m*; bolsa *f*.
baggage *n* bagaje, equipaje *m*.
bail *n* fianza, caución (juratoria) *f*.
bailiff *n* alguacil *m*.
bake *vt* cocer en horno.
bakery *n* panadería *f*.
baking powder *n* levadura *f*.
balance *n* balanza *f*; equilibrio *m*.
balcony *n* balcón *m*.
bald *adj* calvo/va.
ball *n* bola *f*; pelota *f*; baile.
ballad *n* balada *f*.
ballerina *n* bailarina *f*.
ballet *n* ballet *m*.
balloon *n* globo *m*.

ballpoint (pen) *n* bolígrafo *m*.
balm, balsam *n* bálsamo *m*.
balustrade *n* balaustrada *f*.
bamboo *n* bambú *m*.
ban *n* prohibición *f*.
banal *adj* vulgar.
banana *n* plátano *m*.
band *n* faja *f*; cuadrilla *f*.
bandage *n* venda *f*.
bandit *n* bandido/da *m/f*.
bang *n* golpe *m*.
bangle *n* brazalete *m*.
banister(s) *n*(*pl*) pasamanos *m*.
banjo *n* banjo *m*.
bank *n* orilla (de río) *f*; montón de tierra *m*; banco *m*.
bank account *n* cuenta de banco *f*.
bankrupt *adj* insolvente.
banner *n* bandera *f*.
banquet *n* banquete *m*.
baptize *vt* bautizar.
bar *n* bar *m*; barra *f*.
barbecue *n* barbacoa *f*.
barber *n* peluquero *m*.
bare *adj* desnudo/da, descubierto/ta.
barely *adv* apenas.
bargain *n* ganga *f*.
barge *n* barcaza *f*.
bark *n* corteza *f*.
barley *n* cebada *f*.
barn *n* granero *m*.
barometer *n* barómetro *m*.
baron *n* barón *m*.

barracks *npl* cuartel *m*.
barrel *n* barril *m*.
barren *adj* estéril, infructuoso/sa.
barrier *n* barrera *f*; obstáculo *m*.
barter *vi* baratar.
base *n* fondo *m*; base *f*; basa *f*.
baseball *n* béisbol *m*.
basement *n* sótano *m*.
basic *adj* básico/ca.
basin *n* jofaina, bacía *f*.
basis *n* base *f*; fundamento *m*.
basket *n* cesta, canasta *f*.
basketball *n* baloncesto *m*.
bastard *n, adj* bastardo/da *m/f*.
bat *n* murciélago *m*.
batch *n* serie *f*.
bath *n* baño *m*.
bathe *vt* (*vi*) bañar(se).
bathing suit *n* traje de baño *m*.
bathroom *n* (cuarto de) baño *m*.
baths *npl* piscina *f*.
battery *n* batería *f*.
battle *n* combate *m*.
bawdy *adj* indecente.
bay *n* bahía *f*; laurel.
bazaar *n* bazar *m*.
be *vi* ser; estar.
beach *n* playa, orilla *f*.
beacon *n* almenara *f*.
beagle *n* sabueso *m*.
beak *n* pico *m*.
beam *n* rayo de luz *m*; travesaño *m*.
bean *n* haba *f*.
beansprouts *npl* brotes de soja *mpl*.
bear *vt* llevar alguna cosa como carga; sostener; soportar.
bear *n* oso *m*.
beard *n* barba *f*.
bearer *n* portador/a *m/f*.
beast *n* bestia *f*.
beat *vt* golpear; tocar (un tambor).
beatify *vt* beatificar, santificar.
beautiful *adj* hermoso/sa, bello.
beauty *n* hermosura, belleza *f*.
because *conj* porque, a causa de.
bed *n* cama *f*.
bedroom *n* dormitorio *m*.
bee *n* abeja *f*.
beech *n* haya *f*.
beef *n* carne de vaca *f*.
beefburger *n* hamburguesa *f*.
beefsteak *n* bistec *m*.
beeline *n* línea recta *f*.
beer *n* cerveza *f*.
beetle *n* escarabajo *m*.
befall *vi* suceder, acontecer.
before *adv, prep* antes de; delante.

beg *vt* mendigar.
beggar *n* mendigo/ga *m/f*.
begin *vt vi* comenzar, empezar.
beginning *n* principio *m*.
begrudge *vt* envidiar.
behave *vi* comportarse.
behind *prep* detrás; atrás.
beige *adj* color beige.
belch *vi* eructar.
belief *n* fe, creencia *f*.
believe *vt* creer.
believer *n* creyente, fiel.
bell *n* campana *f*.
bellows *npl* fuelle *m*.
belly *n* vientre *m*; panza *f*.
belong *vi* pertenecer.
beloved *adj* querido/da, amado/da.
below *adv, prep* debajo, inferior; abajo.
belt *n* cinturón, cinto *m*.
bench *n* banco *m*.
bend *vt* encorvar, inclinar, plegar.
beneath *adv, prep* debajo, abajo.
benefit *n* beneficio *m*; utilidad *f*; provecho *m*.
benevolence *n* benevolencia *f*.
benevolent *adj* benévolo.
benign *adj* benigno/na.
bent *n* inclinación *f*.
bereave *vt* privar.
bereavement *n* perdida *f*.
beret *n* boina *f*.
berry *n* baya *f*.
beset *vt* acosar.
beside(s) *prep* al lado de; excepto.
best *adj* mejor.
bestial *adj* bestial, brutal.
bestow *vt* dar, conferir.
bestseller *n* bestseller *m*.
bet *n* apuesta *f*.
betray *vt* traicionar.
betroth *vt* contraer esponsales.
betting *n* juego *m*.
between *prep* entre, en medio de.
beverage *n* bebida *f*.
beware *vi* guardarse.
bewitch *vt* encantar, hechizar.
beyond *prep* más allá.
bias *n* propensión.
bib *n* babador *m*.
Bible *n* Biblia *f*.
bibliography *n* bibliografía *f*.
bicycle *n* bicicleta *f*.
bid *vt* mandar, ordenar; ofrecer.
biennial *adj* bienal.
bifocals *npl* anteojos bifocales *mpl*.
big *adj* grande, lleno/na.
bigamist *n* bígamo/ma *m/f*.
bigamy *n* bigamia *f*.

bigot n fanático/ca m/f.
bike n bici f.
bikini n bikini m.
bile n bilis f.
bilingual adj bilingüe.
bill n pico de ave m; billete.
billboard n cartelera f.
billet n alojamiento m.
billfold n cartera.
billiards npl billar m.
billion n billón f.
bin n cubo de la basura m.
binder n encuadernador/a m/f.
bingo n bingo m.
binoculars npl prismáticos mpl.
biographer n biógrafo/fa m/f.
biography n biografía f.
biological adj biológico/ca.
biology n biología f.
birch n abedul m.
bird n ave f; pájaro m.
birth n nacimiento m.
birthday n cumpleaños m invar.
biscuit n bizcocho m.
bishop n obispo m.
bit n bocado m; pedacito m.
bitch n perra f.
bite vt morder; picar.
bitter adj amargo/ga.
bitumen n betún m.
bizarre adj raro/ra.
blab vi chismear.
black adj negro/gra, oscuro/ra.
blackberry n zarzamora f.
blackbird n mirlo m.
blackboard n pizarra f.
blackmail n chantaje m:—vt chantajear.
blacksmith n herrero m.
bladder n vejiga f.
blade n hoja f; filo m.
blame vt culpar.
blameless adj inocente.
blank adj blanco/ca.
blanket n manta f.
blaspheme vt blasfemar, jurar.
blasphemy n blasfemia f.
blatant adj obvio.
blaze n llama f.
bleed vi, vt sangrar.
blemish vt manchar.
bless vt bendecir.
blessing n bendición f.
blight vt arruinar.
blind adj ciego/ga.
blink vi parpadear.
bliss n felicidad (eterna) f.
blister n ampolla f.

blitz n bombardeo aéreo m.
blizzard n huracán m.
bloated adj hinchado/da.
blob n gota f.
bloc n bloque m.
block n bloque m; obstáculo m.
blockade n bloqueo m:—vt bloquear.
blond adj rubio/bia.
blood n sangre f.
blood group n grupo sanguíneo m.
blood poisoning n envenenamiento de la sangre. m.
blood pressure n presión de sangre f.
blood sausage n morcilla f.
blood test n análisis de sangre m.
blood transfusion n transfusion de sangre f.
bloom n flor f; (also fig):—vi florecer.
blossom n flor f.
blot vt manchar.
blotchy adj muy manchado/da.
blouse n blusa f.
blow vi soplar; sonar.
blubber n grasa de ballena f.
blue adj azul.
bluebell n campanilla f.
blueprint n (fig) anteproyecto m.
blunder n desatino m.
blunt adj obtuso/sa; grosero/ra.
blush n rubor m; sonrojo m.
boar n verraco m:—**wild ~** jabalí m.
board n tabla f; mesa f.
boarder n pensionista m.
boarding card n tarjeta de embarque f.
boast vi jactarse.
boat n barco m.
bobsleigh n bob m.
bodice n corsé m.
body n cuerpo m; individuo m; gremio m.
body-building n culturismo m.
bodyguard n guardaespaldas m.
boil vi hervir; bullir.
bold adj ardiente, valiente; audaz.
bolt n cerrojo m.
bomb n bomba f.
bond n ligadura f; vinculo m.
bondage n esclavitud, servidumbre f.
bone n hueso m.
bonfire n hoguera f.
bonny adj bonito/ta.
bonus n cuota, prima f.
book n libro m.
bookcase n armario para libros m.
bookmarker n registro m.
bookstore n librería f.
boom n trueno m.
boon n presente, regalo m.
booth n barraca, cabaña f.

booty n botín m; presa f; saqueo m.
border n orilla f; borde m.
borderline n frontera f.
bore vt taladrar; barrenar; fastidiar.
boredom n aburrimiento m.
borrow vt pedir prestado/da.
bosom n seno, pecho m.
boss n jefe m; patrón/ona m/f.
botany n botánica f.
botch vt chapuzar.
both adj ambos.
bother vt preocupar; fastidiar.
bottle n botella f.
bottom n fondo m.
bough n brazo del árbol m; ramo m.
boulder n canto rodado m.
bounce vi rebotar.
bound n límite m; salto m.
boundary n límite m; frontera f.
bouquet n ramillete de flores m.
bourgeois adj burgués.
bout n ataque m.
bow vt encorvar, doblar.
bow n arco m.
bowels npl intestinos mpl.
bowl n taza; bola f.
bow tie n pajarita f.
box n caja, cajita f.
boxer n boxeador m.
boxing n boxeo m.
box office n taquilla f.
boy n muchacho m; niño m.
boycott vt boicotear:—n boicot m.
boyfriend n novio m.
bra n sujetador m.
bracelet n brazalete m.
bracket n puntal m; paréntesis m.
brag n jactancia f:—vi jactarse.
braid n pliegue m, trenza f:—vt trenzar.
brain n cerebro m.
brake n freno m:—vt vi frenar.
hran n salvado m.
branch n ramo m; rama f.
brand n marca f.
brandy n coñac m.
brass n latón m.
brassiere n sujetador m.
brave adj bravo/va, valiente.
bravery n valor m.
brawl n pelea f.
brazier n brasero m.
breach n rotura f.
bread n pan m.
breadth n anchura f.
break vt romper; quebrantar.
breakage n rotura f.
breakfast n desayuno m:—vi desayunar.

breast n pecho, seno m.
breastbone n esternón m.
breath n aliento m, respiración f; soplo de aire m.
breathe vt vi respirar; exhalar.
breathtaking adj pasmoso/sa.
breed n casta, raza f.
breeze n brisa f.
brevity n brevedad, concisión f.
brew vt hacer; tramar, mezclar.
bribe n cohecho, soborno m.
bribery n cohecho, soborno m.
bric-a-brac n baratijas fpl.
brick n ladrillo m.
bricklayer n albañil m.
bride n novia f.
bridegroom n novio m.
bridesmaid n madrina de boda f.
bridge n puente m/f.
brief adj breve, conciso/sa, sucinto/ta.
briefcase n cartera f.
brigade n (mil) brigada f.
bright adj claro/ra, luciente, brillante.
brighten vt pulir, dar lustre.
brilliant adj brillante.
bring vt llevar, traer.
brisk adj vivo/va, alegre, jovial; fresco/ca.
brisket n pecho (de un animal) m.
briskly adj vigorosamente.
bristle n cerda, seta f:—vi erizarse.
bristly adj cerdoso/sa, lleno/na de cerdas.
brittle adj quebradizo, frágil.
broach vt comenzar a hablar de.
broad adj ancho.
broadcast n emisión f.
broadcasting n radiodifusión f.
broaden vt vi ensanchar(se).
broadly adv anchamente.
broad-minded adj tolerante.
brocade n brocado m.
broccoli n brécol m.
brochure n folleto m.
broil vt asar a la parrilla.
broken adj roto/ta.
broker n corredor/a m/f.
bronchial adj bronquial.
bronchitis n bronquitis f.
bronze n bronce m.
brooch n broche m.
brook n arroyo m.
broom n hiniesta f; escoba f.
broth n caldo m.
brothel n burdel m.
brother n hermano m.
brother-in-law n cuñado m.
brow n caja f; frente f; cima f.
browbeat vt intimidar.

brown adj moreno/na; castaño/ña.
browse vt ramonear.
bruise vt magullar.
brunette n morena f.
brunt n choque m.
brush n cepillo m; escobilla f.
brusque adj brusco/ca.
Brussels sprout n col de Bruselas f.
brutal adj brutal.
brutality n brutalidad f.
brute n bruto m.
bubble n burbuja f.
bubblegum n chicle m.
bucket n cubo, pozal m.
buckle n hebilla f.
bucolic adj bucólico/ca.
bud n pimpollo, botón m:—vi brotar.
Buddhism n Budismo m.
buddy n compañero m.
budge vi moverse.
budgerigar n periquito m.
budget n presupuesto m.
buff n entusiasta m.
buffalo n búfalo m.
buffet n buffet m.
buffoon n bufón, chocarrero m.
bug n chinche m.
bugle(horn) n trompa de caza f.
build vt edificar; construir.
building n edificio m; construcción f.
bulb n bulbo m; cebolla f.
bulge vi combarse:—n bombeo m.
bulk n masa f; volumen m.
bulky adj grueso/sa, grande.
bull n toro m.
bulldog n dogo m.
bulldozer n aplanadora f.
bullet n bala f.
bullfight n corrida de toros f.
bullfighter n toreo m.
bullfighting n los toros mpl.
bullion n oro o plata en barras m o f.
bullock n novillo capado m.
bullring n plaza de toros f.
bully n valentón m:—vt tiranizar.
bumblebee n abejorro m.
bump n hinchazón f.
bun n bollo m; mono m.
bunch n ramo m.
bundle n fardo m, haz m.
bung n tapón m.

bungalow n bungalow m.
bunk n litera f.
bunker n refugio m; bunker m.
burden n carga f:—vt cargar.
bureau n armario m; escritorio m.
bureaucracy n burocracia f.
burglar n ladrón m.
burial n enterramiento m; exequias fpl.
burial place n cementerio m.
burly adj corpulento/ta, fornido/da.
burn vt quemar, abrasar, incendiar:—vi arder:
—n quema dura f.
burner n quemador m; mechero m.
burning adj ardiente.
burrow n conejera f.
bursar n tesorero m.
burse n bolsa, lonja f.
burst vi reventar; abrirse.
bury vt enterrar, sepultar; esconder.
bus n autobús m.
bush n arbusto, espinal m.
busily adv diligentemente, apresuradamente.
business n asunto m; negocios mpl.
businessman n hombre de negocios m.
bust n busto m.
bus-stop n parada de autobuses f.
bustle vi hacer ruido.
busy adj ocupado/da; entrometido/da.
busybody n entrometido m.
but conj pero; mas.
butcher n carnicero m.
butcher's (shop) n carnicería f.
butler n mayordomo m.
butter n mantequilla f.
buttercup n (bot) ranúnculo m.
butterfly n mariposa f.
buttocks npl posaderas fpl.
button n botón m.
buttonhole n ojal m.
buttress n estribo m; apoyo m.
buxom adj frescachona.
buy vt comprar.
buzz n susurro, zumbido m:—vi zumbar.
buzzard n ratonero común m.
buzzer n timbre m.
by prep por; a, en; de; cerca, al lado de.
bypass n carretera de circunvalación f.
by-product n derivado m.
bystander n mirador m.
byte n (comput) byte m.
byword n proverbio, refrán m.

C

cab n taxi m.
cabbage n berza, col f.

cabin n cabaña.
cabinet n consejo á ministros m; gabinete m.

cable *n* (*mar*) cable *m*.
cable car *n* teleférico *m*.
cactus *n* cacto *m*.
cadaver *n* cadáver *m*.
cadet *n* cadete *m*.
cadge *vt* mangar.
cafeteria *n* cantina *f*.
cage *n* jaula *f*.
cake *n* bollo *m*; tortita *f*.
calculate *vt* calcular.
calculator *n* calculadora *f*.
calendar *n* calendario *m*.
calf *n* ternero *m*.
call *vt* llamar, nombrar.
calligraphy *n* caligrafía *f*.
callous *adj* calloso/sa.
calm *n* calma, tranquilidad.
calorie *n* caloría *f*.
Calvinist *n* calvinista *m*.
camel *n* camello *m*.
cameo *n* camafeo *m*.
camera *n* máquina fotográfica *f*.
camomile *n* manzanilla *f*.
camouflage *n* camuflaje *m*.
camp *n* campo *m*.
campaign *n* campana *f*.
camping *n* camping *m*.
campsite *n* camping *m*.
can *vi* poder:—*n* lata *f*.
canal *n* estanque *m*; canal *m*.
cancel *vt* cancelar; anular.
cancer *n* cáncer *m*.
Cancer *n* Cáncer *m* (signo del zodiaco).
candid *adj* cándido/da, sencillo/lla.
candle *n* candela *f*; vela *f*.
candlestick *n* candelero *m*.
candy *n* caramelo *m*.
cane *n* cana *f*; bastón *m*.
cannabis *n* canabis *f*.
cannibal *n* caníbal *m*.
cannibalism *n* canibalismo *m*.
cannon *n* cañón *m*.
canoe *n* canoa *f*.
canon *n* canon *m*; regla *f*.
can opener *n* abrelatas *m invar*.
canopy *n* dosel, pabellón *m*.
canter *n* medio galope *m*.
canvas *n* cañamazo *m*.
canyon *n* cañón *m*.
cap *n* gorra *f*.
capability *n* capacidad *f*.
capable *adj* capaz.
cape *n* cabo, promontorio *m*.
capital *adj* capital; principal.
capitalism *n* capitalismo *m*.
Capitol *n* Capitolio *m*.
capitulate *vi* capitular.

Capricorn *n* Capricornio *m* (signo del zodiaco).
capsule *n* cápsula *f*.
captain *n* capitán *m*.
captivate *vt* cautivar.
capture *n* captura *f*; presa *f*.
car *n* coche, carro *m*; vagón *m*.
carafe *n* garrafa *f*.
caramel *n* caramelo *m*.
carat *n* quilate *m*.
carbohydrates *npl* hidratos de carbono *mpl*.
carcass *n* cadáver *m*.
card *n* naipe *m*; carta *f*.
cardboard *n* cartón *m*.
cardinal *adj* cardinal, principal.
care *n* cuidado *m*; solicitud *f*.
career *n* carrera *f*.
caress *n* caricia *f*.
caretaker *n* portero *m*.
cargo *n* cargamento de navío *m*.
caricature *n* caricatura *f*.
carnal *adj* carnal; sensual.
carnation *n* clavel *m*.
carnival *n* carnaval *m*.
carpenter *n* carpintero *m*.
carpentry *n* carpintería *f*.
carpet *n* alfombra *f*.
carrier *n* portador *m*.
carrot *n* zanahoria *f*.
carry *vt* llevar, conducir.
cart *n* carro *m*; carreta *f*.
cartilage *n* cartílago *m*.
carton *n* caja *f*.
cartoon *n* dibujo animado *m*.
carve *vt* cincelar.
carving *n* escultura *f*.
case *n* caja *f*; maleta *f*.
cash *n* dinero contante *m*.
cashmere *n* cachemira *f*.
cask *n* barril, tonel *m*.
casserole *n* cazuela *f*.
cassette *n* cassette *m*.
cassock *n* sotana *f*.
castanets *npl* castañetas *fpl*.
castaway *n* réprobo *m*.
caste *n* casta *f*.
castigate *vt* castigar.
castle *n* castillo *m*.
castrate *vt* castrar.
castration *n* capadura *f*.
casual *adj* casual.
cat *n* gato *m*; gata *f*.
catalog(ue) *n* catalogo *m*.
cataract *n* cascada *f*; catarata *f*.
catarrh *n* catarro *m*; reuma *f*.
catastrophe *n* catástrofe *f*.
catch *vt* coger.

catchphrase n lema m.
catechism n catecismo m.
categorize vt clasificar.
category n categoría f.
caterpillar n oruga f.
cathedral n catedral f.
catholic adj, n católico m.
Catholicism n catolicismo m.
cattle n ganado m.
cauliflower n coliflor f.
cause n causa f; razón f; motivo m.
causeway n arrecife m.
caustic adj, n cáustico m.
cauterize vt cauterizar.
caution n prudencia.
cavalry n caballería f.
cave n caverna f.
caviar n caviar m.
cease vt parar, suspender.
cedar n cedro m.
cede vt ceder.
ceiling n techo m.
celebrate vt celebrar.
celery n apio m.
celibacy n celibato m.
cell n celdilla f; célula f; cueva f.
cellar n sótano m.
cellophane n celofán m.
cement n cemento.
cemetery n cementerio m.
cenotaph n cenotafio m.
censor n censor m.
census n censo m.
cent n centavo m.
center n centro m.
centigrade n centígrado m.
centiliter n centilitro m.
centimeter n centímetro m.
centipede n escolopendra f.
central adj central.
centralize vt centralizar.
century n siglo m.
ceramic adj cerámico/ca.
ceremony n ceremonia f.
certain adj cierto/ta, evidente.
certificate n certificado, testimonio m.
certify vt certificar, afirmar.
cervical adj cervical.
chaffinch n pinzón m.
chain n cadena f.
chair n silla f.
chamber n cámara f.
chameleon n camaleón m.
champagne n champaña m.
championship n campeonato m.
chance n ventura, suerte f; oportunidad f.
chancellor n canciller m.

change vt cambiar.
channel n canal m.
chant n canto (llano) m.
chaos n caos m.
chapel n capilla f.
chaplain n capellán m.
chapter n capitulo m.
character n carácter m.
charcoal n carbón de leña m.
charge vt cargar; acusar, imputar.
charity n caridad.
charlatan n charlatán/tana m/f.
charm n encanto m.
charter flight n vuelo charter m.
chauffeur n chófer m.
chauvinist n machista m.
cheap adj barato/ta.
cheat vt engañar, defraudar.
check n cheque m.
checkmate n mate m.
checkout n caja f.
cheek n mejilla f.
cheese n queso m.
chef n jefe de cocina m.
chemical adj químico/ca.
chemist n químico m.
cheroot n puro m.
cherry n cereza f.
cherub n querubín m.
chess n ajedrez m.
chest n pecho m.
chestnut n castaña f.
chew vt mascar, masticar.
chewing gum n chicle m.
chicken n pollo m.
chickenpox n varicela f.
chickpea n garbanzo m.
chief adj principal.
chilblain n sabañón m.
child n niño m; niña f.
childhood n infancia, niñez f.
children npl de child niños mpl.
chimney n chimenea f.
chimpanzee n chimpancé m.
chin n barbilla f.
chiropodist n pedicuro m.
chirp vi chirriar.
chlorine n cloro m.
chloroform n cloroformo m.
chocolate n chocolate m.
choice n elección, preferencia f.
choir n coro m.
choke vt sofocar.
cholera n cólera m.
choose vt escoger, elegir.
chop vt tajar, cortar:—n chuleta f.
chore n faena f.

Christ n Cristo m.
christen vt bautizar.
Christianity n cristianismo m; cristiandad f.
Christmas n Navidad f.
chrome n cromo m.
chronicle n crónica f.
chronological adj cronológico/ca.
chubby adj gordo/da.
chunk n trozo m.
church n iglesia f.
churchyard n cementerio m.
cider n sidra f.
cigar n cigarro m.
cigarette n cigarrillo m.
cinder n carbonilla f.
cinema n cine m.
cinnamon n canela f.
circle n círculo m.
circumcize vt circuncidar.
circumcision n circuncisión f.
circumference n circunferencia f; circuito m.
circumflex n acento circunflejo m.
circumstance n circunstancia.
circus n circo m.
cistern n cisterna f.
cite vt citar.
citizen n ciudadano m.
city n ciudad f.
civic adj cívico/ca.
civil adj civil, cortés.
civilization n civilización f.
clairvoyant n clarividente m/f.
clam n almeja f.
clammy adj viscoso/sa.
clamor n clamor m.
clan n familia, tribu, raza f.
clandestine adj clandestino/na.
clap vt aplaudir.
claret n clarete m.
clarify vt clarificar, aclarar.
clarinet n clarinete m.
clarity n claridad f.
class n clase f; orden f.
classic(al) adj clásico/ca:—n autor clásico m.
classify vt clasificar.
classmate n compañero de clase m.
classroom n aula f.
clause n cláusula f.
claw n garra f.
clay n arcilla f.
clean adj limpio/pia; casto/ta:—vt limpiar.
cleanse vt limpiar, purificar; purgar.
clear adj claro/ra.
clemency n clemencia f.
clement adj clemente, benigno/na.
clergy n clero m.
clerical adj clerical, eclesiástico/ca.

clerk n dependiente m; oficinista m.
clever adj listo/ta; hábil.
client n cliente m/f.
cliff n acantilado m.
climate n clima m.
climax n clímax m.
climb vt escalar, trepar.
cling vi colgar, adherirse.
clinic n clínica f.
clip vt cortar.
clique n camarilla f.
cloak n capa f.
cloakroom n guardarropa m.
clock n reloj m.
clog n zueco m.
cloister n claustro, monasterio m.
close vt cerrar; concluir, terminar.
closet n armario m.
close-up n primer plano m.
clot n grumo m; embolia f.
cloth n paño m.
clothe vt vestir.
clothes npl ropa f.
clothes pin n pinza f.
cloud n nube f.
clout n tortazo m.
clove n clavo m.
clover n trébol m.
clown n payaso m.
coach n autocar, autobús m.
coagulate vt coagular, cuajar.
coal n carbón m.
coalition n coalición, confederación f.
coarse adj basto/ta; grosero/ra.
coast n costa f.
coastguard n guardacostas m invar.
coat n chaqueta f; abrigo m.
coat hanger n percha f.
cobbler n zapatero m.
cobweb n telaraña f.
cocaine n cocaína f.
cock n gallo m; macho m.
cockle n caracol de mar m.
cockpit n cabina f.
cockroach n cucaracha f.
cocktail n cóctel m.
cocoa n coco m; cacao m.
coconut n coco m.
cod n bacalao m.
code n código m.
cod-liver oil n aceite de hígado de bacalao m.
coffee n café m.
coffer n cofre m; caja f.
coffin n ataúd m.
cog n diente (de rueda) m.
cognac n coñac m.
cogwheel n rueda dentada f.

cohabit *vi* cohabitar.
coherence *n* coherencia *f*.
cohesion *n* coherencia *f*.
cohesive *adj* cohesivo.
coil *n* rollo *m*.
coin *n* moneda *f*.
coincide *vi* coincidir.
coke *n* coque *m*.
colander *n* colador, pasador *m*.
cold *adj* frío/ría.
cold sore *n* herpes labial *m*.
coleslaw *n* ensalada de col *f*.
colic *n* cólico *m*.
collaborate *vt* cooperar.
collapse *vi* hundirse.
collapsible *adj* plegable.
collar *n* cuello *m*.
collarbone *n* clavícula *f*.
collate *vt* comparar.
collateral *adj* colateral.
colleague *n* colega *m*.
collect *vt* recoger; coleccionar.
collection *n* colección *f*; compilación *f*.
college *n* colegio *m*.
collide *vi* chocar.
colloquial *adj* familiar.
collusion *n* colusión *f*.
colon *n* dos puntos *mpl*; (*med*) colon *m*.
colonel *n* (*mil*) coronel *m*.
colonial *adj* colonial.
colonize *vt* colonizar.
colony *n* colonia *f*.
color *n* color *m*.
colossal *adj* colosal.
colt *n* potro *m*.
column *n* columna *f*.
columnist *n* columnista *m*.
coma *n* coma *f*.
comatose *adj* comatoso/sa.
comb *n* peine *m*:—*vt* peinar.
combat *n* combate *m*.
combination *n* combinación *f*.
combine *vt* combinar.
combustion *n* combustión *f*.
come *vi* venir.
comedy *n* comedia *f*.
comet *n* cometa *m*.
comfort *n* confort *m*.
comfortable *adj* cómodo/da.
comma *n* (*gr*) coma *f*.
command *vt* comandar.
commemorate *vt* conmemorar; celebrar.
commence *vt, vi* comenzar.
commencement *n* principio *m*.
commend *vt* encomendar.
commensurate *adj* proporcionado/da.
comment *n* comentario *m*.

commentator *n* comentador *m*.
commerce *n* comercio *m*.
commercial *adj* comercial.
commiserate *vt* compadecer.
commission *n* comisión *f*.
commit *vt* cometer.
committee *n* comité *m*.
commodity *n* comodidad *f*.
common *adj* común.
commotion *n* tumulto *m*.
communicate *vt* comunicar.
communion *n* comunión *f*.
communism *n* comunismo *m*.
community *n* comunidad *f*.
commute *vt* conmutar.
compact *adj* compacto/ta.
compact disc *n* disco compacto *m*.
companion *n* compañero/ra.
company *n* compañía, sociedad *f*.
compare *vt* comparar.
compartment *n* compartimiento *m*.
compass *n* brújula *f*.
compassion *n* compasión *f*.
compatriot *n* compatriota *m*.
compensate *vt* compensar.
compensation *n* compensación *f*.
compère *n* presentador *m*.
compete *vi* concurrir.
competent *adj* competente.
competition *n* competencia *f*.
competitor *n* competidor, rival *m*.
compilation *n* compilación *f*.
complain *vi* quejarse, lamentarse.
complement *n* complemento *m*.
complex *adj* complejo/ja.
complexion *n* tez *f*; aspecto *m*.
complicate *vt* complicar.
component *adj* componente.
compose *vt* componer.
composer *n* autor *m*.
composite *adj* compuesto/ta.
composition *n* composición *f*.
comprehend *vt* comprender, contener; entender.
compress *vt* comprimir.
comprise *vt* comprender.
compromise *n* compromiso *m*.
compulsive *adj* compulsivo/va.
computer *n* ordenador *m*.
comrade *n* camarada *m*.
con *vt* estafar:—*n* estafa *f*.
concave *adj* cóncavo/va.
conceal *vt* ocultar, esconder.
concede *vt* conceder.
conceit *n* concepto *m*, capricho *m*.
conceive *vt* concebir, comprender.
concentrate *vt* concentrar.

concept n concepto m.
conception n concepción f.
concern vt concernir, importar.
concert n concierto m.
concession n concesión f; privilegio m.
concise adj conciso/sa.
conclude vt concluir.
conclusion n conclusión.
concord n concordia, armonía f.
concrete n concreto m.
concussion n concusión f.
condemn vt condenar.
condensation n condensación f.
condiment n condimento m; salsa f.
condition vt condicionar.
conditional adj condicional.
condom n condón m.
conduct n conducta f.
conductor n conductor m.
conduit n conducto m.
cone n cono m.
confection n confitura f.
confectioner's (shop) n pastelería f.
conference n conferencia f.
confess vt, vi confesar(se).
confession n confesión f.
confessional n confesionario m.
confetti n confeti m.
confidant n confidente.
confide vt, vi confiar; fiarse.
confidence n confianza, seguridad f.
confident adj cierto/ta, seguro/ra; confiado/da.
confine vt limitar; aprisionar.
confirm vt confirmar; ratificar.
confiscate vt confiscar.
conflagration n conflagración f.
conflict n conflicto m; combate m; pelea f.
conflicting adj contradictorio/ria.
confluence n confluencia f.
conform vt, vi conformar(se).
conformity n conformidad f.
confound vt turbar, confundir.
confront vt afrontar; confrontar.
confrontation n enfrentamiento m.
confuse vt confundir.
congeal vt, vi helar, congelar(se).
congenial adj congenial.
congenital adj congénito/ta.
congested adj atestado/da.
congestion n congestión f; acumulación f.
congratulate vt congratular, felicitar.
congratulations npl felicidades fpl.
congratulatory adj congratulatorio/ria.
congregate vt congregar.
congress n congreso m; conferencia f.
congruity n congruencia f.
coniferous adj (bot) conífero/ra.

conjecture n conjetura.
conjugal adj conyugal.
conjugate vt (gr) conjugar.
conjunction n conjunción f.
conjuncture n coyuntura f.
conjure vi conjurar.
con man n timador m.
connect vt juntar, unir.
connection n conexión f.
connivance n connivencia f.
connive vi tolerar.
connoisseur n conocedor/a m/f.
conquer vt conquistar; vencer.
conqueror n vencedor/a, conquistador/a m/f.
conquest n conquista f.
conscience n conciencia f.
consciousness n conciencia f.
conscript n conscripto m.
conscription n reclutamiento m.
consecrate vt consagrar.
consecration n consagración f.
consecutive adj consecutivo/va.
consensus n consenso m.
consent n consentimiento m; aprobación f.
consequence n consecuencia f.
consequent adj consecutivo/va.
conservation n conservación f.
conservative adj conservativo/va.
conservatory n conservatorio m.
conserve vt conservar.
consider vt considerar.
considerable adj considerable.
considerate adj considerado/da.
consideration n consideración f.
consign vt consignar.
consignment n consignación f.
consist vi consistir.
consistency n consistencia f.
consistent adj consistente.
consolation n consolación f; consuelo m.
console vt consolar.
consolidate vt, vi consolidar(se).
consolidation n consolidación f.
consonant adj consonante.
consort n consorte, socio m.
conspicuous adj conspicuo/cua.
conspiracy n conspiración f.
conspirator n conspirador/a m/f.
conspire vi conspirar.
constancy n constancia f.
constant adj constante.
constellation n constelación f.
constipated adj estreñido/da.
constituency n junta electoral f.
constituent n constitutivo m.
constitute vt constituir.
constitution n constitución f.

constitutional *adj* constitucional.
constrict *vt* constreñir, estrechar.
construct *vt* construir, edificar.
construction *n* construcción *f*.
consul *n* cónsul *m*.
consulate, consulship *n* consulado *m*.
consult *vt*, *vi* consultar(se).
consultation *n* consulta *f*.
consume *vt* consumir.
consumer *n* consumidor/a *m/f*.
consumption *n* consumo *m*.
contact *n* contacto *m*.
contact lenses *npl* lentes de contacto *mpl*.
contagious *adj* contagioso/sa.
contain *vt* contener.
container *n* recipiente *m*.
contaminate *vt* contaminar.
contamination *n* contaminación *f*.
contemplate *vt* contemplar.
contemplation *n* contemplación *f*.
contempt *n* desprecio, desdén *m*.
contend *vi* contender.
content *adj* contento/ta, satisfecho/cha.
contention *n* contención, altercación *f*.
contest *vt* contestar, disputar, litigar.
contestant *n* concursante/ta *m/f*.
context *n* contexto *m*.
continent *adj* continente.
contingency *n* contingencia *f*.
contingent *n* contingente *m*; cuota *f*.
continue *vt* continuar.
contort *vt* torcer.
contortion *n* contorsión *f*.
contour *n* contorno *m*.
contraband *n* contrabando *m*.
contraception *n* contracepción *f*.
contraceptive *n* anticonceptivo *m*.
contract *vt* contraer; abreviar; contratar.
contraction *n* contracción *f*; abreviatura *f*.
contradict *vt* contradecir.
contradiction *n* contradicción, oposición *f*.
contraption *n* artilugio *m*.
contrary *adj* contrario/ria, opuesto/ta.
contrast *n* contraste *m*.
contrasting *adj* opuesto/ta.
contributary *adj* contributario/ria.
contribute *vt* contribuir, ayudar.
contrive *vt* inventar, trazar.
control *n* control *m*; inspección *f*:—*vt* controlar; manejar; restringir; gobernar.
controversial *adj* polémico/ca.
controversy *n* controversia *f*.
conurbation *n* urbanización *f*.
convalesce *vi* convalecer.
convalescence *n* convalecencia *f*.
convene *vt* convocar; juntar, unir.
convenient *adj* conveniente.

convent *n* convento *m*.
convention *n* convención *f*.
converge *vi* converger.
conversation *n* conversación *f*.
converse *vi* conversar; platicar.
conversely *adv* mutuamente, recíprocamente.
convert *vt*, *vi* convertir(se).
convertible *adj* convertible.
convex *adj* convexo/xa.
convey *vt* transportar; transmitir, transferir.
conveyance *n* transporte *m*.
conveyancer *n* notario *m*.
conviction *n* convicción *f*.
convince *vt* convencer.
convivial *adj* sociable; hospitalario/ria.
convoke *vt* convocar, reunir.
convoy *n* convoy *m*.
convulse *vt* conmover, convulsionar.
convulsion *n* convulsión *f*.
convulsive *adj* convulsivo/va.
cook *n* cocinero *m*; cocinera *f*:—*vt* cocinar.
cool *adj* fresco/ca; indiferente.
cooperate *vi* cooperar.
cooperation *n* cooperación *f*.
coordinate *vt* coordinar.
coordination *n* coordinación *f*.
cop *n* (*fam*) poli *m*.
copier *n* copiadora *f*.
copious *adj* copioso/sa, abundante.
copper *n* cobre *m*.
copulate *vi* copularse.
copy *n* copia *f*.
copying machine *n* copiadora *f*.
coral *n* coral *m*.
cord *n* cuerda *f*; cable *m*.
cordial *adj* cordial.
corduroy *n* pana *f*.
core *n* cuesco *m*; interior *m*.
cork *n* alcornoque *m*; corcho *m*.
corkscrew *n* tirabuzón *m*.
corn *n* maíz *m*; grano *m*; callo *m*.
corncob *n* mazorca *f*.
cornea *n* córnea *f*.
corner *n* rincón *m*; esquina *f*.
cornet *n* corneta *f*.
cornflakes *npl* copos de maíz *mpl*.
cornice *n* cornisa *f*.
coronary *n* infarto *m*.
coronation *n* coronación *f*.
coroner *n* oficial que hace la inspección jurídica de los cadáveres *m*.
corporation *n* corporación *f*.
corps *n* cuerpo (de ejercito) *m*.
correct *vt* corregir; enmendar.
correctness *n* exactitud *f*.
correspond *vi* corresponder.
correspondence *n* correspondencia *f*.

corridor n pasillo m.
corrode vt corroer.
corrosive adj, n corrosivo m.
corrupt vt corromper; sobornar.
corruption n corrupción f; depravación f.
corset n corsé m.
cosily adv cómodamente.
cosmetic adj cosmético/ca.
cosmic adj cósmico/ca.
cosmonaut n cosmonauta m.
cosmopolitan adj cosmopolita.
cosset vt mimar.
cost n coste, precio m:—vi costar.
costume n traje m.
cosy adj cómodo/da.
cottage n casita, casucha f.
cotton n algodón m.
cotton wool n algodón hidrófilo m.
couch n sofá m.
couchette n litera f.
cough n tos f:—vi toser.
council n concilio, consejo m.
counsel n consejo, aviso m.
count vt contar, numerar; calcular.
counter n mostrador m; ficha f.
counterfeit vt contrahacer, imitar, falsear.
counterpart n parte correspondiente f.
countersign vt refrendar.
countess n condesa f.
countless adj innumerable.
countrified adj rústico/ca.
country n país m; campo m; región f; patria f.
county n condado m.
coup n golpe m.
couple n par m.
couplet n copla f; par m.
coupon n cupón m.
courage n coraje, valor f.
courageous adj corajudo/da, valeroso/sa:—
~**ly** adv valerosamente.
courier n correo, mensajero/ra m/f, expreso m.
course n curso m, carrera f; camino m; ruta f.
court n corte f.
courteous adj cortés.
courtesy n cortesía f.
courthouse n palacio de justicia m.
courtyard n patio m.
cousin n primo m; prima f.
cove n (mar) ensenada, caleta f.
covenant n contrato m.
cover n cubierta f; abrigo m.
cover letter n carta de explicación f.
covert adj cubierto/ta; oculto/ta, secreto/ta.
cover-up n encubrimiento m.
covet vt codiciar.
cow n vaca f.
coward n cobarde m/f.

cowardice n cobardía, timidez f.
cowboy n vaquero m.
cower vi agacharse.
cowherd n vaquero m.
crab n cangrejo m.
crab apple n manzana silvestre f.
crack n crujido m; hendedura, quebraja f.
cracker n buscapiés m invar; galleta f.
crackle vi crujir, chillar.
cradle n cuna f.
craft n arte.
craftsman n artífice, artesano m.
craftsmanship n artesanía f.
crafty adj astuto/ta, artificioso/sa.
cramp n calambre m.
cranberry n arandilla f.
crane n grulla f; grua f.
crash vi estallar.
crash helmet n casco m.
crass adj craso/sa.
crater n cráter m; boca de volcán f.
cravat n pañuelo m.
crave vt rogar, suplicar.
craving adj insaciable.
crawl vi arrastrar.
crayfish n cangrejo de río m.
crayon n lápiz m.
craze n manía f.
craziness n locura f.
crazy adj loco/ca.
cream n crema f.
creamy adj cremoso.
crease n pliegue m.
create vt crear; causar.
creation n creación f; elección f.
creator n creador/a m/f.
creature n criatura f.
credence n creencia, fe f.
credibility n credibilidad f.
credible adj creíble.
credit n crédito m.
creditable adj estimable.
credit card n tarjeta de crédito f.
creed n credo m.
creek n arroyo, río m.
creep vi arrastrar, serpear.
creeper n (bot) enredadera f.
cremate vt incinerar cadáveres.
cremation n cremación f.
crematorium n crematorio m.
crescent adj creciente.
cress n berro m.
crest n cresta f.
crevasse n grieta (de glaciar) f.
crevice n raja, hendedura f.
crew n banda, tropa f.
crib n cuna f; pesebre m.

cricket *n* grillo *m*; criquet *m*.
crime *n* crimen *m*.
criminal *adj* criminal.
crimson *adj, n* carmesí *m*.
cripple *n, adj* cojo/ja *m/f*.
crisis *n* crisis *f*.
crisp *adj* crujiente.
crispness *n* encrespadura *f*.
criss-cross *adj* entrelazado/da.
criterion *n* criterio *m*.
critic *n* crítico *m*; crítica *f*.
criticize *vt* criticar, censurar.
crochet *n* ganchillo *m*.
crockery *n* loza *fl*.
crocodile *n* cocodrilo *m*.
crook *n* (*fam*) ladrón *m*.
crooked *adj* torcido/da; perverso/sa.
cross *n* cruz *f*.
crossbar *n* travesaño *m*.
crossbreed *n* raza cruzada *f*.
cross-country *n* carrera a campo traviesa *f*.
crossing *n* cruce *m*; paso a nivel *m*.
cross-reference *n* contrarreferencia *f*.
crotch *n* entrepierna *f*.
crouch *vi* agacharse, bajarse.
crow *n* cuervo *m*.
crowd *n* publico *m*.
crown *n* corona *f*.
crown prince *n* príncipe real *m*.
crucial *adj* crucial.
crucible *n* crisol *m*.
crucifix *n* crucifijo *m*.
crucifixion *n* crucifixión *f*.
crude *adj* crudo/da, imperfecto/ta.
cruel *adj* cruel.
cruelty *n* crueldad *f*.
cruet *n* vinagrera *f*.
cruiser *n* crucero *m*.
crumb *n* miga *f*.
crumble *vt* desmigajar.
crumple *vt* arrugar.
crunchy *adj* crujiente.
crusade *n* cruzada *f*.
crush *vt* apretar, oprimir.
crust *n* costra *f*; corteza *f*.
crutch *n* muleta *f*.
crux *n* lo esencial.
cry *vt, vi* gritar; exclamar; llorar.
crypt *n* cripta (bóveda subterránea) *f*.
cryptic *adj* enigmático/ca.
crystal *n* cristal *m*.
cub *n* cachorro *m*.
cube *n* cubo *m*.
cuckoo *n* cuclillo, cuco *m*.
cucumber *n* pepino *m*.
cuddle *vt* abrazar.
cudgel *n* garrote, palo *m*.

cue *n* taco (de billar) *m*.
cuff *n* puñada *f*; vuelta *f*.
cull *vt* escoger, elegir.
culminate *vi* culminar.
culpable *adj* culpable.
cult *n* culto *f*.
cultivate *vi* cultivar.
cultivation *n* cultivación *f*.
cultural *adj* cultural.
culture *n* cultura *f*.
cumulative *adj* cumulativo/va.
cunning *adj* astuto/ta; intrigante.
cup *n* taza, jícara *f*; (*bot*) cáliz *m*.
cupboard *n* armario *m*.
curable *adj* curable.
curb *n* freno *m*; bordillo *m*.
curd *n* cuajada *f*.
cure *n* cura *f*; remedio *m*.
curiosity *n* curiosidad *f*; rareza *f*.
curious *adj* curioso/sa:—**~ly** *adv* curiosamente.
curl *n* rizo de pelo *m*.
curly *adj* rizado/da.
currant *n* pasa *f*.
currency *n* moneda *f*.
current *adj* corriente.
current affairs *npl* actualidades *fpl*.
currently *adv* corrientemente; actualmente.
curry *n* curry *m*.
curse *vt* maldecir.
cursor *n* cursor *m*.
curt *adj* sucinto/ta.
curtail *vt* acortar.
curtain *n* cortina *f*; telón (en los teatros) *m*.
curvature *n* curvatura *f*.
curve *vt* encorvar:—*n* curva *f*.
cushion *n* cojín *m*; almohada *f*.
custard *n* natillas *fpl*.
custodian *n* custodio *m*.
custody *n* custodia *f*; prisión *f*.
custom *n* costumbre *f*, uso *m*.
customary *adj* usual, acostumbrado/da, ordinario/ria.
customer *n* cliente *m/f*.
customs *npl* aduana *f*.
customs duty *n* derechos de aduana *mpl*.
customs officer *n* aduanero/ra *m/f*.
cut *vt* cortar; separar.
cutback *n* reducción *f*.
cute *adj* lindo/da.
cutlery *n* cuchillería *f*.
cutlet *n* chuleta *f*.
cut-rate *adj* a precio reducido.
cut-throat *n* asesino *m*:—*adj* encarnizado/da.
cutting *n* cortadura *f*:—*adj* cortante; mordaz.
cyanide *n* cianuro *m*.

cycle *n* ciclo *m*; bicicleta *f*:—*vi* ir en bicicleta.
cycling *n* ciclismo *m*.
cyclist *n* ciclista *m/f*.
cyclone *n* ciclón *m*.
cygnet *n* pollo del cisne *m*.
cylinder *n* cilindro *m*; rollo *m*.
cylindric(al) *adj* cilíndrico/ca.

cymbals *n* címbalo *m*.
cynic(al) *adj* cínico/ca; obsceno/na: —*n* cínico *m* (*filósofo*).
cynicism *n* cinismo *m*.
cypress *n* ciprés *m*.
cyst *n* quiste *m*.
czar *n* zar *m*.

D

dad(dy) *n* papá *m*.
daddy-long-legs *n* típula *m*.
daffodil *n* narciso *m*.
dagger *n* puñal *m*.
daily *adj* diario/ria.
dainty *adj* delicado/da.
dairy *n* lechería *f*.
dairy produce *n* productos lácteos *mpl*.
daisy *n* margarita *f*.
damage *n* daño *m*; perjuicio *m*.
damask *n* damasco *m*.
damn *vt* condenar.
damnation *n* perdición *f*.
damp *adj* húmedo/da.
dampen *vt* mojar.
dampness *n* humedad *f*.
dance *n* danza *f*; baile *m*.
dandelion *n* diente de león *m*.
dandruff *n* caspa *f*.
danger *n* peligro *m*.
dare *vi* atreverse.
daredevil *n* atrevido *m*.
dark *adj* oscuro/ra.
darling *n, adj* querido *m*.
darn *vt* zurcir.
dart *n* dardo *m*.
dartboard *n* diana *f*.
dash *vi* irse de prisa.
dashboard *n* tablero de instrumentos *m*.
data *n* datos *mpl*.
database *n* base de datos *f*.
date *n* fecha *f*; cita *f*.
daughter *n* hija *f*:—~ in-law nuera *f*.
dawn *n* alba *f*:—*vi* amanecer.
day *n* día *m*.
dazzle *vt* deslumbrar.
deacon *n* diácono *m*.
dead *adj* muerto/ta.
deadline *n* fecha tope *f*.
deadlock *n* punto muerto *m*.
deaf *adj* sordo/da.
deal *n* convenio *m*; transacción *f*.
dean *n* deán *m*.
dear *adj* querido/da. caro/ra.
dearness *n* carestía *f*.
death *n* muerte *f*.

debacle *n* desastre *m*.
debar *vt* excluir.
debase *vt* degradar.
debate *n* debate *m*; polémica *f*.
debilitate *vt* debilitar.
debt *n* deuda *f*.
decade *n* década *f*.
decadence *n* decadencia *f*.
decaffeinated *adj* descafeinado/da.
decay *vi* decaer; pudrirse.
deceit *n* engaño *m*.
deceive *vt* engañar.
December *n* diciembre *m*.
decent *adj* decente.
decide *vt, vi* decidir; resolver.
deciduous *adj* (*bot*) de hoja caduca.
decimal *adj* decimal.
decipher *vt* descifrar.
decision *n* decisión.
declare *vt* declarar.
decline *vt* (*gr*) declinar; evitar.
decompose *vt* descomponer.
decorate *vt* decorar, adornar.
decoration *n* decoración *f*.
decorum *n* decoro *m*.
decrease *vt* disminuir.
decree *n* decreto *m*.
dedicate *vt* dedicar; consagrar.
dedication *n* dedicación *f*.
deduce *vt* deducir.
deep *adj* profundo/da.
deep-freeze *n* congeladora *f*.
deer *n* ciervo *m*.
defamation *n* difamación *f*.
defeat *n* derrota *f*:—*vt* derrotar.
defect *n* defecto *m*.
defend *vt* defender.
defense *n* defensa *f*.
defensive *adj* defensivo/va.
defer *vt* aplazar.
deficient *adj* insuficiente.
deficit *n* déficit *m*.
define *vt* definir.
definition *n* definición *f*.
deflate *vt* desinflar.
deflect *vt* desviar.

deform *vt* desfigurar.
defraud *vt* estafar.
defuse *vt* desactivar.
degenerate *vi* degenerar.
degrade *vt* degradar.
degree *n* grado *m*; titulo *m*.
dehydrated *adj* deshidratado/da.
deity *n* deidad, divinidad *f*.
dejection *n* desaliento *m*.
delay *vt* demorar:—*n* retraso *m*.
delegate *vt* delegar:—*n* delegado *m*.
delete *vt* tachar; borrar.
delicacy *n* delicadeza *f*.
delicate *adj* delicado/da.
delicious *adj* delicioso/sa.
delight *n* delicia *f*.
delinquent *n* delincuente *m*.
delirium *n* delirio *m*.
deliver *vt* entregar.
delivery *n* entrega *f*; parto *m*.
delivery truck *n* camioneta *f*.
delude *vt* engañar.
deluge *n* diluvio *m*.
demagog(ue) *n* demagogo *m*.
demand *n* demanda *f*.
demean *vi* rebajarse.
demented *adj* demente.
demise *n* desaparición *f*.
democracy *n* democracia *f*.
democrat *n* demócrata *m/f*.
demolish *vt* demoler.
demon *n* demonio, diablo *m*.
demonstrate *vt* demostrar.
demoralize *vt* desmoralizar.
demote *vt* degradar.
demure *adj* modesto/ta.
den *n* guarida *f*.
denial *n* negación *f*.
denims *npl* vaqueros *mpl*.
denomination *n* valor *m*.
denote *vt* denotar.
denounce *vt* denunciar.
dense *adj* denso/sa.
density *n* densidad *f*.
dental *adj* dental.
dentist *n* dentista *m/f*.
denture *npl* dentadura postiza *f*.
denunciation *n* denuncia *f*.
deny *vt* negar.
deodorant *n* desodorante *m*.
depart *vi* partir(se).
department *n* departamento *m*.
department store *n* gran almacén *m*.
departure lounge *n* sala de embarque *f*.
depend *vi* depender.
depict *vt* pintar, retratar; describir.
deplore *vt* deplorar, lamentar.

deport *vt* deportar.
deposit *vt* depositar.
depositor *n* depositante *m*.
depot *n* depósito *m*.
deprave *vt* depravar.
depravity *n* depravación *f*.
deprecate *vt* lamentar.
depreciate *vi* depreciarse
depreciation *n* depreciación *f*.
depress *vt* deprimir.
depressed *adj* deprimido/da.
depression *n* depresión *f*.
deprivation *n* privación *f*.
deprive *vt* privar.
depth *n* profundidad *f*.
deputation *n* diputación *f*.
deputize *vi* suplir a.
deputy *n* diputado *m*.
derelict *adj* abandonado/da.
deride *vt* burlar.
derision *n* mofa *f*.
derivative *n* derivado *m*.
derive *vt, vi* derivar(se).
derogatory *adj* despectivo/va.
descend *vi* descender.
descendant *n* descendiente *m*.
descent *n* descenso *m*.
describe *vt* describir.
description *n* descripción *f*.
descriptive *adj* descriptivo/va.
desecrate *vt* profanar.
desert *n* desierto *m*.
deserve *vt* merecer.
design *vt* diseñar.
designate *vt* nombrar.
designedly *adv* de propósito.
designer *n* diseñador *m*.
desirable *adj* deseable.
desire *n* deseo *m*.
desk *n* escritorio *m*.
desolate *adj* desierto/ta.
despair *n* desesperación *f*.
desperado *n* bandido *m*.
desperate *adj* desesperado/da.
despise *vt* despreciar.
despite *prep* a pesar de.
despoil *vt* despojar.
despondency *n* abatimiento *m*.
despot *n* déspota *m/f*.
dessert *n* postre *m*.
destination *n* destino *m*.
destine *vt* destinar.
destiny *n* destino *m*; suerte *f*.
destitute *adj* indigente.
destroy *vt* destruir.
destruction *n* destrucción *f*.
detach *vt* separar.

detail *n* detalle *m*.
detain *vt* retener; detener.
detect *vt* detectar.
detection *n* descubrimiento *m*.
detective *n* detective *m/f*.
deter *vt* disuadir.
detergent *n* detergente *m*.
deteriorate *vt* deteriorar.
determination *n* resolución *f*.
determine *vt* determinar.
deterrent *n* fuerza de disuasión *f*.
detest *vt* detestar.
detonate *vi* detonar.
detonation *n* detonación *f*.
detour *n* desviación *f*.
detriment *n* perjuicio *m*.
devaluation *n* devaluación *f*.
devastate *vt* devastar.
develop *vt* desarrollar.
development *n* desarrollo *m*.
deviate *vi* desviarse.
deviation *n* desviación *f*.
device *n* mecanismo *m*.
devil *n* diablo, demonio *m*.
devious *adj* taimado/da.
devise *vt* inventar.
devote *vt* dedicar.
devour *vt* devorar.
devout *adj* devoto/ta.
dew *n* rocío *m*.
dexterity *n* destreza *f*.
diabetes *n* diabetes *f*.
diabetic *n* diabético *m*.
diadem *n* diadema *f*.
diagnosis *n* (*med*) diagnosis *f*.
diagonal *adj*, *n* diagonal (*f*).
diagram *n* diagrama *m*.
dial *n* cuadrante *m*.
dialect *n* dialecto *m*.
dialog(ue) *n* dialogo *m*.
diameter *n* diámetro *m*.
diamond *n* diamante *m*.
diaper *n* pañal *m*.
diaphragm *n* diafragma *m*.
diarrhea *n* diarrea *f*.
diary *n* diario *m*.
dice *npl* dados *mpl*.
dictate *vt* dictar.
dictation *n* dictado *m*.
dictatorship *n* dictadura *f*.
diction *n* dicción *f*
dictionary *n* diccionario *m*.
didactic *adj* didáctico/ca.
die¹ *vi* morir.
die² *n* dado *m*.
diesel *n* diesel *m*.
diet *n* dieta *f*; régimen *m*.

differ *vi* diferenciarse.
difference *n* diferencia *f*.
different *adj* diferente.
difficult *adj* difícil.
dig *vt* cavar.
digest *vt* digerir.
digestion *n* digestión *f*.
digger *n* excavadora *f*.
digit *n* dígito *m*.
digital *adj* digital.
dignity *n* dignidad *f*.
dike *n* dique *m*.
dilate *vt*, *vi* dilatar(se).
dilemma *n* dilema *m*.
dilute *vt* diluir.
dim *adj* turbio/bia.
dimension *n* dimensión, extensión *f*.
diminish *vt*, *vi* disminuir(se).
dimple *n* hoyuelo *m*.
din *n* alboroto *m*.
dine *vi* cenar.
diner *n* café *m*, restaurante (económico) *m*.
dinghy *n* lancha neumática *f*.
dingy *adj* sombrío/ría.
dinner *n* cena *f*.
dinosaur *n* dinosaurio *m*.
diocese *n* diócesis *f*.
dip *vt* mojar.
diphtheria *n* difteria *f*.
diploma *n* diploma *m*.
diplomacy *n* diplomacia *f*.
diplomat *n* diplomático/ca *m/f*.
dire *adj* calamitoso/sa.
direct *adj* directo/ta:—*vt* dirigir.
direction *n* dirección *f*.
directly *adj* directamente.
director *n* director/a *m/f*.
directory *n* guía *f*.
dirt *n* suciedad *f*.
disability *n* incapacidad *f*.
disabled *adj* minusválido/da.
disadvantage *n* desventaja *f*:—*vt* perju-
    dicar.
disagree *vi* no estar de acuerdo.
disappear *vi* desaparecer.
disappoint *vt* decepcionar.
disapprove *vt* desaprobar.
disaster *n* desastre *m*.
disbelieve *vt* desconfiar.
discard *vt* descartar.
discern *vt* discernir, percibir.
discharge *vt* descargar; pagar (una deuda).
disciple *n* discípulo *m*.
discipline *n* disciplina *f*:—*vt* disciplinar.
disclose *vi* revelar.
disco *n* discoteca *f*.
discomfort *n* incomodidad *f*.

discontent *n* descontento *m*:—*adj* malcontento/ta.
discontinue *vi* interrumpir.
discord *n* discordia *f*.
discount *n* descuento *m*; rebaja *f*.
discover *vt* descubrir.
discreet *adj* discreto/ta.
discriminate *vt* distinguir.
discuss *vt* discutir.
discussion *n* discusión *f*.
disease *n* enfermedad *f*.
disembark *vt, vi* desembarcar.
disentangle *vt* desenredar.
disfigure *vt* desfigurar.
disgrace *n* ignominia *f*.
disgruntled *adj* descontento/ta.
disguise *vt* disfrazar.
disgust *n* aversión *f*:—*vt* repugnar.
dish *n* fuente *f*; plato *m*.
disheveled *adj* desarreglado/da.
dishonest *adj* deshonesto/ta.
dishonesty *n* falta de honradez *f*.
dishonor *n* deshonra, ignominia *f*.
dishtowel *n* trapo de fregar *m*.
dishwasher *n* lavaplatos *m*.
disillusion *vt* desilusionar.
disillusioned *adj* desilusionado/da.
disincentive *n* freno *m*.
disinclination *n* aversión *f*.
disinclined *adj* reacio/cia.
disinfect *vt* desinfectar.
disinfectant *n* desinfectante *m*.
disinherit *vt* desheredar.
disintegrate *vi* disgregarse.
disinterested *adj* desinteresado/da.
disjointed *adj* inconexo/xa.
disk *n* disco, disquete *m*.
diskette *n* disco, disquete *m*.
dislike *n* aversión *f*.
dislocate *vt* dislocar.
dislocation *n* dislocación *f*.
dislodge *vt, vi* desalojar.
disloyal *adj* desleal.
disloyalty *n* deslealtad *f*.
dismal *adj* triste.
dismantle *vt* desmontar.
dismay *n* consternación *f*.
dismember *vt* despedazar.
dismiss *vt* despedir.
dismissal *n* despedida *f*.
disobedience *n* desobediencia *f*.
disobedient *adj* desobediente.
disobey *vt* desobedecer.
disorderly *adj* desarreglado/da.
disorganized *adj* desorganizado/da.
disorientated *adj* desorientado/da.
disown *vt* desconocer.

disparage *vt* despreciar.
disparaging *adj* despreciativo/va.
disparity *n* disparidad *f*.
dispassionate *adj* desapasionado/da.
dispatch *vt* enviar.
dispel *vt* disipar.
dispensary *n* dispensario *m*.
dispense *vt* dispensar; distribuir.
disperse *vt* disipersar.
dispirited *adj* desalentado/da.
displace *vt* desplazar.
display *vt* exponer.
displeased *adj* disgustado/da.
displeasure *n* disgusto *m*.
disposable *adj* desechable.
disposal *n* disposición *f*.
dispose *vt* disponer; arreglar.
disposition *n* disposición *f*.
dispossess *vt* desposeer.
disproportionate *adj* desproporcionado/da.
disprove *vt* refutar.
dispute *n* disputa, controversia *f*.
disqualify *vt* incapacitar.
disregard *vt* desatender:—*n* desdén *m*.
disreputable *adj* de mala fama.
disrespectful *adj* irreverente.
disrobe *vt* desnudar.
disrupt *vt* interrumpir.
disruption *n* interrupción *f*.
dissatisfaction *n* descontento/ta.
dissatisfied *adj* insatisfecho/cha.
dissect *vt* disecar.
dissection *n* disección *f*.
dissent *vi* disentir.
dissertation *n* disertación *f*.
dissident *n* disidente *m*.
dissimilar *adj* distinto.
dissolution *n* disolución *f*.
dissolve *vt* disolver.
dissuade *vt* disuadir.
distance *n* distancia *f*:—at a ~ de lejos:—*vt* apartar.
distant *adj* distante.
distillery *n* destilería *f*.
distinct *adj* distinto/ta.
distinction *n* distinción *f*.
distinctive *adj* distintivo/va.
distinguish *vt* distinguir.
distort *vt* retorcer.
distorted *adj* distorsionado/da.
distortion *n* distorción *f*.
distract *vt* distraer.
distracted *adj* distraído/da.
distraction *n* distracción *f*; confusión *f*.
distraught *adj* enloquecido/da.
distress *n* angustia *f*.
distribute *vt* distribuir, repartir.

distribution *n* distribución *f*.
district *n* distrito *m*.
disturb *vt* molestar.
disturbance *n* disturbio *m*.
disturbing *adj* inquietante.
disused *adj* abandonado/da.
ditch *n* zanja *f*.
ditto *adv* ídem.
diuretic *adj* (*med*) diurético/ca.
diver *n* buzo *m*.
diverge *vi* divergir.
diverse *adj* diverso/sa, diferente.
diversion *n* diversión *f*.
diversity *n* diversidad *f*.
divert *vt* desviar; divertir.
divide *vt* dividir:—*vi* dividirse.
divine *adj* divino/na.
divinity *n* divinidad *f*.
divorce *n* divorcio *m*.
DJ *n* pinchadiscos *m*.
do *vt* hacer, obrar.
docile *adj* dócil, apacible.
dockyard *n* (*mar*) astillero *m*.
doctor *n* médico/ca *m/f*.
doctrine *n* doctrina *f*.
document *n* documento *m*.
documentary *adj* documental.
doe *n* gama *f*:—~ **rabbit** coneja *f*.
dog(ue) *n* perro *m*.
do-it-yourself *n* bricolaje *m*.
doll *n* muñeca *f*.
dollar *n* dólar *m*.
dolphin *n* delfín *m*.
dome *n* cúpula *f*.
domestic *adj* doméstico/ca.
domesticity *n* domesticidad *f*.
domicile *n* domicilio *m*.
dominant *adj* dominante.
dominate *vi* dominar.
domineer *vi* dominar.
dominion *n* dominio *m*.
dominoes *npl* domino *m*.
donate *vt* donar.
donation *n* donación *f*.
donkey *n* asno, borrico *m*.
donor *n* donante *m*.
door *n* puerta *f*.
doorbell *n* timbre *m*.
doorman *n* portero *m*.
doormat *n* felpudo *m*.
dormouse *n* lirón *m*.
dose *n* dosis *f*.
dossier *n* expediente *m*.
dot *n* punto *m*.
dote *vi* adorar.
double *adj* doble.
doubly *adj* doblemente.

doubt *n* duda, sospecha *f*.
doubtful *adj* dudoso/sa.
doubtless *adv* sin duda.
dough *n* masa *f*.
douse *vt* apagar.
dove *n* paloma *f*.
dovecot *n* palomar *m*.
dowdy *adj* mal vestido/da.
down *n* plumón *m*; flojel *m*:—*prep* abajo.
downfall *n* ruina *f*.
downhearted *adj* desanimado/da.
downpour *n* aguacero *m*.
downtown *adv* al centro (de la ciudad).
dowry *n* dote *f*.
doze *vi* dormitar.
dozen *n* docena *f*.
dozy *adj* soñoliento/ta.
drab *adj* gris.
draft *n* borrador *m*; quinta *f*; corriente de aire *f*.
dragon *n* dragón *m*.
dragonfly *n* libélula *f*.
drain *vt* desaguar.
drake *n* ánade macho *m*.
drama *n* drama *m*.
dramatic *adj* dramático/ca.
dramatize *vt* dramatizar.
dramatist *n* dramaturgo/ga *m/f*.
drape *vt* cubrir.
drapes *npl* cortinas *fpl*.
drastic *adj* drástico/ca.
draw *vt* tirar; dibujar.
drawback *n* desventaja *f*.
drawer *n* cajón *m*.
drawing *n* dibujo *m*.
drawing room *n* salón *m*.
dread *n* terror, espanto *m*:—*vt* temer.
dreadful *adj* espantoso/sa.
dream *n* sueno *m*:—*vi* sonar.
drench *vt* empapar.
dress *vt* vestir:—*n* vestido *m*.
dresser *n* aparador *m*.
dressing gown *n* bata *f*.
dressing table *n* tocador *m*.
dressmaker *n* modista *f*.
dried *adj* seco/ca.
drill *n* taladro *m*.
drink *vt*, *vi* beber.
drinkable *adj* potable.
drip *vi* gotear.
drive *vt* manejar.
driver *n* conductor *m*.
driveway *n* entrada *f*.
drizzle *vi* lloviznar.
droop *vi* decaer.
drop *n* gota *f*.
drought *n* seguía *f*.

drown *vt* anegar.
drowsiness *n* somnolencia *f*.
drowsy *adj* soñoliento/ta.
drudgery *n* trabajo monótono *m*.
drug *n* droga *f*:—*vt* drogar.
drug addict *n* drogadicto *m*.
drug store *n* farmacia *f*.
drum *n* tambor *m*:—*vi* tocar el tambor.
drummer *n* batería *m*.
drumstick *n* palillo de tambor *m*.
drunk *adj* borracho/cha.
drunkard *n* borracho *m*.
drunkenness *n* borrachera *f*.
dry *adj* seco/ca. * *vt* secar.
dry goods store *n* mercería, camisería *f*.
dry rot *n* podredumbre *f*.
dual *adj* doble.
dubbed *adj* doblado/da.
dubious *adj* dudoso/sa.
duck *n* pato *m*.
duckling *n* patito *m*.
dud *adj* estropeado/da.
due *adj* debido/da.
duel *n* duelo *m*.
duet *n* (*mus*) duo *m*.
dull *adj* lerdo/da. insípido/da.
duly *adv* debidamente; puntualmente.
dumb *adj* mudo/da.
dumbbell *n* pesa *f*.
dumbfounded *adj* pasmado/da.
dummy *n* maniquí *m*; imbécil *m*.

dumpling *n* bola de masa *f*.
dumpy *adj* gordito/ta.
dunce *n* zopenco *m*.
dune *n* duna *f*.
dung *n* estiércol *m*.
dungarees *npl* mono *m*.
dungeon *n* calabozo *m*.
dupe *n* hobo *m*.
duplicity *n* duplicidad *f*.
durability *n* durabilidad *f*.
durable *adj* duradero/ra.
duration *n* duración *f*.
during *prep* mientras, durante el tiempo que.
dusk *n* crepúsculo *m*.
dust *n* polvo *m*.
duster *n* plumero *m*.
dutch courage *n* valor fingido *m*.
duteous *adj* fiel, leal.
dutiful *adj* obediente.
duty *n* deber *m*; obligación *f*.
dwarf *n* enano *m*; enana *f*.
dwell *vi* habitar, morar.
dwelling *n* habitación *f*; domicilio *m*.
dwindle *vi* mermar, disminuirse.
dye *vt* teñir:—*n* tinte *m*.
dynamic *adj* dinámico/ca.
dynamite *n* dinamita *f*.
dynamo *n* dinamo *f*.
dynasty *n* dinastía *f*.
dysentery *n* disentería *f*.
dyspepsia *n* (*med*) dispepsia *f*.

E

each *pn* cada uno, cada una.
eager *adj* entusiasmado/da.
eagle *n* águila *f*.
eaglet *n* aguilucho *m*.
ear *n* oreja *f*.
earache *n* dolor de oídos *m*.
eardrum *n* tímpano (del oído) *m*.
early *adj* temprano/na.
earn *vt* ganar; conseguir.
earnest *adj* serio/ria.
earth *n* tierra *f*.
earthenware *n* loza de barro *f*.
earthquake *n* terremoto *m*.
earthworm *n* lombriz *f*.
earthy *adj* sensual.
earwig *n* tijereta *f*.
ease *n* comodidad *f*; facilidad *f*.
easel *n* caballete *m*.
easily *adv* fácilmente.
east *n* este *m*; oriente *m*.
Easter *n* Pascua de Resurrección *f*.
easterly *adj* del este.

eastern *adj* del este, oriental.
easy *adj* fácil; cómodo/da.
easy chair *n* sillón *m*.
eat *vt* comer.
ebb *n* reflujo *m*.
ebony *n* ébano *m*.
eccentric *adj* excéntrico/ca.
echo *n* eco *m*.
eclectic *adj* ecléctico/ca.
eclipse *n* eclipse *m*.
ecology *n* ecología *f*.
economics *npl* economía *f*.
economy *n* economía *f*.
ecstasy *n* éxtasis *m*.
eczema *n* eczema *m*.
eddy *n* reflujo de agua *m*.
edge *n* filo *m*.
edict *n* edicto, mandato *m*.
edit *vt* dirigir; redactar.
edition *n* edición *f*.
editor *n* director *m*.
educate *vt* educar.

education *n* educación *f*.
eel *n* anguila *f*.
effect *n* efecto *m*.
effective *adj* eficaz..
effeminate *adj* afeminado/da.
effervescence *n* efervescencia *f*.
efficacy *n* eficacia *f*.
efficient *adj* eficaz.
effigy *n* efigie, imagen *f*.
effort *n* esfuerzo *m*.
egg *n* huevo *m*.
eggplant *n* berenjena *f*.
ego(t)ist *n* egoísta *m/f*.
eight *num* ocho.
eighteen *num* dieciocho.
eighth *adj* octavo.
eighty *num* ochenta.
either *pn* cualquiera.
eject *vt* expeler, desechar.
elastic *adj* elástico/ca.
elation *n* regocijo *m*.
elbow *n* codo *m*.
elder *n* saúco *m* (árbol):—*adj* mayor.
elect *vt* elegir.
election *n* elección *f*.
electrician *n* electricista *m/f*.
electricity *n* electricidad *f*.
elegance *n* elegancia *f*.
elegant *adj* elegante, delicado/da.
elegy *n* elegía *f*.
element *n* elemento *m*.
elephant *n* elefante *m*.
elevate *vt* elevar, alzar.
elevator *n* ascensor *m*.
eleven *num* once.
eleventh *adj* onceno, undécimo.
elf *n* duende *m*.
elicit *vt* sacar de.
eligible *adj* elegible.
eliminate *vt* eliminar, descartar.
elk *n* alce *m*.
elm *n* olmo *m*.
elocution *n* elocución *f*.
elongate *vt* alargar.
elope *vi* escapar, huir.
elopement *n* fuga *f*.
eloquence *n* elocuencia *f*.
else *pn* otro/ra.
elsewhere *adv* en otra parte.
elude *vt* eludir, evitar.
embargo *n* prohibición *f*.
embark *vt* embarcar.
embarrass *vt* avergonzar.
embarrassment *n* desconcierto *m*.
embassy *n* embajada *f*.
embed *vt* empotrar; clavar.
embellish *vt* hermosear.

embers *npl* rescoldo *m*.
embezzle *vt* desfalcar.
embitter *vt* amargar.
emblem *n* emblema *m*.
embrace *vt* abrazar.
embroider *vt* bordar.
embroil *vt* embrollar; confundir.
embryo *n* embrión *m*.
emerald *n* esmeralda *f*.
emerge *vi* salir, proceder.
emergency *n* emergencia *f*.
emery *n* esmeril *m*.
emigrant *n* emigrante *m*.
emigrate *vi* emigrar.
eminent *adj* eminente.
emission *n* emisión *f*.
emit *vt* emitir.
emotion *n* emoción *f*.
emperor *n* emperador *m*.
emphasis *n* énfasis *m*.
emphasize *vt* hablar con énfasis.
empire *n* imperio *m*.
employ *vt* emplear, ocupar.
employee *n* empleado *m*.
employer *n* patrón *m*; empresario *m*.
empress *n* emperatriz *f*.
empty *adj* vacío/cía.
emulate *vt* emular.
emulsion *n* emulsión *f*.
enable *vt* capacitar.
enact *vt* promulgar.
enamel *n* esmalte *m*.
enchant *vt* encantar.
enchanting *adj* encantador.
encircle *vt* cercar, circundar.
enclose *vt* cercar, circunvalar.
encore *adv* otra vez, de nuevo.
encounter *n* encuentro *m*.
encourage *vt* animar.
encouragement *n* estímulo, patrocinio *m*.
encroach *vt* usurpar.
encumber *vt* embarazar, cargar.
encyclopedia *n* enciclopedia *f*.
end *n* fin *m*.
endanger *vt* peligrar.
endear *vt* encarecer.
endeavor *vi* esforzarse; intentar.
endemic *adj* endémico/ca.
ending *n* conclusión.
endive *n* (*bot*) endibia *f*.
endless *adj* infinito/ta.
endorse *vt* endosar; aprobar.
endow *vt* dotar.
endure *vt* sufrir, soportar.
enemy *n* enemigo/ga.
energetic *adj* enérgico/ca.
energy *n* energía, fuerza *f*.

enforce *vt* hacer cumplir.
engine *n* motor *m*; locomotora *f*.
engineer *n* ingeniero *m*.
engrave *vt* grabar.
enhance *vt* aumentar.
enigma *n* enigma *m*.
enjoy *vt* gozar.
enjoyment *n* disfrute *m*; placer *m*.
enlarge *vt* engrandecer.
enlist *vt* alistar.
enliven *vt* animar.
enmity *n* enemistad *f*; odio *m*.
enormous *adj* enorme.
enough *adv* bastante; basta.
enrage *vt* enfurecer.
enrapture *vt* arrebatar.
enrich *vt* enriquecer.
enrol *vt* registrar.
enrolment *n* inscripción *f*.
ensign *n* (*mil*) bandera *f*.
enslave *vt* esclavizar.
ensue *vi* seguirse.
ensure *vt* asegurar.
entangle *vt* enmarañar.
enter *vt* entrar; admitir.
enterprise *n* empresa *f*.
entertain *vt* divertir; hospedar.
entertainer *n* artista *m/f*.
entertainment *n* entretenimiento, pasatiempo *m*.
enthralling *adj* cautivador.
enthusiasm *n* entusiasmo *m*.
entice *vt* tentar; seducir.
entire *adj* entero/ra, completo/ta.
entitle *vt* intitular; conferir algún derecho.
entity *n* entidad *f*.
entrance *n* entrada *f*.
entreat *vt* rogar, suplicar.
entrepreneur *n* empresario *m*.
entrust *vt* confiar.
entry *n* entrada *f*.
entwine *vt* entrelazar.
envelop *n* envolver.
envelope *vt* sobre *m*.
enviable *adj* envidiable.
environment *n* medio ambiente *m*.
environs *npl* vecindad *f*.
envisage *vt* prever; concebir.
envoy *n* enviado *m*.
envy *n* envidia.
ephemeral *adj* efímero/ra.
epic *adj* épico/ca.
epidemic *adj* epidémico/ca.
epilogue *n* epílogo *m*.
Epiphany *n* Epifanía *f*.
episcopacy *n* episcopado *m*.
episcopal *adj* episcopal.

episcopalian *n* anglicano *m*.
episode *n* episodio *m*.
epistle *n* epístola *f*.
epithet *n* epíteto *m*.
epoch *n* época *f*.
equal *adj* igual.
equalize *vt* igualar.
equality *n* igualdad, uniformidad *f*.
equally *adv* igualmente.
equate *vt* equiparar (con).
equation *n* ecuación *f*.
equator *n* ecuador *m*.
equatorial *adj* ecuatorial.
equestrian *adj* ecuestre.
equilibrium *n* equilibrio *m*.
equinox *n* equinoccio *m*.
equip *vt* equipar.
equipment *n* equipaje *m*.
equitable *adj* equitativo/va.
equity *n* equidad *f*.
equivalent *adj*, *n* equivalente *m*.
era *n* era *f*.
eradicate *vt* desarraigar.
eradication *n* extirpación *f*.
erase *vt* borrar.
eraser *n* goma de borrar *f*.
erect *vt* erigir; establecer.
ermine *n* armiño *m*.
erode *vt* erosionar.
erotic *adj* erótico/ca.
err *vi* vagar, errar.
errand *n* recado.
erratic *adj* errático/ca.
erroneous *adj* erróneo/nea.
error *n* error *m*.
erudite *adj* erudito/ta.
erupt *vi* entrar en erupción; hacer erupción.
eruption *n* erupción *f*.
escalate *vi* extenderse.
escalator *n* escalera móvil *f*.
escapade *n* travesura *f*.
escape *vt* evitar; escapar.
escapism *n* escapismo *m*.
escort *n* escolta *f*:—*vt* escoltar.
esoteric *adj* esotérico/ca.
especial *adj* especial.
essay *n* ensayo *m*.
essence *n* esencia *f*.
essential *n* esencia *f*:—*adj* esencial.
establish *vt* establecer.
establishment *n* establecimiento *m*.
estate *n* estado *m*.
esteem *vt* estimar, apreciar.
estimate *vt* estimar, apreciar.
estuary *n* estuario.
etch *vt* grabar al aguafuerte.
eternal *adj* eterno/na.

eternity *n* eternidad *f*.
ether *n* éter *m*.
ethical *adj* ético/ca.
ethics *npl* ética *f*.
ethnic *adj* étnico/ca.
ethos *n* genio *m*.
etiquette *n* etiqueta *f*.
etymology *n* etimología *f*.
Eucharist *n* Eucaristía *f*.
eulogy *n* elogio *m*.
eunuch *n* eunuco *m*.
euphemism *n* eufemismo *m*.
evacuate *vt* evacuar.
evacuation *n* evacuación *f*.
evade *vt* evadir.
evaluate *vt* evaluar.
evangelical *adj* evangélico/ca.
evaporate *vt* evaporar.
evasion *n* evasión *f*.
evasive *adj* evasivo/va.
eve *n* víspera *f*.
even *adj* llano/na, igual; par, semejante:—
    adv aun; aun cuando, supuesto que; no
    obstante.
evening *n* tarde *f*.
event *n* acontecimiento, evento *m*.
eventuality *n* eventualidad *f*.
ever *adv* siempre.
every *adj* cada uno o cada una.
evict *vt* desahuciar.
eviction *n* desahucio *m*.
evidence *n* evidencia *f*.
evil *adj* malo/la, depravado/da.
evocative *adj* sugestivo/va.
evoke *vt* evocar.
evolution *n* evolución *f*.
evolve *vt, vi* evolucionar.
ewe *n* oveja *f*.
exacerbate *vt* exacerbar.
exact *adj* exacto/ta.
exacting *adj* exigente.
exaggerate *vt* exagerar.
exaggeration *n* exageración *f*.
exalt *vt* exaltar.
exaltation *n* exaltación.
examination *n* examen *m*.
examine *vt* examinar.
examiner *n* inspector/a *m/f*.
example *n* ejemplar *m*; ejemplo *m*.
excavate *vt* excavar.
excavation *n* excavación *f*.
exceed *vt* exceder.
exceedingly *adv* extremamente, en sumo
    grado.
excel *vt* sobresalir.
excellence *n* excelencia *f*.
excellent *adj* excelente.

except *vt* exceptuar, excluir:—~(ing) *prep*
    excepto, a excepción de.
exception *n* excepción, exclusión *f*.
exceptional *adj* excepcional.
excerpt *n* extracto *m*.
excess *n* exceso *m*.
excessive *adj* excesivo/va.
exchange *vt* cambiar; trocar.
exchange rate *n* tipo de cambio *m*.
excitability *n* excitabilidad *f*.
excitable *adj* excitable.
excite *vt* excitar; estimular.
excited *adj* emocionado/da.
excitement *n* estímulo *m*, excitación *f*.
exclaim *vi* exclamar.
exclamation *n* exclamación *f*.
exclamation mark *n* punto de admiración *m*.
exclamatory *adj* exclamatorio/ria.
exclude *vt* excluir; exceptuar.
exclusion *n* exclusión, *f*.
exclusive *adj* exclusivo/va.
excommunicate *vt* excomulgar.
excommunication *n* excomunión *f*.
excrement *n* excremento *m*.
excruciating *adj* atroz.
excursion *n* excursión *f*.
excusable *adj* excusable.
excuse *vt* disculpar.
execute *vt* ejecutar.
execution *n* ejecución *f*.
executioner *n* ejecutor/a.
executive *adj* ejecutivo/va.
executor *n* testamentario/ria, albacea *m/f*.
exemplary *adj* ejemplar.
exemplify *vt* ejemplificar.
exempt *adj* exento/ta.
exemption *n* exención *f*.
exercise *n* ejercicio *m*.
exercise book *n* cuaderno *m*.
exertion *n* esfuerzo *m*.
exhale *vt* exhalar.
exhaust *n* escape *m*.
exhausted *adj* agotado/da.
exhaustion *n* agotamiento *m*.
exhaustive *adj* comprensivo/va.
exhibit *vt* exhibir; mostrar.
exhibition *n* exposición *f*.
exhilarating *adj* estimulante.
exhort *vt* exhortar, excitar.
exhume *vt* exhumar.
exile *n* destierro *m*.
exist *vi* existir.
existence *n* existencia *f*.
exit *n* salida *f*:—*vi* hacer mutis.
exit ramp *n* vía de acceso *f*.
exodus *n* éxodo *m*.
exonerate *vt* exonerar.

exhorbitant *adj* exorbitante.
exorcize *vt* exorcizar, conjurar.
exorcism *n* exorcismo *m*.
exotic *adj* exótico/ca.
expand *vt* extender, dilatar.
expatriate *vt* expatriar.
expect *vt* esperar.
expectant mother *n* mujer encinta *f*.
expediency *n* conveniencia *f*.
expedition *n* expedición *f*.
expel *vt* expeler, desterrar.
expend *vt* expender.
expendable *adj* prescindible.
expenditure *n* gasto, desembolso *m*.
expense *n* gasto *m*; coste *m*.
experience *n* experiencia *f*; practica *f*.
experienced *adj* experimentado/da.
experiment *n* experimento *m*.
expert *adj* experto/ta.
expertise *n* pericia *f*.
expiration *n* expiración *f*.
expire *vi* expirar.
explain *vt* explanar, explicar.
explanation *n* explanación, explicación *f*.
expletive *adj* expletivo/va.
explicit *adj* explícito/ta.
explode *vt*, *vi* estallar, explotar.
exploit *vt* explotar.
exploitation *n* explotación *f*.
exploration *n* exploración *f*.
exploratory *adj* exploratorio/ria.
explore *vt* explorar.
explorer *n* explorador *m*.
explosion *n* explosión *f*.
explosive *adj*, *n* explosivo *m*.
exponent *n* (*math*) exponente *m*.
export *vt* exportar.
expose *vt* exponer; mostrar.
exposed *adj* expuesto/ta.
exposition *n* exposición *f*.
expostulate *vi* debatir, contender.
exposure *n* exposición *f*.
expound *vt* exponer.
express *vt* exprimir; representar.
expression *n* expresión *f*.
expressionless *adj* sin expresión (cara).

expressway *n* autopista *f*.
expulsion *n* expulsión *f*.
expurgate *vt* expurgar.
exquisite *adj* exquisito/ta.
extend *vt* extender.
extension *n* extensión *f*.
extensive *adj* extenso/sa.
extent *n* extensión *f*.
extenuate *vt* extenuar.
exterior *adj*, *n* exterior *m*.
exterminate *vt* exterminar.
extermination *n* exterminación *f*.
external *adj* externo/na.
extinct *adj* extinto/ta.
extinction *n* extinción *f*.
extinguish *vt* extinguir.
extinguisher *n* extintor *m*.
extol *vt* alabar, magnificar.
extort *vt* sacar por fuerza.
extortion *n* extorsión *f*.
extortionate *adj* excesivo/va.
extra *adv* extra.
extract *vt* extraer.
extracurricular *adj* extraescolar.
extradition *n* (*law*) extradición *f*.
extramarital *adj* extramatrimonial.
extraneous *adj* extraño/ña.
extraordinary *adj* extraordinario/ria.
extravagance *n* extravagancia *f*.
extravagant *adj* extravagante.
extreme *adj* extremo/ma.
extremist *adj*, *n* extremista *m/f*.
extremity *n* extremidad *f*.
extrovert *adj*, *n* extrovertido *m*.
exuberance *n* exuberancia *f*.
exuberant *adj* exuberante.
exult *vt* exultar.
exultation *n* exultación *f*; regocijo *m*.
eye *n* ojo *m*:—*vt* ojear, contemplar, observar.
eyeball *n* globo del ojo *m*.
eyebrow *n* ceja *f*.
eyelash *n* pestaña *f*.
eyelid *n* párpado *m*.
eyesight *n* vista *f*.
eyewitness *n* testigo ocular *m*.
eyrie *n* aguilera *f*.

F

fabric *n* tejido *m*.
fabricate *vt* fabricar.
fabulous *adj* fabuloso/sa.
facade *n* fachada *f*.
face *n* cara, faz *f*; superficie *f*.
facet *n* faceta *f*.
facetious *adj* chistoso/sa.

facile *adj* fácil.
facilitate *vt* facilitar.
facility *n* facilidad *f*.
facsimile *n* facsímile *m*; telefax *m*.
fact *n* hecho *m*.
faction *n* facción *f*.
factor *n* factor *m*.

factory *n* fabrica *f*.
faculty *n* facultad *f*.
fad *n* moda , manía *f*.
fade *vi* decaer.
fail *vt* suspender, reprobar; fallar a.
failure *n* falta *f*; culpa *f*.
faint *vi* desmayarse, debilitarse.
faint-hearted *adj* cobarde.
fair *adj* hermoso/sa, bello/la; blanco/ca;
  rubio/bia; claro/ra, sereno/na; favorable;
  recto/ta, justo/ta; franco/ca:—*adv* limpio:
  —*n* feria *f*.
fairly *adv* justamente.
fairy *n* hada *f*.
faith *n* fe *f*; dogma de fe *m*.
faithfulness *n* fidelidad *f*.
fake *n* falsificación *f*.
falcon *n* halcón *m*.
fall¹ *n* otoño *m*.
fall² *vi* caer(se).
fallacy *n* falacia *f*.
fallible *adj* falible.
false *adj* falso/sa.
falsify *vt* falsificar.
fame *n* fama *f*.
famed *adj* celebrado/da, famoso/sa.
familiar *adj* familiar.
family *n* familia *f*.
famine *n* hambre *f*; carestía *f*.
famous *adj* famoso/sa.
fan *n* abanico *m*; aficionado *m*.
fanatic *adj*, *n* fanático *m*.
fanciful *adj* imaginativo/va.
fancy *n* fantasía, imaginación *f*.
fanfare *n* (*mus*) fanfarria *f*.
fang *n* colmillo *m*.
fantastic *adj* fantástico/ca.
fantasy *n* fantasía *f*.
far *adv* lejos.
faraway *adj* remoto/ta.
farce *n* farsa *f*.
fare *n* precio *m*; tarifa *f*.
farm *n* finca *f*, granja *f*.
farmer *n* estanciero *m*; granjero *m*.
fascinate *vt* fascinar, encantar.
fascism *n* fascismo.
fashion *n* moda *f*; forma.
fashionable *adj* a la moda.
fashion show *n* desfile de modelos *m*.
fast *vi* ayunar; *adv* rápidamente.
fasten *vt* abrochar.
fastidious *adj* fastidioso/sa.
fat *adj* gordo/da.
fatal *adj* fatal.
fate *n* hado, destino *m*.
fateful *adj* fatídico/ca.
father *n* padre *m*.

father-in-law *n* suegro *m*.
fatherland *n* patria *f*.
fathom *n* braza (medida) *f*.
fatigue *n* fatiga *f*.
fatty *adj* graso/sa.
faucet *n* espita *f*.
fault *n* falta, culpa *f*.
fauna *n* fauna *f*.
faux pas *n* plancha *f*.
favor *n* favor.
favorite *n* favorito *m*.
fawn *n* cervato *m*.
fax *n* facsímil(e) *m*; telefax *m*.
fear *vi* temer:—*n* miedo *m*.
fearful *adj* medroso/sa, temeroso/sa.
feasible *adj* factible.
feast *n* banquete.
feat *n* hecho *m*.
feather *n* pluma *f*.
feature *n* característica *f*; rasgo *m*.
February *n* febrero *m*.
federal *adj* federal.
federalist *n* federalista *m/f*.
federation *n* federación *f*.
fed-up *adj* harto/ta.
fee *n* honorarios *mpl*.
feeble *adj* flaco/ca, débil.
feed *vt* nutrir; alimentar.
feedback *n* reacción *f*.
feel *vt* sentir; tocar.
feign *vt* inventar, fingir.
feline *adj* gatuno/na.
fellowship *n* compañerismo *m*.
felon *n* criminal *m/f*.
felony *n* crimen *m*.
felt *n* fieltro *m*.
female *n* hembra *f*:—*adj* femenino/na.
feminine *adj* femenino/na.
feminist *n* feminista *m/f*.
fence *n* cerca *f*; defensa *f*.
fennel *n* (*bot*) hinojo *m*.
fern *n* (*bot*) helecho *m*.
ferocious *adj* feroz.
ferret *n* hurón *m*.
ferry *n* barca de pasaje *f*.
fertile *adj* fértil, fecundo/da.
fester *vi* enconarse.
festival *n* fiesta *f*; festival *m*.
fetch *vt* ir a buscar.
fete *n* fiesta *f*.
fetus *n* feto *m*.
feud *n* riña, contienda *f*.
feudal *adj* feudal.
fever *n* fiebre *f*.
feverish *adj* febril.
few *adj* poco/ca.
fewer *adj* menor.

fewest *adj* los menos.
fiancé *n* novio *m*.
fiancée *n* novia *f*.
fib *n* mentira *f*.
fibre *n* fibra, hebra *f*.
fickle *adj* voluble.
fiction *n* ficción *f*.
fiddle *n* violín *m*; trampa *f*.
fidelity *n* fidelidad *f*.
field *n* campo *m*.
fieldmouse *n* ratón de campo *m*.
fierce *adj* fiero/ra, feroz.
fierceness *n* fiereza, ferocidad *f*.
fiery *adj* ardiente; apasionado/da.
fifteen *adj*, *n* quince.
fifteenth *adj*, *n* decimoquinto/ta.
fifth *adj*, *n* quinto/ta.
fiftieth *adj*, *n* quincuagésimo/ma.
fifty *adj*, *n* cincuenta.
fig *n* higo *m*.
fight *vt*, *vi* reñir; batallar; combatir.
fig-leaf *n* hoja de higuera *f*.
figurative *adj* figurativo/va.
figure *n* figura.
filament *n* filamento *m*.
fill *vt* llenar; hartar.
fillet *n* filete *m*.
filling station *n* estación de servicio *f*.
fillip *n* (*fig*) estimulo *m*.
filly *n* potra *f*.
film *n* película *f*; film *m*.
filter *n* filtro *m*.
filth(iness) *n* inmundicia, porquería *f*.
fin *n* aleta *f*.
final *adj* final, último/ma.
finalize *vt* concluir.
finance *n* fondos *mpl*.
financier *n* financiero *m*.
find *vt* hallar, descubrir.
finesse *n* sutileza *f*.
finger *n* dedo *m*.
fingernail *n* uña *f*.
finish *vt* acabar, terminar, concluir.
finite *adj* finito/ta.
fir *n* abeto *m*.
fire *n* fuego *m*; incendio *m*.
firearm *n* arma de fuego *f*.
firefly *n* luciérnaga *f*.
firewood *n* leña *f*.
fireworks *npl* fuegos artificiales *mpl*.
firm *adj* firme, estable.
firmament *n* firmamento *m*.
firmness *n* firmeza *f*.
first *adj* primero/ra.
fiscal *adj* fiscal.
fish *n* pez *m*.
fishbone *n* espina *f*.

fisherman *n* pescador *m*.
fishy *adj* (*fig*) sospechoso/sa.
fist *n* puño *m*.
fitness *n* salud *f*.
five *adj*, *n* cinco.
fix *vt* fijar.
fixation *n* obsesión *f*.
fizzy *adj* gaseoso/sa.
flabbergasted *adj* pasmado/da.
flabby *adj* blando/da.
flaccid *adj* flojo/ja.
flag *n* bandera *f*.
flagpole *n* asta de bandera *f*.
flagrant *adj* flagrante; notorio/ria.
flagship *n* navío almirante *m*.
flair *n* aptitud especial *f*.
flake *n* copo *m*.
flamboyant *adj* vistoso/sa.
flame *n* llama *f*.
flamingo *n* flamenco *m*.
flammable *adj* inflamable.
flank *n* ijada *f*.
flannel *n* franela *f*.
flare *vi* lucir, brillar.
flash *n* flash *m*.
flashlight *n* antorcha *f*.
flask *n* frasco *m*.
flat *adj* llano/na, plano/na.
flatness *n* llanura *f*.
flatten *vt* allanar.
flatter *vt* adular.
flattery *n* adulación *f*.
flatulence *n* (*med*) flatulencia *f*.
flaunt *vt* ostentar.
flavor *n* sabor *m*.
flavorless *adj* soso/sa.
flaw *n* falta *m*.
flawless *adj* sin defecto.
flax *n* lino *m*.
flea *n* pulga *f*.
fleck *n* mota *f*.
flee *vt* huir de.
fleece *n* vellón *m*.
fleet *n* flota *f*.
flesh *n* carne *f*.
flex *n* cordón *m*.
flexibility *n* flexibilidad *f*.
flexible *adj* flexible.
flight *n* vuelo *m*.
flight attendant *n* tripulante auxiliar *m*.
flimsy *adj* débil; fútil.
flinch *vi* encogerse.
fling *vt* lanzar.
flint *n* pedernal *m*.
flip *vt* arrojar.
flippant *adj* petulante.
flipper *n* aleta *f*.

flirt *vi* coquetear:—*n* coqueta *f*.
flirtation *n* coquetería *f*.
flock *n* manada *f*.
flog *vt* azotar.
flogging *n* tunda, zurra *f*.
flood *n* diluvio *m*; inundación *f*.
flooding *n* inundación *f*.
floodlight *n* foco *m*.
floor *n* suelo, piso *m*.
floorboard *n* tabla *f*.
flop *n* fracaso *m*.
floppy *adj* flojo/ja.
flora *n* flora *f*.
floral *adj* floral.
florescence *n* florescencia *f*.
florid *adj* florido/da.
florist *n* florista *m/f*.
florist's (shop) *n* florería *f*.
flotilla *n* (*mar*) flotilla *f*.
flounder *n* platija (pez de mar) *f*.
flour *n* harina *f*.
flourish *vi* florecer.
flout *vt* burlarse de.
flow *vi* fluir.
flower *n* flor *f*.
flowerbed *n* cuadro (en un jardín) *m*.
flowerpot *n* tiesto de flores *m*.
flowery *adj* florido/da.
fluctuate *vi* fluctuar.
fluctuation *n* fluctuación *f*.
fluency *n* fluidez *f*.
fluent *adj* fluido/da.
fluff *n* pelusa *f*.
fluid *adj*, *n* fluido/da *m*.
fluidity *n* fluidez *f*.
fluke *n* (*sl*) chiripa *f*.
fluoride *n* fluoruro *m*.
flurry *n* ráfaga *f*; agitación *f*.
flute *n* flauta *f*.
flutter *vi* revolotear; estar en agitación.
flux *n* flujo *m*.
fly *vt* pilotar; transportar:—*vi* volar.
flying saucer *n* platillo volante *m*.
foal *n* potro *m*.
foam *n* espuma *f*.
foamy *adj* espumoso/sa.
focus *n* foco.
fodder *n* forraje *m*.
foe *n* adversario/ria *m/f*, enemigo *m*.
fog *n* niebla *f*.
foggy *adj* nebuloso/sa.
fold *n* redil *m*; pliegue *m*.
folder *n* carpeta *f*.
folding *adj* plegable.
foliage *n* follaje *m*.
folio *n* folio *m*.
folk *n* gente *f*.

folklore *n* folklore *m*.
folk song *n* canción folklórica *f*.
follow *vt* seguir; acompañar.
follower *n* seguidor/a *m/f*.
following *adj* siguiente.
folly *n* extravagancia *f*.
foment *vt* fomentar.
fond *adj* cariñoso/sa.
fondle *vt* acariciar.
fondness *n* gusto *m*; cariño *m*.
font *n* pila bautismal *f*.
food *n* comida *f*.
food mixer *n* batidora *f*.
food poisoning *n* botulismo *m*.
fool *n* loco/ca, tonto/ta *m/f*.
foolish *adj* bobo/ba, tonto/ta.
foolscap *n* papel tamaño folio *m*.
foot *n* pie *m*; pata *f*.
footage *n* imágenes *fpl*.
footnote *n* nota de pie *f*.
footpath *n* senda *f*.
footprint *n* huella *f*.
for *prep* por, a causa de; para.
forbid *vt* prohibir.
force *n* fuerza *f*; poder, vigor *m*.
forced *adj* forzado/da.
forceful *adj* enérgico/ca.
forceps *n* fórceps *m*.
ford *n* vado *m*.
fore *n*:—**to the ~** en evidencia.
forearm *n* antebrazo *m*.
foreboding *n* presentimiento *m*.
forecast *vt* pronosticar.
forecourt *n* patio *m*.
forefather *n* abuelo, antecesor *m*.
forefinger *n* índice *m*.
forefront *n*:—**in the ~ of** en la vanguardia de.
forego *vt* ceder.
foreground *n* delantera *f*.
forehead *n* frente *f*.
foreign *adj* extranjero/ra; extraño/ña.
foreigner *n* extranjero/ra, forastero/ra *m/f*.
foreign exchange *n* divisas *fpl*.
foreleg *n* pata delantera *f*.
foreman *n* capataz *m*.
foremost *adj* principal.
forensic *adj* forense.
forerunner *n* precursor/a *m/f*.
foresee *vt* prever.
foresight *n* previsión *f*.
forest *n* bosque *m*; selva *f*.
forester *n* guardabosque *m*.
forestry *n* silvicultura *f*.
foretaste *n* muestra *f*.
foretell *vt* predecir, profetizar.
forethought *n* providencia *f*.
forever *adv* para siempre.

foreword n prefacio m.
forfeit n confiscación f.
forge n fragua f; fabrica de metales f.
forger n falsificador/a m/f.
forgery n falsificación f.
forget vt olvidar.
forgetful adj olvidadizo/za.
forget-me-not n (bot) nomeolvides m.
forgive vt perdonar.
forgiveness n perdón m.
fork n tenedor m.
form n forma f; modelo m; modo m.
formal adj formal.
formality n formalidad f.
format n formato m.
formation n formación f.
formative adj formativo/va.
former adj precedente; anterior.
formidable adj formidable.
formula n fórmula f.
formulate vt formular.
forsake vt dejar.
fort n castillo m.
forthright adj franco/ca.
forthwith adv inmediatamente.
fortieth adj, n cuadragésimo m.
fortification n fortificación f.
fortify vt fortificar.
fortitude n fortaleza f.
fortnight n quince días mpl.
fortress n (mil) fortaleza f.
fortuitous adj impensado/da.
fortunate adj afortunado/da.
fortune n fortuna, suerte f.
fortune-teller n sortílego/ga.
forty adj, n cuarenta.
forum n foro m.
forward adj avanzado/da; delantero/ra.
forwardness n precocidad f; audacia f.
fossil adj, n fósil m.
foster vt criar.
foul adj sucio/cia, puerco/ca; impuro/ra.
found vt fundar, establecer.
foundation n fundación f.
founder n fundador/a m/f.
foundling n niño expósito m, niña expósita f.
foundry n fundería f.
fount, fountain n fuente f.
fountainhead n origen de fuente m.
four adj, n cuatro.
fourfold adj cuádruple.
fourteen adj, n catorce.
fourteenth adj, n decimocuarto/ta.
fourth adj, n cuarto/ta:—n cuarto m: —~ly adv en cuarto lugar.
fowl n ave f.
fox n zorra f.

fracas n riña f.
fraction n fracción f.
fracture n fractura f.
fragile adj frágil; débil.
fragility n fragilidad f.
fragment n fragmento m.
fragrance n fragancia f.
fragrant adj fragante, oloroso/sa.
frail adj frágil, débil.
frailty n fragilidad f; debilidad f.
frame n armazón m; marco, cerco m.
franchise n sufragio m.
frank adj franco/ca, liberal.
frankly adv francamente.
frantic adj frenético/ca.
fraternize vi hermanarse.
fraternity n fraternidad f.
fraud n fraude m.
fraudulent adj fraudulento/ta.
fraught adj cargado/da, lleno/na.
freak n monstruo m; fenómeno m.
freckle n peca f.
freckled adj pecoso/sa.
free adj libre; liberal; suelto/ta.
freedom n libertad f.
freehold n propiedad vitalicia f.
free-for-all n riña general f.
freelance adj, adv por cuenta propia.
freemason n francmasón m.
freemasonry n francmasonería f.
freeway n autopista f.
freewheel vi ir en punto muerto.
freeze vi helar(se).
freezer n congeladora f.
freight n carga f; flete m.
freighter n fletador m.
frenzy n frenesí m; locura f.
frequency n frecuencia f.
fresco n fresco m.
fresh adj fresco/ca; nuevo/va.
freshly adv nuevamente.
freshman n novicio m.
freshwater adj de agua dulce.
fret vi agitarse.
friar n fraile m.
friction n fricción f.
Friday n viernes m:—**Good ~** Viernes Santo m.
friend n amigo m; amiga f.
friendship n amistad f.
frieze n friso m.
frigate n (mar) fragata f.
fright n espanto, terror m.
frighten vt espantar.
frigid adj frío/ría, frígido/da.
fringe n franja f.
frisk vt cachear.
frivolity n frivolidad f.

frock *n* vestido *m*.
frog *n* rana *f*.
frolic *vi* juguetear.
from *prep* de; después; desde.
front *n* parte delantera *f*; fachada *f*; paseo marítimo *m*; frente *m*.
frontal *adj* de frente.
frontier *n* frontera *f*.
frost *n* helada *f*; hielo *m*.
froth *n* espuma (de algún líquido) *f*.
frown *vt* mirar con ceño.
frozen *adj* helado/da.
fruit *n* fruta *f*; fruto *m*.
fruiterer *n* frutero *m*.
fruiterer's (shop) *n* frutería *f*.
fruit juice *n* jugo de fruta *m*.
fruitless *adj* estéril; inútil.
fruit salad *n* ensalada de frutas *f*.
fruit tree *n* frutal *m*.
frustrate *vt* frustrar; anular.
fry *vt* freír.
frying pan *n* sartén *f*.
fuchsia *n* (*bot*) fucsia *f*.
fuel *n* combustible *m*.
fuel tank *n* deposito *m*.
fugitive *adj, n* fugitivo *m*.
fulcrum *n* fulcro *m*.
fulfill *vt* cumplir; realizar.
fulfillment *n* cumplimiento *m*.
full *adj* lleno/na.
full moon *n* plenilunio *m*; luna llena *f*.

fulsome *adj* exagerado/da.
fumble *vi* manejar torpemente.
fume *vi* humear; encolerizarse.
fun *n* diversión *f*; alegría *f*.
function *n* función *f*.
functional *adj* funcional.
fund *n* fondo *m*.
fundamental *adj* fundamental.
funeral *n* funerales *mpl*.
fungus *n* hongo *m*; seta *f*.
funnel *n* embudo *m*.
funny *adj* divertido/da; curioso/sa.
fur *n* piel *f*.
furious *adj* furioso/sa.
furnace *n* horno *m*; hornaza *f*.
furnish *vt* amueblar.
furnishings *npl* muebles *mpl*.
furniture *n* muebles *mpl*.
furrow *n* surco *m*.
furry *adj* peludo/da.
furthermore *adv* además.
fury *n* furor *m*; furia *f*; ira *f*.
fuse *vt, vi* fundir; derretirse.
fuse box *n* caja de fusibles *f*.
fusion *n* fusión *f*.
fuss *n* lío *m*; alboroto *m*.
fussy *adj* jactancioso/sa.
futile *adj* fútil, frívolo/la.
futility *n* futilidad *f*.
future *adj* futuro/ra.
fuzzy *adj* borroso/sa; muy rizado/da.

G

gable *n* aguilón *m*.
gag *n* mordaza *f*; chiste *m*.
gage *n* calibre *m*.
gaiety *n* alegría *f*.
gain *n* ganancia *f*.
gala *n* fiesta *f*.
galaxy *n* galaxia *f*.
gale *n* vendaval *m*.
gallant *adj* galante.
gallery *n* galería *f*.
gallon *n* galón *m* (medida).
gallop *n* galope *m*.
gallows *n* horca *f*.
galore *adv* en abundancia.
gambit *n* estrategia *f*.
gamble *vi* jugar; especular *f*.
gambler *n* jugador *m*.
game *n* juego *m*; pasatiempo *m*.
gamekeeper *n* guardabosques *m*.
gaming *n* juego *m*.
gammon *n* jamón *m*.
gander *n* ganso *m*.

gang *n* pandilla, banda *f*.
gangrene *n* gangrena *f*.
gangster *n* gangster *m*.
gangway *n* pasarela *f*.
gap *n* hueco *m*; claro *m*; intervalo *m*.
garage *n* garaje *m*.
garbage *n* basura *f*.
garbage can *n* cubo de la basura *m*.
garden *n* jardín *m*.
gargoyle *n* gárgola *f*.
garish *adj* ostentoso/sa.
garland *n* guirnalda *f*.
garlic *n* ajo *m*.
garment *n* prenda *f*.
garnish *vt* guarnecer *m*.
garter *n* liga *f*.
gas *n* gas *m*.
gasoline, gas *n* gasolina *f*.
gash *n* cuchillada *f*.
gasp *vi* jadear.
gastric *adj* gástrico/ca.
gastronomic *adj* gastronómico/ca.

gate n puerta f.
gateway n puerta f.
gather vt recoger.
gathering n reunión f.
gaudy adj chillón/ona.
gauze n gasa f.
gay adj alegre; vivo/va; gay.
gazelle n gacela f.
gazette n gaceta f.
gazetteer n gacetero m.
gear n atavío m; vestido m.
gearbox n caja de cambios f.
gel n gel m.
gelatin(e) n jaletina, jalea f.
gelignite n gelignita f.
gem n joya f
Gemini n Géminis m (signo del zodiaco).
gender n género m.
gene n gen m.
genealogy n genealogía f.
general adj general, común.
generalize vt generalizar.
generation n generación f.
generic adj genérico/ca.
generosity n generosidad.
generous adj generoso/sa.
genetics npl genética f.
genial adj genial.
genitals npl genitales mpl.
genius n genio m.
genteel adj refinado, elegante.
gentile n gentil.
gentle adj suave.
gentleman n caballero m.
gentry n alta burguesía f.
gents n aseos mpl.
genuine adj genuino/na.
genus n genero m.
geographer n geógrafo/fa m/f.
geography n geografía f.
geology n geología f.
geometry n geometría f.
geranium n (bot) geranio m.
germ n (bot) germen m.
germinate vi brotar.
gesticulate vi gesticular.
gesture n gesto m.
get vt ganar; conseguir, obtener.
geyser n géiser m m.
ghastly adj espantoso/sa.
gherkin n pepinillo m.
ghost n fantasma m.
ghostly adj fantasmal.
giant n gigante m.
giddy adj vertiginoso/sa.
gift n regalo m.
giggle vi reírse tontamente.

gin n ginebra f.
ginger n jengibre m.
ginger-haired adj pelirrojo/ja.
giraffe n jirafa f.
girl n muchacha, chica f.
girlfriend n amiga f; novia f.
giro n giro postal m.
girth n cincha f; circunferencia f.
give vt, vi dar.
glacier n glaciar m.
glad adj alegre, contento/ta.
gladiator n gladiator m.
glamor n encanto m.
gland n glándula f.
glare n deslumbramiento f.
glass n vidrio.
glean vt espigar; recoger.
glee n alegría f; gozo m.
glib adj con poca sinceridad, elocuente pero falso.
glide vi resbalar.
glimmer n vislumbre f.
glimpse n vislumbre f.
glint vi centellear.
glisten, glitter vi relucir, brillar.
gloat vi ojear con admiración.
global adj mundial.
globe n globo m; esfera f.
gloom, gloominess n oscuridad f; melancolía.
glorify vt glorificar, celebrar.
glory n gloria, fama, celebridad f.
gloss n glosa f; lustre m.
glossary n glosario m.
glove n guante m.
glow vi arder; inflamarse; relucir.
glower vi mirar con ceño.
glue n cola f.
glum adj abatido/da, triste.
glut n hartura, abundancia f.
gluttony n glotonería f.
glycerine n glicerina f.
gnarled adj nudoso/sa.
gnash vt, vi rechinar; crujir los dientes.
gnat n mosquito m.
gnaw vt roer.
gnome n gnomo m.
go vi ir, irse.
goal n meta f; fin m.
goaltender n portero m.
go-between n mediador/a m/f.
goblet n copa f.
goblin n espíritu ambulante, duende m.
God n Dios m.
godchild n ahijado, hijo de pila m.
goddaughter n ahijada, hija de pila f.
goddess n diosa f.

godfather *n* padrino *m*.
godmother *n* madrina *f*.
godsend *n* don del cielo *m*.
godson *n* ahijado *m*.
goggle-eyed *adj* bizco/ca.
goggles *npl* anteojos *mpl*.
gold *n* oro *m*.
goldfish *n* pez de colores *m*.
gold-plated *adj* chapado/da en oro.
golf *n* golf *m*.
golf course *n* campo de golf *m*.
golfer *n* golfista *m/f*.
gondolier *n* gondolero/ra *m/f*.
gone *adj* ido/da; perdido/da; pasado/da; gastado/da; muerto/ta.
gong *n* atabal chino *m*.
good *adj* bueno/na.
goodbye ! *excl* ¡adiós!
Good Friday *n* Viernes Santo *m*.
good-looking *adj* guapo/pa.
goodness *n* bondad *f*.
goodwill *n* benevolencia, bondad *f*.
goose *n* ganso *m*; oca *f*.
gooseberry *n* grosella espinosa *f*.
gorge *n* barranco *m*.
gorgeous *adj* maravilloso/sa.
gorilla *n* gorila *m*.
gorse *n* aulaga *f*.
gory *adj* sangriento/ta.
goshawk *n* azor *m*.
gospel *n* evangelio *m*.
gossamer *n* vello *m*.
gossip *n* charla *f*.
gothic *adj* gótico/ca.
gout *n* gota *f* (enfermedad).
govern *vt* gobernar, dirigir.
governess *n* gobernadora *f*.
government *n* gobierno *m*.
governor *n* gobernador *m*.
gown *n* toga *f*.
grab *vt* agarrar.
grace *n* gracia *f*.
graceful *adj* gracioso/sa.
gracious *adj* gracioso/sa.
gradation *n* gradación *f*.
grade *n* grado *m*.
grade crossing *n* paso a nivel *m*.
gradient *n* (*rail*) pendiente *f*.
gradual *adj* gradual.
graduate *vi* graduarse.
graduation *n* graduación *f*.
graffiti *n* pintadas *fpl*.
graft *n* injerto *m*.
grain *n* grano *m*.
gram *n* gramo *m* (peso).
grammar *n* gramática *f*.
granary *n* granero *m*.

grand *adj* grande, ilustre.
grandchild *n* nieto *m*; nieta *f*.
grandad *n* abuelo *m*.
granddaughter *n* nieta *f*.
grandeur *n* grandeza *f*.
grandfather *n* abuelo *m*.
grandiose *adj* grandioso/sa.
grandma *n* abuelita *f*.
grandmother *n* abuela *f*.
grandparents *npl* abuelos *mpl*.
grand piano *n* piano de cola *m*.
grandson *n* nieto *m*.
grandstand *n* tribuna *f*.
granite *n* granito *m*.
granny *n* abuelita *f*.
grant *vt* conceder.
granule *n* gránulo *m*.
grape *n* uva *f*:—**bunch of ~s** racimo de uvas *m*.
grapefruit *n* toronja *f*.
graph *n* gráfica *f*.
graphics *n* artes gráficas *fpl*; gráficos *mpl*.
grasp *vt* empuñar.
grass *n* hierba *f*.
grasshopper *n* saltamontes *m*.
grassland *n* pampa , pradera *f*.
grass snake *n* culebra *f*.
gratify *vt* contentar; gratificar.
gratifying *adj* grato/ta.
grating *n* rejado *m*.
gratis *adv* gratis.
gratitude *n* gratitud *f*.
grave *n* sepultura *f*.
gravel *n* cascajo *m*.
gravestone *n* piedra sepulcra *f*.
graveyard *n* cementerio *m*.
gravity *n* gravedad *f*.
gravy *n* jugo de la carne *f*; salsa *f*.
gray *adj* gris.
graze *vt* pastorear.
grease *n* grasa *f*:—*vt* untar.
greasy *adj* grasiento/ta.
great *adj* gran, grande.
greatcoat *n* sobretodo *m*.
greatness *n* grandeza *f*.
greedily *adv* vorazmente.
greediness, greed *n* gula *f*; codicia *f*.
Greek *n* griego (idioma) *m*.
green *adj* verde.
greengrocer *n* verdulero *m*.
greenhouse *n* invernadero *m*.
greet *vt* saludar, congratular.
greeting *n* saludo *m*.
greeting(s) card *n* tarjeta de felicitaciones *f*.
grenade *n* (*mil*) granada *f*.
grenadier *n* granadero *m*.
greyhound *n* galgo *m*.

greyish *adj* pardusco/ca.
grid *n* reja *f*; red *f*.
grief *n* dolor *m*.
grieve *vt* agraviar.
grievous *adj* doloroso/sa.
griffin *n* grifo *m*.
grill *n* parrilla *f*.
grim *adj* feo, fea.
grimace *n* visaje *m*.
grime *n* porquería *f*.
grin *n* mueca *f*.
grind *vt* moler.
grinder *n* molinero *m*.
grip *n* asimiento *m*.
grisly *adj* horroroso/sa.
gristle *n* tendón, nervio *m*.
grit *n* gravilla *f*; valor *m*.
groan *vi* gemir, suspirar.
grocer *n* tendero/ra, abarrotero/ra *m/f*.
groceries *npl* comestibles *mpl*.
groin *n* ingle *f*.
groom *n* establero *m*.
groove *n* ranura *f*.
gross *adj* grueso/sa.
grotesque *adj* grotesco/ca.
grotto *n* gruta *f*.
ground *n* tierra *f*.
ground floor *n* planta baja *f*.
group *n* grupo *m*..
grouse *n* urogallo *m*:—*vi* quejarse.
grove *n* arboleda *f*.
grovel *vi* arrastrarse.
grow *vt* cultivar:—*vi* crecer, aumentarse.
growl *vi* regañar, gruñir.
grown-up *n* adulto *m*.
grub *n* gusano *m*.
grubby *adj* sucio/cia.
grudge *n* rencor, odio *m*; envidia *f*:—*vt, vi* envidiar.
gruesome *adj* horrible.
gruff *adj* brusco/ca.
grumble *vi* gruñir; murmurar.

grunt *vi* gruñir.
G-string *n* taparrabo *m*.
guarantee *n* garantía *f*.
guard *n* guardia *f*.
guardianship *n* tutela *f*.
guerrilla *n* guerrillero *m*.
guess *vt, vi* conjeturar; adivinar; suponer.
guest *n* huésped/a.
guffaw *n* carcajada *f*.
guide *vt* guiar, dirigir:—*n* guía *m*.
guidebook *n* guía *f*.
guild *n* gremio *m*.
guile *n* astucia *f*.
guilt *n* culpabilidad *f*.
guilty *adj* reo, rea, culpable.
guinea pig *n* cobayo *m*.
guise *n* manera *f*.
guitar *n* guitarra *f*.
gulf *n* golfo *m*.
gull *n* gaviota *f*.
gullet *n* esófago *m*.
gullible *adj* crédulo/la.
gully *n* barranco *m*.
gulp *n* trago *m*.
gum *n* goma *f*.
gum tree *n* árbol gomero *m*.
gun *n* pistola *f*; escopeta *f*.
gunboat *n* cañonera *f*.
gunpowder *n* pólvora *f*.
gunshot *n* escopetazo *m*.
gurgle *vi* gorgotear.
guru *n* gurú *m*.
gush *vi* brotar.
gusset *n* escudete *m*.
gut *n* intestino *m*.
gutter *n* canalón *m*; arroyo *m*.
guy *n* tío *m*; tipo *m*.
gym(nasium) *n* gimnasio *m*.
gymnast *n* gimnasta *m/f*.
gynecologist *n* ginecólogo/ga *m/f*.
Gypsy *n* gitano/na *m/f*.
gyrate *vi* girar.

H

haberdasher *n* camisero/ra, mercero/ra *m/f*.
habit *n* costumbre *f*.
habitable *adj* habitable.
habitat *n* hábitat *m*.
habitual *adj* habitual.
haddock *n* merlango *m*.
hag *n* bruja *f*.
hail *n* granizo *m*.

hair *n* pelo; cabello *m*.
hairbrush *n* cepillo *m*.
haircut *n* corte de pelo *m*.
hairdresser *n* peluquero *m*.
hairdryer *n* secador de pelo *m*.
hairspray *n* laca *f*.
hairstyle *n* peinado *m*.
half *n* mitad *f*.
half-caste *adj* mestizo/za.

hall *n* vestíbulo *m*.
hallow *vt* consagrar, santificar.
hallucination *n* alucinación *f*.
halo *n* halo *m*.
halt *vi* parar.
halve *vt* partir por mitad.
ham *n* jamón *m*.
hamburger *n* hamburguesa *f*.
hamlet *n* aldea *f*.
hammer *n* martillo *m*.
hammock *n* hamaca *f*.
hamper *n* cesto *f*.
hamstring *vt* desjarretar.
hand *n* mano *f*.
handbag *n* cartera *f*.
handful *n* puñado *m*.
handicap *n* desventaja *f*.
handicraft *n* artesanía *f*.
handkerchief *n* pañuelo *m*.
handle *n* mango, puño *m*; asa; manija *f*.
handshake *n* apretón de manos *m*.
handsome *adj* guapo/pa.
handwriting *n* letra *f*.
handy *adj* practico/ca.
hang *vt* colgar.
hanger *n* percha *f*.
hangover *n* resaca *f*.
happen *vi* pasar; acontecer.
happiness *n* felicidad *f*.
happy *adj* feliz.
harass *vt* cansar, fatigar.
harbinger *n* precursor *m*.
harbor *n* puerto *m*.
hard *adj* duro/ra, firme.
harden *vt, vi* endurecer(se).
hardiness *n* robustez *f*.
hardly *adv* apenas.
hardship *n* penas *fpl*.
hard-up *adj* sin plata.
hardware store *n* ferretería *f*.
hardy *adj* fuerte.
hare *n* liebre *f*.
hare-lipped *adj* labihendido/da.
haricot *n* alubia *f*.
harlequin *n* arlequín *m*.
harm *n* mal, daño *m*.
harmful *adj* perjudicial.
harmless *adj* inocuo/cua.
harmonic *adj* armónico/ca.
harmonious *adj* armonioso/sa.
harmonize *vt* armonizar.
harmony *n* armonía *f*.
harp *n* arpa *f*.
harpoon *n* arpón *m*.
harsh *adj* duro/ra; austero/ra.
harvest *n* cosecha *f*.
harvester *n* cosechadora *f*.

hash *n* hachís *m*.
hassock *n* cojín de paja *m*.
haste *n* apuro *m*.
hasten *vt* acelerar.
hasty *adj* apresurado/da.
hat *n* sombrero *m*.
hatch *vt* incubar; tramar *f*.
hatchet *n* hacha *f*.
hatchway *n* (*mar*) escotilla *f*.
hate *n* odio.
hateful *adj* odioso/sa.
hatred *n* odio, aborrecimiento *m*.
haughty *adj* altanero/ra, orgulloso/sa.
haul *vt* tirar:—*n* botín *m*.
hauler *n* transportista *m/f*.
haunch *n* anca *f*.
haunt *vt* frecuentar, rondar.
have *vt* haber; tener, poseer.
haven *n* asilo *m*.
havoc *n* estrago *m*.
hawk *n* halcón *m*.
hawthorn *n* espino blanco *m*.
hay *n* heno *m*.
hazard *n* riesgo *m*.
haze *n* niebla *f*.
hazel *n* avellano *m*.
hazelnut *n* avellana *f*.
hazy *adj* oscuro/ra.
he *pn* el. **head** *n* cabeza *f*.
head *n* cakeza *f*.
headache *n* dolor de cabeza *m*.
headlamp *n* faro *m*.
headline *n* titular *m*.
headmaster *n* director *m*.
headphones *npl* auriculares *mpl*.
heal *vt, vi* curar.
health *n* salud *f*
healthy *adj* sano/na.
heap *n* montón *m*.
hear *vt* oír; escuchar.
hearing *n* oído *m*.
hearing aid *n* audífono *m*.
hearse *n* coche fúnebre *m*.
heart *n* corazón *m*.
heart attack *n* infarto *m*.
heartburn *n* acedia *f*.
hearth *n* hogar *m*.
heartily *adv* sinceramente.
heartless *adj* cruel.
hearty *adj* cordial.
heat *n* calor *m*.
heater *n* calentador *m*.
heathen *n* pagano *m*.
heating *n* calefacción *f*.
heatwave *n* ola de calor *f*.
heaven *n* cielo *m*.
heavily *adv* pesadamente.

heavy *adj* pesado/da.
Hebrew *n* hebreo *m*.
heckle *vt* interrumpir.
hectic *adj* agitado/da.
hedge *n* seto *m*.
hedgehog *n* erizo *m*.
heed *vt* hacer caso de.
heedless *adj* descuidado/da.
heel *n* talón *m*.
hefty *adj* grande.
heifer *n* ternera *f*.
height *n* altura *f*; altitud *f*.
heinous *adj* atroz.
heir *n* heredero/ra *m/f*.
heirloom *n* reliquia de familia *f*.
helicopter *n* helicóptero *m*.
hell *n* infierno *m*.
helm *n* (*mar*) timón *m*.
helmet *n* casco *m*.
help *vt, vi* ayudar, socorrer.
helper *n* ayudante *m*.
helpful *adj* útil.
helping *n* ración *f*.
helpless *adj* indefenso/sa.
hem *n* ribete *m*.
he-man *n* macho *m*.
hemisphere *n* hemisferio *m*.
hemorrhage *n* hemorragia *f*.
hemorrhoids *npl* hemorroides *mpl*.
hemp *n* cáñamo *m*.
hen *n* gallina *f*.
henchman *n* secuaz *m*.
henceforth, henceforward *adv* de aquí en adelante.
her *pn* su; ella; de ella; a ella.
herald *n* heraldo *m*.
heraldry *n* heráldica *f*.
herb *n* hierba *fl*.
herbaceous *adj* herbáceo/cea.
herbalist *n* herbolario *m*.
herbivorous *adj* herbívoro/ra.
herd *n* rebaño *m*.
here *adv* aquí, acá.
hereabout(s) *adv* aquí alrededor.
hereafter *adv* en el futuro.
hereby *adv* por esto.
hereditary *adj* hereditario/ria.
heresy *n* herejía *f*.
heretic *n* hereje *m/f*.
heritage *n* patrimonio *m*.
hermetic *adj* hermético/ca.
hermit *n* ermitaño/ña *m/f*.
hermitage *n* ermita *f*.
hernia *n* hernia *f*.
hero *n* héroe *m*.
heroic *adj* heroico/ca.
heroine *n* heroína *f*.

heroism *n* heroísmo *m*.
heron *n* garza *f*.
herring *n* arenque *m*.
herself *pn* ella misma.
hesitant *adj* vacilante.
hesitate *vt* dudar; tardar.
heterosexual *adj, n* heterosexual *m*.
hew *vt* tajar; cortar.
heyday *n* apogeo *m*.
hi *excl* ¡hola!
hiatus *n* (*gr*) hiato *m*.
hibernate *vi* invernar.
hiccup *n* hipo *m*.
hickory *n* noguera americana *f*.
hide *vt* esconder *f*.
hideaway *n* escondite *m*.
hideous *adj* horrible.
hierarchy *n* jerarquía *f*.
hieroglyphic *adj* jeroglífico/ca.
hi-fi *n* estéreo, hi-fi *m*.
high *adj* alto/ta; elevado/da.
highlight *n* punto culminante *m*.
highway *n* carretera *f*.
hike *vi* ir de excursión.
hijack *vt* secuestrar.
hilarious *adj* alegre.
hill, hillock *n* colina *f*.
him *pn* le, lo, el.
himself *pn* el mismo, se, si mismo.
hinder *vt* impedir.
hindrance *n* impedimento, obstáculo *m*.
hinge *n* bisagra *f*.
hip *n* cadera *f*.
hippopotamus *n* hipopótamo *m*.
hire *vt* alquilar.
his *pn* su, suyo, de el.
Hispanic *adj* hispano/na; hispánico/ca.
hiss *vt, vi* silbar.
historian *n* historiador *m*.
history *n* historia *f*.
hit *vt* golpear.
hitch *vt* atar.
hitch-hike *vi* hacer autostop.
hive *n* colmena *f*.
hoax *n* trampa *f*.
hobble *vi* cojear.
hobby *n* pasatiempo *m*.
hockey *n* hockey *m*.
hodge-podge *n* mezcolanza *f*.
hoe *n* azadón *m*.
hog *n* cerdo, puerco *m*.
hoist *vt* alzar.
hold *vt* tener; detener; contener.
hole *n* agujero *m*.
holiday *n* día de fiesta *m*:—~s *pl* vacaciones *fpl*.
hollow *adj* hueco/ca.

holly n (bot) acebo m.
hollyhock n malva hortense f.
holocaust n holocausto m.
holster n pistolera f.
holy adj santo/ta.
holy week n semana santa f.
homage n homenaje m.
home n casa f.
home address n domicilio m.
homely adj casero/ra.
homeopathist n homeopatista m/f.
homeopathy n homeopatía f.
homesick adj nostálgico/ca.
homework n deberes mpl.
homicide n homicidio m; homicida m.
homosexual adj, n homosexual m.
honest adj honrado/da.
honesty n honradez f.
honey n miel f.
honeycomb n panal m.
honeymoon n luna de miel f.
honeysuckle n (bot) madreselva f.
honor n honra f; honor m:—vt honrar.
honorary adj honorario/ria.
hood n capo m; capucha f.
hoof n pezuña f.
hook n gancho m.
hooligan n gamberro m.
hoop n aro m.
hooter n sirena f.
hop n (bot) lúpulo.
hope n esperanza f.
horde n horda f.
horizon n horizonte m.
horizontal adj horizontal.
hormone n hormona f.
horn n cuerno m.
hornet n avispón m.
horny adj calloso/sa.
horoscope n horóscopo m.
horrendous adj horrendo/da.
horrible adj horrible.
horrid adj horrible.
horrific adj horroroso/sa.
horrify vt horrorizar.
horror n horror, terror m.
hors d'oeuvre n entremeses mpl.
horse n caballo m
horse chestnut n castaño de Indias m.
horsefly n moscarda f.
horseradish n rábano silvestre m.
horticulture n horticultura, jardinería f.
horticulturist n jardinero/ra m/f.
hosepipe n manga f.
hosiery n calcetería f.
hospital n hospital m.
hospitality n hospitalidad f.

host n anfitrión m; hostia f.
hostage n rehén m.
hostess n anfitriona f.
hostile adj hostil.
hot adj caliente; cálido/da.
hotbed n semillero m.
hotel n hotel m.
hotelier n hotelero/ra m/f.
hour n hora f.
hour-glass n reloj de arena m.
house n casa f.
household n familia f.
houseless adv sin casa.
housewife n ama de casa f.
hovel n choza, cabaña f.
hover vi flotar.
how adv cómo.
howl vi aullar.
hub n centro m.
hue n color m.
hug vt abrazar:—n abrazo m.
huge adj vasto/ta, enorme.
hum vi canturrear.
human adv humano/na.
humane adv humano/na.
humanist n humanista m/f.
humanitarian adj humanitario/ria.
humanity n humanidad f.
humble adj humilde.
humid adj húmedo/da.
humidity n humedad f.
humiliate vt humillar.
humming-bird n colibrí m.
humor n sentido del humor m.
humorist n humorista m./f
humorous adj gracioso/sa.
hundred adj ciento.
hundredth adj centésimo.
hundredweight n quintal m.
hunger n hambre f.
hunt vt cazar; perseguir.
hunter n cazador/a m/f.
hurdle n valla f.
hurricane n huracán m.
hurt vt hacer daño; ofender.
hurtful adj dañoso/sa:—ly adv dañosamente.
husband n marido m.
hush! excl ichitón!, isilencio!.
husk n cáscara f.
hut n cabaña f.
hutch n conejera f.
hyacinth n jacinto m.
hydraulic adj hidráulico/ca.
hydrofoil n aerodeslizador m.
hydrogen n hidroala f.
hyena n hiena f.

hygiene *n* higiene *f*.
hymn *n* himno *m*.
hypermarket *n* hipermercado *m*.
hyphen *n* (*gr*) guión *m*.

hypocrisy *n* hipocresía *f*.
hypocrite *n* hipócrita *m/f*.
hysterical *adj* histérico/ca.
hysterics *npl* histeria *f*.

I

I *pn* yo.
ice *n* hielo *m*:—*vt* helar.
ice cream *n* helado *m*.
ice rink *n* pista de hielo *f*.
icicle *n* carámbano *m*.
idea *n* idea *f*.
ideal *adj* ideal.
identical *adj* idéntico/ca.
identification *n* identificación *f*.
identify *vt* identificar.
identity *n* identidad *f*.
ideology *n* ideología *f*.
idiom *n* idioma *m*.
idiosyncrasy *n* idiosincrasia *f*.
idiot *n* idiota, necio *m*.
idiotic *adj* tonto/ta, bobo/ba.
idle *adj* desocupado/da.
idol *n* ídolo *m*.
idolatry *n* idolatría *f*.
idyllic *adj* idílico/ca.
i.e. *adv* esto es.
if *conj* si, aunque.
ignite *vt* encender.
ignoble *adj* innoble.
ignorance *n* ignorancia *f*.
ignorant *adj* ignorante.
ignore *vt* no hacer caso de.
ill *adj* malo/la, enfermo/ma.
ill-advised *adj* imprudente.
illegal *adj* ~ly *adv* ilegal(mente).
illegible *adj* ilegible.
illegitimate *adj* ilegítimo/ma.
ill feeling *n* rencor *m*.
illiterate *adj* analfabeto/ta.
illness *n* enfermedad *f*.
illogical *adj* ilógico/ca.
illuminate *vt* iluminar.
illusion *n* ilusión *f*.
illustrate *vt* ilustrar.
illustration *n* ilustración *f*.
image *n* imagen *f*.
imagination *n* imaginación *f*.
imagine *vt* imaginarse.
imbalance *n* desequilibrio *m*.
imbecile *adj* imbécil.
imitate *vt* imitar, copiar.
imitation *n* imitación, copia *f*.

immaculate *adj* inmaculado/da.
immature *adj* inmaduro/ra.
immediate *adj* inmediato/ta.
immense *adj* inmenso/sa.
immigrant *n* inmigrante *m*.
immigration *n* inmigración *f*.
imminent *adj* inminente.
immodest *adj* inmodesto/ta.
immoral *adj* inmoral.
immortal *adj* inmortal.
immune *adj* inmune.
imp *n* diablillo, duende *m*.
impact *n* impacto *m*.
impair *vt* disminuir.
impartial *adj* ~ly *adv* imparcial(mente).
impatience *n* impaciencia *f*.
impede *vt* estorbar.
impel *vt* impeler.
impending *adj* inminente.
imperative *adj* imperativo/va.
imperfect *adj* imperfecto/ta
imperial *adj* imperial.
impersonal *adj*, ~ly *adv* impersonal-(mente).
impetus *n* ímpetu *m*.
impiety *n* irmpiedad *f*.
implant *vt* implantar.
implement *n* herramienta.
implore *vt* suplicar.
imply *vt* suponer.
impolite *adj* maleducado/da.
import *vt* importar.
importance *n* importancia *f*.
important *adj* importante.
impose *vt* imponer.
impostor *n* impostor *m*.
impotence *n* impotencia *f*.
impotent *adj* impotente.
impound *vt* embargar.
impoverish *vt* empobrecer.
impractical *adj* poco práctico/ca.
imprecise *adj* impreciso/sa.
impress *vt* impresionar.
impression *n* impresión *f*; edición *f*.
impressive *adj* impresionante.
imprint *n* sello *m*:—*vt* imprimir; estampar.
improbable *adj* improbable.

improper *adj* impropio/pia.
improve *vt, vi* mejorar.
improvise *vt* improvisar.
impulse *n* impulso *m*.
impure *adj* impuro/ra.
impurity *n* impureza *f*.
in *prep* en.
inability *n* incapacidad *f*.
inaccessible *adj* inaccesible.
inaccurate *adj* inexacto/ta.
inadequate *adj* inadecuado/da, defectuoso/sa.
inadmissible *adj* inadmisible.
inadvertently *adv* sin querer.
inappropriate *adj* impropio/pia.
inaudible *adj* inaudible.
inaugurate *vt* inaugurar.
in-between *adj* intermedio/dia.
inborn, inbred *adj* innato/ta.
incapable *adj* incapaz.
incarcerate *vt* encarcelar.
incarnation *n* encarnación *f*.
incendiary *n* bomba incendiaria *f*.
incense *n* incienso *m*.
incentive *n* incentivo *m*.
incessant *adj* incesante.
incest *n* incesto *m*.
inch *n* pulgada *f*.
incident *n* incidente *m*.
incinerator *n* incinerador *m*.
inclination *n* inclinación.
incline *vt, vi* inclinar(se).
include *vt* incluir.
inclusive *adj* inclusivo/va.
incognito *adv* de incógnito.
incoherent *adj* incoherente.
income *n* renta *f*
incompatible *adj* incompatible.
incompetence *n* incompetencia *f*.
incomplete *adj* incompleto/ta.
incomprehensible *adj* incomprensible.
inconceivable *adj* inconcebible.
incontinence *n* incontinencia *f*.
inconvenience *n* incomodidad *f*.
incorrect *adj* incorrecto/ta.
increase *vt* acrecentar, aumentar
incredible *adj* increíble.
incubate *vi* incubar.
incubator *n* incubadora *f*.
incurable *adj* incurable.
indecency *n* indecencia *f*.
indecent *adj* indecente:—**~ly** *adv* indecentemente.
indecisive *adj* indeciso/sa.
indeed *adv* verdaderamente, de veras.
independence *n* independencia *f*.
independent *adj* independiente.
indescribable *adj* indescriptible.

index *n* índice *m*.
indicate *vt* indicar.
indifference *n* indiferencia *f*.
indigenous *adj* indígena.
indigestion *n* indigestión *f*.
indignation *n* indignación *f*.
indigo *n* añil *m*.
indirect *adj* indirecto/ta.
indiscreet *adj* indiscreto/ta.
indispensable *adj* indispensable.
indistinguishable *adj* indistinguible.
individual *adj* individual *m*.
indoors *adv* dentro.
indulge *vt, vi* conceder; ser indulgente.
industrialist *n* industrial *m*.
industry *n* industria *f*.
inedible *adj* no comestible.
ineffective, ineffectual *adj* ineficaz.
inefficiency *n* ineficacia *f*.
ineligible *adj* ineligible.
inept *adj* incompetente.
inequality *n* desigualdad *f*.
inevitable *adj* inevitable.
inexpensive *adj* económico/ca.
inexperience *n* inexperiencia *f*.
inexpert *adj* inexperto/ta.
inexplicable *adj* inexplicable.
infallible *adj* infalible.
infamy *n* infamia *f*.
infancy *n* infancia *f*.
infant *n* niño/ña *m/f*.
infantile *adj* infantil.
infantry *n* infantería *f*.
infatuation *n* infatuación *f*.
infect *vt* infectar.
infection *n* infección *f*.
inferior *adj* inferior.
infernal *adj* infernal.
inferno *n* infierno *m*.
infest *vt* infestar.
infidelity *n* infidelidad *f*.
infinite *adj* infinito/ta.
infinitive *n* infinitivo *m*.
infinity *n* infinito *m*; infinidad *f*.
infirm *adj* enfermo/ma.
infirmary *n* enfermería *f*.
infirmity *n* fragilidad, enfermedad *f*.
inflammation *n* inflamación *f*.
inflatable *adj* inflable.
inflate *vt* inflar, hinchar.
inflation *n* inflación *f*.
inflict *vt* imponer.
influence *n* influencia *f*.
influenza *n* gripe *f*.
inform *vt* informar.
informal *adj* informal.
information *n* información *f*.

infrastructure *n* infraestructura *f*.
infuriate *vt* enfurecer.
infusion *n* infusión *f*.
ingenious *adj* ingenioso/sa.
ingenuity *n* ingeniosidad *f*.
ingot *n* barra de metal *f*.
ingrained *adj* inveterado/da.
ingratitude *n* ingratitud *f*.
ingredient *n* ingrediente *m*.
inhabit *vt, vi* habitar.
inhabitant *n* habitante *m*.
inhale *vt* inhalar.
inherent *adj* inherente.
inherit *vt* heredar.
inheritance *n* herencia *f*.
inhibit *vt* inhibir.
inhospitable *adj* inhospitalario/ria.
inhuman *adj* inhumano/na.
inhumanity *n* inhumanidad, crueldad *f*.
initial *adj* inicial.
initiate *vt* iniciar.
initiative *n* iniciativa *f*.
inject *vt* inyectar.
injection *n* inyección *f*.
injure *vt* herir.
injury *n* daño *m*.
injustice *n* injusticia *f*.
ink *n* tinta *f*.
inkling *n* sospecha *f*.
inlaid *adj* taraceado/da.
in-laws *npl* suegros *mpl*.
inlay *vt* taracear.
inlet *n* entsenada *f*.
inmate *n* preso *m*.
inn *n* posada *f*; mesón *m*.
innkeeper *n* posadero/ra, mesonero/ra *m/f*.
innocence *n* inocencia *f*.
innocent *adj* inocente.
innovate *vt* innovar.
innovation *n* innovación *f*.
innuendo *n* indirecta, insinuación *f*.
inoffensive *adj* inofensivo/va.
inorganic *adj* inorgánico/ca.
inpatient *n* paciente interno *m*.
input *n* entrada *f*.
inquest *n* encuesta judicial *f*.
inquire *vt, vi* preguntar.
inquiry *n* pesquisa *f*.
inquisition *n* inquisición *f*.
inquisitive *adj* curioso/sa.
insane *adj* loco/ca, demente.
insanity *n* locura *f*.
inscription *n* inscripción *f*.
inscrutable *adj* inescrutable.
insect *n* insecto *m*.
insecticide *n* insecticida *m*.

insecure *adj* inseguro/ra.
insensitive *adj* insensible.
inseparable *adj* inseparable.
insert *vt* introducir.
insertion *n* inserción *f*.
inside *n* interior *m*:—*adv* dentro.
inside out *adv* al revés; a fondo.
insignia *npl* insignias *fpl*.
insignificant *adj* insignificante.
insincere *adj* poco sincero/ra.
insipid *adj* insípido/da.
insist *vi* insistir.
insole *n* plantilla *f*.
insolence *n* insolencia *f*.
insoluble *adj* insoluble.
insomnia *n* insomnio *m*.
insomuch *conj* puesto que.
inspect *vt* examinar, inspeccionar.
inspection *n* inspección *f*.
inspire *vt* inspirar.
instability *n* inestabilidad *f*.
instance *n* ejemplo *m*.
instant *adj* inmediato/ta.
instead (of) *pr* por, en lugar de, en vez de.
instill *vt* inculcar.
instinct *n* instinto *m*.
instinctive *adj* instintivo/va.
institute *vt* establecer:—*n* instituto *m*.
institution *n* institución *f*.
instruct *vt* instruir, enseñar.
instruction *n* instrucción *f*.
instrument *n* instrumento *m*.
instrumental *adj* instrumental.
insufferable *adj* insoportable.
insufficient *adj* insuficiente.
insulate *vt* aislar.
insulin *n* insulina *f*.
insult *vt* insultar:—*n* insulto *m*.
insurance *n* (*com*) seguro *m*.
insure *vt* asegurar.
intact *adj* intacto/ta.
integral *adj* íntegro/gra.
integrate *vt* integrar.
integrity *n* integridad *f*.
intellect *n* intelecto *m*.
intelligence *n* inteligencia *f*.
intend *vi* tener intención.
intense *adj* intenso/sa.
intensity *n* intensidad *f*.
intention *n* intención *f*.
inter *vt* enterrar.
interaction *n* interacción *f*.
intercourse *n* relaciones sexuales *fpl*.
interest *vt* interesar.
interesting *adj* interesante.
interest rate *n* tipo de interés *m*.
interfere *vi* entrometerse.

interference *n* interferencia *f*.
interior *adj* interior.
interlude *n* intermedio *m*.
intermediate *adj* intermedio/dia.
interment *n* entierro *m*; sepultura *f*.
intermission *n* descanso *m*.
intermittent *adj* intermitente.
internal *adj* interno/na.
international *adj* internacional.
interpret *vt* interpretar.
interpretation *n* interpretación *f*.
interpreter *n* intérprete *m/f*.
interregnum *n* interregno *m*.
interrelated *adj* interrelacionado/da.
interrogate *vt* interrogar.
interrogation *n* interrogatorio *m*.
interrogative *adj* interrogativo/va.
interrupt *vt* interrumpir.
interruption *n* interrupción *f*.
intersect *vi* cruzarse.
intersection *n* cruce *m*.
intersperse *vt* esparcir.
intertwine *vt* entretejer.
interval *n* intervalo *m*.
intervene *vi* intervenir.
intervention *n* intervención *f*.
interview *n* entrevista *f*.
interviewer *n* entrevistador/a *m/f*.
intestine *n* intestino *m*.
intimacy *n* intimidad *f*.
intimate *n* amigo/ga íntimo/ma.
intimidate *vt* intimidar.
into *prep* en, dentro, adentro.
intolerable *adj* intolerable.
intolerance *n* intolerancia *f*.
intoxicate *vt* embriagar.
intravenous *adj* intravenoso/sa.
intrepid *adj* intrépido/da.
intricate *adj* intricado/da.
intrigue *n* intriga *f*:—*vi* intrigar.
intriguing *adj* fascinante.
intrinsic *adj* intrínseco/ca.
introduce *vt* introducir.
introduction *n* introducción *f*.
introvert *n* introvertido *m*.
intrude *vi* entrometerse.
intruder *n* intruso/sa *m/f*.
intuition *n* intuición *f*.
intuitive *adj* intuitivo/va.
inundate *vt* inundar.
inundation *n* inundación *f*.
invade *vt* invadir.
invalid *adj* inválido/da.
invalidate *vt* invalidar, anular.
invaluable *adj* inapreciable.
invariable *adj* invariable.
invariably *adv* invariablemente.

invasion *n* invasión *f*.
invent *vt* inventar.
invention *n* invento *m*.
inventor *n* inventor *m*.
inventory *n* inventario *m*.
inversion *n* inversión *f*.
invert *vt* invertir.
invest *vt* invertir.
investigate *vt* investigar.
investment *n* inversión *f*.
invigilate *vt* vigilar.
invigorating *adj* vigorizante.
invincible *adj* invencible.
invisible *adj* invisible.
invitation *n* invitación *f*.
invite *vt* invitar.
invoice *n* (com) factura *f*.
involuntarily *adv* involuntariamente.
involve *vt* implicar.
involvement *n* compromiso *m*.
iodine *n* (chem) yodo *m*.
IOU (I owe you) *n* vale *m*.
irate, ireful *adj* enojado/da.
iris *n* iris *m*.
irksome *adj* fastidioso/sa.
iron *n* hierro *m*:—*adj* férreo/rea:—*vt* planchar.
ironic *adj* irónico/ca:—~**ly** *adv* con ironía.
ironwork *n* herraje *m*:—~**s** *pl* herrería *f*.
irony *n* ironía *f*.
irradiate *vt* irradiar.
irrational *adj* irracional.
irreconcilable *adj* irreconciliable.
irregular *adj* ~**ly** *adv* irregular(mente).
irrelevant *adj* impertinente.
irreparable *adj* irreparable.
irresistible *adj* irresistible.
irresponsible *adj* irresponsable.
irrigate *vt* regar.
irrigation *n* riego *m*.
irritable *adj* irritable.
irritant *n* (med) irritante *m*.
irritate *vt* irritar.
island *n* isla *f*.
isle *n* isla *f*.
isolate *vt* aislar.
issue *n* asunto *m*.
it *pn* el, ella, ello, lo, la, le.
italic *n* cursiva *f*.
itch *n* picazón *f*:—*vi* picar.
item *n* artículo *m*.
itemize *vt* detallar.
itinerary *n* itinerario *m*.
its *pn* su, suyo.
itself *pn* el mismo, la misma, lo mismo.
ivory *n* marfil *m*.
ivy *n* hiedra *f*.

J

jab *vt* clavar.
jabber *vi* farfullar.
jack *n* gato *m*; sota *f*.
jackal *n* chacal *m*.
jackboots *npl* botas militares *fpl*.
jackdaw *n* grajo *m*.
jacket *n* chaqueta *f*.
jack-knife *vi* colear.
jackpot *n* premio gordo *m*.
jade *n* jade *m*.
jagged *adj* dentado/da.
jaguar *n* jaguar *m*.
jail *n* cárcel *f*.
jailer *n* carcelero/ra *m/f*.
jam *n* conserva *f*; mermelada de frutas *f*.
jangle *vi* sonar.
January *n* enero *m*.
jargon *n* jerigonza *f*.
jasmine *n* jazmín *m*.
jaundice *n* ictericia *f*.
jaunt *n* excursión *f*.
jaunty *adj* alegre.
javelin *n* jabalina *f*.
jaw *n* mandíbula *f*.
jay *n* arrendajo *m*.
jazz *n* jazz *m*.
jealous *adj* celoso/sa.
jealousy *n* celos *mpl*; envidia *f*.
jeans *npl* vaqueros *mpl*.
jeep *n* jeep *m*.
jeer *vi* befar.
jelly *n* jalea, gelatina *f*.
jellyfish *n* aguamar *m*; medusa *f*.
jeopardize *vt* arriesgar.
jersey *n* jersey *m*.
jest *n* broma *f*.
jester *n* bufón/ona *m/f*.
Jesuit *n* jesuita *m*.
Jesus *n* Jesús *m*.
jet *n* avión a reacción *m*.
jettison *vt* desechar.
jetty *n* muelle *m*.
Jew *n* judío/día *m/f*.
jewel *n* joya *f*.
jewelry *n* joyería *f*.
Jewish *adj* judío/día.
jib *n* (*mar*) foque *m*.
jibe *n* mofa *f*.
jig *n* giga *f*.
jigsaw *n* rompecabezas *m*.
jilt *vt* dejar.
job *n* trabajo *m*.
jockey *n* jinete *m/f*.
jocular *adj* jocoso/sa, alegre.

jog *vi* hacer footing.
jogging *n* footing *m*.
join *vt* juntar, unir.
joiner *n* carpintero/ra *m/f*.
joinery *n* carpintería *f*.
joint *n* articulación *f*.
jointly *adv* conjuntamente.
joke *n* broma *f*:—*vi* bromear.
joker *n* comodín *m*.
jollity *n* alegría *f*.
jolly *adj* alegre.
jolt *vt* sacudir:—*n* sacudida *f*.
jostle *vt* codear.
journal *n* revista *f*.
journalism *n* periodismo *m*.
journalist *n* periodista *m/f*.
journey *n* viaje *m*:—*vt* viajar.
jovial *adj* jovial.
joy *n* alegría *f*; jubilo *m*.
jubilant *adj* jubiloso/sa.
jubilation *n* jubilo/la, regocijo *m*.
jubilee *n* jubileo *m*.
Judaism *n* judaísmo *m*.
judge *n* juez/a *m/f*:—*vt* juzgar.
judgment *n* juicio *m*.
judicial *adj* ~ly *adv* judicial(mente).
judiciary *n* judicatura *m*.
judicious *adj* prudente.
judo *n* judo *m*.
juggle *vi* hacer juegos malabares.
juggler *n* malabarista *m/f*.
juice *n* jugo *m*; suco *m*.
juicy *adj* jugoso/sa.
jukebox *n* gramola *f*.
July *n* julio *m*.
jumble *vt* mezclar.
jump *vi* saltar.
jumper *n* suéter *m*.
jumpy *adj* nervioso/sa.
juncture *n* coyuntura *f*.
June *n* junio *m*.
jungle *n* selva *f*.
junior *adj* más joven.
juniper *n* (*bot*) enebro *m*.
junk *n* basura *f*; baratijas *fpl*.
junta *n* junta *f*.
jurisdiction *n* jurisdicción *f*.
jurisprudence *n* jurisprudencia *f*.
jurist *n* jurista *m/f*.
jury *n* jurado *m*.
just *adj* justo/ta.
justice *n* justicia *f*.
justification *n* justificación *f*.
justify *vt* justificar.

justly *adv* justamente.
justness *n* justicia *f*.
jut *vi*:—to ~ out sobresalir.

jute *n* yute *m*.
juvenile *adj* juvenil.
juxtaposition *n* yuxtaposición *f*.

K

kaleidoscope *n* calidoscopio *m*.
kangaroo *n* canguro *m*.
karate *n* karate *m*.
kebab *n* pincho *m*.
keel *n* (*mar*) quilla *f*.
keen *adj* agudo/da; vivo/va.
keep *vt* mantener; guardar; conservar.
keeper *n* guardián/ana *m/f*.
keepsake *n* recuerdo *m*.
keg *n* barril *m*.
kennel *n* perrera *f*.
kernel *n* fruta *f*; meollo *m*.
kerosene *n* kerosene *m*.
ketchup *n* catsup *m*.
kettle *n* hervidor *m*.
key *n* llave *f*; (*mus*) clave *f*; tecla *f*.
keyboard *n* teclado *m*.
keyhole *n* ojo de la cerradura *m*.
key ring *n* llavero *m*.
khaki *n* caqui *m*.
kick *vt*, *vi* patear.
kid *n* chico *m*.
kidnap *vt* secuestrar.
kidnapper *n* secuestrador/a *m/f*.
kidney *n* riñón *m*.
killer *n* asesino/na *m/f*.
killing *n* asesinato *m*.
kiln *n* horno *m*.
kilo *n* kilo *m*.
kilobyte *n* kilocteto *m*.
kilogram *n* kilo *m*.
kilometer *n* kilómetro *m*.
kilt *n* falda escocesa *f*.
kin *n* parientes *mpl*.
kind *adj* cariñoso/sa:—*n* genero *m*.
kind-hearted *adj* bondadoso/sa.
kindle *vt*, *vi* encender.
kindly *adj* bondadoso/sa.
kindness *n* bondad *f*.

kindred *adj* emparentado/da.
kinetic *adj* cinético/ca.
king *n* rey *m*.
kingdom *n* reino *m*.
kingfisher *n* martín pescador *m*.
kiosk *n* quiosco *m*.
kiss *n* beso *m*:—*vt* besar.
kit *n* equipo *m*.
kitchen *n* cocina *f*.
kite *n* cometa *f*.
kitten *n* gatillo *m*.
knack *n* don *m*.
knapsack *n* mochila *f*.
knave *n* bribón
knead *vt* amasar.
knee *n* rodilla *f*.
kneel *vi* arrodillarse.
knell *n* toque de difuntos *m*.
knife *n* cuchillo *m*.
knight *n* caballero *m*.
knit *vt*, *vi* tejer.
knitting needle *n* aguja de tejer *f*.
knitwear *n* prendas de punto *fpl*.
knob *n* bulto *m*.
knock *vt*, *vi* golpear.
knocker *n* aldaba *f*.
knock-kneed *adj* patizambo/ba.
knock-out *n* K.O. *m*.
knoll *n* cima de una colina *f*.
knot *n* nudo *m*; lazo *m*:—*vt* anudar.
knotty *adj* escabroso/sa.
know *vt*, *vi* conocer; saber.
know-all *n* sabelotodo *m/f*.
know-how *n* conocimientos *mpl*.
knowing *adj* entendido/da:—~ly *adv* a
sabiendas.
knowledge *n* conocimiento *m*.
knowledgeable *adj* bien informado/da.
knuckle *n* nudillo *m*.

L

label *n* etiqueta *f*.
laboratory *n* laboratorio *m*.
laborious *adj* laborioso/sa.
labor *n* trabajo *m*.
laborer *n* peón *m*.
labyrinth *n* laberinto *m*.
lace *n* cordón.

lacerate *vt* lacerar.
lack *vt*, *vi* faltar.
lacquer *n* laca *f*.
lad *n* muchacho *m*.
ladder *n* escalera *f*.
ladle *n* cucharón *m*.
lady *n* señora *f*.

lag vi quedarse atrás.
lager n cerveza (rubia) f.
lagoon n laguna f.
lake n lago m.
lamb n cordero m:—vi parir.
lame adj cojo/ja.
lament vt, vi lamentar(se).
lamp n lámpara f.
lampoon n sátira f.
lampshade n pantalla f.
lance n lanza f.
lancet n lanceta f.
land n país m; tierra f.
landing n desembarco m.
landmark n lugar conocido m.
landscape n paisaje m.
lane n callejuela f.
language n lengua f; lenguaje m.
lank adj lacio/cia.
lanky adj larguirucho.
lantern n linterna f; farol m.
lap n regazo m.
lapel n solapa f.
lapse n lapso m.
larceny n latrocinio m.
larch n alerce m.
lard n manteca de cerdo f.
larder n despensa f.
large adj grande.
lark n alondra f.
larva n larva, oruga f.
laryngitis n laringitis f.
larynx n laringe f.
lascivious adj lascivo/va.
laser n láser m.
lash n latigazo m.
lasso n lazo m.
last adj último/ma.
lasting adj duradero/ra, permanente.
latch n picaporte m.
late adj tarde; difunto/ta.
latent adj latente.
lathe n torno m.
lather n espuma f.
latitude n latitud f.
latter adj último/ma.
lattice n celosía f.
laugh vi reir.
laughter n risa f.
launch vt, vi lanzar(se):—n (mar) lancha f.
launching n lanzamiento m.
launder vt lavar.
laundry n lavandería f.
laurel n laurel m.
lava n lava f.
lavatory n water m.
lavender n (bot) espliego m, lavándula f.

lavish adj pródigo/ga:—~ly adv pródiga-
   mente:—vt disipar.
law n ley f; derecho m.
law court n tribunal m.
lawn n pasto m.
lawnmower n cortacésped m.
law suit n proceso m.
lawyer n abogado/da m/f.
laxative n laxante m.
lay vt poner.
layabout n vago/ga m/f.
layer n capa f.
layout n composición f.
laze vi holgazanear.
laziness n pereza f.
lazy adj perezoso/sa.
lead n plomo m.
leader n jefe/fa m/f.
leaf n hoja f.
leaflet n folleto m.
league n liga, alianza f.
leak n escape m.
lean vt, vi apoyar(se).
leap vi saltar.
leap year n año bisiesto m.
learn vt, vi aprender.
lease n arriendo m:—vt arrendar.
leash n correa f.
least adj mínimo/ma.
leather n cuero m.
leave n licencia f; permiso m.
lecherous adj lascivo/va.
lecture n conferencia f.
ledge n reborde m.
ledger n (com) libro mayor m.
leech n sanguijuela f.
leek n (bot) puerro m.
left adj izquierdo/da.
left-handed adj zurdo/da.
leftovers npl sobras fpl.
leg n pierna f
legacy n herencia f.
legal adj legal.
legalize vt legalizar.
legend n leyenda f.
legendary adj legendario/ria.
legible adj legible.
legion n legión f.
legislate vt legislar.
legislation n legislación f.
leisure n ocio m:—~ly adj sin prisa: —at ~
   desocupado/da.
lemon n limón m.
lemonade n limonada f.
lend vt prestar.
length n largo m; duración f.
lenient adj indulgente.

lens *n* lente *f*.
Lent *n* Cuaresma *f*.
lentil *n* lenteja *f*.
leopard *n* leopardo *m*.
leotard *n* leotardo *m*.
leper *n* leproso/sa *m/f*.
leprosy *n* lepra *f*.
lesbian *n* lesbiana *f*.
less *adj* menor.
lesson *n* lección *f*.
let *vt* dejar, permitir.
lethal *adj* mortal.
lethargy *n* letargo *m*.
letter *n* letra *f*; carta *f*.
lettuce *n* lechuga *f*.
leukemia *n* leucemia *f*.
level *adj* llano/na, igual.
lever *n* palanca *f*.
leverage *n* influencia *f*.
levy *n* leva (de tropas) *f*.
lexicon *n* léxico *m*.
liability *n* responsabilidad *f*.
liable *adj* sujeto/ta; responsable.
liaise *vi* enlazar.
liaison *n* enlace *m*.
liar *n* embustero *m*.
libel *n* difamación *f*:—*vt* difamar.
liberal *adj* liberal.
liberate *vt* libertar.
liberation *n* liberación *f*.
liberty *n* libertad *f*.
Libra *n* Libra *f*.
librarian *n* bibliotecario *m*.
library *n* biblioteca *f*.
license *n* licencia *f*.
lick *vt* lamer.
lid *n* tapa *f*.
lie *n* mentira *f*.
life *n* vida *f*.
lifelike *adj* natural.
life preserver *n* chaleco salvavidas *m*.
lift *vt* levantar.
ligament *n* ligamento *m*.
light *n* luz *f*.
light bulb *n* foco *m*; bombilla *f*.
lighter *n* encendedor *m*.
lighthouse *n* (*mar*) faro *m*.
lightning *n* relámpago *m*.
like *adj* semejante; igual.
likeness *n* semejanza *f*.
lilac *n* lila *f*.
lily *n* lirio *m*.
lima beans *npl* haba gruesa *f*.
limb *n* miembro *m*.
lime *n* cal *f*; lima *f*.
limestone *n* piedra caliza *f*.
limit *n* limite *m*.

line *n* línea *f*.
linen *n* lino *m*.
liner *n* transatlántico *m*.
linger *vi* persistir.
lingerie *n* ropa interior *f*.
linguist *n* lingüista *m*.
lining *n* forro *m*.
link *n* eslabón *m*.
linoleum *n* linóleo *m*.
lintel *n* dintel *m*.
lion *n* león *m*.
lip *n* labio *m*.
liqueur *n* licor *m*.
liquid *adj* líquido/da.
liquor *n* licor *m*.
liquorice *n* orozuz *m*; regaliz *a f*.
lisp *vi* cecear.
list *n* lista *f*.
listen *vi* escuchar.
literature *n* literatura *f*.
lithe *adj* ágil.
lithograph *n* litografía *f*.
litigation *n* litigio *m*.
liter *n* litro *m*.
litter *n* litera *f*.
little *adj* pequeño/ña, poco/ca.
live *vi* vivir; habitar.
liver *n* hígado *m*.
livestock *n* ganado *m*.
living *n* vida *f*:—*adj* vivo/va.
living room *n* sala de estar *f*.
lizard *n* lagarto *m*.
load *vt* cargar.
loaf *n* pan *m*.
loam *n* marga *f*.
loan *n* préstamo *m*.
loathe *vt* aborrecer.
loathing *n* aversión *f*.
lobby *n* vestíbulo *m*.
lobe *n* lóbulo *m*.
lobster *n* langosta *f*.
local *adj* local.
locality *n* localidad *f*.
locate *vt* localizar.
location *n* situación *f*.
loch *n* lago *m*.
lock *n* cerradura *f*.
locker *n* vestuario *m*.
locket *n* medallón *m*.
locomotive *n* locomotora *f*.
locust *n* langosta *f*.
loft *n* desván *m*.
lofty *adj* alto/ta.
log *n* leño *m*.
logic *n* lógica *f*.
logo *n* logotipo *m*.
loiter *vi* merodear.

lollipop *n* pirulí *m*.
loneliness *n* soledad *f*.
long *adj* largo/ga.
longitude *n* longitud *f*.
look *vi* mirar *f*.
looking glass *n* espejo *m*.
loop *n* lazo *m*.
loose *adj* suelto/ta.
loot *vt* saquear:—*n* botín *m*.
lop *vt* desmochar.
lord *n* señor *m*.
lose *vt* perder.
loss *n* perdida *f*.
lotion *n* loción *f*.
lottery *n* lotería *f*.
loud *adj* fuerte:——**ly** *adv* fuerte.
loudspeaker *n* altavoz *m*.
lounge *n* salón *m*.
louse *n* piojo (*pl* **lice**) *m*.
lout *n* gamberro *m*.
love *n* amor, cariño *m*.
lovely *adj* hermoso/sa.
lover *n* amante *m*.
low *adj* bajo/ja.
loyal *adj* leal; fiel.
lozenge *n* pastilla *f*.
lubricant *n* lubricante *m*.

lubricate *vt* lubricar.
luck *n* suerte *f*; fortuna *f*.
lucrative *adj* lucrativo/va.
ludicrous *adj* absurdo/da.
lug *vt* arrastrar.
luggage *n* equipaje *m*.
lull *vt* acunar:—*n* tregua *f*.
lullaby *n* nana *f*.
lumbago *n* lumbago *m*.
lumber *n* madera de construccion *f*
luminous *adj* luminoso/sa.
lump *n* terrón *m*.
lunacy *n* locura *f*.
lunar *adj* lunar.
lunatic *adj* loco/ca.
lunch, luncheon *n* merienda *f*.
lungs *npl* pulmones *mpl*.
luscious *adj* delicioso/sa.
lush *adj* exuberante.
lust *n* lujuria, sensualidad *f*.
luster *n* lustre *m*.
luxurious *adj* lujoso/sa.
luxury *n* lujo *m*.
lymph *n* linfa *f*.
lynx *n* lince *m*.
lyrical *adj* lírico/ca.
lyrics *npl* letra *f*.

M

macaroni *n* macarrones *mpl*.
macaroon *n* almendrado *m*.
mace *n* maza *f*; macis *f*.
machine *n* maquina *f*.
machinery *n* maquinaria, mecanica *f*.
mackerel *n* escombro *m*.
mad *adj* loco, furioso, rabioso.
madam *n* madama, senora *f*.
madhouse *n* casa de locos *f*.
madness *n* locura *f*.
magazine *n* revista *f*.
maggot *n* gusano *m*.
magic *n* magia *f*.
magician *n* mago *m*
magistrate *n* magistrado *m*.
magnet *n* iman *m*.
magnetic *adj* magnetico.
magnificent *adj* magnifico.
magnify *vt* aumentar.
magnifying glass *n* lupa *f*.
magnitude *n* magnitud *f*.
magpie *n* urraca *f*.
mahogany *n* caoba *f*.
mail *n* correo *m*.

mailman *n* cartero *m*.
maim *vt* mutilar.
main *adj* principal.
maintain *vt* mantener.
maintenance *n* mantenimiento *m*.
maize *n* maiz *m*.
majesty *n* majestad *f*.
major *adj* principal
make *vt* hacer, crear.
make-up *n* maquillaje *m*.
malaria *n* malaria *f*.
male *adj* masculino:—*n* macho *m*.
malice *n* malicia *f*.
malicious *adj* malicioso.
mall *n* centro comercial *m*.
malleable *adj* maleable.
mallet *n* mazo *m*.
mallows *n* (*bot*) malva *f*.
malnutrition *n* desnutricion *f*.
malpractice *n* negligencia *f*.
malt *n* malta *f*.
maltreat *vt* maltratar.
mammal *n* mamifero *m*.
mammoth *adj* gigantesco.

man *n* hombre *m*.
manage *vt, vi* manejar, dirigir.
management *n* direccion *f*.
manager *n* director *m*.
mandate *n* mandato *m*.
mane *n* crines del caballo *fpl*.
maneuvre *n* maniobra *f*.
mangle *n* rodillo *m*.
mangy *adj* sarnoso.
manhood *n* edad viril *f*.
mania *n* mania *f*.
maniac *n* maniaco *m*.
manipulate *vt* manejar.
mankind *n* genero humano *m*.
man-made *n* artificial.
manner *n* manera *f*; modo *m*
mansion *n* palacio *m*.
mantelpiece *n* repisa de chimenea *f*.
manual *adj, n* manual *m*.
manufacture *n* fabricacion *f*.
manufacturer *n* fabricante *m*.
manuscript *n* manuscrito *m*.
many *adj* muchos, muchas.
map *n* mapa *m*.
maple *n* arce *m*.
mar *vt* estropear.
marathon *n* maraton *m*.
marble *n* marmol *m*.
March *n* marzo *m*.
mare *n* yegua *f*.
margarine *n* margarina *f*.
margin *n* margen *m*; borde *m*.
marigold *n* (*bot*) calendula *f*.
marijuana *n* marijuana *f*.
marine *adj* marino*m*.
marital *adj* marital.
mark *n* marca *f*.
market *n* mercado *m*.
marmalade *n* mermelada de naranja *f*.
maroon *adj* marron.
marquee *n* entoldado *m*.
marriage *n* matrimonio *m*
marrow *n* medula *f*.
marry *vi* casar(se).
marsh *n* pantano *m*.
marshy *adj* pantanoso.
martyr *n* martir *m*.
marvel *n* maravilla *f*.
marvelous *adj* maravilloso.
marzipan *n* mazapan *m*.
mascara *n* rimel *m*.
masculine *adj* masculino.
mask *n* mascara *f*.
masochist *n* masoquista *m*.
mason *n* albanil *m*.
mass *n* masa *f*; misa *f*;
massacre *n* carniceria, matanza *f*.

massage *n* masaje *m*.
massive *adj* enorme.
mast *n* mastil *m*.
masterpiece *n* obra maestra *f*.
masticate *vt* masticar.
mat *n* estera *f*.
match *n* fosforo *m*, cerilla *f*.
mate *n* companero *m*:—*vt* acoplar.
mathematics *npl* matematicas *fpl*.
matinee *n* funcion de la tarde *f*.
mating *n* aparejamiento *m*.
matriculate *vt* matricular.
matriculation *n* matriculacion *f*.
matt *adj* mate.
matter *n* materia, substancia *f*.
mattress *n* colchon *m*.
mature *adj* maduro.
maximum *n* maximo *m*.
May *n* mayo *m*.
mayonnaise *n* mayonesa *f*.
mayor *n* alcalde *m*.
maze *n* laberinto *m*.
me *pn* me; mi.
meal *n* comida *f*; harina *f*.
mean *adj* tacano.
meander *vi* serpentear.
meaning *n* sentido, significado *m*.
meantime, meanwhile *adv* mientras tanto.
measles *npl* sarampion *m*.
measurement *n* medida *f*.
meat *n* carne *f*.
mechanic *n* mecanico *m*.
mechanism *n* mecanismo *m*.
medal *n* medalla *f*.
media *npl* medios de comunicacion *mpl*.
medical *adj* medico.
medicate *vt* medicinar.
medicine *n* medicina *f*.
medieval *adj* medieval.
mediocre *adj* mediocre.
meditate *vi* meditar.
meditation *n* meditacion *f*.
Mediterranean *adj* mediterraneo.
medium *n* medio *m*.
meet *vt* encontrar.
meeting *n* reunion *f*.
megaphone *n* megafono *m*.
melancholy *n* melancolia *f*.
mellow *adj* maduro.
mellowness *n* madurez *f*.
melody *n* melodia *f*.
melon *n* melon *m*.
melt *vt* derretir.
member *n* miembro *m*.
membrane *n* membrana *f*.
memento *n* memento *m*.

memoir n memoria f.
memorandum n memorandum m.
memorial n monumento conmemorativo m.
memory n memoria f; recuerdo m.
menace n amenaza f.
menagerie n casa de fieras f.
mend vt reparar.
menial adj domestico.
meningitis n meningitis f.
menopause n menopausia f.
menstruation n menstruacion f.
mental adj mental.
mention n mencion f.
mentor n mentor m.
menu n menu m; carta f.
merchandise n mercancia f.
merchant n comerciante m.
mercury n mercurio m.
mercy n compasion f.
mere adj mero.
meridian n meridiano m.
merit n merito m.
mermaid n sirena f.
merry adj alegre.
merry-go-round n tiovivo m.
mesh n malla f.
mesmerize vt hipnotizar.
mess n lio m.
message n mensaje m.
metabolism n metabolismo n.
metal n metal m.
metallic adj metalico.
metamorphosis n metamorfosis f.
metaphor n metafora f.
meteor n meteoro m.
meteorological adj meteorológico.
meteorology n meteorologia f.
meter[1] n medidor m.
meter[2] n metro m.
method n metodo m.
methodical adj metodico.
Methodist n metodista m.
metric adj metrico.
metropolis n metropoli f.
metropolitan adj metropolitano.
mettle n valor m.
mew vi maullar.
mezzanine n entresuelo m.
microbe n microbio m.
microphone n microfono m.
microchip n microplaqueta f.
microscope n microscopio m.
microwave n horno microondas m.
mid adj medio.
midday n mediodia m.
middle adj mediom.
midge n mosca f.

midget n enano m.
midnight n medianoche f.
midst n medio, centro m.
midsummer n pleno verano m.
midwife n partera f.
might n poder m; fuerza f.
mighty adj fuerte.
migraine n jaqueca f.
migrate vi emigrar.
migration n emigracion f.
mike n microfono m.
mild adj apacible; suave.
mildew n moho m.
mileage n kilometraje m.
milieu n ambiente m.
militant adj militante.
military adj militar.
milk n leche f.
milkshake n batido m
milky adj lechoso:—**M~ Way** n Via Lactea f.
mill n molino m.
millennium n milenio m.
miller n molinero m.
milligram n miligramo m.
milliliter n mililitro m.
millimeter n milimetro m.
milliner n sombrerero.
million n millon m.
millionaire n millonario m.
millionth adj millonésimo.
mime n mimo m.
mimic vt imitar.
mince vt picar.
mind n mente f.
mine pn mio, mia, mi:—n mina:—vi minar.
miner n minero m.
mineral adj, n mineral m.
mineral water n agua mineral f.
mingle vt mezclar.
miniature n miniatura f.
minimal adj minimo.
minimum n minimum m.
mining n explotacion minera f.
minister n ministro m.
mink n vison m.
minnow n pecicillo m (pez).
minor adj menor.
mint n (bot) menta f.
minus adv menos.
minute adj diminuto.
minute n minuto m.
miracle n milagro m.
mirage n espejismo m.
mire n fango m.
mirror n espejo m.
mirth n alegria f.

misbehave *vi* portarse mal.
miscarry *vi* abortar.
miscellaneous *adj* varios, varias.
miser *n* avaro *m*.
miserable *adj* miserable.
miserly *adj* mezquino, tacano.
misery *n* miseria *f*.
mislay *vt* extraviar.
mislead *vt* enganar.
misogynist *n* misogino *m*.
Miss *n* senorita *f*.
miss *vt* perder; echar de menos.
missile *n* misil *m*.
mission *n* mision *f*.
missionary *n* misionero *m*.
mist *n* niebla *f*.
mistake *vt* entender mal
Mister *n* Senor *m*.
mistletoe *n* (*bot*) muerdago *m*.
mistress *n* amante *f*.
mistrust *vt* desconfiar.
mitigate *vt* mitigar.
mitigation *n* mitigacion *f*.
miter *n* mitra *f*.
mittens *npl* manoplas *fpl*.
mix *vt* mezclar.
mixer *n* licuadora *f*.
mixture *n* mezcla *f*.
moan *n* gemido *m*.
moat *n* foso *m*.
mob *n* multitud *f*.
mobile *adj* movil.
mode *n* modo *m*.
model *n* modelo *m*.
moderate *adj* moderado.
moderation *n* moderacion *f*.
modern *adj* moderno.
modernize *vt* modernizar.
modest *adj* modesto.
modesty *n* modestia *f*.
modify *vt* modificar.
module *n* modulo *m*.
mogul *n* magnate *m*.
mohair *n* mohair *m*.
moist *adj* humedo.
moisture *n* humedad *f*.
mold *n* molde *m*.
mole *n* topo *m*.
molecule *n* molecula *f*.
molest *vt* importunar.
mom *n* mama *f*.
moment *n* momento *m*.
momentum *n* impetu *m*.
mommy *n* mama *f*.
monarch *n* monarca *m*.
monarchy *n* monarquia *f*.
monastery *n* monasterio *m*.

Monday *n* lunes *m*.
monetary *adj* monetario.
money *n* moneda *f*; dinero *m*.
mongol *n* mongolico *m*.
mongrel *adj*, *n* mestizo *m*.
monk *n* monje *m*.
monkey *n* mono *m*.
monopoly *n* monopolio *m*.
monotonous *adj* monotono.
monsoon *n* (*mar*) monzon *m*.
monster *n* monstruo *m*.
month *n* mes *m*.
monthly *adj*, *adv* mensual (mente).
monument *n* monumento *m*.
mood *n* humor *m*.
moody *adj* malhumorado.
moon *n* luna *f*.
moor *n* paramo *m*.
moorland *n* paramo *m*.
moose *n* alce *m*.
mop *n* fregona *f*.
mope *vi* estar triste.
moped *n* ciclomotor *m*.
morality *n* etica, moralidad *f*.
morbid *adj* morboso.
more *adj*, *adv* mas.
moreover *adv* ademas.
morgue *n* deposito de cadaveres *m*.
morning *n* manana *f*:—**good** ~ buenos dias *mpl*.
moron *n* imbecil *m*.
morphine *n* morfina *f*.
morse *n* morse *m*.
morsel *n* bocado *m*.
mortal *adj* mortal
mortality *n* mortalidad *f*.
mortar *n* mortero *m*.
mortgage *n* hipoteca *f*.
mortify *vt* mortificar.
mortuary *n* deposito de cadaveres *m*.
mosaic *n* mosaico *m*.
mosque *n* mezquita *f*.
mosquito *n* mosquito *m*.
moss *n* (*bot*) musgo *m*.
most *adj* la mayoria de.
motel *n* motel *m*.
moth *n* polilla *f*.
mother *n* madre *f*.
mother-in-law *n* suegra *f*.
mother-of-pearl *n* nacar *m*.
motif *n* tema *m*.
motion *n* movimiento *m*.
motive *n* motivo *m*.
motor *n* motor *m*.
motorbike *n* moto *f*.
motorcycle *n* motocicleta *f*.
motor vehicle *n* automovil *m*.

motto n lema m.
mount n monte m.
mountain n montana f.
mountaineering n montañismo m.
mourn vt lamentar.
mourner n doliente m.
mourning n luto m.
mouse n (pl mice) raton m.
mousse n mousse f.
mouth n boca f;
mouthful n bocado m.
mouthwash n enjuague m.
mouthwatering adj apetitoso.
move vt mover.
movement n movimiento m.
movies n pelicula f; el cine
moving adj conmovedor.
mow vt segar.
mower n cortacesped m; mocion f.
Mrs n senora f.
much adj, adv mucho.
muck n suciedad f.
mucous adj mocoso.
mud n barro m.
muddle vt confundir m; confusion f.
muffle vt embozar.
mug n jarra f.
mulberry n mora f.
mule n mulo m, mula f.
multiple adj multiplo m.
multiplication n multiplicacion f.
multiply vt multiplicar.
multitude n multitud f.
mumble vt, vi refunfunar.
mummy n momia f.
mumps npl paperas fpl.
munch vt mascar.

mundane adj trivial.
municipal adj municipal.
municipality n municipalidad f.
mural n mural m.
murder n asesinato m; homicidio m.
murky adj sombrio.
murmur n murmullo.
muscle n musculo m.
muse vi meditar.
museum n museo m.
mushroom n (bot) seta f; champinon m.
music n musica f.
musician n musico m.
musk n musco m.
muslin n muselina f.
mussel n marisco m.
must v aux estar obligado.
mustache n bigote m.
mustard n mostaza f.
mute adj mudo, silencioso.
mutilate vt mutilar.
mutter vt, vi murmurar.
mutton n carnero m.
mutual adj mutuo, mutual.
muzzle n bozal m.
my pn mi, mis; mio, mia; mios, mias.
myriad n miriada f.
myrrh n mirra f.
myrtle n mirto, arrayan m.
myself pn yo mismo.
mysterious adj misterioso.
mystery n misterio m.
mystic(al) adj mistico.
mystify vt dejar perplejo.
mystique n misterio m.
myth n mito m.
mythology n mitologia f.

N

nag n jaca f:—vt reganar.
nagging adj persistente.
nail n una f; garra f; clavo m.
naive adj ingenuo.
naked adj desnudo.
name n nombre m.
nameless adj anonimo.
namely adv a saber.
namesake n tocayo m.
nanny n ninera f.
nap n sueno ligero m.
nape n nuca f.
napkin n servilleta f.
narcissus n (bot) narciso m.

narcotic adj, n narcotico m.
narrate vt narrar.
narrative adj narrativo.
narrow adj angosto, estrecho.
nasal adj nasal.
nasty adj sucio, puerco.
natal adj nativo; natal.
nation n nacion f.
nationalize vt nacionalizar.
nationalism n nacionalismo m.
nationalist adj, n nacionalista m.
nationality n nacionalidad f.
native adj nativo m.
native language n lengua materna f.

Nativity n Navidad f.
natural adj natural.
naturalize vt naturalizar.
naturalist n naturalista m.
nature n naturaleza f.
naught n cero m.
naughty adj malo.
nausea n nausea.
nauseous adj fastidioso.
nautic(al), naval adj nautico, naval.
nave n nave (de la iglesia) f.
navel n ombligo m.
navigate vi navegar.
navigation n navegacion f.
navy n marina f.
Nazi n nazi m.
near prep cerca de.
nearby adj cercano.
nearly adv casi.
near-sighted adj miope.
nebulous adj nebuloso.
necessarily adv necesariamente.
necessary adj necesario.
necessity n necesidad f.
neck n cuello m.
necklace n collar m.
necktie n corbata f.
nectar n nectar m.
need n necesidad f.
needle n aguja f.
needless adj superfluo.
needlework n costura f.
needy adj necesitado, pobre.
negation n negacion f.
negative adj negativo.
neglect vt descuidar.
negligee n salto de cama m.
negligence n negligencia f.
negligible adj insignificante.
negotiate vt, vi negociar (con).
negotiation n negociacion f; negocio m.
Negress n negra f.
Negro adj, n negro m.
neighbor n vecino m.
neighborhood n vecindad f; vecin- dario m.
neither conj ni:—pn ninguno.
neon n neon m.
neon light n luz de neon f.
nephew n sobrino m.
nepotism n nepotismo m.
nerve n nervio m; valor m.
nerve-racking adj espantoso.
nervous adj nervioso; nervudo.
nervous breakdown n crisis nerviosa f.
nest n nido m.
nest egg n (fig) ahorros mpl.
nestle vt anidarse.

net n red f.
netball n basquet m.
nettle n ortiga f.
network n red f.
neurosis n neurosis f invar.
neurotic adj, n neurotico m.
neuter adj (gr) neutro.
neutral adj neutral.
neutrality n neutralidad f.
neutron n neutron m.
never adv nunca, jamas.
nevertheless adv no obstante.
new adj nuevo.
news npl novedad, noticias fpl.
newscaster n presentador m.
newspaper n periodico m.
next adj proximo.
nib n pico m.
nibble vt picar.
nice adj simpatico.
niche n nicho m.
nickel n niquel m
nickname n mote.
nicotine n nicotina f.
niece n sobrina f.
niggling adj insignificante.
night n noche f.
nightclub n cabaret m.
nightfall n anochecer m.
nightingale n ruisenor m.
nightmare n pesadilla f.
nihilist n nihilista m.
nimble adj ligero, activo, listo, agil.
nine adj, n nueve.
nineteen adj, n diecinueve.
nineteenth adj, n decimonono.
ninetieth adj, n nonagesimo.
ninety adj, n noventa.
ninth adj, n nono, noveno.
nip vt pellizcar; morder.
nipple n pezon m; tetilla f.
nit n liendre f.
nitrogen n nitrogeno m.
no adv no.
nobility n nobleza f.
noble adj noble.
nobleman n noble m.
nobody n nadie, ninguna persona f.
nocturnal adj nocturnal.
noise n ruido m.
noisy adj ruidoso, turbulento.
nominate vt nombrar.
nomination n nominacion f.
nominee n candidato m.
non-alcoholic adj no alcoholico.
nonchalant adj indiferente.
nondescript adj no descrito.

none *adj* nadie, ninguno.
nonentity *n* nulidad *f*.
nonetheless *adv* sin embargo.
nonsense *n* disparate *m*.
noodles *npl* fideos *mpl*.
noon *n* mediodia *m*.
noose *n* lazo corredizo *m*.
nor *conj* ni.
normal *adj* normal.
north *n* norte *m*.
North America *n* America del Norte *f*.
northeast *n* nor(d)este *m*.
northerly, northern *adj* norteno.
North Pole *n* polo artico *m*.
northwest *n* nor(d)oeste *m*.
nose *n* nariz *f*.
nosebleed *n* hemorragia nasal *f*.
nostalgia *n* nostalgia *f*.
nostril *n* ventana de la nariz *f*.
not *adv* no.
notable *adj* notable.
notably *adv* especialmente.
notary *n* notario *m*.
notch *n* muesca *f*.
note *n* nota, marca *f*.
notebook *n* librito de apuntes *m*.
noted *adj* afamado, celebre.
nothing *n* nada *f*.
notice *n* noticia *f*; aviso *m*.
notification *n* notificacion *f*.
notify *vt* notificar.
notion *n* nocion *f*.
notoriety *n* notoriedad *f*.
notwithstanding *conj* no obstante, aunque.
nougat *n* turron *m*.
nought *n* cero *m*.
noun *n* (*gr*) sustantivo *m*.

nourish *vt* nutrir, alimentar.
novel *n* novela *f*.
novelist *n* novelista *m*.
novelty *n* novedad *f*.
November *n* noviembre *m*.
novice *n* novicio *m*.
now *adv* ahora.
nowadays *adv* hoy (en) dia.
nowhere *adv* en ninguna parte.
noxious *adj* nocivo, danoso.
nozzle *n* boquilla *f*.
nuance *n* matiz *m*.
nuclear *adj* nuclear.
nucleus *n* nucleo *m*.
nude *adj* desnudo.
nudge *vt* dar un codazo a.
nudist *n* nudista *m*.
nudity *n* desnudez *f*.
null *adj* nulo.
nullify *vt* anular.
numb *adj* entorpecido.
number *n* numero *m*.
numerous *adj* numeroso.
nun *n* monja *f*.
nunnery *n* convento de monjas *m*.
nuptial *adj* nupcial *fpl*.
nurse *n* enfermera *f*.
nursery *n* guarderia infantil *f*.
nursery rhyme *n* cancion infantil *f*.
nursery school *n* parvulario *m*.
nursing home *n* clinica de reposo *f*.
nurture *vt* criar.
nut *n* nuez *f*.
nutcrackers *npl* cascanueces *m*.
nutmeg *n* nuez moscada *f*.
nutritious *adj* nutritivo.
nut shell *n* cascara de nuez *f*.
nylon *n* nilon *m*.

O

oak *n* roble *m*.
oar *n* remo *m*.
oasis *n* oasis *f*.
oat *n* avena *f*.
oath *n* juramento *m*.
obedience *n* obediencia *f*.
obese *adj* obeso, gordo.
obey *vt* obedecer.
obituary *n* necrologia *f*.
object *n* objeto *m*:—*vt* objetar.
objective *adj*, *n* objetivo *m*.
oblige *vt* obligar.
obliterate *vt* borrar.

oblivion *n* olvido *m*.
oblong *adj* oblongo.
obnoxious *adj* odioso.
oboe *n* oboe *m*.
obscene *adj* obsceno.
obscenity *n* obscenidad *f*.
obscure *adj* oscuro.
observatory *n* observatorio *m*.
observe *vt* observar, mirar.
obsess *vt* obsesionar.
obsolete *adj* en desuso.
obstacle *n* obstaculo *m*.
obstinate *adj* obstinado.

obstruct *vt* obstruir; impedir.
obtain *vt* obtener, adquirir.
obvious *adj* obvio, evidente.
occasion *n* ocasion *f*.
occupant, occupier *n* ocupador *m*
occupation *n* ocupacion *f*; empleo *m*.
occupy *vt* ocupar.
occur *vi* pasar.
ocean *n* oceano *m*; alta *mar f*.
ocher *n* ocre *m*.
octave *n* octava *f*.
October *n* octubre *m*.
octopus *n* pulpo *m*.
odd *adj* impar.
oddity *n* singularidad.
odious *adj* odioso.
odor *n* olor *m*.
of *prep* de.
off *adv* desconectado; apagado.
offence *n* ofensa *f*.
offend *vt* ofender.
offensive *adj* ofensivo.
offer *vt* ofrecer.
offering *n* sacrificio *m*.
office *n* oficina *f*.
officer *n* oficial, empleado *m*.
official *adj* oficial.
offspring *n* prole *f*.
ogle *vt* comerse con los ojos.
oil *n* aceite *m*.
oil painting *n* pintura al oleo *f*.
oil rig *n* torre de perforacion *f*.
oil tanker *n* petrolero *m*.
ointment *n* unguento *m*.
OK, okay *excl* vale.
old *adj* viejo; antiguo.
old age *n* vejez *f*.
olive *n* olivo *m*.
omelet *n* tortilla de huevos *f*.
omen *n* agüero.
ominous *adj* ominoso.
omission *n* omisión *f*.
omit *vt* omitir.
omnipotence *n* omnipotencia *f*.
on *prep* sobre, encima, en; de; a.
one *adj* un, uno.
oneself *pn* si mismo; si misma.
ongoing *adj* continuo.
onion *n* cebolla *f*.
onlooker *n* espectador *m*.
only *adj* unico, solo.
onus *n* responsabilidad *f*.
onwards *adv* adelante.
opaque *adj* opaco.
open *adj* abierto; *vi* abrirse.
open-minded *adj* imparcial.
opera *n* opera *f*.

operate *vi* obrar.
operation *n* operacion *f*.
operational *adj* operacional.
operative *adj* operativo.
operator *n* operario *m*; operador *m*.
ophthalmic *adj* oftálmico.
opinion *n* opinion *f*.
opinion poll *n* sondeo *m*.
opponent *n* antagonista *m*.
opportune *adj* oportuno.
opportunity *n* oportunidad *f*.
oppose *vt* oponerse.
opposite *adj* opuesto; contrario.
opposition *n* oposicion *f*.
oppress *vt* oprimir.
oppression *n* opresion *f*.
optic(al) *adj* optico *f*.
optician *n* optico *m*.
optimist *n* optimista *m*.
optimum *adj* optimum.
option *n* opcion *f*; deseo *m*.
opulent *adj* opulento.
or *conj* o; u.
oracle *n* oraculo *m*.
oral *adj* oral.
orange *n* naranja *f*.
orbit *n* orbita *f*.
orchard *n* huerto *m*.
orchestra *n* orquesta *f*.
orchid *n* orquidea *f*.
order *n* orden *mf*; regla *f*; mandar.
ordinary *adj* ordinario.
ore *n* mineral *m*.
organ *n* organo *m*.
organic *adj* organico.
organization *n* organizacion *f*.
organize *vt* organizar.
organism *n* organismo *m*.
organist *n* organista *m*.
orgasm *n* orgasmo *m*.
orgy *n* orgia *f*.
oriental *adj* oriental.
orifice *n* orificio *m*.
origin *n* origen *m*.
original *adj* original.
originate *vi* originar.
ornament *n* ornamento *m*.
ornate *adj* adornado.
orphan *adj*, *n* huerfano *m*.
orphanage *n* orfanato *m*.
orthodox *adj* ortodoxo.
orthopedic *adj* ortopedico.
oscillate *vi* oscilar.
osprey *n* aguila marina *f*.
ostensibly *adv* aparentemente.
ostentatious *adj* ostentoso.
osteopath *n* osteopata *m*.

ostrich *n* avestruz *m*.
other *pn* otro.
otter *n* nutria *f*.
ouch *excl* ¡ay!
ought *v aux* deber, ser menester.
ounce *n* onza *f*.
our, ours *pn* nuestro, nuestra, nuestros, nuestras.
ourselves *pn pl* nosotros mismos.
out *adv* fuera.
outbreak *n* erupcion *f*.
outcast *n* paria *m*.
outcome *n* resultado *m*.
outcry *n* clamor *m*.
outdo *vt* exceder a otro, sobrepujar.
outer *adj* exterior.
outermost *adj* extremo; lo mas exterior.
outfit *n* vestidos *mpl*; ropa *f*.
outlet *n* enchufe *m*.
outline *n* contorno *m*
outlook *n* perspectiva *f*.
out-of-date *adj* caducado; pasado de moda.
outpatient *n* paciente externo *m*.
output *n* rendimiento *m*.
outrage *n* ultraje *m*.
outrageous *adj* ultrajoso.
outside *n* superficie *f*; exterior *m*.
outsider *n* forastero *m*.
outskirts *npl* alrededores *mpl*.
outstanding *adj* excepcional.
outwit *vt* enganar a uno a fuerza de tretas.
oval *n* ovalo *m*:—*adj* oval.
ovary *n* ovario *m*.
oven *n* horno *m*.

ovenproof *adj* resistente al horno.
over *prep* sobre, encima.
overbearing *adj* despotico.
overcharge *vt* sobrecargar.
overcoat *n* abrigo *m*.
overdose *n* sobredosis *f*.
overdue *adj* retrasado.
overeat *vi* atracarse.
overflow *vt, vi* inundar.
overhaul *vt* revisar.
overkill *n* exceso de medios *m*.
overlap *vi* traslaparse.
overleaf *adv* al dorso.
overload *vt* sobrecargar.
overpower *vt* predominar, oprimir.
overseas *adv* en ultramar:—*adj* extranjero.
oversee *vt* inspeccionar.
overshadow *vt* eclipsar.
overstate *vi* exagerar.
overstep *vt* exceder, pasar de.
overtake *vt* sobrepasar.
overtime *n* horas extra *fpl*.
overtone *n* tono *m*.
owe *vt* deber.
owl *n* buho *m*.
own *adj* propio.
owner *n* dueno, propietario *m*.
ownership *n* posesion *f*.
ox *n* buey *m*.
oxidize *vt* oxidar.
oxygen *n* oxigeno *m*.
oyster *n* ostra *f*.
ozone *n* ozono *m*.

P

pa *n* papa *m*.
pace *n* paso *m*.
pacemaker *n* marcapasos *m*.
pacific(al) *adj* pacifico.
pacify *vt* pacificar.
package *n* paquete *m*.
packet *n* paquete *m*.
packing *n* embalaje *m*.
pact *n* pacto *m*.
pad *n* bloc *m*.
paddle *vi* remar.
paddock *n* corral *m*.
paddy *n* arrozal *m*.
pagan *adj, n* pagano *m*.
page *n* pagina *f*.
pain *n* pena *f*; castigo *m*; dolor *m*.
painkiller *n* analgesico *m*.

paint *vt* pintar.
paintbrush *n* pincel *m*.
painter *n* pintor *m*.
painting *n* pintura *f*.
pair *n* par *m*.
pajamas *npl* pijama *m*.
palatial *adj* palatino.
pale *adj* palido; claro.
pallet *n* pallet *m*.
palliative *adj, n* paliativo *m*.
pallid *adj* palido.
pallor *n* palidez *f*.
palm *n* (*bot*) palma *f*.
Palm Sunday *n* Domingo de Ramos *m*.
palpable *adj* palpable.
paltry *adj* irrisorio; mezquino.
pamphlet *n* folleto *m*.

pan n cazuela f.
pancake n bunuelo m.
pandemonium n jaleo m.
pane n cristal m.
panel n panel m
pang n angustia f.
panic adj, n panico m.
pansy n (bot) pensamiento m.
pant vi jadear.
panther n pantera f.
pantry n despensa f.
pants npl pantalones mpl.
papacy n papado m.
papal adj papal.
paper n papel m.
paperback n libro de bolsillo m.
paper clip n clip m.
paperweight n sujetapapeles m.
paprika n pimienta hungara f.
parachute n paracaidas m.
paradise n paraiso m.
paradox n paradoja f.
paragon n modelo perfecto m.
paragraph n parrafo m.
parallel adj paralelo.
paralysis n paralisis f.
paralytic(al) adj paralitico.
paralyze vt paralizar.
paramedic n ambulanciero m.
paramount adj supremo.
paranoid adj paranoico.
parasite n parásito m.
parasol n parasol m.
parcel n paquete m.
parch vt resecar.
pardon n perdon m.
parent n padre m; madre f.
parentage n parentela f.
parental adj paternal.
parenthesis n parentesis m.
parish n parroquia f.
parity n paridad f.
park n parque m.
parliament n parlamento m.
parlor n sala de recibimiento f.
parody n parodia f.
parrot n papagayo m.
parsley n (bot) perejil m.
parsnip n (bot) chirivia f.
part n parte f.
participate vi participar (en).
particle n particula f.
particular adj particular.
parting n separacion f.
partition n particion.
partner n socio, companero m.
partridge n perdiz f.

party n partido m; fiesta f.
pass vt pasar.
passage n pasaje m
passbook n libreta de depositos f.
passenger n pasajero m.
passion n pasion f
passionate adj apasionado.
passive adj pasivo.
Passover n Pascua f.
passport n pasaporte m.
password n contrasena f.
past adj pasado.
pasta n pasta f.
paste n pasta f.
pastime n pasatiempo m f.
pastor n pastor m.
pastry n pasteleria f.
pasture n pasto m.
patch n remiendo m; parche m.
patent adj patente.
pathetic adj patetico.
patience n paciencia f.
patient adj paciente.
patio n patio m.
patriot n patriota m.
patriotism n patriotismo m.
patrol n patrulla f.
patron n patron m.
patronize vt patrocinar.
pattern n patron m; dibujo m.
pauper n pobre m.
pause n pausa f.
pave vt empedrar.
pavilion n pabellon m.
paw n pata f.
pay vt pagar.
pea n guisante m.
peace n paz f.
peach n melocoton m.
peacock n pavon, pavo real m.
peak n cima f.
peanut n cacahuete m.
pear n pera f.
pearl n perla f.
peasant n campesino m.
pebble n guija f.
peculiar adj peculiar.
pedal n pedal m.
pedestal n pedestal m.
pedestrian n peaton m.
pedigree n genealogia f.
peel vt pelar.
peg n clavija f.
pelican n pelicano m.
pen n boligrafo m; pluma f.
penal adj penal.
pence n d pl of penny.

pencil n lapiz m.
pendulum n pendulo m.
penetrate vt penetrar.
penguin n pinguino m.
penicillin n penicilina f.
peninsula n peninsula f.
penis n pene m.
penitence n penitencia f.
penitentiary n encierro m.
penknife n navaja f.
penny n penique m.
pension n pension f.
pensive adj pensativo.
Pentecost n Pentecostes m.
penthouse n atico m.
people n pueblo m; nacion f; gente f.
pepper n pimienta f.
peppermint n menta f.
perceive vt percibir.
percentage n porcentaje m.
perception n percepcion f.
percolator n cafetera de filtro f.
percussion n percusion f; golpe m.
perennial adj perenne; perpetuo.
perfect adj perfecto.
perform vt ejecutar.
performance n ejecucion f.
perfume n perfume m; fragancia f:—vt per-
    fumar.
perhaps adv quiza, quizas.
peril n peligro m.
period n periodo m.
periodical n jornal, periodico m.
perk n extra m.
perm n permanente f.
permanent adj, ~ly adv perma-nente
    (mente).
permissible adj licito.
permission n permiso m.
permit vt permitir.
perplex vt confundir.
persecute vt perseguir.
persevere vi perseverar.
persist vi persistir.
person n persona f.
personality n personalidad f.
personnel n personal m.
perspective n perspectiva f.
perspiration n transpiracion f.
perspire vi transpirar.
persuade vt persuadir.
perturb vt perturbar.
peruse vt leer.
perverse adj perverso.
pessimist n pesimista m.
pester vt molestar.
pet n animal domestico m.

petal n (bot) petalo m.
petition n presentacion, peticion f.
petroleum n petroleo m.
petticoat n enaguas fpl.
pewter n peltre m.
phantom n fantasma m.
pharmacist n farmacéutico m.
pharmacy n farmacia f.
phase n fase f.
pheasant n faisan m.
phenomenon n fenomeno m.
phial n redomilla f.
philosopher n filosofo m.
philosophy n filosofia f.
phlegm n flema f.
phobia n fobia f.
phone n telefono m.
photocopier n fotocopiadora f.
photocopy n fotocopia f.
photograph n fotografia f:—vt fotografiar.
photographic adj fotografico.
photography n fotografia f.
phrase n frase f.
physical adj fisico.
physician n medico m.
physicist n fisico m.
physiotherapy n fisioterapia f.
physique n fisico m.
pianist n pianista m, f.
piano n piano m.
piccolo n flautin m.
pick vt escoger, elegir.
pickle n escabeche m.
picnic n comida, merienda f.
picture n pintura f.
picturesque adj pintoresco.
pie n pastel m; tarta f.
piece n pedazo m; pieza f.
pierce vt penetrar, agujerear.
pig n cerdo m.
pigeon n paloma f.
pigtail n trenza f.
pike n lucio m; pica f.
pile n estaca f; pila f; monton m.
pilgrim n peregrino m.
pill n pildora f.
pillar n pilar m.
pillow n almohada f.
pilot n piloto m.
pimple n grano m.
pin n alfiler m.
pinball n fliper m.
pincers n pinzas fpl.
pinch vt pellizcar.
pine n (bot) pino m.
pineapple n pina f, ananas m.

pink n rosa f.
pinnacle n cumbre f.
pint n pinta f.
pioneer n pionero m.
pious adj pio.
pip n pepita f.
pipe n tubo.
pirate n pirata m.
pirouette n pirueta.
Pisces n Piscis m (signo del zodiaco).
piss n (sl) meados mpl.
pistol n pistola f.
piston n embolo m.
pit n hoyo m; mina f.
pitcher n cantaro, jarro m.
pitchfork n horca f.
pity n piedad, compasion f.
pivot n eje m.
pizza n pizza f.
placard n pancarta f.
placate vt apaciguar.
place n lugar, sitio m.
placid adj placido.
plagiarism n plagio m.
plague n peste, plaga f.
plaice n platija f (pez).
plaid n tartan m.
plain adj liso, llano
plaintiff n (law) demandador m.
plan n plano m.
plane n avion m; plano m.
planet n planeta m.
plank n tabla f.
plant n planta f.
plantation n plantacion f.
plaque n placa f.
plaster n yeso m.
plastic adj plastico.
plate n plato m.
plateau n meseta f.
platform n plataforma f.
platinum n platino m.
platoon n (mil) peloton m.
play n juego m.
playboy n playboy m.
player n jugador m
plea n defensa f.
pleasant adj agradable.
please vt agradar.
pleasure n gusto, placer m.
pleat n pliegue m.
plentiful adj copioso.
plethora n pletora, replecion f.
pleurisy n pleuresia f.
pliers npl alicates mpl.
plinth n plinto m.
plough n arado m.

ploy n truco m.
plug n tapon m.
plum n ciruela f.
plumage n plumaje m.
plumb n plomada f.
plumber n plomero m.
plume n pluma f.
plump adj gordo.
plunder vt saquear.
plunge vi sumergir(se), precipitarse.
pluperfect n (gr) pluscuamperfecto m.
plural adj, n plural m.
plus n signo de mas m.
plush adj de felpa.
plutonium n plutonio m.
plywood n madera contrachapada f.
pneumatic adj neumatico.
pneumonia n pulmonia f.
poach vt escalfar.
pocket n bolsillo m.
pod n vaina f.
poem n poema m.
poet n poeta m.
poetry n poesia f.
poignant adj punzante.
point n punta f; punto m.
point-blank adv directamente.
poise n peso m; equilibrio m.
poison n veneno m.
poker n atizador m; poker m.
polar adj polar.
pole n polo m.
police n policia f.
policy n politica f.
polio n polio f.
polish vt pulir, alisar.
polite adj pulido, cortes.
politician n politico m.
politics npl politica f.
polka n polca f.
pollen n (bot) polen m.
pollute vt ensuciar.
pollution n polucion, contaminacion f.
polo n polo m.
polyester n poliester m.
polytechnic n politecnico m.
pomegranate n granada f.
pomp n pompa f; esplendor m.
pompom n borla f.
pompous adj pomposo.
pond n estanque m.
ponder vt ponderar, considerar.
ponderous adj ponderoso, pesado.
pontoon n ponton m.
pony n jaca f.
pool n charca f; piscina f.
poor adj pobre.

pop *n* papá *m*.
popcorn *n* palomitas *fpl*.
Pope *n* papa *m*.
poplar *n* alamo *m*.
poppy *n* (*bot*) amapola *f*.
popular *adj*, ~ly *adv* popular(mente).
populate *vi* poblar.
population *n* poblacion *f*.
porcelain *n* porcelana *f*.
porch *n* portico *m*.
porcupine *n* puerco espin *m*.
pore *n* poro *m*.
pork *n* carne de puerco *f*.
pornography *n* pornografia *f*.
porous *adj* poroso.
porpoise *n* marsopa *f*.
porridge *n* gachas de avena *fpl*.
port *n* puerto *m m*.
portable *adj* portatil.
portal *n* portal *m f*.
porter *n* portero *m*.
portfolio *n* cartera *f*.
porthole *n* portilla *f*.
portico *n* portico *m*.
portion *n* porcion *f*.
portly *adj* rollizo.
portrait *n* retrato *m*.
portray *vt* retratar.
pose *n* postura *f*; pose *f*.
posh *adj* elegante.
position *n* posicion *f*.
positive *adj* positivo.
posse *n* peloton *m*.
possess *vt* poseer.
possession *n* posesion *f*.
possibility *n* posibilidad *f*.
possible *adj* posible.
post *n* correo *m*; puesto *m*.
postage stamp *n* sello *m*.
postcard *n* tarjeta postal *f*.
poster *n* cartel *m*.
posterior *n* trasero *m*.
posterity *n* posteridad *f*.
postgraduate *n* posgraduado *m*.
posthumous *adj* postumo.
post office *n* correos *m*.
postpone *vt* diferir.
posture *n* postura *f*.
posy *n* ramillete de flores *m*.
pot *n* marmita *f*.
potato *n* patata *f*; papa *f*.
potent *adj* potente.
potential *adj* potencial.
pothole *n* bache *m*.
potion *n* pocion *f*.
potter *n* alfarero *m*.
pottery *n* cerámica *f*.

pouch *n* bolsa *f*.
poultice *n* cataplasma *f*.
poultry *n* aves caseras *fpl*.
pound *n* libra *f*; libra esterlina *f*.
pour *vt* echar; servir.
pout *vi* ponerse cenudo.
poverty *n* pobreza *f*.
powder *n* polvo *m*.
power *n* poder *m*.
practicable *adj* practicable; hacedero.
practical *adj* práctico:——ly *adv* prácticamente.
practicality *n* factibilidad *f*.
practice *n* practica *f*.
pragmatic *adj* pragmático.
prairie *n* pampa *f*.
praise *n* renombre *m*.
prattle *vi* charlar:—*n* charla *f*.
prawn *n* gamba *f*.
pray *vi* rezar.
prayer *n* oracion *f*.
preach *vi* predicar.
preacher *n* pastor *m*.
precaution *n* precaucion *f*.
precede *vt* anteceder.
precious *adj* precioso.
precise *n* preciso.
precision *n* precision *f*.
preconception *n* preocupacion *f*.
predator *n* animal de rapina *m*.
predict *vt* predecir.
prediction *n* prediccion *f*.
predominant *adj* predominante.
predominate *vt* predominar.
preface *n* prefacio *m*.
prefer *vt* preferir.
preference *n* preferencia *f*.
prefix *vt* prefijar.
pregnancy *n* embarazo *m*.
pregnant *adj* embarazada.
prehistoric *adj* prehistorico.
prejudice *n* perjuicio *m*.
preliminary *adj* preliminar.
prelude *n* preludio *m*.
premature *adj* prematuro.
premier *n* primer ministro *m*.
premises *npl* establecimiento *m*.
premium *n* premio *m*.
premonition *n* presentimiento *m*.
prepare *vt* preparar(se).
preposition *n* preposicion *f*.
preposterous *adj* prepostero; absurdo.
prerequisite *n* requisito *m*.
prerogative *n* prerrogativa *f*.
prescribe *vi* prescribir; recetar.
prescription *n* prescripcion *f*.
present *n* regalo *m*.

presentation n presentacion f.
preservation n preservacion f.
preservative n preservativo m.
preserve vt preservar.
preside vi presidir.
presidency n presidencia f.
president n presidente m.
press vt empujar n prensa.
pressure n presion f.
prestige n prestigio m.
presume vt presumir, suponer.
pretence n pretexto m; pretension f.
pretend vi pretender.
preterite n preterito m.
pretext n pretexto m.
pretty adj lindo.
prevent vt prevenir.
preview n preestreno m.
previous adj previo.
prey n presa f.
price n precio m; premio m.
prick vt punzar, picar.
pride n orgullo m.
priest n sacerdote m.
priggish adj afectado.
prim adj peripuesto.
primary adj primario.
primate n primado m.
primeval adj primitivo.
primitive adj primitivo.
primrose n (bot) primula f.
prince n principe m.
princess n princesa f.
principle n principio m.
printer n impresor m.
prior adj anterior.
priority n prioridad f.
priory n priorato m.
prism n prisma m.
prison n prision, carcel f.
prisoner n prisionero m.
pristine adj pristino.
privacy n soledad f.
private adj secreto, privado; particular.
private eye n detective privado m.
privet n alhena f.
privilege n privilegio m.
prize n premio m.
probability n probabilidad f.
probable adj probable.
probation n prueba f.
problem n problema m.
procedure n procedimiento
proceed vi proceder.
process n proceso m.
procession n procesion f.
proclaim vt proclamar.

proclamation n proclamacion f.
procure vt procurar.
prod vt empujar.
prodigal adj prodigo.
prodigious adj prodigioso.
prodigy n prodigio m.
produce vt producir
product n producto m; obra f; efecto m.
production n produccion f.
profane adj profano.
profess vt profesar.
profession n profesion f.
professor n profesor, catedrático m.
proficient adj proficiente.
profile n perfil m.
profit n ganancia f.
profound adj profundo.
profuse adj profuso.
program n programa m.
progress n progreso m.
prohibit vt prohibir.
project vt proyectar
prominent adj prominente, saledizo.
promiscuous adj promiscuo.
promise n promesa f.
promontory n promontorio m.
promote vt promover.
promotion n promocion f.
prone adj inclinado.
prong n diente m.
pronoun n pronombre m.
pronounce vt pronunciar.
proof n prueba f.
propaganda n propaganda f.
propel vt impeler.
propeller n helice f.
propensity n propension f.
proper adj propio.
property n propiedad f.
prophecy n profecia f.
prophesy vt profetizar.
prophet n profeta m.
prophetic adj profetico.
proportion n proporcion f.
proportional adj proporcional.
proposal n propuesta f.
propose vt proponer.
proposition n proposicion f.
proprietor n propietario m.
propriety n propiedad f.
pro rata adv a prorrateo.
prosaic adj prosaico.
prose n prosa f.
prosecute vt proseguir.
prosecution n prosecucion f.
prosecutor n acusador m.
prospect n perspectiva f.

prospectus *n* prospecto *m*.
prosper *vi* prosperar.
prosperity *n* prosperidad *f*.
prostitute *n* prostituta *f*.
prostitution *n* prostitucion *f*.
prostrate *adj* postrado.
protagonist *n* protagonista *m*.
protect *vt* proteger.
protection *n* proteccion *f*.
protective *adj* protectorio.
protector *n* protector, patrono *m*.
protege *n* protegido *m*.
protein *n* proteina *f*.
protest *vi* protestar.
Protestant *n* protestante *m*.
protester *n* manifestante *m*.
protocol *n* protocolo *m*.
prototype *n* prototipo *m*.
protracted *adj* prolongado.
protrude *vi* sobresalir.
proud *adj* soberbio, orgulloso.
prove *vt* probar.
proverb *n* proverbio *m*.
provide *vt* proveer.
provided *conj*:—~ that con tal que.
providence *n* providencia *f*.
province *n* provincia *f*
provincial *adj, n* provincial *m*.
provision *n* provision *f*.
proviso *n* estipulacion *f*.
provocation *n* provocacion *f*.
provocative *adj* provocativo.
provoke *vt* provocar.
prowess *n* proeza *f*.
prowl *vi* rondar.
proximity *n* proximidad *f*.
proxy *n* poder *m*; apoderado *m*.
prudence *n* prudencia *f*.
prudent *adj* prudente.
prudish *adj* gazmono.
prussic acid *n* acido prúsico *m*.
pry *vi* espiar, acechar.
psalm *n* salmo *m*.
pseudonym *n* seudonimo *m*.
psyche *n* psique *f*.
psychiatrist *n* psiquiatra *m*.
psychiatry *n* psiquiatria *f*.
psychic *adj* psiquico.
psychoanalysis *n* psicoanalisis *m*.
psychoanalyst *n* psicoanalista *m*.
psychological *adj* psicologico.
psychologist *n* psicologo *m*.
psychology *n* psicologia *f*.
puberty *n* pubertad *f*.
public *adj* publico
publicize *vt* publicitar.

publicity *n* publicidad *f*.
publish *vt* publicar.
publisher *n* publicador *m*.
pucker *vt* arrugar, hacer pliegues.
puddle *n* charco *m*.
puff *n* soplo *m*.
pull *vt* tirar.
pulley *n* polea *f*.
pullover *n* jersey *m*.
pulp *n* pulpa *f*.
pulpit *n* pulpito *m*.
pulsate *vi* pulsar.
pulse *n* pulso *m*; legumbres *fpl*.
pumice *n* piedra pomez *f*.
pummel *vt* aporrear.
pump *n* bomba *f*.
pumpkin *n* calabaza *f*.
pun *n* equivoco, chiste *m*.
punch *n* punetazo *m*.
punctual *adj* puntual.
punctuate *vi* puntuar.
punctuation *n* puntuacion *f*.
pungent *adj* picante.
punish *vt* castigar.
punishment *n* castigo *m*.
punk *n* punki *m*.
punt *n* barco llano *m*.
pup *n* cachorro *m*.
pupil *n* alumno *m*.
puppet *n* titere *m*.
puppy *n* perrito *m*.
purchase *vt* comprar.
pure *adj* puro.
puree *n* pure *m*.
purification *n* purificacion *f*.
purify *vt* purificar.
puritan *n* puritano *m*.
purity *n* pureza *f*.
purple *adj* purpureo.
purpose *n* intencion *f*.
purr *vi* ronronear.
purse *n* bolsa *f*; cartera *f*.
pursue *vi* perseguir.
pursuit *n* perseguimiento *m*.
purveyor *n* abastecedor *m*.
push *vt* empujar
pusher *n* traficante de drogas *m*.
push-up *n* plancha *f*.
put *vt* poner, colocar.
putrid *adj* podrido.
putty *n* masilla *f*.
puzzle *n* acertijo *m*.
puzzling *adj* extrano.
pylon *n* torre de conduccion electrica *f*.
pyramid *n* piramide *f*.
python *n* piton atigrado *m*.

Q

quack *vi* graznar.
quadrangle *n* cuadrangulo *m*.
quadrant *n* cuadrante *m*.
quadrilateral *adj* cuadrilatero.
quadruped *n* cuadrupedo *m*.
quadruple *adj* cuadruplo.
quadruplet *n* cuatrillizo *m*.
quagmire *n* tremedal *m*.
quail *n* codorniz *f*.
quaint *adj* pulido; exquisito.
quake *vi* temblar; tiritar.
qualification *n* calificacion *f*.
qualify *vt* calificar.
quality *n* calidad *f*.
qualm *n* escrupulo *m*.
quandary *n* incertidumbre *f*.
quantitative *adj* cuantitativo.
quantity *n* cantidad *f*.
quarantine *n* cuarentena *f*.
quarrel *n* rina, contienda *f*.
quarrelsome *adj* pendenciero.
quarry *n* cantera *f*.
quarter *n* cuarto *mr*.
quarterly *adj* trimestral.
quartermaster *n* (*mil*) comisario *m*.
quartet *n* (*mus*) cuarteto *m*.
quartz *n* (*min*) cuarzo *m*.
quash *vt* fracasar; anular.
quay *n* muelle *m*.
queasy *adj* nauseabundo.
queen *n* reina *f*.
queer *adj* extrano.
quell *vt* calmar.

quench *vt* apagar.
query *n* cuestion.
quest *n* pesquisa *f*.
question *n* pregunta *f*; cuestion *f*.
questionable *adj* cuestionable.
question mark *n* punto de interrogación *m*.
questionnaire *n* cuestionario *m*.
quibble *vi* buscar evasivas.
quick *adj* rapido.
quicken *vt* apresurar.
quicksand *n* arena movediza *f*.
quicksilver *n* azogue, mercurio *m*.
quick-witted *adj* agudo, perspicaz.
quiet *adj* callado.
quinine *n* quinina *f*.
quintet *n* (*mus*) quinteto *m*.
quintuple *adj* quintuplo.
quintuplet *n* quintillizo *m*.
quip *n* indirecta *f*:—*vt* echar pullas.
quirk *n* peculiaridad *f*.
quit *vt* dejar.
quite *adv* bastante.
quits *adv* ¡en paz!.
quiver *vi* temblar.
quixotic *adj* quijotesco.
quiz *n* concurso *m*.
quizzical *adj* burlon.
quota *n* cuota *f*.
quotation *n* citacion, cita *f*.
quotation marks *npl* comillas *fpl*.
quote *vt* citar.
quotient *n* cociente *m*.

R

rabbi *n* rabi *m*.
rabbit *n* conejo *m*.
rabble *n* gentuza *f*.
rabid *adj* rabioso.
rabies *n* rabia *f*.
race *n* raza.
rack *n* rejilla *f*.
racket *n* ruido *m*; raqueta *f*.
racy *adj* picante.
radiance *n* brillantez *f*.
radiant *adj* radiante.
radiate *vt*, *vi* radiar.
radiation *n* radiacion *f*.

radiator *n* radiador *m*.
radical *adj*, ~ly *adv* radical(mente).
radio *n* radio *f*.
radioactive *adj* radioactivo.
radish *n* rabano *m*.
radius *n* radio *f*.
raffle *n* rifa *f*.
raft *n* balsa *f*.
rafter *n* par *m*; viga *f*.
rag *n* trapo *m*.
rage *n* rabia *f*.
raid *n* incursion *f*.
rail *n* baranda, barandilla *f*.

railroad, railway n ferrocarril m.
rain n lluvia f.
rainbow n arco iris m.
raise vt levantar, alzar.
raisin n pasa f.
rake n rastro m.
ram n carnero m.
ramble vi divagar.
ramification n ramificacion f.
ramp n rampa f.
rampant adj exuberante.
ramshackle adj en ruina.
ranch n hacienda f.
rancid adj rancio.
rancor n rencor m.
random adj fortuito, sin orden.
range vt colocar, ordenar.
ransack vt saquear.
ransom n rescate m.
rape n violacion f.
rapid adj rapido.
rapist n violador m.
rapture n rapto m.
rare adj raro.
rascal n picaro m.
rash adj precipitado m; erupción (cutánea) f.
raspberry n frambuesa f.
rat n rata f.
rate n tasa f, precio, valor m.
rather adv mas bien; antes.
ratification n ratificacion f.
ratify vt ratificar.
ratio n razon f.
ration n racion f.
rational adj racional.
ravage vt saquear.
rave vi delirar.
raven n cuervo m.
ravine n barranco m.
ravish vt encantar.
ravishing adj encantador.
raw adj crudo.
ray n rayo de luz m; raya f (pez).
raze vt arrasar.
razor n navaja.
reach vt alcanzar.
react vi reaccionar.
reaction n reaccion f.
read vt leer.
readable adj legible.
reader n lector m.
readjust vt reajustar.
ready adj listo, pronto.
real adj real.
realization n realizacion f.
realize adv darse cuenta de; realizar.
reality n realidad f.

realm n reino m.
ream n resma f.
reap vt segar.
reappear vi reaparecer.
rear n parte trasera fr.
rearmament n rearme m.
reason n razon f; causa f:—vt, vi razonar.
reassure vt tranquilizar, alentar; (com) asegurar.
rebel n rebelde m/f.
rebellion n rebelion f.
rebound vi rebotar.
rebuke vt reprender.
rebut vi repercutir.
recede vi retroceder.
receipt n recibo m.
receive vt recibir.
recent adj reciente.
reception n recepcion f.
recess n descanso m.
recession n retirada f; (com) recesion f.
recipe n receta f.
recipient n recipiente m.
recital n recital m.
recite vt recitar.
reckless adj temerario.
reckon vt contar.
recline vt, vi reclinar(se).
recluse n recluso/a m/f.
recognize vt reconocer.
recommend vt recomendar.
recommendation n recomendacion f.
recompense n recompensa f.
reconcile vt reconciliar.
reconsider vt considerar de nuevo.
record vt registrar; grabar.
recourse n recurso m.
recover vt recobrar; recuperar.
recovery n convalecencia f; recobro m.
recreation n recreacion f; recreo m.
recruit vt reclutar.
rectangle n rectangulo m.
rectify vt rectificar.
rectilinear adj rectilineo.
rector n rector m.
recur vi repetirse.
red adj rojo; tinto:—n rojo m.
redeem vt redimir.
redemption n redencion f.
redhot adj candente, ardiente.
redress vt corregir.
reduce vt reducir.
reduction n reduccion f.
reed n cana f.
reek n mal olor.
refectory n refectorio m.
refer vt, vi referir.

referee n arbitro m.
reference n referencia.
refine vt refinar.
refit vt reparar.
reflect vt, vi reflejar.
reflection n reflexion f.
reflex adj reflejo.
reform vt, vi reformar(se).
refresh vt refrescar.
refreshment n refresco.
refrigerator n nevera f.
refuge n refugio, asilo m.
refugee n refugiado m/f.
refund vt devolver.
refurbish vt restaurar.
refusal n negativa f.
refuse vt rehusar.
refute vt refutar.
regal adj real.
regard vt estimar.
regardless adv a pesar de todo.
regatta n regata f.
regime n regimen m.
region n region f.
register n registro m.
registrar n registrador m.
registration n registro m.
registry n registro m.
regular adj regular.
regulation n regulacion f.
reign n reinado, reino m.
reinforce vt reforzar.
reinstate vt reintegrar.
reject vt rechazar.
rejection n rechazo m.
rejoice vt, vi regocijar(se).
relapse vi recaer.
relate vt, vi relatar.
relation n relacion f.
relationship n parentesco m; relacion f.
relative adj relativo.
relax vt, vi relajar.
release vt soltar, libertar.
relic n reliquia f.
relief n relieve m.
relieve vt aliviar.
religion n religion f.
rely vi confiar en; contar con.
remain vi quedar.
remains npl restos mpl.
remark n observacion, nota f.
remedial adv curativo.
remedy n remedio m.
remember vt acordarse de; recordar.
remind vt recordar.
remit vt, vi remitir.
remorse n remordimiento m.

remote adj remoto.
remove vt quitar.
renew vt renovar.
renovate vt renovar.
rent n renta f.
rental n alquiler m.
repair vt reparar.
repeat vt repetir.
repel vt repeler.
repetition n repeticion f.
replace vt reemplazar.
reply n respuesta f.
repose vt, vi reposar.
represent vt representar.
reproduce vt reproducir.
reproduction n reproduccion f.
reptile n reptil m.
republic n republica f.
repugnance n repugnancia f.
repulse vt repulsar.
request n peticion.
require vt requerir.
rescue vt librar.
research vt investigar.
resemble vt asemejarse.
resent vt resentirse.
reserve vt reservar.
residence n residencia f.
resign vt, vi resignar.
resin n resina f.
resist vt resistir, oponerse.
resolve vt, vr resolver(se).
resort vi recurrir.
resource n recurso m.
respect n respecto m.
respite n suspension f.
respond vt responder.
rest n reposo m.
restless adj insomne.
restore vt restaurar.
restrict vt restringir.
result vi resultar.
resume vt resumir.
résumé n curriculum m.
resurrection n resurreccion f.
resuscitate vt resucitar.
retail vt revender f.
retain vt retener.
reticence n reticencia f.
retina n retina f.
retire vt, vi retirar(se).
retreat n retirada f.
return vt retribuir; restituir; devolver.
reveal vt revelar.
revenge vt vengar:—n venganza f.
revenue n renta f.
revere vt reverenciar.

reverse *vt* trastrocar.
review *vt* rever.
revise *vt* rever; repasar.
revival *n* restauracion *f*.
revolt *vi* rebelarse.
revolution *n* revolucion *f*.
revolve *vt* revolver.
revue *n* revista *f*.
reward *n* recompensa *f*.
rheumatism *n* reumatismo *m*.
rhinoceros *n* rinoceronte *m*.
rhombus *n* rombo *m*.
rhubarb *n* ruibarbo *m*.
rhyme *n* rima *f*.
rhythm *n* ritmo *m*.
rib *n* costilla *f*.
ribbon *n* liston *m*.
rice *n* arroz *m*.
rich *adj* rico.
riches *npl* riqueza *f*.
rickets *n* raquitis *f*.
rid *vt* librar.
riddle *n* enigma *m*.
ride *vi* cabalgar.
ridge *n* espinazo.
ridiculous *adj* ridiculoso.
rifle *n* rifle *m*.
right *adj* derecho, recto; justo.—*n* derecho *m*; título *m*; privilegio *m*.
rigid *adj* rigido.
rigor *n* rigor *m*.
rind *n* corteza *f*.
rinse *vt* lavar, limpiar.
rise *vi* levantarse.
risk *n* riesgo, peligro *m*.
rite *n* rito *m*.
ritual *adj*, *n* ritual *m*.
rival *adj* emulo.
river *n* rio *m*.
road *n* camino *m*.
roadsign *n* senal de trafico *f*.
roar *vi* rugir.
roast *vt* asar.
rob *vt* robar.
robber *n* robador, ladron *m*.
robbery *n* robo *m*.
robust *adj* robusto.
rock *n* roca *f*.
rocket *n* cohete *m*.
rodent *n* roedor *m*.
rogue *n* bribon *m*.
roll *vt* rodar.
Roman Catholic *adj*, *n* catolico/a *m/f* (romano/a).
romance *n* romance *m*.
roof *n* tejado *m*.
room *n* habitacion, sala *f*.

roomy *adj* espacioso.
root *n* raiz *f*.
rope *n* cuerda *f*.
rosary *n* rosario *m*.
rose *n* rosa *f*.
rosebed *n* campo de rosales *m*.
rosebud *n* capullo de rosa *m*.
rosemary *n* (*bot*) romero *m*.
rosette *n* roseta *f*.
rot *vi* pudrirse.
rotten *adj* podrido.
rouble *n* rublo *m*.
rouge *n* arrebol *m*.
rough *adj* aspero.
roulette *n* ruleta *f*.
round *adj* redondo.
rouse *vt* despertar.
route *n* ruta *f*.
routine *adj* rutinario.
row *n* camorra *f*.
row *n* (line) hilera, fila *f*:—*vt* (*mar*) remar, bogar.
royal *adj* real.
royalty *n* realeza, dignidad real *f*.
rub *vt* estregar, fregar, frotar.
rubber *n* caucho *m*, goma *f*.
rubber-band *n* goma, gomita *f*.
rubric *n* rubrica *f*.
ruby *n* rubi *m*.
rudder *n* timon *m*.
rude *adj* rudo, brutal.
rudiment *n* rudimentos *mpl*.
rue *vi* compadecerse.
rug *n* alfombra *f*.
rugby *n* rugby *m*.
ruin *n* ruina *f*.
ruinous *adj* ruinoso.
rule *n* mando *m*; regla *f*.
ruler *n* gobernador *m*; regla *f*.
rum *n* ron *m*.
rumor *n* rumor *m*.
run *vt* dirigir; organizar, *vi* correr.
runaway *n* fugitivo.
rung *n* escalon.
runway *n* pista de aterrizaje *f*.
rupture *n* rotura *f*.
rural *adj* rural.
ruse *n* astucia *f*.
rush *n* junco *m*; rafaga *f*.
rusk *n* galleta *f*.
russet *adj* bermejo.
rust *n* herrumbre *f*.
rustic *adj* rustico.
rustle *vi* crujir.
rut *n* celo *m*.
ruthless *adj* cruel.
rye *n* (*bot*) centeno *m*.

S

Sabbath *n* sabado *m*.
sabotage *n* sabotaje *m*.
saccharin *n* sacarina *f*.
sachet *n* sobrecito *m*.
sack *n* saco *m*:—*vt* despedir.
sacrament *n* sacramento *m*.
sacred *adj* sagrado.
sacredness *n* santidad *f*.
sacrifice *n* sacrificio *m*.
sacrilege *n* sacrilegio *m*.
sad *adj* triste.
saddle *n* silla *f*.
sadness *n* tristeza *f*.
safari *n* safari *m*.
safe *adj* seguro; *n* caja fuerte *f*.
safety *n* seguridad *f*
saffron *n* azafran *m*.
sage *n* (*bot*) salvia *f*.
Sagittarius *n* Sagitario *m* (signo del zodiaco).
sago *n* (*bot*) zagu *m*.
sail *n* vela *f*.
sailor *n* marinero *m*.
saint *n* santo *m*; santa *f*.
sake *n* causa, razon *f*.
salad *n* ensalada *f*.
salamander *n* salamandra *f*.
salary *n* sueldo *m*.
sale *n* venta *f*.
sales clerk *n* dependiente *m*.
salient *adj* saliente.
saline *adj* salino.
saliva *n* saliva *f*.
salmon *n* salmon *m*.
salmon trout *n* trucha salmonada *f*.
saloon *n* bar *m*.
salt *n* sal *f*.
salubrious *adj* salubre.
salutation *n* salutacion *f*.
salute *vt* saludar.
same *adj* mismo, idéntico/a
sample *n* muestra *f*; ejemplo *m*.
sanctify *vt* santificar.
sanctuary *n* santuario *m*.
sand *n* arena *f*.
sandal *n* sandalia *f*.
sandstone *n* piedra arenisca *f*.
sandwich *n* bocadillo *m*.
sane *adj* sapo.
sanitarium *n* sanatorio *m*.
sanity *n* juicio sano *m*.
sap *n* savia *f*.
sapling *n* arbolito *m*.
sapphire *n* zafir *m*.

sarcasm *n* sarcasmo *m*.
sarcophagus *n* sarcofago.
sardine *n* sardina *f*.
Satan *n* Satanas *m*.
satchel *n* mochila *f*.
satellite *n* satelite *m*.
satin *n* raso *m*.
satire *n* satira *f*.
satisfaction *n* satisfaccion *f*.
satisfy *vt* satisfacer.
Saturday *n* sabado *m*.
satyr *n* satiro *m*.
sauce *n* salsa *f*.
saucepan *n* cazo *m*.
saucer *n* platillo *m*.
sausage *n* salchicha *f*.
savage *adj* salvaje
savagery *n* crueldad *f*.
savannah *n* sabana *f*.
save *vt* salvar.
saveloy *n* chorizo *m*.
Savior *n* Salvador *m*.
savory *adj* sabroso.
saw *n* sierra *f*.
saxophone *n* saxofono *m*.
say *vt* decir.
saying *n* dicho *m*.
scab *n* rona *f*.
scald *vt* escaldar.
scale *n* balanza *f*.
scalp *n* cabellera *f*.
scamp *n* bribon.
scampi *npl* gambas *fpl*.
scan *vt* escudrinar.
scandal *n* escandalo *m*.
scandalize *vt* escandalizar.
scar *n* cicatriz *f*.
scarce *adj* raro.
scare *vt* espantar.
scarf *n* bufanda *f*.
scarlet *n* escarlata *f*.
scarp *n* escarpa *f*.
scene *n* escena *f*.
scenery *n* vista *f*.
schedule *n* horario *m*.
scheme *n* proyecto, plan *m*.
schism *n* cisma *m*.
scholar *n* estudiante *m*
school *n* escuela *f*.
schoolteacher *n* maestro, tra *m/f*; profesor, ra *m/f*.
science *n* ciencia *f*.
scientist *n* cientifico, ca *m/f*.
scissors *npl* tijeras *fpl*.

scooter n moto f.
scorch vt quemar.
scorn vt, vi despreciar.
Scorpio n Escorpion m (signo del zodiaco).
scorpion n escorpion m.
Scotch n whisky escoces m.
scoundrel n picaro m.
scramble vi arrapar.
scrap n migaja f; sobras fpl.
scrape vt, vi raer, raspar.
scraper n rascador m.
scratch vt rascar.
scrawl vt, vi garrapatear.
scream, screech vi chillar.
screen n pantalla f.
screenplay n guion m.
screw n tornillo m.
screwdriver n destornillador m.
scribble vt escarabajear.
scribe n escritor m.
script n guion m; letra f.
Scripture n Escritura sagrada f.
scruffy adj desalinado.
scruple n escrupulo m.
scullery n fregadero m.
sculptor n escultor, ra m/f.
sculpture n escultura f.
scum n espuma f; escoria f.
scurvy n escorbuto m.
scythe n guadana f.
sea n mar m;—adj de mar.
sea breeze n viento de mar m.
seafood n mariscos mpl.
sea front n paseo maritimo m.
seagull n gaviota f.
sea horse n hipocampo m.
seal n sello m; foca f.
seam n costura f.
seaman n marinero m.
sea plane n hidroavion m.
sear vt cauterizar.
search vt examinar, buscar.
seashore n ribera f, litoral m.
seasick adj mareado.
season n estacion f.
seasoning n condimento m.
seat n asiento m; silla f.
seat belt n cinturon de seguridad m.
seaweed n alga marina f.
seclude vt apartar.
seclusion n separacion f.
second adj segundo.
secondary adj secundario.
secondhand n segunda mano f.
secret adj, n secreto m.
secretary n secretario, ria m/f.
sect n secta f.

section n seccion f.
sector n sector m.
secular adj secular.
secure adj seguro.
security n seguridad f.
sedate adj sosegado.
sedative n sedativo m.
sedge n (bot) junco m.
sediment n sedimento m
sedition n sedicion f.
seduce vt seducir.
seducer n seductor m.
seduction n seduccion f.
seductive adj seductivo.
see vt, vi ver
seed n semilla.
seedy adj desaseado.
seek vt, vi buscar.
seem vi parecer.
seemliness n decensia f.
seesaw n vaiven m.
seethe vi hervir.
segment n segmento m.
seize vt asir.
seizure n captura f.
seldom adv raramente.
select vt elegir.
selection n seleccion f.
self n uno mismo.
selfish adj egoista.
self-portrait n autorretrato m.
selfsame adj identico.
sell vt, vi vender.
semen n semen m.
semester n semestre m.
semicircle n semicirculo m.
semicircular adj semicircular.
semicolon n punto y coma m.
seminary n seminario m.
senate n senado m.
senator n senador, ra m/f.
send vt enviar.
sender n remitente m.
senile adj senil.
senior n mayor m.
senna n (bot) sena f.
sensation n sensacion f.
sense n sentido m.
sensibility n sensibilidad f.
sensible adj sensato/a, juicioso/a..
sensitive adj sensitivo.
sensual, sensuous adj sensual.
sensuality n sensualidad f.
sentence n oracion f; sentencia f.
sentiment n sentimiento m.
sentinel, sentry n centinela m.
separate vt (vi) separar(se).

separation *n* separacion *f*.
September *n* se(p)tiembre *m*.
sepulcher *n* sepulcro *m*.
sequel *n* continuacion *f*.
sequence *n* serie *f*.
seraph *n* serafin *m*.
serenade *n* serenata *f*.
serene *adj* seneno.
serenity *n* serenidad *f*.
serf *n* siervo *m*.
sergeant *n* sargento *m*.
serial *adj* consecutivo.
series *n* serie *f*.
serious *adj* serio, grave.
sermon *n* sermon *f*.
serious *adj* seroso.
serpent *n* serpiente *f*.
serpentine *adj* serpentino.
serrated *adj* serrado.
serum *n* suero *m*.
servant *n* criado *m*; criada *f*.
serve *vt*, *vi* servir.
service *n* servicio *m*.
servile *adj* scrvil.
session *n* junta *f*; sesion *f*.
set *vt* poner, colocar, fijar.
setter *n* perro de muestra *m*.
seven *adj*, *n* siete.
seventeen *adj*, *n* diez y siete, diecisiete.
seventeenth *adj*, *n* decimoseptimo.
seventh *adj*, *n* septimo.
seventieth *adj*, *n* septuagesimo.
seventy *adj*, *n* setenta.
sever *vt*, *vi* separar.
several *adj*, *pn* varios.
severance *n* separacion *f*.
severe *adj* severo.
severity *n* severidad *f*.
sew *vt*, *vi* coser.
sewer *n* albanal *m*.
sex *n* sexo *m*.
sexist *adj n* sexista *m/f*.
sexual *adj* sexual.
sexy *adj* sexy.
shade *n* sombra *f*.
shadow *n* sombra *f*.
shaft *n* flecha, saeta *f*.
shake *vt* sacudir; agitar.
shallow *adj* somero.
sham *vt* enganar.
shame *n* verguenza *f*.
shamefaced *adj* vergonzoso.
shampoo champu *m*.
shamrock *n* trebol *m*.
shank *n* pierna *f*.
shanty *n* chabola *f*.
shantytown *n* barrio de chabolas *m*.

shape *vt*, *vi* formar; *n* forma *m*.
shapeless *adj* informe.
shapely *adj* bien hecho.
share *n* parte, porcion *f*; compartir.
shark *n* tiburon *m*.
sharp *adj* agudo.
shatter *vt* destrozar.
shave *vt* afeitar.
shaver *n* maquina de afeitar *f*.
shawl *n* chal *m*.
she *pn* ella.
sheaf *n* gavilla *f*
shear *vt* atusar.
sheath *n* vaina *f*.
shed *vt* verter; cabana *f*.
sheen *n* resplandor *m*.
sheep *n* oveja *f*.
sheer *adj* puro, claro.
sheet *n* sabana *f*.
sheet lightning *n* relampagueamiento *m*.
shelf *n* anaquel *m*.
shell *n* cascara *f*; concha *f*.
shelter *n* guardia *f*; amparo *m*.
shepherd *n* pastor *m*.
sherbet *n* sorbete *m*.
sheriff *n* sherif *m*.
sherry *n* jerez *m*.
shield *n* escudo *m*.
shift *vi* cambiarse.
shinbone *n* espinilla *f*.
shine *vi* lucir, brillar.
shiny *adj* brillante.
ship *n* nave *f*; barco *m*.
shipwreck *n* naufragio *m*.
shirt *n* camisa *f*.
shit *excl* (*sl*) imierda!
shiver *vi* tiritar de frio.
shoal *n* banco *m*.
shock *n* choque *m*.
shock absorber *n* amortiguador *m*.
shoddy *adj* de pacotilla.
shoe *n* zapato *m*.
shoelace *n* correa de zapato *f*.
shoemaker *n* zapatero *m*.
shoot *vt* tirar.
shopper *n* comprador, ra *m/f*.
shopping *n* compras *fpl*.
shopping mall *n* centro comercial *m*.
shore *n* costa, ribera *f*.
short *adj* corto breve.
short-sighted *adj* corto de vista.
shot *n* tiro *m*.
shotgun *n* escopeta *f*.
shoulder *n* hombro *m*.
shout *vi* gritar, aclamar.
shove *vt*, *vi* empujar.
shovel *n* pala *f*.

show *vt* mostrar.
shower *n* nubada *f*; llovizna *f*; ducha *f*.
showy *adj* ostentoso.
shred *n* cacho, pedazo.
shrewd *adj* astuto.
shriek *vt*, *vi* chillar
shrimp *n* camaron *m*.
shrine *n* relicario *m*.
shrink *vi* encogerse.
shroud *n* cubierta *f*.
Shrove Tuesday *n* martes de carnaval *m*.
shrub *n* arbusto *m*.
shrug *vt* encogerse de hombros.
shun *vt* huir, evitar.
shut *vt* cerrar.
shutter *n* contraventana *f*.
shuttle *n* lanzadera *f*.
shuttlecock *n* volante *m*.
shy *adj* timido.
shyness *n* timidez *f*.
sick *adj* malo, enfermo.
sickle *n* hoz *f*.
sickness *n* enfermedad *f*.
side *n* lado *m*.
sideboard *n* aparador *m*; alacena *f*.
sidewalk *n* calzada *f*.
siege *n* (*mil*) sitio *m*.
sieve *n* tamiz *m*.
sift *vt* cerner.
sigh *vi* suspirar.
sight *n* vista *f*.
sightseeing *n* excursionismo, turismo *m*.
sign *n* senal *f*.
signal *n* senal *f*.
signature *n* firma *f*.
significance *n* importancia *f*.
signify *vt* significar.
signpost *n* indicador *m*.
silence *n* silencio *m*.
silk *n* seda *f*.
silky *adj* hecho de seda; sedeno.
sill *n* repisa *f*.
silly *adj* tonto.
silver *n* plata *f*.
similar *adj* similar; semejante.
similarity *n* semejanza *f*.
simile *n* simil *m*.
simmer *vi* hervir a fuego lento.
simple *adj* simple.
simplicity *n* sencillez *ff*.
simulate *vt* simular.
simulation *n* simulacion *f*.
sin *n* pecado *m*.
since *adv* desde.
sincerity *n* sinceridad *f*.
sinew *n* tendon *m*; nervio *m*.
sing *vi*, *vt* cantar.

singe *vt* chamuscar.
singer *n* cantor *m*; cantora *f*.
single *adj* solo; soltero, soltera.
singly *adv* separadamente.
singular *adj* singular.
sinister *adj* siniestro.
sink *vi* hundirse.
sinner *n* pecador *m*; pecadora *f*.
sinus *n* seno *m*.
sip *vt* sorber:—*n* sorbo *m*.
siphon *n* sifon *m*.
sir *n* senor *m*.
siren *n* sirena *f*.
sister *n* hermana *f*.
sister-in-law *n* cunada *f*.
sisterly *adj* con hermandad.
sit *vi* sentarse.
site *n* sitio *m*; situacion *f*.
sit-in *n* ocupacion *f*.
sitting room *n* sala de estar *f*.
situation *n* situacion *f*.
six *adj*, *n* seis.
sixteen *adj*, *n* diez y seis, dieciseis.
sixteenth *adj*, *n* decimosexto.
sixth *adj*, *n* sexto.
sixtieth *adj*, *n* sexagesimo.
sixty *adj*, *n* sesenta.
size *n* tamano *m*.
skate *n* patin *m*:—*vi* patinar.
skeleton *n* esqueleto *m*.
skeptic *n* esceptico.
skepticism *n* escepticismo *m*.
sketch *n* esbozo *m*.
ski *n* esqui *m*:—*vi* esquiar.
skid *n* patinazo *m*.
skill *n* destreza *f*.
skim *vt* espumar.
skin *n* piel *f*; cutis *m/f*.
skip *vi* saltar, brincar.
skirt *n* falda.
skittle *n* bolo *m*.
skulk *vi* escuchar, acechar.
skull *n* craneo *m*.
sky *n* cielo *m*.
skyscraper *n* rascacielos *m invar*.
slab *n* losa *f*.
slack *adj* flojo.
slag *n* escoria *f*.
slander *vt* calumniar *f*.
slang *n* argot *m f*.
slap *n* manotada *f*.
slate *n* pizarra *f*.
slave *n* esclavo *m*.
slaver *n* baba *f*:—*vi* babosear.
slay *vt* matar.
sled, sleigh *n* trineo *m*.
sleek *adj* liso.

sleep *vi* dormir.
sleeping bag *n* saco de dormir *m*.
sleeping pill *n* somnifero *m*.
sleepwalking *n* sonambulismo *m*.
sleet *n* aguanieve *f*.
sleeve *n* manga *f*.
slender *adj* delgado.
slice *n* rebanada *f*.
slide *vi* resbalar, deslizarse.
slight *adj* ligero.
slim *adj* delgado.
slime *n* lodo *m/f*.
slimy *adj* viscoso, pegajoso.
sling *n* honda *f*; cabestrillo *m*.
slingshot *n* catapulta *f*.
slip *vi* resbalar; escapar.
slipper *n* zapatilla *f*.
slogan *n* eslogan, lema *m*.
slope *n* cuesta *f*.
slow *adj* tardio, lento, torpe.
slum *n* tugurio *m*.
slump *n* depresion *f*.
slur *vt* ensuciar; calumniar.
slut *n* marrana *f*.
sly *adj* astuto.
smack *n* sabor, gusto *m*; chasquido de latigo *m*.
small *adj* pequeno.
smallpox *n* viruelas *fpl*.
smalltalk *n* charla, prosa *f*.
smart *adj* elegante; listo.
smash *vt* romper, quebrantar
smell *vt*, *vi* oler.
smile *vi* sonreirse:—*n* sonrisa *f*.
smoke *n* humo *m*; fumar
smoker *n* fumador, ra *m/f*.
smooth *adj* liso.
smug *adj* presumido.
smut *n* tizon *m*.
snack *n* bocado *m*.
snag *n* problema *m*.
snail *n* caracol *m*.
snake *n* culebra *f*.
snap *vt*, *vi* romper.
snapdragon *n* (*bot*) antirrino *m*.
snatch *vt* arrebatar.
sneeze *vi* estornudar.
sniff *vt* oler:—*vi* resollar con fuerza.
snob *n* (e)snob *m/f*.
snore *vi* roncar.
snow *n* nieve *f*.
snowdrop *n* (*bot*) campanilla blanca *f*.
snowman *n* figura de nieve *f*.
snub *vt* reprender.
snuff *n* rape *m*.
so *adv* asi; de este modo; tan.
soap *n* jabon *m*.

soap opera *n* telenovela *f*.
soar *vi* remontarse.
sob *n* sollozo *m*:—*vi* sollozar.
soccer *n* balon *m*; fútbol *m*.
soccer player *n* futbolista *m/f*.
sociable *adj* sociable.
social *adj* social.
socialism *n* socialismo *m*.
society *n* sociedad *f*.
sociologist *n* sociologo, ga *m/f*.
sociology *n* sociologia *f*.
sock *n* calcetin *m*.
sod *n* cesped *m*.
soda *n* sosa *f*.
sofa *n* sofa *m*.
soft *adj* blando.
soil *vt* ensuciar, tierra *f*.
solar *adj* solar.
soldier *n* soldado *m*.
sole *n* planta del pie *f*.
solemn *adj*, **~ly** *adv* solemne(mente).
solicitor *n* representante, agente *m/f*.
solid *adj* solido.
solitaire *n* solitario *m*; grueso diamante *m*.
solitude *n* soledad *f*.
solo *n* (*mus*) solo *m*.
solstice *n* solsticio *m*.
soluble *adj* soluble.
solution *n* solucion *f*.
solve *vt* resolver.
some *adj* algo de, un poco, algun, alguno, alguna, unos, pocos, ciertos.
somebody *n* alguien *m*.
something *n* alguna cosa, algo.
sometimes *adv* a veces.
somnambulism *n* somnambulismo *m*.
somnambulist *n* somnambulo *m*.
somnolence *n* somnolencia *f*.
son *n* hijo *m*.
sonata *n* (*mus*) sonata *f*.
song *n* cancion.
son-in-law *n* yerno *m*.
sonnet *n* soneto *m*.
soon *adv* pronto.
soot *n* hollin *m*.
soothe *vt* adular; calmar.
sop *n* sopa *f*.
sophisticate *vt* sofisticar.
sophisticated *adj* sofisticado.
sorcerer *n* hechicero *m*.
sorcery *n* hechizo *m*.
sordid *adj* sordido.
sore *n* llaga, ulcera *f*.
sorrow *n* pesar *m*; tristeza *f*.
sorry *adj* triste.
soul *n* alma *f*.
sound *adj* sano; sonido, *vi* sonar.

soup *n* sopa *f*.
sour *adj* agrio.
souvenir *n* recuerdo *m*.
south *n* sur *m*.
sovereign *adj*, *n* soberano, na (*m/f*).
sovereignty *n* soberania *f*.
sow *n* puerca *f*.
sow *vt* sembrar.
space *n* espacio *m*.
spacious *adj* espacioso.
spade *n* laya.
spaghetti *n* espaguetis *mpl*.
span *n* palmo *m*.
spangle *n* lentejuela *f*.
spaniel *n* perro de aguas *m*.
Spanish *adj* espanol(a)
spar *n* palo *m*.
spark *n* chispa *f*.
sparkle *n* centella.
sparrow *n* gorrion *m*.
sparse *adj* delgado.
spasm *n* espasmo *m*.
spatula *n* espatula *f*.
spawn *n* freza *f*.
speak *vt*, *vi* hablar.
spear *n* lanza *f*.
special *adj* especial.
species *n* especie *f*.
specific *adj* especifico *m*.
specimen *n* muestra *f*.
spectacle *n* espectaculo *m*.
spectator *n* espectador, ra *m/f*.
specter *n* espectro *m*.
speculate *vi* especular.
speculation *n* especulacion *f*.
speed *n* prisa *f*; velocidad *f*.
spell *n* hechizo *m*.
spelling *n* ortografia *f*.
spend *vt* gastar.
sperm *n* esperma *f*.
spew *vi* (*sl*) vomitar.
sphere *n* esfera *f*.
spherical *adj* esferico.
spice *n* especia *f*.
spicy *adj* aromatico.
spider *n* arana *f*.
spike *n* espigon *m*.
spill *vt* derramar.
spin *vt* hilar.
spinach *n* espinaca *f*.
spinal *adj* espinal.
spine *n* espinazo *m*.
spinster *n* soltera *f*.
spiral *adj* espiral.
spire *n* espira *f*.
spirit *n* aliento *m*; espiritu *m*.
spiritual *adj*, ~ly *adv* espiritual(men-te).

spiritualist *n* espiritualista *m*.
spit *n* asador *m*; saliva *f*.
spite *n* rencor *m*.
splash *vt* salpicar.
spleen *n* bazo *m*.
splendid *adj* esplendido.
splendor *n* esplendor *m*.
splint *n* tablilla *f*.
splinter *n* cacho *m*.
split *n* hendedura *f*.
spoil *vt* despojar.
spoke *n* rayo de la rueda *m*.
spokesman *n* portavoz *m*.
sponge *n* esponja *f*.
sponsor *n* fiador *m*.
spontaneity *n* espontaneidad *f*.
spool *n* carrete *m*.
spoon *n* cuchara *f*.
spoonful *n* cucharada *f*.
sport *n* deporte *m*
spot *n* mancha *f*.
spouse *n* esposo *m*; esposa *f*.
sprain *adj* descoyuntar.
sprat *n* meleta, nuesa *f* (*pez*).
sprawl *vi* revolcarse.
spray *n* rociada *f*; espray *m*.
spread *vt* extender
spree *n* fiesta *f*; juerga *f*.
sprig *n* ramito *m*.
sprinkle *vt* rociar.
spur *n* espuela *f*.
spurn *vt* despreciar.
spy *n* espia *m*.
squad *n* escuadra *f*.
squadron *n* (*mil*) escuadron *m*.
squalid *adj* sucio.
squall *n* rafaga *f*.
squalor *n* porqueria *f*.
squander *vt* malgastar.
square *adj* cuadrado *m*; plaza *f*.
squash *vt* aplastar.
squaw *n* hembra de un indiano *f*.
squeak *vi* planir.
squeamish *adj* fastidioso.
squeeze *vt* apretar.
squid *n* calamar *m*.
squint *adj* bizco.
squirrel *n* ardilla *f*.
stable *n* establo *m*.
stack *n* pila *f*.
staff *n* personal *m*.
stag *n* ciervo *m*.
stage *n* etapa *f*; escena *f*.
stagnate *vi* estancarse.
stain *vt* manchar.
stair *n* escalon *m*.
staircase *n* escalera *f*.

stale *adj* anejo.

stalk, tronco *m*.

stall *n* pesebre *m*; tienda portatil *f*.

stallion *n* semental *m*.

stamina *n* resistencia *f*.

stammer *vi* tartamudear.

stamp estampar, imprimir; sello *m*.

stampede *n* estampida *f*.

stand *vi* estar de pie o derecho; stand *m*.

standard *n* estandarte *m*.

staple *n* grapa *f*.

star *n* estrella *f*.

starch *n* almidon *m*.

stark *adj* fuerte, aspero.

starling *n* estornino *m*.

start *vi* empezar.

startle *vt* sobresaltar.

starvation *n* hambre *f*.

state *n* estado *m*; condicion *f*.

statement *n* afirmacion *f*.

static *adj* estatico.

station *n* estacion *f*.

stationary *adj* estacionario, fijo.

stationery *n* papeleria *f*.

statistics *npl* estadistica *f*.

statuary *n* estatuario *m*.

statue *n* estatua *f*.

stature *n* estatura *f*.

statute *n* estatuto *m*.

stay *n* estancia *f*.

steak *n* filete *m*; bistec *m*.

steal *vt, vi* robar.

stealth *n* hurto *m*.

steam *n* vapor *m*.

steel *n* acero *m*.

steep *adj* escarpado.

steeple *n* torre *f*; campanario *m*.

steer *n* novillo *m*:—*vt* manejar, conducir.

steering wheel *n* volante *m*.

stem *n* vastago.

stench *n* hedor *m*.

stencil *n* cliche *m*.

stenographer *n* taquigrafo, fa *m/f*.

stenography *n* taquigrafia *f*.

step *n* paso, escalon *m*.

stepbrother *n* hermanastro *m*.

stepdaughter *n* hijastra *f*.

stepfather *n* padrastro *m*.

stepmother *n* madrastra *f*.

stepsister *n* hermanastra *f*.

stepson *n* hijastro *m*.

stereo *n* estereo *m*.

stereotype *n* estereotipo *m*.

sterile *adj* esteril.

sterling *n* libras esterlinas *fpl*.

stethoscope *n* (*med*) estetoscopio *m*.

stew *vt* estofar *f*.

steward *n* mayordomo *m*

stick *n* palo, pegarse.

stiff *adj* tieso.

stifle *vt* sufocar.

stigma *n* estigma *m*.

stigmatize *vt* infamar.

stiletto *n* estilete *m*

still tranquilo; *adv* todavia.

stillborn *adj* nacido muerto.

stilts *npl* zancos *mpl*.

stimulant *n* estimulante *m*.

stimulate *vt* estimular.

stimulus *n* estimulo *m*.

sting *vt* picar o morder (un insecto).

stingy *adj* mezquino.

stink *vi* heder.

stint *n* tarea *f*.

stipulate *vt* estipular.

stipulation *n* estipulacion *f*.

stir *vt* agitar.

stirrup *n* estribo *m*.

stitch *vt* coser.

stoat *n* comadreja *f*.

stock *n* ganado *m*; caldo *m*.

stockbroker *n* agente de bolsa *m/f*.

stock exchange *n* bolsa *f*.

stocking *n* media *f*.

stock market *n* bolsa *f*.

stoic *n* estoico *m*.

stoical *adj* estoico.

stole *n* estola *f*.

stomach *n* estomago *m*.

stone *n* piedra *f*.

stop *vt* detener, parar.

stopwatch *n* cronometro *m*.

store *n* provision *f*; almacen *m*.

stork *n* ciguena *f*.

storm *n* tempestad.

story *n* historia *f*.

stout *adj* robusto.

stove *n* estufa *f*.

straight *adj* derecho.

strain *vt* colar, filtrar; *n* tension *f*.

strainer *n* colador *m*.

strange *adj* raro/a, extranjero.

stranger *n* desconocido *m*; extranjero, ra *m/f*.

strangle *vt* ahogar.

strap *n* correa *f*.

strapping *adj* abultado.

stratagem *n* estratagema *f*; astucia *f*.

strategic *adj* estrategico *m*.

strategy *n* estrategia *f*.

stratum *n* estrato *m*.

straw *n* paja *m*; pajita *f*.

strawberry *n* fresa *f*.

stray *vi* extraviarse.

streak n raya.
street n calle f.
streetcar n tranvia f.
strength n fuerza.
strenuous adj arduo.
stress n presion f; estres m.
stretch vt, vi extender.
stretcher n camilla f.
strew vt esparcir.
strict adj estricto.
stride n tranco m.
string n cordon m.
stringent adj astringente.
strip vt desnudar.
stripe n raya.
strive vi esforzarse.
stroll n paseo.
strong adj fuerte.
strongbox n cofre fuerte m.
structure n estructura f.
struggle vi esforzarse.
strum vt (mus) rasguear.
strut vi pavonearse.
stubborn adj obstinado.
stucco n estuco m.
stud n corchete m.
student n estudiante m/f.
studio n estudio de un artista m.
studious adj estudioso.
study n estudio m.
stuff n materia f.
stuffing n relleno m.
stumble vi tropezar
stump n tronco m.
stun vt aturdir.
stunt n vuelo acrobático m; truco publi-
  citario m.
stuntman n especialista m.
stupid adj estupido.
sturdy adj fuerte.
sturgeon n esturion m.
stutter vi tartamudear.
sty n zahurda f.
stye n orzuelo m.
style n estilo m.
stylish adj elegante.
suave adj afable.
subdivide vt subdividir.
subdue vt sojuzgar, sujetar.
subject adj sujeto.
subjunctive n subjuntivo m.
sublime adj sublime.
submarine adj submarino.
submerge vt sumergir.
submit vt, (vi) someter(se).
subordinate adj subordinado, inferior:—vt
  subordinar.

subscribe vt, vi suscribir.
subsequent adj, ~ly adv subsiguien-te
  (mente).
subservient adj subordinado.
subside vi sumergirse.
subsidence n derrumbamiento m.
subsidiary adj subsidiario.
subsidize vt subvencionar.
subsidy n subvencion f.
substance n substancia f.
substitute vt sustituir.
substratum n lecho m.
subterranean adj subterraneo.
subtitle n subtitulo m.
subtle adj sutil.
suburb n suburbio m.
subversion n subversion f.
subway n metro m.
succeed vt, vi seguir; conseguir, lograr, tener
  exito.
success n exito m.
succumb vi sucumbir.
such adj tal.
suck vt, vi chupar.
sudden adj repentino, no previsto.
sue vt poner por justicia; suplicar.
suede n ante m.
suffer vt, vi sufrir, padecer.
sufficient adj suficiente.
suffocate vt sofocar.
suffrage n sufragio.
sugar n azucar m.
sugar cane n cana de azucar f.
suggest vt sugerir.
suggestion n sugestion f.
suicide n suicidio m.
suit n conjunto m; traje m.
suitcase n maleta f.
suitor n suplicante m.
sultan n sultan m.
sultana n sultana f.
sum n suma f.
summary adj, n sumario (m).
summer n verano m.
summit n apice m.
summon vt citar.
summons n citacion f.
sumptuous adj suntuoso.
sun n sol m.
sunbathe vi tomar el sol.
Sunday n domingo m.
sundial n reloj de sol m.
sundry adj varios.
sunflower n girasol m.
sunglasses npl gafas o antojos de sol
  mpl.
sunlight n luz del sol f.

sunrise *n* salida del sol *f*.
sunset *n* puesta del sol *f*.
sunshade *n* quitasol *m*.
sunstroke *n* insolacion *f*.
suntan *n* bronceado *m*.
suntan oil *n* aceite bronceador *m*.
superb *adj* magnifico.
superficial *adj* superficial.
superfluity *n* superfluidad *f*.
superior *adj*, *n* superior (*m*).
supermarket *n* supermercado *m*.
supernatural *n* sobrenatural.
superpower *n* superpotencia *f*.
superstition *n* supersticion *f*.
supertanker *n* superpetrolero *m*.
supervise *vt* inspeccionar.
supper *n* cena *f*.
supple *adj* flexible.
supplement *n* suplemento *m*.
supplementary *adj* adicional.
suppleness *n* flexibilidad *f*.
suppli(c)ant *n* suplicante *m*.
supplicate *vt* suplicar.
supplication *n* suplica, suplicacion *f*.
supplier *n* distribuidor, ra *m/f*.
supply *vt* suministrar; suplir, completar;
   surtir:—*n* provision *f*; suministro *m*.
support *vt* sostener; soportar, asistir: —*n*
   apoyo *m*.
supportable *adj* soportable.
supporter *n* partidario, ria; aficionado,
   da *m/f*.
suppose *vt*, *vi* suponer.
supposition *n* suposicion *f*.
suppress *vt* suprimir.
suppression *n* supresion *f*.
supremacy *n* supremacia *f*.
supreme *adj* supremo:—~ly *adv* suprema-
   mente.
surcharge *vt* sobrecargar:—*n* sobretasa *f*.
sure *adj* seguro, cierto; firme; estable:—to
   be ~ sin duda; ya se ve:—~ly *adv* cierta-
   mente, seguramente, sin duda.
sureness *n* certeza, seguridad *f*.
surety *n* seguridad *f*; fiador *m*.
surf *n* (*mar*) resaca *f*.
surface *n* superficie *f*:—*vt* revestir:—*vi* salir
   a la superficie.
surfboard *n* plancha (de surf) *f*.
surfeit *n* exceso *m*.
surge *n* ola, onda *f*:—*vi* avanzar en tropel.
surgeon *n* cirujano, na *m/f*.
surgery *n* cirujia *m*.
surgical *adj* quirurgico.
surliness *n* mal humor *m*.
surly *adj* aspero de genio.
surmise *vt* sospechar:—*n* sospecha *f*.

surmount *vt* sobrepujar.
surmountable *adj* superable.
surname *n* apellido, sobrenombre *m*.
surpass *vt* sobresalir, sobrepujar, exceder,
   aventajar.
surpassing *adj* sobresaliente.
surplice *n* sobrepelliz *f*.
surplus *n* excedente *m*; sobrante *m*:—*adj*
   sobrante.
surprise *vt* sorprender:—*n* sorpresa *f*.
surprising *adj* sorprendente.
surrender *vt*, *vi* rendir; ceder; rendirse:—*n*
   rendicion *f*.
surreptitious *adj* subrepticio:—~ly *adv*
   subrepticiamente.
surrogate *vt* subrogar:—*n* subrogado *m*.
surrogate mother *n* madre portadora *f*.
surround *vt* circundar, cercar, rodear.
survey *vt* inspeccionar, examinar; apear: —
   n inspeccion *f*; apeo (de tierras) *m*.
survive *vi* sobrevivir:—*vt* sobrevivir a.
survivor *n* sobreviviente *m/f*.
susceptibility *n* susceptibilidad *f*.
susceptible *adj* susceptible.
suspect *vt*, *vi* sospechar:—*n* sospechoso, sa
   m/f.
suspend *vt* suspender.
suspense *n* suspense *m*; detencion *f*; incertidumbre *f*.
suspension *n* suspension *f*.
suspension bridge *n* puente colgante o
   colgado *m*.
suspicion *n* sospecha *f*.
suspicious *adj* suspicaz:—~ly *adv* sospe-
   chosamente.
suspiciousness *n* suspicacia *f*.
sustain *vt* sostener, sustentar, mantener;
   apoyar; sufrir.
sustenance *n* sostenimiento, sustento *m*.
suture *n* sutura, costura *f*.
swab *n* algodon *m*; frotis *m* invar.
swaddle *vt* fajar.
swaddling-clothes *npl* panales *mpl*.
swagger *vi* baladronear.
swallow *n* golondrina *f*:—*vt* tragar, engullir.
swamp *n* pantano *m*.
swampy *adj* pantanoso.
swan *n* cisne *m*.
swap *vt* canjear:—*n* intercambio *m*.
swarm *n* enjambre *m*; gentio *m*; hormi-
   guero *m*:—*vi* enjam brar; hormiguear de
   gente; abundar.
swarthy *adj* atezado.
swarthiness *n* tez morena *f*.
swashbuckling *adj* fanfarron.
swath *n* tranco *m*.

swathe *vt* fajar:—*n* faja *f*.

sway *vt* mover:—*vi* ladearse, inclinarse:—*n* balanceo *m*; poder, imperio, influjo *m*.

swear *vt, vi* jurar; hacer jurar; juramentar.

sweat *n* sudor *m*:—*vi* sudar; trabajar con fatiga.

sweater, sweatshirt *n* sueter *m*.

sweep *vt, vi* barrer; arrebatar; deshollinar; pasar o tocar liger amente; oscilar:—*n* barredura *f*; vuelta *f*; giro *m*.

sweeping *adj* rapido:—~s *pl* barreduras *fpl*.

sweepstake *n* loteria *f*.

sweet *adj* dulce, grato, gustoso; suave; oloroso; melodioso; hermoso; amable:—*adv* dulcemente, suavemente.

sweetbread *n* mellejas de ternera *fpl*.

sweeten *vt* endulzar; suavizar; aplacar; perfumar.

sweetener *n* edulcorante *m*.

sweetheart *n* novio, via *m/f*; querida *f*.

sweetmeats *npl* dulces secos *mpl*.

sweetness *n* dulzura, suavidad *f*.

swell *vi* hincharse; ensoberbecerse; embravecerse:—*vt* hin char, inflar, agravar:—*n* marejada *f*:—*adj* (*fam*) estupendo, fenomenal.

swelling *n* hinchazon *f*; tumor *m*.

swelter *vi* ahogarse de calor.

swerve *vi* vagar; desviarse.

swift *adj* veloz, ligero, rapido:—*n* vencejo, *m*.

swiftly *adv* velozmente.

swiftness *n* velocidad, rapidez *f*.

swill *vt* beber con exceso:—*n* bazofia *f*.

swim *vi* nadar; abundar en:—*vt* pasar a nado:—*n* nadada *f*.

swimming *n* natacion *f*; vertigo *m*.

swimming pool *n* piscina *f*.

swimsuit *n* traje de bano *m*.

swindle *vt* estafar.

swindler *n* trampista *m*.

swine *n* puerco, cochino *m*.

swing *vi* balancear, columpiarse; vibrar; agitarse:—*vt* colum piar; balancear; girar:—*n* vibracion *f*; balanceo *m*.

swinging *adj* (*fam*) alegre.

swinging door *n* puerta giratoria *f*.

swirl *n* hacer remolinos (en el agua).

switch *n* varilla *f*; interruptor *m*; (*rail*) aguja *f*:—*vt* cambiar de:—to ~ off apagar; parar:—to ~ on encender, prender.

switchboard *n* centralita (de teléfonos) *f*.

swivel *vt* girar.

swoon *vi* desmayarse:—*n* desmayo, deliquio, pasmo *m*.

swoop *vi* calarse:—*n* calada; redada *f*:— in one ~ de un golpe.

sword *n* espada *f*.

swordfish *n* pez espada *f*.

swordsman *n* guerrero *m*.

sycamore *n* sicomoro *m* (arbol).

sycophant *n* sicofante *m*.

syllabic *adj* silabico.

syllable *n* silaba *f*.

syllabus *n* programa de estudios *m*.

syllogism *n* silogismo *m*.

sylph *n* silfio *m*; silfida *f*.

symbol *n* simbolo *m*.

symbolic(al) *adj* simbolico.

symbolize *vt* simbolizar.

symmetrical *adj* simetrico:—~ly *adv* con simetria.

symmetry *n* simetria *f*.

sympathetic *adj* simpatico:—~ally *adv* simpaticamente.

sympathize *vi* compadecerse.

sympathy *n* simpatia *f*.

symphony *n* sinfonia *f*.

symposium *n* simposio *m*.

symptom *n* sintoma *m*.

synagogue *n* sinagoga *f*.

synchronism *n* sincronismo *m*.

syndicate *n* sindicato *m*.

syndrome *n* sindrome *m*.

synod *n* sinodo *m*.

synonym *n* sinonimo *m*.

synonymous *adj* sinonimo:—~ly *adv* con sinonimia.

synopsis *n* sinopsis *f*; sumario *m*.

synoptical *adj* sinoptico.

syntax *n* sintaxis *f*.

synthesis *n* sintesis *f*.

syringe *n* jeringa, lavativa *f*:—*vt* jeringar.

system *n* sistema *m*.

systematic *adj* sistematico:—~ally *adv* sistematicamente.

systems analyst *n* analista de sistemas *m/f*.

T

table *n* mesa *f m*.

tablecloth *n* mantel *m*.

tablespoon *n* cuchara para comer *f*.

tablet *n* tableta *f m*.

table tennis *n* ping-pong *m*.

taboo *adj* tabu.

tacit *adj* tacito.

taciturn *adj* taciturno.

tack *n* tachuela *f.*
tact *n* tacto *m.*
tactician *n* tactico *m.*
tactics *npl* tactica *f.*
tadpole *n* ranilla *f.*
taffeta *n* tafetan *m.*
tag *n* herrete *m.*
tail *n* cola *f.*
tailor *n* sastre *m.*
tailor-made *adj* hecho a la medida.
taint *vt* tachar.
take *vt* tomar, coger.
takeoff *n* despegue *m.*
takings *npl* ingresos *mpl.*
talc *n* talco *m.*
talent *n* talento *m.*
talisman *n* talisman *m.*
talk *vi* hablar.
talkative *adj* locuaz.
tall *adj* alto.
talon *n* garra de ave de rapina *f.*
tambourine *n* pandereta *f.*
tame *adj* amansado.
tamper *vi* tocar.
tampon *n* tampon *m.*
tan *vt* broncear.
tang *n* sabor fuerte *m.*
tangerine *n* mandarina *f.*
tangle *vt* enredar.
tank *n* cisterna *f;* aljibe *m.*
tanned *adj* bronceado.
tantrum *n* rabieta *f.*
tape *n* cinta *f.*
tape measure *n* metro *m.*
tapestry *n* tapiz *mf.*
tar *n* brea *f.*
target *n* blanco *m* (para tirar).
tariff *n* tarifa *f.*
tarmac *n* pista *f.*
tarnish *vt* deslustrar.
tarpaulin *n* alquitranado *m.*
tarragon *n* (*bot*) estragon *m.*
tartan *n* tela escocesa *f.*
tartar *n* tartaro *m.*
task *n* tarea *f.*
tassel *n* borlita *f.*
taste *n* gusto *m;* sabor *m.*
tasty *adj* sabroso.
tattoo *n* tatuaje *m.*
taunt *vt* mofar.
Taurus *n* Tauro *m.*
tax *n* impuesto *m.*
taxi *n* taxi *m.*
tea *n* te *m.*
teach *vt* ensenar.
teacher *n* profesor, ra *m/f.*
teak *n* teca *f* (arbol).

team *n* equipo *m.*
teamster *n* camionero *m.*
teapot *n* tetera *f.*
tear *vt* despedazar, rasgar.
tear *n* lagrima *f.*
tease *vt* tomar el pelo.
teaspoon *n* cucharita *f.*
teat *n* ubre, teta *f.*
technical *adj* tecnico.
technician *n* tecnico *m.*
technique *n* tecnica *f.*
technology *n* tecnologia *f.*
teddy (bear) *n* osito de felpa *m.*
tedious *adj* tedioso.
tedium *n* tedio *m.*
tee-shirt *n* camiseta *f.*
teeth *npl* de tooth.
telegraph *n* telegrafo *m.*
telegraphic *adj* telegrafico.
telepathy *n* telepatia *f.*
telephone *n* telefono *m.*
telescope *n* telescopio *m.*
telescopic *adj* telescopico.
television *n* television *f.*
tell *vt* decir.
teller *n* cajero *m.*
temper *vt* templar:—*n* mal genio *m.*
temperament *n* temperamento *m.*
temperate *adj* templado.
temperature *n* temperatura *f.*
template *n* plantilla *f.*
temple *n* templo *m.*
temporary *adj* temporal.
tempt *vt* tentar.
temptation *n* tentacion *f.*
ten *adj, n* diez.
tenacity *n* tenacidad *f.*
tenancy *n* tenencia *f.*
tenant *n* arrendador *m.*
tend *vt* guardar.
tendency *n* tendencia *f.*
tender *adj* tierno, estimar.
tendon *n* tendon *m.*
tennis *n* tenis *m.*
tense *adj* tieso, tenso.
tension *n* tension *f.*
tent *n* tienda de campana *f.*
tentacle *n* tentaculo *m.*
tenth *adj, n* decimo.
tenure *n* tenencia *f.*
tepid *adj* tibio.
term *n* termino *m.*
terminal *adj* mortal.
termination *n* terminacion *f.*
terminus *n* terminal *m.*
terrace *n* terraza *f.*
terrain *n* terreno *m.*

terrestrial *adj* terrestre.
terrible *adj* terrible.
terrier *n* terrier *m*.
terrific *adj* fantastico.
terrify *vt* aterrar.
territorial *adj* territorial.
territory *n* territorio, distrito *m*.
terror *n* terror *m*.
terrorism *n* terrorismo *m*.
test *n* examen *m*.
testament *n* testamento *m*.
testicles *npl* testiculos *mpl*.
testify *vt* testificar.
testimony *n* testimonio *m*.
tetanus *n* tetano *m*.
tether *vt* atar.
text *n* texto *m*.
textiles *npl* textiles *mpl*.
texture *n* textura *f*.
than *adv* que, de.
thank *vt* agradecer.
thanks *npl* gracias *fpl*.
that *pn* aquel, aquello, aquella; que; este.
thaw *n* deshielo *m*.
the *art* el, la, lo; los, las.
theater *n* teatro *m*.
theft *n* robo *m*.
their *pn* su, suyo, suya; de ellos, de ellas:—
~s el suyo, la suya, los suyos, las suyas; de
ellos, de ellas.
them *pn* los, las, les; ellos, ellas.
theme *n* tema *m*.
themselves *pn pl* ellos mismos, ellas
mismas; si mismos; se.
then *adv* entonces, despues.
theology *n* teologia *f*.
theory *n* teoria *f*.
therapist *n* terapeuta *m*.
therapy *n* terapia *f*.
there *adv* alli, alla.
thermal *adj* termal.
thermometer *n* termometro *m*.
thesaurus *n* tesoro *m*.
these *pn pl* estos, estas.
thesis *n* tesis *f*.
they *pn pl* ellos, ellas.
thick *adj* espeso.
thicken *vi* espesar.
thief *n* ladron *m*.
thigh *n* muslo *m*.
thimble *n* dedal *m*.
thin *adj* delgado.
thing *n* cosa *f*.
think *vi* pensar.
third *adj* tercero.
thirst *n* sed *f*.
thirteen *adj*, *n* trece.

thirteenth *adj*, *n* decimotercio.
thirtieth *adj*, *n* trigesimo.
thirty *adj*, *n* treinta.
this *adj* este, esta, esto:—*pn* este, esta, esto.
thorn *n* espino *m*; espina *f*.
those *pn pl* esos, esas; aquellos, aquellas:—
adj esos, esas; aquellos, aquellas.
thought *n* pensamiento *m*.
thousand *adj*, *n* mil.
thousandth *adj*, *n* milesimo.
thrash *vt* golpear.
thread *n* hilo *m*.
threat *n* amenaza *f*.
threaten *vt* amenazar.
three *adj*, *n* tres.
threshold *n* umbral *m*.
thrifty *adj* economico.
thrill *vt* emocionar.
thrive *vi* prosperar.
throat *n* garganta *f*.
throb *vi* palpitar.
throne *n* trono *m*.
through *prep* por; durante; mediante.
throw *vt* echar.
thrush *n* tordo *m* (ave).
thrust *vt* empujar.
thug *n* gamberro *m*.
thumb *n* pulgar *m*.
thump *n* golpe *m*.
thunder *n* trueno *m*.
Thursday *n* jueves *m*.
thus *adv* asi, de este modo.
thyme *n* (*bot*) tomillo *m*.
thyroid *n* tiroides *m*.
tiara *n* tiara *f*.
tic *n* tic *m*.
ticket *n* billete *m* .
tickle *vt* hacer cosquillas.
tidal *adj* (*mar*) de marea.
tide *n* marea *f*.
tidy *adj* ordenado.
tie *vt* anudar, atar
tiger *n* tigre *m*.
tight *adj* tirante, apretado/a.
tile *n* azulejo *m*.
till *n* caja *f*:—*vt* cultivar.
time *n* tiempo; epoca *f*.
timer *n* interruptor *m*.
timid *adj* timido.
timidity *n* timidez *f*.
tin *n* estano *m*.
tinfoil *n* papel de estano *m*.
tinsel *n* oropel *m*.
tint *n* tinte *m*.
tiny *adj* pequeno, chico.
tip *n* punta, extremidad *f*; propina *f*.
tire *vt* cansar, fatigar:—*n* neumático *m*.

tissue n tejido m.
title n titulo m.
titular adj titular.
to prep a; para; por; de; hasta; en; con; que.
toad n sapo m.
toadstool n (bot) hongovejin m.
toast vt tostar; brindar.
toaster n tostadora f.
tobacco n tabaco m.
tobacco shop n tabaqueria f.
today adv hoy.
toe n dedo del pie m.
together adv juntamente.
toilet paper n papel higienico m.
token n senal f.
tolerate vt tolerar.
tomato n tomate m.
tomb n tumba f.
tomboy n muchachota f.
tombstone n piedra sepulcral f.
tomcat n gato m.
tomorrow adv, n manana f.
ton n tonelada f.
tongs npl tcnacillas fpl.
tongue n lengua f.
tonic n (med) tonico.
tonight adv, n esta tarde (f).
tonsil n amigdala f.
too adv demasiado; tambien.
tool n herramienta f.
tooth n diente m.
toothache n dolor de muelas m.
top n cima.
topaz n topacio m.
topic n tema m.
topless adj topless.
topographic(al) adj topografico.
topography n topografia f.
torment vt atormentar.
tornado n tornado m.
torrent n torrente m.
torrid adj apasionado.
tortoise n tortuga f.
tortoiseshell adj de carey.
tortuous adj tortuoso.
torture n tortura f.
toss vt tirar, lanzar.
total adj total.
totalitarian adj totalitario.
totality n totalidad f.
totter vi vacilar.
touch vt tocar.
touchdown n aterrizaje m.
touching adj patetico, conmovedor.
tough adj duro.
toupee n tupe m.
tour n viaje m.

touring n viajes turisticos mpl.
tourism n turismo m.
tourist n turista m/f.
tourist office n oficina de turismo f.
tournament n torneo m.
tow n remolque m.
toward(s) prep, adv hacia.
towel n toalla f.
tower n torre m.
town n ciudad f.
town hall n ayuntamiento m.
toy n juguete m.
toy store n jugueteria f.
trace n huella f:—vt trazar.
trade n comercio m; ocupacion f.
trade(s) union n sindicato m.
tradition n tradicion f.
traditional adj tradicional.
traffic n trafico m.
traffic lights npl semaforo m.
tragedy n tragedia f.
tragic adj tragico.
trail vt, vi rastrear:— n senda f.
trailer n caravana f.
train vt entrenar * n tren m.
trainee n aprendiz m.
trainer n entrenador m.
trait n rasgo m.
traitor n traidor m.
tramp n vagabundo m.
trample vt pisotear.
trampoline n trampolin m.
trance n rapto m.
tranquil adj tranquilo.
tranquillizer n tranquilizante m.
transact vt negociar.
transaction n transaccion f.
transatlantic adj transatlántico.
transcription n traslado m.
transfer vt transferir.
transform vt transformar.
transformation n transformacion f.
transfusion n transfusion f.
transit n transito m.
transition n transito m; transicion f.
translate vt traducir.
translation n traduccion f.
translator n traductor, ra m/f.
transmit vt transmitir.
transparent adj transparente.
transpire vi resultar.
transplant vt trasplantar.
transport vt transportar.
trap n trampa f.
trapeze n trapecio m.
trappings npl adornos mpl.
trash n pacotilla f; basura f.

travel *vi* viajar.
trawler *n* pesquero de arrastre *m*.
tray *n* bandeja *f*.
treachery *n* traicion *f*.
tread *vi* pisar.
treason *n* traicion *n*.
treasure *n* tesoro *m*.
treasurer *n* tesorero *m*.
treat *vt* tratar.
treatise *n* tratado *m*.
treatment *n* trato *m*.
treaty *n* tratado *m*.
treble *adj* triple.
treble clef *n* clave de sol *f*.
tree *n* arbol *m*.
trellis *n* enrejado *m*.
tremble *vi* temblar.
tremendous *adj* tremendo.
tremor *n* temblor *m*.
trench *n* foso *m*.
trend *n* tendencia *f*.
trendy *adj* de moda.
trespass *vt* transpasar.
tress *n* trenza *f*.
trestle *n* caballete de serrador *m*.
trial *n* proceso *m*.
triangle *n* triangulo *m*.
triangular *adj* triangular.
tribal *adj* tribal.
tribe *n* tribu *f*.
tribunal *n* tribunal *m*.
tributary *adj, n* tributario *m*.
tribute *n* tributo *m*.
trice *n* momento, tris *m*.
trick *n* engano *m*.
trickle *vi* gotear.
tricky *adj* dificil.
tricycle *n* triciclo *m*.
trifle *n* bagatela.
trigger *n* gatillo *m*.
trigonometry *n* trigonometria *f*.
trim *adj* aseado.
Trinity *n* Trinidad *f*.
trinket *n* joya.
trio *n (mus)* trio *m*.
trip *vt* hacer caer; viaje corto *m*.
tripe *n* callos *mpl*.
triple *adj* triple.
triplets *npl* trillizos *mpl*.
triplicate *n* triplicado *m*.
tripod *n* tripode *m*.
triumph *n* triunfo *m*.
triumphal *adj* triunfal.
triumphant *adj* triunfante.
trivia *npl* trivialidades *fpl*.
trivial *adj* trivial.
trolley *n* carrito *m*.

trombone *n* trombon *m*.
trophy *n* trofeo *m*.
tropical *adj* tropico.
trot *n* trote *m*.
trouble *vt* afligir.
trough *n* abrevadero *m*.
trout *n* trucha *f*.
trowel *n* paleta *f*.
truce *n* tregua *f*.
truck *n* camion *m*.
true *adj* verdadero.
truffle *n* trufa *f*.
truly *adv* en verdad.
trumpet *n* trompeta *f*.
trunk *n* baul, cofre *m*; trompa *f*.
trust *n* confianza *f*.
truth *n* verdad *f*.
try *vt* examinar, tentar.
tub *n* balde, cubo *m*.
tuba *n* tuba *f*.
tube *n* tubo *m*.
tuberculosis *n* tuberculosis *f*.
Tuesday *n* martes *m*.
tuition *n* enseñanza. *f*.
tulip *n* tulipan *m*.
tumble *vi* caer.
tumbler *n* vaso *m*.
tummy *n* barriga *f*.
tumor *n* tumor *m*.
tumultuous *adj* tumultuoso.
tuna *n* atun *m*.
tune *n* tono *m*.
tunic *n* tunica *f*.
tunnel *n* tunel *m*.
turban *n* turbante *m*.
turbine *n* turbina *f*.
turbulence *n* turbulencia *f*.
tureen *n* sopera *f*.
turf *n* cesped *m*.
turgid *adj* pesado.
turkey *n* pavo *m*.
turmoil *n* disturbio *m*.
turn *vi* volver.
turncoat *n* desertor *m*.
turnip *n* nabo *m*.
turnover *n* facturacion *f*.
turnstile *n* torniquete *m*.
turpentine *n* trementina *f*.
turquoise *n* turquesa *f*.
turret *n* torrecilla *f*.
turtle *n* galapago *m*.
turtledove *n* tortola *f*.
tusk *n* colmillo *m*.
tussle *n* pelea *f*.
tutor *n* tutor *m*.
tuxedo *n* smoking *m*.
twang *n* gangueo *m*.

tweezers *npl* tenacillas *fpl.*
twelfth *adj, n* duodecimo.
twelve *adj, n* doce.
twentieth *adj, n* vigesimo.
twenty *adj, n* veinte.
twice *adv* dos veces.
twig *n* ramita *f:—vi* caer en la cuenta.
twilight *n* crepusculo *m.*
twin *n* gemelo *m.*
twist *vt* torcer.
twit *n (col)* tonto *m.*

twitch *vi* moverse nerviosamente.
two *adj, n* dos.
two-faced *adj* falso.
tycoon *n* magnate *m.*
type *n* tipo *m*; letra *f*; modelo *m:—vt* escribir a maquina.
typewriter *n* maquina de escribir *f.*
typical *adj* tipico.
tyrannical *adj* tiranico.
tyranny *n* tirania *f.*
tyrant *n* tirano *m.*

U

ubiquitous *adj* ubicuo.
udder *n* ubre *f.*
ugh *excl* ¡uf!
ugliness *n* fealdad *f.*
ugly *adj* feo; peligroso.
ulcer *n* ulcera *f.*
ulterior *adj* ulterior.
ultimate *adj* ultimo.
ultimatum *n* ultimatum *m.*
umbrella *n* paraguas *m invar.*
umpire *n* arbitro *m.*
unable *adj* incapaz.
unaccompanied *adj* solo.
unaccustomed *adj* desacostumbrado.
unanimity *n* unanimidad *f.*
unanimous *adj* unanime.
unanswerable *adj* incontrovertible.
unapproachable *adj* inaccesible.
unbearable *adj* intolerable.
unbecoming *adj* indecente.
unbutton *vt* desabotonar.
uncanny *adj* extraordinario.
unchanged *adj* no alterado.
uncharitable *adj* nada caritativo.
uncle *n* tio.
uncomfortable *adj* incomodo.
uncommon *adj* raro.
uncompromising *adj* irreconciliable.
unconscious *adj* inconsciente.
unconventional *adj* poco convencional.
uncork *vt* destapar.
uncouth *adj* grosero.
uncover *vt* descubrir.
undaunted *adj* intrepido.
under *prep* debajo de.
under-age *adj* menor de edad.
underclothing *n* ropa intima *f.*
underdeveloped *adj* subdesarrollado.
underdog *n* desvalido *m.*
underestimate *vt* subestimar.
undergo *vt* sufrir.
undergraduate *n* estudiante *m.*

underground *n* movimiento clandestino *m.*
underline *vt* subrayar.
underpaid *adj* mal pagado.
undershirt *n* camiseta *f.*
understand *vt* entender, comprender.
understatement *n* subestimacion *f.*
underwear *n* ropa intima *f.*
underworld *n* hampa *f.*
undetermined *adj* indeterminado, indeciso.
undigested *adj* indigesto.
undisciplined *adj* indisciplinado.
undismayed *adj* intrepido.
undisputed *adj* incontestable.
undisturbed *adj* quieto, tranquilo.
undivided *adj* indiviso, entero.
undo *vt* deshacer, destar.
undoubted *adj* indudable.
undress *vi* desnudarse.
undue *adj* indebido.
undulating *adj* ondulante.
unduly *adv* indebidamente.
undying *adj* inmortal.
unearth *vt* desenterrar.
uneasy *adj* inquieto.
uneducated *adj* ignorante.
unemployed *adj* parado.
unemployment *n* paro *m.*
unenlightened *adj* no iluminado.
unenviable *adj* poco envidiable.
unequal *adj* desigual.
unequaled *adj* incomparable.
uneven *adj* desigual.
unexpected *adj* inesperado.
unexplored *adj* inexplorado.
unfair *adj* injusto.
unfaithful *adj* infiel.
unfamiliar *adj* desacostumbrado.
unfashionable *adj* pasado de moda.
unfasten *vt* desatar.
unfavorable *adj* desfavorable.
unfeeling *adj* insensible.

unfit *adj* indispuesto.
unfold *vt* desplegar.
unforeseen *adj* imprevisto.
unforgettable *adj* inolvidable.
unforgivable *adj* imperdonable.
unforgiving *adj* implacable.
unfortunate *adj* desafortunado.
unfounded *adj* sin fundamento.
unfriendly *adj* antipatico.
unfruitful *adj* esteril; infructuoso.
unfurnished *adj* sin muebles.
ungrateful *adj* ingrato.
unhappily *adv* infelizmente.
unhappy *adj* infeliz.
unhealthy *adj* malsano.
unhook *vt* desenganchar; descolgar; desabrochar.
unhoped(-for) *adj* inesperado.
unhurt *adj* ileso.
unicorn *n* unicornio *m*.
uniform *adj* uniforme:—*n* uniforme *m*.
uniformity *adj* uniformidad *f*.
unify *vt* unificar.
unimaginable *adj* inimaginable.
unimportant *adj* nada importante.
uninformed *adj* ignorante.
uninhabitable *adj* inhabitable.
uninhabited *adj* inhabitado, desierto.
uninjured *adj* ileso, no danado.
unintelligible *adj* ininteligible.
unintentional *adj* involuntario.
uninterested *adj* desinteresado.
uninteresting *adj* poco interesante.
uninvited *adj* no convidado.
union *n* union *f*; sindicato *m*.
unionist *n* unitario *m*.
unique *adj* unico, uno, singular.
unit *n* unidad *f*.
unite *vt vi* unir(se), juntarse.
United States (of America) *npl* Estados Unidos (de América) *mpl*.
unity *n* unidad *f*.
universal *adj* universal.
universe *n* universo *m*.
university *n* universidad *f*.
unjust *adj* injusto.
unkind *adj* poco amable.
unknown *adj* incognito.
unlawful *adj* ilícito/a.
unless *conj* a menos que, si no.
unload *vt* descargar.
unluckily *adv* desafortunadamente.
unlucky *adj* desafortunado.
unmarried *adj* soltero; soltera.
unmerited *adj* desmerecido.
unmistakable *adj* evidente.
unmoved *adj* inmoto, firme.

unnatural *adj* antinatural.
unnecessary *adj* inutil, innecesario.
unnoticed *adj* no observado.
unobserved *adj* no observado.
unobtrusive *adj* invertido/a.
unobtainable *adj* inconseguible.
unobtrusive *adj* modesto.
unoccupied *adj* desocupado.
unofficial *adj* no oficial.
unpack *vt* desempacar; desenvolver.
unpaid *adj* no pagado.
unpleasant *adj* desagradable.
unpopular *adj* no popular.
unpracticed *adj* inexperto.
unprecedented *adj* sin ejemplo.
unpredictable *adj* imprevisible.
unprepared *adj* no preparado.
unprofitable *adj* inútil, vano; poco lucrativo.
unpunished *adj* impune.
unqualified *adj* sin titulos; total.
unquestionable *adj* indubitable.
unravel *vt* desenredar.
unrealistic *adj* poco realista.
unreasonable *adv* irracionalmente.
unrelated *adj* sin relacion; inconexo.
unrelenting *adj* incompasivo, inflexible.
unreliable *adj* poco fiable.
unrestrained *adj* desenfrenado; ilimitado.
unripe *adj* inmaduro.
unrivaled *adj* sin rival.
unroll *vt* desenrollar.
unsafe *adj* inseguro.
unsatisfactory *adj* insatisfactorio.
unscrew *vt* destornillar.
unscrupulous *adj* sin escrupulos.
unseemly *adj* indecente.
unseen *adj* invisible.
unselfish *adj* desinteresado.
unsettle *vt* perturbar.
unshaken *adj* firme, estable.
unskilled *adj* inhabil.
unsociable *adj* insociable.
unspeakable *adj* inefable.
unstable *adj* instable, inconstante.
unsteady *adj* inestable.
unsuccessful *adj* infeliz, desafortunado.
unsuitable *adj* inapropiado; inoportuno.
unsure *adj* inseguro.
unsympathetic *adj* inompasivo.
untapped *adj* sin explotar.
untenable *adj* insostenible.
unthinkable *adj* inconcebible.
unthinking *adj* desatento, irreflexivo.
untidiness *n* desalino *m*.
untidy *adj* desordenado; sucio.
untie *vt* desatar, deshacer, soltar.
until *prep* hasta:—*conj* hasta que.

untimely *adj* intempestivo.
untiring *adj* incansable.
untold *adj* nunca dicho; indecible; incalculable.
untouched *adj* intacto.
untoward *adj* impropio; adverso.
untried *adj* no ensayado o probado.
untroubled *adj* no perturbado, tranquilo.
untrue *adj* falso.
untrustworthy *adj* indigno de confianza.
untruth *n* falsedad, mentira *f*.
unused *adj* isin usar, no usado.
unusual *adj* inusitado, raro:—**~ly** *adv* inusitadamente, raramente.
unveil *vt* quitar el velo, descubrir.
unwavering *adj* inquebrantable.
unwelcome *adj* desagradable, inoportuno.
unwell *adj* enfermizo, malo.
unwieldy *adj* pesado.
unwilling *adj* desinclinado:—**~ly** *adv* de mala gana.
unwillingness *n* mala gana, repugnancia *f*.
unwind *vt* desenredar, desenmaranar: —*vi* relajarse.
unwlse *adj* imprudente.
unwitting *adj* inconsciente.
unworkable *adj* poco practico.
unworthy *adj* indigno.
unwrap *vt* desenvolver.
unwritten *adj* no escrito.
up *adv* arriba, en lo alto; levantado:—*prep* hacia; hasta.
upbringing *n* educacion *f*.
update *vt* poner al dia.
upheaval *n* agitacion *f*.
uphill *adj* dificil, penoso:—*adv* cuesta arriba.
uphold *vt* sos tener, apoyar.
upholstery *n* tapiceria *f*.
upkeep *n* mantenimiento *m*.
uplift *vt* levantar.
upon *prep* sobre, encima.
upper *adj* superior; mas elevado.
upper-class *adj* de la clase alta.
upper-hand *n* (*fig*) superioridad *f*.
uppermost *adj* mas alto, supremo:—**to be ~** predominar.
upright *adj* derecho, perpendicular, recto; puesto en pie; hon rado.
uprising *n* sublevacion *f*.

uproar *n* tumulto, alboroto *m*.
uproot *vt* desarraigar.
upset *vt* trastornar; derramar, volcar:—*n* reves *m*; trastorno *m*:—*adj* molesto; revuelto.
upshot *n* remate *m*; fin *m*; conclusion *f*.
upside-down *adv* de arriba abajo.
upstairs *adv* de arriba.
upstart *n* advenedizo *m*.
uptight *adj* nervioso.
up-to-date *adj* al dia.
upturn *n* mejora *f*.
upward *adj* ascendente:—**~s** *adv* hacia arriba.
urban *adj* urbano.
urbane *adj* cortes.
urchin *n* golfillo *m*.
urge *vt* animar:—*n* impulso *m*; deseo *m*.
urgency *n* urgencia *f*.
urgent *adj* urgente.
urinal *n* orinal *m*.
urinate *vi* orinar.
urine *n* orina *f*.
urn *n* urna *f*.
us *pn* nos; nosotros.
usage *n* tratamiento *m*; uso *m*.
use *n* uso *m*; utilidad, practica *f*:—*vt* usar, emplear.
used *adj* usado.
useful *adj*, **~ly** *adv* util(mente).
usefulness *n* utilidad *f*.
useless *adj* inútil:—**~ly** *adv* inútilmente.
uselessness *n* inutilidad *f*.
user-friendly *adj* amistoso.
usher *n* ujier *m*; acomodador *m*.
usherette *n* acomodadora *f*.
usual *adj* usual, comun, normal:—**~ly** *adv* normalmente.
usurer *n* usurero *m*.
usurp *vt* usurpar.
usury *n* usura *f*.
utensil *n* utensilio *m*.
uterus *n* utero *m*.
utilize *vt* utilizar.
utility *n* utilidad *f*.
utmost *adj* extremo, sumo; ultimo.
utter *adj* total; todo; entero:—*vt* proferir; expresar; publicar.
utterance *n* expresion *f*.
utterly *adv* enteramente, del todo.

V

vacancy *n* cuarto libre *m*.
vacant *adj* vacio; desocupado.
vacate *vt* desocupar.

vacation *n* vacaciones *fpl*.
vaccinate *vt* vacunar.
vaccination *n* vacunacion *f*.

vaccine n vacuna f.
vacuous adj necio/a, bobo/a.
vacuum n vacio m.
vagina n vagina f.
vagrant n vagabundo.
vague adj vago.
vain adj vano.
valet n criado m.
valiant adj valiente.
valid adj valido.
valley n valle m.
valor n valor m.
valuable adj precioso.
valuation n tasa, valuacion f.
value n valor.
valued adj apreciado.
valve n valvula f.
vampire n vampiro m.
vandal n gamberro m.
vandalize vt danar.
vandalism n vandalismo m.
vanguard n vanguardia f.
vanilla n vainilla f.
vanish vi desvanecerse.
vanity n vanidad f.
vanquish vt vencer.
vantage point n punto panoramico m.
vapor n vapor m.
variable adj variable.
variance n discordia f.
variation n variacion f.
varicose vein n variz f.
varied adj variado.
variety n variedad f.
various adj vario.
varnish n barniz m.
vary vt, vi variar.
vase n florero m.
vast adj vasto.
vat n tina f.
vault n boveda f.
veal n ternera f.
veer vi (mar) virar.
vegetable adj vegetal, n ~s pl legumbres fpl.
vegetable garden n huerta f.
vegetarian n vegetariano, na m/f.
vegetate vi vegetar.
vegetation n vegetacion f.
vehemence n vehemencia f.
vehement adj vehemente.
vehicle n vehiculo m.
veil n velo m.
vein n vena f.
velocity n velocidad f.
velvet n terciopelo m.
vendor n vendedor m.

veneer n chapa f.
venerable adj venerable.
venerate vt venerar.
veneration n veneracion f.
venereal adj venereo.
vengeance n venganza f.
venial adj venial.
venison n (carne de) venado f.
venom n veneno m.
venomous adj venenoso.
vent n respiradero m; salida f.
ventilate vt ventilar.
ventilation n ventilacion f.
ventilator n ventilador m.
ventriloquist n ventrilocuo m.
venture n empresa f:—vi aventurarse.
venue n lugar de reunion m.
veranda(h) n terraza f.
verb n (gr) verbo m.
verbal adj verbal.
verdict n (law) veredicto m.
verification n verificacion f.
verify vt verificar.
veritable adj verdadero.
vermin n bichos mpl.
vermouth n vermut m.
versatile adj versatil.
verse n verso m.
versed adj versado.
version n version f.
versus prep contra.
vertebra n vertebra f.
vertebra, vertebrate adj vertebral.
vertical adj , ~ly adv vertical(mente).
vertigo n vertigo m.
very adj adv muy, mucho.
vessel n vasija f.
vest n chaleco m.
vestibule n vestibulo m.
vestige n vestigio m.
vestry n sacristia f.
veteran adj, n veterano (m).
veterinary adj veterinario.
veto n veto m.
vex vt molestar.
via prep por.
viaduct n viaducto m.
vial n redoma f.
vibrate vi vibrar.
vibration n vibracion f.
vicarious adj sustituto.
vice n vicio m.
vice versa adv viceversa.
vicinity n vecindad f.
vicious adj vicioso.
victim n victima f.
victimize vt victimizar.

victor *n* vencedor *m*.
victorious *adj* victorioso.
victory *n* victoria *f*.
video *n* videofilm *m*; video cassette *f*; video-grabadora *f*.
video tape *n* cinta de video *f*.
vie *vi* competir.
view *n* vista *f*.
viewpoint *n* punto de vista *m*.
vigilance *n* vigilancia *f*.
vigilant *adj* vigilante.
vigorous *adj* vigoroso.
vigor *n* vigor *m*.
vile *adj* vil.
vilify *vt* envilecer.
villa *n* chalet *m*.
village *n* aldea *f*.
villain *n* malvado *m*.
vindicate *vt* vindicar.
vindication *n* vindicacion *f*.
vindictive *adj* vengativo.
vine *n* vid *f*.
vinegar *n* vinagre *m*.
vineyard *n* vina *f*.
vintage *n* vendimia *f*.
vinyl *n* vinilo *m*.
viola *n* (*mus*) viola *f*.
violate *vt* violar.
violation *n* violacion *f*.
violence *n* violencia *f*.
violent *adj* violento.
violet *n* (*bot*) violeta *f*.
violin *n* (*mus*) violin *m*.
viper *n* vibora *f*.
virgin *n* virgen *f*.
virginity *n* virginidad *f*.
Virgo *n* Virgo *f* (signo del zodiaco).
virile *adj* viril.
virility *n* virilidad *f*.
virtual *adj* , ~ly *adv* virtual(mente).
virtue *n* virtud *f*.
virtuous *adj* virtuoso.
virulent *adj* virulento.
virus *n* virus *m*.
visa *n* visado *m*, visa *f*.
vis-a-vis *prep* con respecto a.
visibility *n* visibilidad *f*.
visible *adj* visible.
vision *n* vista *f*.

visit *vt* visitar:—*n* visita *f*.
visitor *n* visitante *m/f*.
visor *n* visera *f*.
vista *n* vista, perspectiva *f*.
visual *adj* visual.
visualize *vt* imaginarse.
vital *adj* vital.
vitality *n* vitalidad *f*.
vitamin *n* vitamina *f*.
vitiate *vt* viciar.
vivacious *adj* vivaz.
vivid *adj* vivo.
vivisection *n* viviseccion *f*.
vocabulary *n* vocabulario *m*.
vocal *adj* vocal.
vocation *n* vocacion *f*.
vociferous *adj* vocinglero.
vodka *n* vodka *m*.
vogue *n* moda *f*; boga *f*.
voice *n* voz *f*:—*vt* expresar.
void *adj* nulo:—*n* vacio *m*.
volatile *adj* volatil; voluble.
vulcanic *adj* volcanico.
volcano *n* volcan *m*.
volition *n* voluntad *f*.
volley *n* descarga *f*; salva *f*; rociada *f*; volea *f*.
volleyball *n* voleibol *m*.
volt *n* voltio *m*.
voltage *n* voltaje *m*.
voluble *adj* locuaz.
volume *n* volumen *m*.
voluntarily *adv* voluntariamente.
voluntary *adj* voluntario.
volunteer *n* voluntario *m*.
voluptuous *adj* voluptuoso.
vomit *vt*, *vi* vomitar.
vortex *n* remolino *m*.
vote *n* voto.
voter *n* votante *m/f*.
voting *n* votacion *f*.
voucher *n* vale *m*.
vow *n* voto *m*.
vowel *n* vocal *f*.
voyage *n* viaje *m*.
vulgar *adj* ordinario.
vulgarity *n* groseria.
vulnerable *adj* vulnerable.
vulture *n* buitre *m*.

W

wad *n* fajo *m*.
waddle *vi* anadear.
wade *vi* vadear.
wafer *n* galleta *f*.

waffle *n* gofre *m*.
wag *vt* menear.
wage *n* salario *m*.
waggon *n* carro *m*.

wail n lamento m.
waist n cintura f.
wait vi esperar.
waiter n camarero m.
waiting list n lista de espera f.
waiting room n sala de espera f.
waive vt suspender.
wake vi despertarse.
waken vt, (vi) despertar(se).
walk vt, vi pasear; andar.
walking stick n baston m.
wall n pared f; muralla f; muro m.
wallflower n (bot) aleli m.
wallpaper n papel pintado m.
walnut n nogal m; nuez f.
walrus n morsa f.
waltz n vals m (baile).
wan adj palido.
wand n varita magica f.
wane vi menguar.
want vt querer.
wanton adj lascivo.
war n guerra f.
ward n sala f.
wardrobe n guardarropa f.
warehouse n almacen m.
warm adj calido; caliente.
warm-hearted adj afectuoso.
warmth n calor m.
warn vt avisar.
warning n aviso m.
warp vi torcerse.
warrant n orden judicial f.
warranty n garantia f.
warren n conejero m.
warrior n guerrero m.
wart n verruga f.
wary adj cauto.
wash vt lavar.
washbowl n lavabo m.
washing machine n lavadora f.
washing-up n fregado m.
washroom n servicios mpl.
wasp n avispa f.
waste vt malgastar.
watch n reloj m; vigilar.
watchdog n perro guardian m.
water n agua f.
watercolor n acuarela f.
waterfall n cascada f.
watering-can n regadera f.
waterlily n ninfea f.
water melon n sandia f.
watertight adj impermeable.
watt n vatio m.
wave n ola, onda f.
waver vi vacilar.

wax n cera f.
way n camino m; via f.
we pn nosotros, nosotras.
weak adj , ~ly adv debil(mente).
wealth n riqueza f.
wealthy adj rico.
weapon n arma f.
wear vt gastar, consumir; usar, llevar.
weary adj cansado.
weasel n comadreja f.
weather n tiempo m.
weave vt tejer; trenzar.
weaving n tejido m.
web n telarana f.
wed vt, vi casar(se).
wedge n cuna f.
Wednesday n miercoles m.
wee adj pequenito.
weed n mala hierba f.
week n semana f.
weekend n fin de semana m.
weekly adj semanal.
weep vt, vi llorar.
weeping willow n sauce lloron m.
weigh vt, vi pesar.
weight n peso m.
welcome adj recibido con agrado:—~! ibienvenido!.
weld vt soldar.
welfare n prosperidad f.
well n fuente f adv bien.
wench n mozuela f.
west n oeste, occidente m.
wet adj humedo, mojado.
whale n ballena f.
wharf n muelle m.
what pn que, qué?, el que, la que, lo que.
whatever pn cualquier o cualquiera cosa que.
wheat n trigo m.
wheel n rueda f.
wheelbarrow n carretilla f.
wheelchair n sillita de ruedas f.
wheeze vi jadear.
when adv cuando.
whenever adv cuando; cada vez que.
where adv dónde? conj donde.
whether conj si.
which pn que; lo que; el que, el cual; cual: —adj qué?; cuyo.
while n rato m; vez f:—conj durante; mientras; aunque.
whim n antojo m.
whine vi llorar, lamentar
whinny vi relinchar.
whip n azote m; latigo m.
whirlpool n vortice m.
whirlwind n torbellino m.

whiskey n whisky m.
whisper vi cuchichear.
whistle vi silbar.
white adj blanco.
who pn quién?, que.
whoever pn quienquiera, cualquiera.
whole adj todo.
wholemeal adj integral.
wholly adv enteramente.
whom pn quién? que.
whooping cough n tos ferina f.
whore n puta f.
why n por qué?
wick n mecha f.
wicked adj malvado.
wide adj ancho.
widen vt ensanchar.
widow n viuda f.
widower n viudo m.
width n anchura f.
wield vt manejar.
wife n esposa f.
wig n peluca f.
wild adj silvestre.
wilderness n desierto m.
wild life n fauna f.
will n voluntad f.
willful adj deliberado; testarudo.
willow n sauce m (arbol).
willpower n fuerza de voluntad f.
wilt vi marchitarse.
wily adj astuto.
win vt ganar.
wince vi encogerse, estremecerse.
winch n torno m.
wind n viento m.
wind vt enrollar.
windfall n golpe de suerte m.
winding adj tortuoso.
windmill n molino de viento m.
window n ventana f.
window box n jardinera de ventana f.
window ledge n repisa f.
window pane n cristal m.
window sill n repisa f.
windpipe n traquea f.
windshield n parabrisas m invar.
windy adj de mucho viento.
wine n vino m.
wine cellar n bodega f.
wine glass n copa f.
wing n ala f.
winged adj alado.
wink vi guinar.
winner n ganador.
winter n invierno m.
wintry adj invernal.

wipe vt limpiar.
wire n telegrama m.
wisdom n sabiduria f.
wisdom teeth npl muelas de juicio fpl.
wise adj sabio.
wisecrack n broma f.
wish vt querer.
wishful adj deseoso.
wit n entendimiento m.
witch n bruja f.
witchcraft n brujeria f.
with prep con; por, de, a.
withdraw vt quitar.
withdrawal n retirada f.
withdrawn adj reservado.
withhold vt detener.
within prep dentro de.
without prep sin.
withstand vt resistir.
witless adj necio.
witness n testigo m.
witticism n ocurrencia f.
wittily adv ingeniosamente.
witty adj ingenioso.
wizard n brujo m.
woe n dolor m; miseria f.
woeful adj triste.
wolf n lobo m.
woman n mujer f.
womb n utero m.
wonder n milagro m.
wonderful adj maravilloso.
won't abrev de will not.
woo vt cortejar.
wood n bosque m; selva f; madera f; lena f.
woodland n arbolado m.
woodlouse n cochinilla f.
woodpecker n picamaderos m invar.
woodworm n carcoma f.
wool n lana f.
woolen adj de lana.
word n palabra f.
wordy adj verboso.
work vi trabajar; obrar.
world n mundo m.
worm n gusano m.
worn-out adj gastado.
worried adj preocupado.
worry vt preocupar.
worse adj, adv peor.
worship n culto m; adoracion f.
worst adj el/la peor.
worth n valor m.
worthwhile adj que vale la pena; valioso.
worthy adj digno.
wound n herida f.
wrangle vi renir f.

wrap *vt* envolver.
wrath *n* ira *f*.
wreath *n* corona *f*.
wreck *n* naufragio *m*; ruina *f*.
wreckage *n* restos *mpl*.
wren *n* reyezuelo *m* (avecilla).
wrestle *vi* luchar; disputar.
wrestling *n* lucha *f*.
wretched *adj* infeliz, miserable.
wring *vt* torcer.
wrinkle *n* arruga *f*.
wrist *n* muneca *f*.
wristband *n* puno de camisa *m*.

wristwatch *n* reloj de pulsera *m*.
writ *n* escrito *m*; escritura *f*.
write *vt* escribir.
write-off *n* perdida total *f*.
writer *n* escritor, ra, *m/f*; autor, ra *m/f*.
writhe *vi* retorcerse.
writing *n* escritura *f*
writing desk *n* escritorio *m*.
writing paper *n* papel para escribir *m*.
wrong *n* injuria *f*; injusticia *f*.
wrongful *adj* injusto.
wrongly *adv* injustamente.
wry *adj* ironico.

XYZ

Xmas *n* Navidad *f*.
X-ray *n* radiografia *f*.
xylophone *n* xilofano *m*.
yacht *n* yate *m*.
yachting *n* balandrismo *m*.
Yankee *n* yanqui *m*.
yard *n* corral *m*; yarda *f*.
yardstick *n* criterio *m*.
yarn *n* estambre *m*; hilo de lino *m*.
yawn *vi* bostezar
yeah *adv* si.
year *n* ano *m*.
yearling *n* primal *m*, ala *f*.
yearly *adj* anual.
yearn *vi* anorar.
yearning *n* anoranza *f*.
yeast *n* levadura *f*.
yell *vi* aullar.
yellow *adj* amarillo.
yelp *vi* latir, ganir.
yes *adv*, *n* si (*m*).
yesterday *adv*, *n* ayer (*m*).
yet *conj* sin embargo; pero:—*adv* todavia.
yew *n* tejo *m*.
yield *vt* dar, producir.
yoga *n* yoga *m*.
yog(h)urt *n* yogur *m*.
yoke *n* yugo *m*.
yolk *n* yema de huevo *f*.
yonder *adv* alla.

you *pn* vosotros, tu, usted, ustedes.
young *adj* joven.
youngster *n* jovencito, ta *m/f*.
your(s) *pn* tuyo, vuestro, suyo:—**sincerely**
  ~s su seguro ser vidor.
yourself *pn* tu mismo, usted mismo, vosotros mismos, ustedes mismos.
youth *n* juventud *f*.
youthful *adj* juvenil.
youthfulness *n* juventud *f*.
yuppie *adj*, *n* yuppie *m/f*.
zany *adj* estrafalario.
zap *vt* borrar.
zeal *n* celo *m*; ardor *m*.
zealous *adj* celoso.
zebra *n* cebra *f*.
zenith *n* cenit *m*.
zero *n* zero, cero *m*.
zest *n* animo *m*.
zigzag *n* zigzag *m*.
zinc *n* zinc *m*.
zip, zipper *n* cremallera *f*.
zodiac *n* zodiaco *m*.
zone *n* banda, faja *f*; zona *f*.
zoo *n* zoo *m*.
zoological *adj* zoologico.
zoologist *n* zoologo, ga *m/f*.
zoology *n* zoologia *f*.
zoom *vi* zumbar.
zoom lens *n* zoom *m*.

Verbos Irregulares en Ingles

Present tense	Past tense	Past participle
arise	arose	arisen
awake	awoke	awaked, awoke
be [I am, you/we/they are, he/she/it is, gerund being]		
	was, were	been
bear	bore	borne
beat	beat	beaten
become	became	become
begin	began	begun
behold	beheld	beheld
bend	bent	bent
beseech	besought, beseeched	besought, beseeched
beset	beset	beset
bet	bet, betted	bet, betted
bid	bade, bid	bid, bidden
bite	bit	bitten
bleed	bled	bled
bless	blessed, blest	blessed, blest
blow	blew	blown
break	broke	broken
breed	bred	bred
bring	brought	brought
build	built	built
burn	burnt, burned	burnt, burned
burst	burst	burst
buy	bought	bought
can	could	(been able)
cast	cast	cast
catch	caught	caught
choose	chose	chosen
cling	clung	clung
come	came	come
cost	cost	cost
creep	crept	crept
cut	cut	cut
deal	dealt	dealt
dig	dug	dug
do [he/she/it does]	did	done
draw	drew	drawn
dream	dreamed, dreamt	dreamed, dreamt

Present tense	Past tense	Past participle
drink	drank	drunk
drive	drove	driven
dwell	dwelt, dwelled	dwelt, dwelled
eat	ate	eaten
fall	fell	fallen
feed	fed	fed
feel	felt	felt
fight	fought	fought
find	found	found
flee	fled	fled
fling	flung	flung
fly [he/she/it flies]	flew	flown
forbid	forbade	forbidden
forecast	forecast	forecast
forget	forgot	forgotten
forgive	forgave	forgiven
forsake	forsook	forsaken
forsee	foresaw	foreseen
freeze	froze	frozen
get	got	got, gotten (US)
give	gave	given
go [he/she/it goes]	went	gone
grind	ground	ground
grow	grew	grown
hang	hung, hanged	hung, hanged
have [I/you/we/they have, he/she/it has, gerund having]		
	had	had
hear	heard	heard
hide	hid	hidden
hit	hit	hit
hold	held	held
hurt	hurt	hurt
keep	kept	kept
kneel	knelt	knelt
know	knew	known
lay	laid	laid
lead	led	led
lean	leant, leaned	leant, leaned
leap	leapt, leaped	leapt, leaped
learn	learnt, learned	learnt, learned
leave	left	left
lend	lent	lent
let	let	let
lie [gerund lying]	lay	lain
light	lighted, lit	lighted, lit

Present tense	Past tense	Past participle
lose	lost	lost
make	made	made
may	might	—
mean	meant	meant
meet	met	met
mistake	mistook	mistaken
mow	mowed	mowed, mown
must	(had to)	(had to)
overcome	overcame	overcome
pay	paid	paid
put	put	put
quit	quit, quitted	quit, quitted
read	read	read
rid	rid	rid
ride	rode	ridden
ring	rang	rung
rise	rose	risen
run	ran	run
saw	sawed	sawn, sawed
say	said	said
see	saw	seen
seek	sought	sought
sell	sold	sold
send	sent	sent
set	set	set
sew	sewed	sewn, sewed
shake	shook	shaken
shall	should	—
shear	sheared	sheared, shorn
shed	shed	shed
shine	shone	shone
shoot	shot	shot
show	showed	shown, showed
shrink	shrank	shrunk
shut	shut	shut
sing	sang	sung
sink	sank	sunk
sit	sat	sat
slay	slew	slain
sleep	slept	slept
slide	slid	slid
sling	slung	slung
smell	smelt, smelled	smelt, smelled
sow	sowed	sown, sowed
speak	spoke	spoken

Present tense	Past tense	Past participle
speed	sped, speeded	sped, speeded
spell	spelt, spelled	spelt, spelled
spend	spent	spent
spill	spilt, spilled	spilt, spilled
spin	spun	spun
spit	spat	spat
split	split	split
spoil	spoilt	spoilt
spread	spread	spread
spring	sprang	sprung
stand	stood	stood
steal	stole	stolen
stick	stuck	stuck
sting	stung	stung
stink	stank	stunk
stride	strode	stridden
strike	struck	struck
strive	strove	striven
swear	swore	sworn
sweep	swept	swept
swell	swelled	swelled, swollen
swim	swam	swum
swing	swung	swung
take	took	taken
teach	taught	taught
tear	tore	torn
tell	told	told
think	thought	thought
throw	threw	thrown
thrust	thrust	thrust
tread	trod	trodden, trod
understand	understood	understood
upset	upset	upset
wake	woke	woken
wear	wore	worn
weave	wove,	wove, woven
wed	wedded	wed, wedded
weep	wept	wept
win	won	won
wind	wound	wound
withdraw	withdrew	withdrawn
withhold	withheld	withheld
withstand	withstood	withstood
wring	wrung	wrung
write	wrote	written

Spanish Verbs

Regular

	comprar	temer	partir
	to buy	to fear	to divide
Gerund	comprando	temiendo	partiendo
Part participle	comprado	temido	partido
Present indicative	compro	temo	parto
	compras	temes	partes
	compra	teme	parte
	compramos	tememos	partimos
	compráis	teméis	partís
	compran	temen	parten
Imperfect indicative	compraba	temía	partía
	comprabas	temías	partías
	compraba	temía	partía
	comprábamos	temíamos	partíamos
	comprabais	temíais	partíais
	compraban	temían	partían
Past absolute	compré	temí	partí
(or preterit)	compraste	temiste	partiste
	compró	temió	partió
	compramos	temimos	partimos
	comprasteis	temisteis	partisteis
	compraron	temieron	partieron
Future	compraré	temeré	partiré
	comprarás	temerás	partirás
	comprará	temerá	partirá
	compraremos	temeremos	partiremos
	compraréis	temeréis	partiréis
	comprarán	temerán	partirán
Conditional	compraría	temería	partiría
	comprarías	temerías	partirías
	compraría	temería	partiría
	compraríamos	temeríamos	partiríamos
	compraríais	temeríais	partiríais
	comprarían	temerían	partirían

Imperative	compra	teme	parte
	compre	tema	parta
	compremos	temamos	partamos
	comprad	temed	partid
	compren	teman	partan
Present subjunctive	compre	tema	parta
	compres	temas	partas
	compre	tema	parta
	compreemos	temamos	partamos
	compreéis	temáis	partáis
	compren	teman	partan
Imperfect subjunctive	comprara	temiera	partiera
	ase	iese	iese
	compraras	temieras	partieras
	ases	ieses	ieses
	comprara	temiera	partiera
	ase	iese	iese
	compráramos	temiéramos	partiéramos
	ásemos	iésemos	iésemos
	comprarais	temierais	partierais
	aseis	ieseis	ieseis
	compraran	temieran	partieran
	asen	iesen	iesen

Auxiliary Verbs

Infinitive	haber	ser	tener	estar
	to have	to be	to have	to be
Gerund	habiendo	siendo	teniendo	estando
Part participle	habido	sido	tenido	estado
Present indicative	he	soy	tengo	estoy
	has	eres	tienes	estás
	ha	es	tiene	está
	hemos	somos	tenemos	estamos
	habéis	sois	tenéis	estáis
	han	son	tienen	están
Imperfect indicative	había	era	tenía	estaba
	habías	eras	tenías	estabas
	había	era	tenía	estaba
	habíamos	éramos	teníamos	estábamos
	habíais	erais	teníais	estabais
	habían	eran	tenían	estaban

Past absolute	hube	fui	tuve	estuve
(or preterit)	hubiste	fuiste	tuviste	estuviste
	hubo	fue	tuvo	estuvo
	hubimos	fuimos	tuvimos	estuvimos
	hubisteis	fuisteis	tuvisteis	estuvisteis
	hubieron	fueron	tuvieron	estuvieron
Future	habré	seré	tendré	estaré
	habrás	serás	tendrás	estarás
	habrá	será	tendrá	estará
	habremos	seremos	tendremos	estaremos
	habréis	seréis	tendréis	estaréis
	habrán	serán	tendrán	estarán
Conditional	habría	sería	tendría	estaría
	habrías	serías	tendrías	estarías
	habría	sería	tendría	estaría
	habríamos	seríamos	tendríamos	estaríamos
	habríais	seríais	tendríais	estaríais
	habrían	serían	tendrían	estarían
Imperative	–	sé(tu)	ten(tu)	está(tu)
Present subjunctive	haya	sea	tenga	esté
	hayas	seas	tengas	estés
	haya	sea	tenga	esté
	hayamos	seamos	tengamos	estémos
	hayáis	seáis	tengáis	estéis
	hayan	sean	tengan	estén
Imperfect subjunctive	hubiera	fuera	tuviera	estuviera
	iese	ese	iese	iese
	hubieras	fueras	tuvieras	estuvieras
	ieses	eses	ieses	ieses
	hubiera	fuera	tuviera	estuviera
	iese	ese	iese	iese
	hubiéramos	fuéramos	tuviéramos	estuviéramos
	iésemos	ésemos	iésemos	iésemos
	hubierais	fuerais	tuvierais	estuvierais
	ieseis	eseis	ieseis	ieseis
	hubieran	fueran	tuvieran	estuvieran
	iesen	esen	iesen	iesen